GO BIG RED

ALSO BY MIKE BABCOCK

The Nebraska Football Legacy

*Huskers on the Hardwood: 100 Years of
Nebraska Basketball History*

Devaney

GO BIG RED

The Complete Fan's Guide
to Nebraska Football

MIKE BABCOCK

🦁 ST. MARTIN'S GRIFFIN ☙ NEW YORK

Title page photo: Captain Ed Weir of the University of Nebraska football team plays tackle. November 27, 1925. (Photo Courtesy of UPI/CORBIS-BETTMANN)

GO BIG RED: THE COMPLETE FAN'S GUIDE TO NEBRASKA FOOTBALL. Copyright © 1998 by Mike Babcock. All rights reserved. Printed in the United States of America. No part of this book may be used or reproduced in any manner whatsoever without written permission except in the case of brief quotations embodied in critical articles or reviews. For information address St. Martin's Press, 175 Fifth Avenue, New York, N.Y. 10010.

Design by Maureen Troy

Library of Congress Cataloging-in-Publication Data

Babcock, Mike.
    Go big red : the complete fan's guide to Nebraska football / Mike Babcock.—1st St. Martin's Griffin ed.
        p.   cm.
    ISBN 0-312-19457-9
    1. Nebraska Cornhuskers (Football team)—History.   2. University of Nebraska—Lincoln—History.   I. Title.
GV958.U53B32   1998
796.332'63'09782293—dc21
    [B]   98-23499
                                                                                                          CIP

First St. Martin's Griffin Edition: September 1988

10   9   8   7   6   5   4   3   2   1

CONTENTS

PREFACE

In early October 1958, I attended my first University of Nebraska football game. The Cornhuskers defeated Iowa State 7–6 at Memorial Stadium. I went with a neighborhood friend. We sat in the knothole section at the south end and cheered the second of Nebraska's three victories that season.

The next week, my parents took me to the Band Day game. We sat high in the west stands and watched the Cornhuskers lose to Kansas State. The score was 23–6. I looked it up to be sure. On the cover of the game program was a stick player—except that the sticks were two-color neckties.

The colors were those of the schools in the Big Seven Conference. That I remember vividly.

My interest in Nebraska football might have taken root then. I don't know. But at some point back then I began paying attention to the fortunes of the Cornhuskers—or misfortunes, as the case may be.

Among the many benefits of being a student at Nebraska was the opportunity to buy football tickets. I had tickets in the south stands as a sophomore and low in the west stands as a graduate student.

The remainder of my post–high school education occurred elsewhere.

I was among those at Pershing Auditorium in Lincoln to watch, in disappointment if not disbelief, on closed-circuit television when the Cornhuskers lost to Oklahoma 34–6 in 1962.

I was among those at the NU Coliseum when Richard Nixon presented Bob Devaney and cocaptains Dan Schneiss and Jerry Murtaugh with a national championship proclamation in January 1971.

And I was among those standing at the back of the end zone at Faurot Field in Columbia, Missouri, when Tom Osborne suffered his first loss as a head coach in 1973: 13–12 against Missouri.

I was an instructor at Parkland Community College in Champaign, Illinois, then. I enjoyed teaching. But I thought, if I could do anything I wanted, I would be a sportswriter. And if I could live anywhere I wanted, I would live in Lincoln, Nebraska. My logic was fairly transparent. For one thing, I like Lincoln. For another, a sportswriter who lived in Lincoln logically would cover the Cornhuskers.

By chance, I was hired by the *Lincoln Journal Star* in August 1978. Less than a month later, I was at Legion Field in Birmingham, Alabama, covering the Cornhuskers' 20–3 loss against Bear Bryant's Alabama Crimson Tide. I have lived in Lincoln and written about Nebraska football ever since.

I have covered 20 consecutive Cornhusker bowl games and missed only a handful of regular-season games.

I have not worked a day, in the traditional sense, for 20 years.

I would describe this project as a labor of love, except that I consider "labor of love" a contradiction in terms, as well as a cliché. The love part fits, but there is no labor. As with my coming to Lincoln in 1978, the opportunity to write this book was a result of good fortune rather than coming about by design.

To write about Cornhusker football and its traditions? It couldn't get any better as far as I'm concerned.

Mike Babcock
Lincoln, Nebraska
January 1998

ACKNOWLEDGMENTS

What follows is not so much the result of research as it is of my having grown up a Nebraska football fan and spent the past 20 years writing about the Cornhuskers, first for the *Lincoln Journal Star* and currently for *Huskers Illustrated*, among other publications.

My thanks go to every player and coach, past and present, who has represented Nebraska on the football field. They produced this book. I have been little more than an intermediary, by virtue of the fact that I have been around Cornhusker football for a long time—and tried to pay attention.

Special thanks to Tom Osborne and his assistants, all of whom have answered my questions, even when they would rather have been watching film. Special thanks also to Bob Devaney, whom I came to regard as a friend, as well as to Don Bryant, whose knowledge of this subject far exceeds mine.

The players who have contributed directly or indirectly to this book would number in the hundreds. They would include those with whom you are familiar and many with whom you are not.

I would like to thank Nebraska sports information director Chris Anderson and her staff, including Keith Mann; the editor at *Huskers Illustrated*, Chris Greer; and those with whom I worked at the *Journal Star*, including (but not limited to) Ken Hambleton, Curt McKeever, Steve Sipple, and Brian Hill, and before them Chuck Sinclair and Randy York, among many others. Special thanks to Virgil Parker, the sports editor who hired me, and to Dave Wohlfarth, who followed him.

I appreciate the friendship and shared ideas of Lee Barfknecht, Tom Shatel, and Eric Olson of the *Omaha World-Herald*, as well as those of Ward Jacobson, Scott Young, and the people at KFOR radio; Joe and Timmo, Bill Barker, and Tim Reischl at "The Eagle," KTGL radio; and Jim Carmichael, Steve Alvis, and Bill Doleman at NETV. They all have treated me as if I knew something about Nebraska football.

Finally, special thanks to John P. Holms, who conceived and sold the idea of this book—and who, as a student at Nebraska, tipped a few with Jim Baffico, one of the myriad players to whom I am indebted. And thanks to Pete Wolverton at St. Martin's Press for his patience on this project.

A heartfelt thanks to my parents, Bab and Dorothy, my brother, Jim, my wife, Barb, and my children, Chad and Heather, all of whom, at one time or another, have pretended to care about some of the trivial matters relating to Cornhusker football over which I too often have been enthused.

INTRODUCTION

I was sitting at the study table with Gerald Armstrong, a walk-on. We were put in alphabetical order. We were freshmen. And I was thinking, Man, this isn't going so well. I'm redshirted. I'm getting pounded in practice every day. I mean just pounded. I was just feeling sorry for myself, acting like a baby.

We started talking. I'll never forget it. Gerald told me he had a big family, and he talked about how he had worked all summer in order to pay for school. He didn't know how long he'd be able to play at Nebraska because he just didn't have much money. He said it was such an honor to be there.

I think he told me if he didn't get a scholarship by his sophomore year, he'd have to quit playing. I realized how lucky I was to be on scholarship when guys were working to pay for college.

That's what University of Nebraska football means to guys like Gerald who grew up around it.

That's what it came to mean for me, a transplanted Iowan who now is a Cornhusker.

If I had gone to Iowa, I don't know. You never know how it would have turned out. I think I would have been a good player there. But I don't think I would have grown as much as an individual.

My parents and I didn't really believe that Nebraska would want me. I guess my dad wanted to know if they really thought I could play there. John Melton recruited me. He had mentioned one time that Coach Osborne was visiting some people, and my dad said, "Well, you know, he's never come here to Cedar Falls. If he really thought that highly of Trev, wouldn't he make a trip here?"

Sure enough, Coach Osborne got on a plane and flew to Cedar Falls.

You have to understand the background. Growing up in Iowa, it was well understood that if you ever got a scholarship to Iowa, you were going to Iowa. I mean, my parents, we were big Iowa fans. So it was almost like a slap in the face in the beginning to even talk to another team. I committed orally to Iowa. I was interviewed, and I said if I ever got a scholarship offer to Iowa, I would definitely go there.

Well, after Coach Osborne's visit, my dad said, "I think you definitely ought to take a trip out there, you know, just to see what they have. You'll still go to Iowa." To be honest, when we went to Nebraska, drove the family Cadillac—a big old boat that was my grandpa's—out to Lincoln, it was well understood: "We're just going out there for a free trip. They'll wine and dine us. It'll be neat."

I'll never forget getting off the interstate and driving down Cornhusker Highway. Man, Cornhusker Highway . . . it was Big Red this and Big Red that. It was pretty clear this town was run by the Big Red. I don't remember a lot about my recruiting trip except that.

I do remember the first thing, the very first thing, they did was sit me down with the dean of general studies because I didn't know what to major in. My mom was pretty impressed. It was pretty clear academics wasn't just something they talked about at Nebraska.

I remember going into Coach Osborne's office and his asking me, "Have you made a decision, Trev? Are you going to come here?" It was kind of like the final pressure on the recruit.

I was like, "Well, golly Coach, you know . . . boy, you know, I'd sure like to . . ." That's how I was. "Gee, Coach, I don't know. I'd have to talk with my ma and pa about that one." It's true.

I didn't know what my mom and dad were going to say. But I knew after that little trip I wanted to go to Nebraska because I was just enamored with the facilities and everything.

We got back in the car, and nothing was really said for half of the trip home. I think my parents could sense, it was kind of hitting them, that their son might be leaving and going to Nebraska.

We got to about Des Moines, and the first words out of my dad's mouth were, "You know, Trev, we would like to see you at Iowa. But we want you to know that we would understand, and as a matter of fact, we would almost suggest it would be better if you went to Nebraska."

It was really hard for them to do that. Otherwise, I would have been only an hour away from home. But I think they knew, they were able to listen to their heads more than their hearts.

You talk about a place for a kid, hopefully, to grow into a man: This would be *the* place.

In my heart, I felt Nebraska was the right place for me. I called Coach Osborne and told him I was coming to Nebraska. I was all excited. He said, "Well, that's good news, Trev."

I thought to myself, Well, geez, maybe he's reconsidered since I left. Maybe the character exam came in and I wasn't quite up to par or something. His enthusiasm wasn't quite up to the level of mine. I found out later that he just has a different way of showing enthusiasm, obviously.

The greatest thing about him, win, lose or draw, is—and I know it's been said so many times, but you can't understand unless you've experienced it—he was always the same Tom Osborne.

You think about kids, and all they want is just a steady atmosphere, one where it's safe. And we had that feeling at Nebraska. That's why a lot of guys viewed Coach Osborne as a little bit of a father figure. Some of the guys came from broken homes, where it was just chaos. You came to Nebraska and there was just a steady, constant atmosphere. It was always on an even keel. Coach Osborne promoted that.

I mean, he never wanted us to get too high or too low, win or lose.

My mom's great. She thinks Coach Osborne walks on water. My parents just wish they had more kids who had gotten to play for him. I'm glad it worked out the way it did. But I would like to think that had I never played a down, had I had a miserable football experience at Nebraska, I would still think the same way about Coach Osborne. I know other guys feel the same way about him.

When Bob Devaney passed away, I sat at his funeral listening to Jerry Tagge talk about him, and the thing that hit me was, the day Tom Osborne passes and someone asks me about him, there's nothing new that I can come up with to say about him. Everything has been said.

The only thing I ever thought of that summed it up for me was, is, the man is just real. He's real. So many people aren't real, even myself sometimes. But Tom Osborne is real. More than anything else, that sums up the man for me, and by association that sums up Nebraska football.

Because Tom Osborne and Nebraska football are one and the same.

That's why it's appropriate a book such as this would be published now. With Osborne's retirement, one of the greatest eras of Cornhusker football has come to a close. The timing is perfect.

It's worth remembering the rich tradition a relative few of us have experienced.

And in case you're not up on your Nebraska football history, Gerald Armstrong earned a scholarship and lettered three seasons as a tight end. He and I were among the cocaptains in 1993.

Trev Albert
Lincoln, Nebraska
January 1998
ROLB 1990–93
Butkus Award 1993
Consensus All-American 1993

1

CHEER ON THE BUGEATERS:

The Early Years

Dry-goods stores in Lincoln did a brisk business in ribbon sales. It was a "boom," a local newspaper reported. "But only the stock of scarlet and cream was depleted to any extent."

Scarlet and cream were the colors of the University of Nebraska, which was about to play a football game against the University of Illinois on a Saturday in late October 1892.

They were the new school colors, replacing old gold. And "everybody in the remotest degree in sympathy with the Nebraska team" wore them, the newspaper account said. Spectators arrived in carriages "decked out in red and white . . . university professors wore the colors, carried flags and got as excited as anyone. Flags with every combination of scarlet and white were swung to the breeze on canes. Red neckties were common, and one fellow even wore a vest half red and half white."

It was a festive event, attracting an estimated 800, including a small but vocal group of students from Doane College in nearby Crete, Nebraska. Illinois had defeated Doane during its visit to Nebraska 20–0 in a game at Omaha, and the Doane students had come to cheer for—and bet on—Illinois.

Nebraska had played only six football games in its two-year history, and four of them were against Doane. In 1891, the schools had met three times, with Nebraska winning twice.

The rivalry between the schools was brief, lasting only until 1896. But it was spirited enough that the Doane students would make the 20-plus-mile trip in order to lend their support to Illinois.

The football game was Nebraska's first in Lincoln against an out-of-state opponent, and a handful of amateur photographers were on hand to record the activity surrounding the historic occasion. The contest met expectations, according to the *Daily Nebraska State Journal.*

An unidentified reporter, in the hyperbole of the times, described the game as the best "ever seen in Nebraska." That meant it was better than any of the previous six involving Nebraska.

Illinois and Nebraska, referred to in the newspaper account as the "bug eaters," were evenly matched. The bugeaters managed the only score in 90

Vike Francis of Nebraska goes across the goal line for a touchdown in the
1941 Rose Bowl against Stanford.
(Photo Courtesy of UPI/CORBIS-BETTMANN)

minutes of play, a touchdown worth four points and a two-point conversion.
The key play on the scoring possession was a 25-yard run by George Flippin,
the fifth African-American athlete to attend a white university, according to *A
Hard Road to Glory,* Arthur Ashe's history of African-American athletes.

Ironically, Flippin, the son of a freed slave from Port Isabelle, Ohio, didn't
earn a degree at Nebraska. He completed his undergraduate work at the University of Illinois and attended medical school in Chicago, then returned to
Nebraska to set up practice and establish a hospital in Stromsburg.

Flippin helped coach the Nebraska team in 1892. J. S. Williams, an attorney
from Omaha, also worked with the bugeaters early in the season, without pay.
But they had no coach until 1893, when Frank Crawford, a Yale graduate, was
hired at a salary reported to be between $300 and $500.

Crawford's compensation came at least in part in the form of a tuition
waiver.

In any case, Flippin's run set up Nebraska's touchdown in the 1892 victory
against Illinois. As the teams were leaving the field immediately after the game,
George Huff, "the heavyweight of the Illinois team," punched Nebraska's A. B.
Jones in the face, "knocking him flat and bringing the blood freely."

Huff's behavior, punctuated by laughter, nearly precipitated a riot. "Had it not been for the chancellor and several professors, violence would have been done the perpetrator," the *Daily Nebraska State Journal* reported. Police took the names of witnesses and considered arresting Huff.

Nebraska had intended to play host to the Illinois team at a local theater that night, a common courtesy extended to visiting teams. The bugeaters went to the theater, but Illinois, which never issued an apology for the actions of its player, did not. Such was football before the turn of the century.

Quiz 1: There Were Coaches Before Devaney and Osborne

1. Match the Nebraska coaches with the schools at which they played.

1.___	Tom Osborne	A. Western Reserve
2.___	Bob Devaney	B. Nebraska
3.___	E. N. Robinson	C. Brown
4.___	Fielding Yost	D. Oklahoma
5.___	W. C. Booth	E. Illinois
6.___	E. O. Stiehm	F. Wisconsin
7.___	E. J. Stewart	G. Hastings College
8.___	E. E. Bearg	H. Princeton
9.___	D. X. Bible	I. Carson-Newman
10.___	Glenn Presnell	J. Pittsburgh
11.___	Bill Glassford	K. Alma College
12.___	Bill Jennings	L. Lafayette

2. Three Cornhusker coaches played collegiately at Michigan. Name them.

3. Match the Nebraska coaches with their nicknames.

1. Fielding Yost ( )	A. Snap-It-Up
2. W. C. Booth ( )	B. Potsy
3. W. C. Cole ( )	C. Ernie
4. E. O. Stiehm ( )	D. Jumbo
5. E. J. Stewart ( )	E. Bummy
6. Fred Dawson ( )	F. Biff
7. Henry Schulte ( )	G. Pa, Indian
8. E. E. Bearg ( )	H. Doc
9. Lawrence McCeney Jones ( )	I. Hurry-Up
10. George Clark ( )	J. King

4. Bill Glassford's nickname was the same as one of those above, but he was never referred to by his nickname at Nebraska because Cornhusker fans had a special place in their hearts for the coach who produced Nebraska's first bowl team. What was Glassford's nickname?

5. Glassford came to Nebraska from what eastern school? Hint: It's a state university, which plays in Division I-AA of the NCAA. Its nickname is Wildcats. This is tough.

6. This Cornhusker coach had a penchant for quoting Scripture. He was a southern gentleman, born and raised in Tennessee. He left to become coach and athletic director at Texas. Who was he?

7. Nebraska's first football coach came from Harvard. He was an instructor in agriculture and bacteriology. He wasn't paid to be the football coach. In fact, he had the title because he brought a football with him from Harvard, to which he returned, probably before Nebraska's second football game against Doane College in February 1891. Who was he?

8. D. X. Bible was Nebraska's football coach from 1929 to 1936. What did his initials stand for?

9. Frank Crawford was Nebraska's first paid football coach, receiving compensation of between $300 and $500, at least part of which was in the form of a tuition waiver. Crawford coached the team in 1893 and 1894, when there were complaints on campus about insufficient funds to pay him. However, after Nebraska lost to Doane in the second game of the 1894 season, it hired the Doane coach to assist Crawford. In 1895, the assistant became the head coach. Who was he?

10. This Cornhusker head coach played for Fielding Yost at Michigan after playing at Marietta College. He was king of the hill at Nebraska from 1907 until 1910. Who was he?

11. This Nebraska head coach came from Oregon State—which Nebraska played in Portland in his first season—and installed a unique offense in which there was no quarterback. There were two fullbacks and two halfbacks. The center called the signals and passed the ball sideways, instead of back between his legs, to the player who would carry it. Who was this coach?

12. After his Cornhuskers defeated Pop Warner's Pittsburgh team 10–0 at Pittsburgh in 1921, a sportswriter described them as "man-eating mastadons." Who was he?

13. Before he came to Nebraska, he was an assistant coach under Bob Zuppke at Illinois. While he was there, he worked with Red Grange, "the Galloping Ghost." Who was this coach?

14. This Cornhusker coach was known as the Little Colonel. Who was he?

15. Biff Jones was the coach of Nebraska's Rose Bowl team. What was his army rank?

16. In 1911, Nebraska tied Michigan 6–6 in Lincoln. Michigan's head coach had earlier spent one season as the head coach at Nebraska. Who was this famous coach?

17. What coach has the best winning percentage in Nebraska history (.913)?

18. Frank Crawford was the first paid football coach in Nebraska history. But Nebraska didn't have a full-time football coach until two decades later. Who was he?

19. D. X. Bible's record as Nebraska's head coach was 50–15–7, a winning percentage of .743. Ten of the 15 losses were against two teams. Bible's record against them was 0–10–2. Name the teams. Hint: They regularly appeared on the schedule but were not conference opponents.

20. The student newspaper wrote of this coach: "He raised Nebraska from a second-rate team among those of the Missouri Valley to a position where even the leaders of the conference look upon her as an opponent to be feared." He had been a practicing attorney in New York City. He coached Nebraska to two undefeated and untied seasons. Name him.

21. By December, 1998, six coaches who spent at least one season as head coach at Nebraska will have been inducted into the National Football Foundation Hall of Fame. Name them.

22. This coach spent two pre-1900 seasons at Nebraska. He was known as the Walter Camp of Brown Football. This is a tough one. Name him. Hint: His middle name was North.

23. Nebraska didn't have a football coach in 1891. But before it played Iowa at Omaha, the Iowa coach spent time working with Nebraska. As a result, Nebraska's records list him as the coach for that season. Despite his help, Iowa defeated Nebraska 22–0. Name this Yale graduate.

24. After Ernie Bearg resigned following the 1928 season, Nebraska went looking for a new head coach. The Cornhuskers hired D. X. Bible at the suggestion of perhaps the most famous coach in college football history. Nebraska had contacted this coach to see if he would be interested. He has the highest winning percentage all-time among coaches with 10 or more seasons. Name him.

25. In 1909, Nebraska lost to Haskell Indian School 16–5 at Lawrence, Kansas. The Haskell coach was a former Cornhusker who earned five football letters. Name him.

The Afro-American Legacy

George Flippin was a big man, weighing 200 pounds. He might not have survived three football seasons at Nebraska otherwise. His race was an issue throughout a distinguished career.

Missouri forfeited to Nebraska in 1892 rather than compete against Flippin, and when Nebraska played Iowa at Omaha in the last of five games that season, the hotel at which the team planned to stay balked at accepting Flippin. "There was the usual row over the admission of Flippin," said a Lincoln newspaper.

"But the boys are bent on seeing that the civil rights bill is enforced so far as hotels are concerned."

Flippin's teammates "manfully stood up for their fellow student. The result was that the management yielded so far as to actually allow Flippin to eat in the hotel and pay for it."

The hotel provided a "private dining room," though certainly not as a courtesy to the team, which spent the night in rooms at the Omaha YMCA before returning to Lincoln the next day.

Flippin was the focus on the field as well as off. Nebraska played the Denver Athletic Club at Denver in 1893, and the Denver players "had a special pick at him," according to a newspaper account. "He was kicked, slugged and jumped on, but never knocked out, and gave as good as he received."

The Denver Athletic Club's penchant for punching determined the game's outcome in Nebraska's favor. With 10 minutes remaining and the score tied, the umpire awarded Nebraska possession of the ball as a result of a slugging foul. The Denver team left the field in protest, and the game was forfeited.

Flippin even had to deal with discrimination on his own team. Remarks directed at Flippin attributed to Frank Crawford, Nebraska's first paid football coach, were blatantly bigoted.

At least three other African-Americans played on Nebraska's football teams prior to 1917, when the university established a policy that prohibited African-Americans from participating in extracurricular activities. They were William Newton Johnson, Robert Taylor, and Clint Ross.

William Johnson, a graduate of Lincoln High School, earned letters at Nebraska in 1900, 1904, 1905, and 1906, playing for teams coached by Bummy Booth and Amos Foster, about whom he once said, "That man, he teaches too much trickery." Johnson helped coach and also wrote about the team for the student yearbook. His senior inscription read, "What he nobly thought, he bravely dared."

Taylor came from York County, Nebraska, as did Flippin (after moving from Ohio), and earned one letter, when he was a freshman. He didn't play in every game in 1905 because Nebraska was a member of a loosely organized conference that included Doane and conference rules prohibited the use of freshmen in conference games. The 208-pound Taylor apparently went out for the team again in 1906, but according to the student yearbook, "changes in the rules in some respects lessened the value of his weight on offense and Nebraska coaches worked out no scheme by which they could use the ponderous guard."

Ross also earned only one letter, playing for Jumbo Stiehm's 8–0 team in 1913. Nebraska posted four shutouts and allowed only 28 points total that season. Ross played tackle in a line that included Vic Halligan, who would be the first Cornhusker to earn All-America recognition in 1914.

Based on available records, Ross appears to be the last African-American athlete at Nebraska until the late 1940s, when Tom Carodine, a running back from Los Angeles by way of Boys Town High School, Nebraska, played for Coach Bill Glassford. Carodine did not earn a letter, however.

Dog

Earl Eager, a three-year letterman for Coach Bummy Booth from 1903 to 1905, was a 135-pound halfback whose nickname was Dog. The game was such then that when the Cornhuskers were near the goal line, they sometimes lifted up Dog and attempted to throw him into the end zone.

The strategy of tossing a teammate over the line of scrimmage was commonplace. Some canvas jerseys included straps on the sides that could be used as handles to lift or pull ball carriers.

Eager was none the worse for the experience. In 1906, he was appointed general manager of athletics for the university, a position he held until 1912. When he assumed the newly created position, Nebraska's athletic association was $400 in debt. Within a year, the association showed a $1,000 balance.

Under Eager's direction, Nebraska Field was built. Local businessmen John McDonald and Colonel C. J. Bills made substantial contributions toward construction costs of the playing field, which ran east and west and was located just south of where the South Stadium offices are now.

Nebraska's football teams had played on a makeshift field laid out by a civil engineering class on the northwest corner of the campus. In 1908, and in the early years, the Cornhuskers played at Lincoln's M Street Ball Park—in the area where the municipal swimming pool is now. On October 23, 1909, the first game was played at Nebraska Field. The Cornhuskers and Iowa tied at 6.

Nebraska defeated Notre Dame 14–6 in the final game at Nebraska Field on November 30, 1922.

Winded

Nebraska defeated Oklahoma 24–0 in the first game played at Memorial Stadium on October 13, 1923. Dave Noble, the Cornhusker captain, scored the first touchdown there, on a four-yard run.

On the kickoff following Noble's touchdown, the ball deflated and had to be replaced.

You Are What You Eat

Coach Bummy Booth established the first training table for the football team in 1901. An account in a newspaper explained: "Fatty substances and rich foods are forbidden, as well as tobacco in any form. In order that no man will be tempted beyond his power to resist, the training table has been established."

The Missouri Valley Intercollegiate Athletic Association, which was organized in 1907 and evolved into the Big Eight, prohibited training tables for a time, allowing them again in the late 1930s.

Bill Glassford, Nebraska's head coach from 1949 to 1955, established a "fat-man's table" during preseason practice at the dreaded "Camp Curtis." Players whom Glassford considered too heavy were required to eat at the fat-man's table. In the fall of 1951, Wayne "the Bear" Handshy, a 240-pound tackle from Hollywood, California, was convicted by a kangaroo court of taking an extra piece of chicken at the Camp Curtis fat-man's table. Glassford was the prosecutor at Handshy's "trial."

Handshy's teammates Cliff Hopp and Nick Adducci served as judge and defense attorney, respectively. Adducci's defense was imaginative but ineffective. He argued that Handshy could have taken an extra helping of potatoes, which would have meant starch overload, but he opted for the chicken.

Hopp ruled against Handshy and in favor of his coach, of course. Handshy's sentence, which was imposed by Glassford, the prosecutor, was to sing for the team and to run extra laps at practice. The singing constituted cruel and unusual punishment, Handshy's teammates argued—for them.

Dick Goll, a 6-foot-2, 196-pound guard from Tekamah, Nebraska, ate 21 pieces of chicken in one sitting at Camp Curtis in the fall of 1951 without punishment. He was not seated at the fat-man's table.

Quiz 2: Some Things Old

1. He was known as the Sutton Comet because he was from Sutton, Nebraska. Who was he?

2. Nebraska's most decisive football victory ever occurred in the final game of the 1910 season. Whom did Nebraska defeat? What was the score? Who was Nebraska's coach? Hint: The opposing team came from Lawrence, Kansas.

3. The score of E. O. "Jumbo" Stiehm's first game as the Cornhuskers' coach in 1911 nearly equaled that of the final game in 1910. What was the score? Against whom was the game played? Hint: The opponent now has something in common with the University of Nebraska–Lincoln.

4. By the way, Stiehm's nickname, Jumbo, was not a result of his 6-foot-4 height. Why was he known as Jumbo? Actually, most people who knew him well called him Eddie. Extra credit: What was his given first name? In other words, what did the initial E stand for?

5. Nebraska didn't lose a game during Jumbo Stiehm's final three seasons as coach. The Cornhuskers were 23–0–1. They were tied 0–0 by South Dakota in Lincoln in the second game of the 1914 season, then won 14 games in a row, a streak that increased to 19 under Stiehm's successor, E. J. Stewart. Stiehm's Nebraska teams lost only twice in five seasons, once in

1911 and once in 1912. The same opponent defeated the Cornhuskers. Name that opponent.

6. This player was a member of Stiehm's first team and went on to serve as an assistant coach at Nebraska for several years. He was from the Grand Island, Nebraska, area, and many old-timers considered him to be the best football player ever to come from Hall County, better even than Bobby Reynolds, "Mr. Touchdown," some 40 years later. Who was he?

7. Stiehm's departure was less than amicable. He was hired away by a school in the Western Conference, which increased his salary substantially. Stiehm was making $3,500 at Nebraska, and the salary increase was reported to be between $750 and $1,000. What school hired him?

8. Stiehm further alienated himself from Nebraska's athletic association by attempting to hire one of his Cornhuskers to coach at his new school. The Cornhusker in question was a three-year letterman and captain of Stiehm's final team at Nebraska in 1915. Who was he?

9. The Missouri Valley Intercollegiate Athletic Association (MVIAA) was established in January of 1907. Name the five original members of the MVIAA.

10. The Big Six Conference was established in 1928, though its official name was the Missouri Valley Intercollegiate Athletic Association until the 1960s, when it was formally changed to the Big Eight. What were the original members of the Big Six Conference?

11. In 1947, the Big Six became the Big Seven. What school was added? From what conference did it come? In 1957, the Big Seven became the Big Eight. What school was added?

12. In 1889, one year before Nebraska's first football game, another school challenged it to a game. Nebraska didn't accept the challenge, however. What was the school?

13. Name Nebraska's first football captain in 1890.

14. Nebraska joined with three other schools in forming the Nebraska Inter-collegiate Athletic Association in 1890. The loosely organized conference was short-lived. Name the other three schools. Hint: Two of the three still exist and have football teams, but not at Nebraska's level.

15. In 1908, Earl Eager, a former player and Nebraska's enterprising general manager of athletics, scheduled a postseason game for Coach King Cole's 7–1–1 Cornhuskers. Despite protests from some faculty members, who considered such a game indicative of an overemphasis on athletics, and a bitterly cold day in December, a crowd of 5,000 watched Nebraska lose 37–6. The Cornhuskers' opponent included a player who was regarded as the greatest athlete of his time. Who was the player? For what team did he play that afternoon?

16. The first game at Memorial Stadium was played on October 13,

1923. Nebraska won 24–0. The stadium wasn't dedicated until the next Saturday, which was Homecoming. Whom did Nebraska defeat in the first game at Memorial Stadium? Whom did the Cornhuskers play in the dedication game? What was the outcome of that game? Who was Nebraska's coach?

17. The opposing coach for the dedication game at Nebraska's Memorial Stadium would later coach the Cornhuskers for two seasons, in 1945 and 1948. Name him.

18. A Chicago newspaper reporter described this Cornhusker as "more than an end to his team; he combined in his ability that of a stellar end and a great back." Lincoln sportswriter Cy Sherman called him the "most brilliant player ever developed in the annals of Missouri Valley football." He was Nebraska's first consensus All-American football player. Name him.

19. He played in the Roaring Twenties, and he was the first Cornhusker football player to earn All-America honors in two seasons. He was from Superior, Nebraska. Who was he?

20. Nebraska needed a head football coach in 1919, after a university professor took over the 1918 team following E. J. "Doc" Stewart's departure because of World War I. The Cornhuskers' choice for a football coach was Missouri's track-and-field coach at the time. He served as Nebraska's head football coach for only two seasons, but continued as an assistant. His specialty was the line. Among those with whom he worked was Ed Weir. Name him and the professor he succeeded. Hint: The north field house at Memorial Stadium is named in his honor.

Sartorial Similarity, or You Are What You Wear

Prior to the 1982 Orange Bowl game against Clemson, Glen Abbott replaced the gray face masks on Nebraska's helmets with red ones. It was a nice touch, and something that has remained a part of the Cornhuskers' look. But it also was an element in a disappointing 22–15 loss.

A couple of years later, Abbott, Nebraska's veteran equipment manager, jokingly accepted some of the responsibility for the loss. "I'm not saying it was my fault, but everybody was so excited about the face masks, and congratulating me on the idea, they forgot about the game," he said.

Even so, studies have shown there might be a correlation between the colors a team wears and its performance. Teams that wear black, for example, seem to be more aggressive.

Outfitting athletic teams has become something of a science, shaped by marketing and coaching contract considerations. It was not always so, however. A history of Cornhusker football included in Nebraska's athletic yearbook for 1922, *Tales of the Cornhuskers,* recounted that at the turn of the century, "football fans cannot recall seeing an entire Nebraska team with each man wearing the same kind of uniform. Scarlet and cream jerseys were much admired and cherished by the lucky few who got them, but most of the teammates had to be satisfied with other kinds of sweaters."

To describe what players wore as "uniforms" was a misnomer. Their outfits were hardly uniform. When Nebraska played Missouri at Lincoln in 1899, the *Daily Nebraska State Journal* reported that "Missouri made a striking contrast to the home team, with their trim suits and striped sweaters, while the Nebraska boys wore not two suits that resembled one another." They were a motley crew.

Nebraska's first football team in 1890 wore canvas uniforms and black stockings—scarlet and cream weren't the school colors until 1893 (and they weren't officially designated the school colors until after 1900). The cost of outfitting that first football team was approximately $35.

In 1904, Bummy Booth's Cornhuskers were outfitted in jerseys with broad, horizontal stripes, appropriate for prison wear. In the late 1920s, their jerseys had similar stripes, except that the stripes were vertical. And in the 1930s, the fronts of Nebraska's jerseys were taken up by an "N."

In the early 1900s, of course, many players didn't wear the leather headgear that made those who did look like gladiators. By the 1920s, leather helmets were commonplace, and by the late 1930s, they included sponge-rubber padding and elements of what became suspension helmets.

Molded plastic and vinyl helmets, post–World War II vintage, provided greater protection and allowed for the addition of color and design. In the late 1950s, Nebraska's helmets were red with white stripes. Bob Devaney's early teams wore white helmets with black numbers but no stripes.

The use of numbers on helmets, as well as on the sleeves and shoulders of jerseys, has become commonplace because of television, which also is a reason players' names often are included on the backs of jerseys. Numbers on the shoulders of jerseys are sometimes called "TV numbers."

In 1966, red stripes were put on Cornhusker helmets, along with a red "NU" on the side and players' numbers on the back. In 1969, a black-and-white "100" decal was added to the fronts of Nebraska's helmets, commemorating the one hundredth anniversary of college football—and creating clutter.

The Cornhusker helmets were changed again for the 1970 season (the "NU" was replaced with just an "N"), but they have remained essentially the same since then, except for the red face masks.

Nebraska's uniforms haven't changed dramatically since Tom Osborne replaced Devaney as head coach in 1973. In fact, the Cornhuskers dress about the same now as they did in the national championship seasons of 1970 and 1971. The most significant difference is probably that the 1970 and 1971 jerseys had double stripes around each shoulder: white on red at home, red on white away.

Jersey manufacturers occasionally refer to such adornment as "UCLA stripes" because UCLA was among the first major colleges to wear stripes around the shoulders of its football jerseys.

Until the NCAA ruled them illegal in the early 1980s because of safety considerations, Nebraska's skill-position players wore unadorned tearaway jerseys. Mike Rozier, the Cornhuskers' Heisman Trophy winner in 1983, left many a defender grasping only a shred of his number 30 tearaway jersey.

Nebraska has worn red pants for away games since the early 1960s. Only on occasion have the Cornhuskers worn white on white. In 1986, they wore red on red at Memorial Stadium for the Oklahoma game, a surprise for the Sooners and the fans but not for the Cornhuskers or Osborne.

The seniors suggested wearing the red pants, and Osborne gave his okay. Even though Nebraska may have gotten a psychological lift from the switch, the Cornhuskers still lost 20–17.

Garnet, Would You Believe?

When Nebraska played at South Carolina in 1986, the number 87 jersey of Cornhusker tight end Tom Banderas turned up missing. Glen Abbott, Nebraska's equipment manager, improvised. He borrowed a South Carolina white road jersey and put Banderas's name on the back.

The numbers were South Carolina's garnet, a slightly different shade of red than Nebraska's scarlet. Considering the alternative, however, that was of little concern.

Abbott has resolved many such crises. On the day before Nebraska played Houston in the 1980 Cotton Bowl, six Cornhusker jerseys turned up missing. So Abbott had to find a sporting goods store in Dallas that stayed open until 5 P.M. on New Year's Eve. He finally found one, bought six white cotton jerseys— Nebraska was the visiting team—and had player names and numbers ironed on them.

Win One for . . . Don Ho?

It doesn't get any worse, not in Nebraska football history, anyway. The day lives in infamy: September 17, 1955. The scoreboard on the face of Schulte Fieldhouse read: HAWAII 6, NEBRASKA 0.

The Cornhuskers have never endured a more embarrassing defeat. Don Bryant, sports editor of the *Lincoln Star*, wrote the next day, "A defeat by any team, good, bad or indifferent, used to send the fans home sad. But Saturday, the folks leaving Memorial Stadium were laughing. . . ."

The laughter, more figurative than real, was directed not so much at the players as at their coach, Bill Glassford. And it might have been more a projection of the news media's attitude toward Glassford than the opinion of the fans. Objectivity as it related to Glassford was in short supply by 1955.

Hawaii came to Memorial Stadium for Nebraska's season opener as part of an agreement that took the Cornhuskers to Honolulu for a game at the end of the 1954 regular season. Nebraska won that game 50–0, six days after losing at Oklahoma 55–7 and five weeks before losing to Duke 34–7 in the Orange Bowl. A no-repeat rule prevented Big Seven champion Oklahoma from returning to Miami.

The Cornhuskers were regarded as 40- to 50-point favorites to win the rematch with Hawaii, even though Glassford cautioned, "There's no such thing as a sure thing in football."

Glassford should have prepared his team with that in mind. Instead, the Cornhuskers focused on the next week's game against defending Big 10 and Rose Bowl champion Ohio State. Seven days later, still smarting from the embarrassment of the Hawaii loss, Nebraska played the sixth-ranked Buckeyes to a standoff at Columbus, Ohio, finally falling 28–20. Ohio State, which featured future Heisman Trophy winner halfback Howard Cassady, would finish 7–2 and repeat as Big 10 champion in 1955.

Duke was the only other opponent to score as many as 20 points against the powerful Buckeyes. The Blue Devils handed Ohio State one of its two losses, 20–14.

Henry Vasconcellos, Hawaii's head coach and athletic director, brought 28 players to Nebraska. They were not "the top players in the islands," Vasconcellos told reporters. "The big stars are sent to the mainland by wealthy alumni. These are just kids—most of them from the outer islands."

The Rainbows played for the fun of it, Vasconcellos said. He had no scholarships to offer them and no paid assistants to help coach them. (One of his assistants was a lawyer in Honolulu.)

To make matters seem more hopeless for the visitors, if that were possible, Hawaii's quarterback, Dick Hadama, had suffered broken fingers and couldn't play. A 19-year-old sophomore, Fred Nagata, took his place. Nagata suffered a back injury returning a kick in the fourth quarter and had to be replaced by the third-string quarterback, junior Ed Kawawaki, who directed the winning drive.

The Rainbows also lost their top running back to injury in the fourth quarter: Skippy Dyer, a 160-pound ex-marine from New Orleans whose ball carrying was a significant factor in Hawaii's 318–219 advantage in total yards. Dyer distinguished himself defensively as well throughout the afternoon.

The final score might have been worse had Hawaii not lost two fumbles and had two passes intercepted. One of the fumbles came after the Rainbows had driven to the Nebraska seven-yard line.

The Cornhuskers, who didn't turn over the ball, were at slightly less than full strength because of players being suspended and declared ineligible for participating in a panty raid. But Glassford had told reporters during spring practice that the team appeared to be "the best I've had at Nebraska."

A crowd of 23,000 watched in disbelief as the outweighed and overmatched visitors held their own for three quarters, then punched in a touchdown in the final period. Even though the temperature at game time was 93 degrees, the Rainbows didn't wilt, despite having two barely full units.

Hawaii which had defeated a high school all-star team 33–7 before coming to Nebraska, finished with a 7–4 record in 1955. But the Nebraska victory was its only one against a collegiate team.

Vasconcellos was gracious in victory, explaining that the 50–0 loss against the Cornhuskers the previous season had been misleading. "We were as flat as poi," he said.

Quiz 3: Are You Paying Attention?

The Ohio State team to which Nebraska was looking ahead when it lost to Hawaii had a young coach with whom you should be familiar. Name him. The Cornhuskers also had been looking ahead to a game against Texas A&M at Memorial Stadium two weeks after the Ohio State game. The Aggies defeated Nebraska 27–0. Afterward, the Texas A&M coach praised Bill Glassford and his staff for their near upset of Ohio State. Who was the Aggies' coach? Hint: He also coached against Bob Devaney and Tom Osborne. Devaney was 1–2 against him. Osborne was 1–1.

Doesn't Get Any Worse Than This

Nebraska's 6–0 loss to Hawaii in 1955 was arguably the worst in Cornhusker history. But the 19–10 loss against Iowa State at Ames, Iowa, in 1992, would be a close second.

Nebraska went to Ames with a number seven national ranking, after back-to-back victories against Colorado and Kansas by a combined score of 101–14. The Cornhuskers had 14 consecutive victories against Iowa State, and considering the Cyclones were 3–6, there was no reason to think the streak would end.

Iowa State, coached by former Nebraska assistant Jim Walden, controlled the ball, using an option attack under the direction of quarterback Marvin Seiler, a fifth-year senior who had never started a game as a collegian until that day. He had rushed for 51 yards total during his career.

Against Nebraska, Seiler rushed for 144 yards on 24 carries, and sophomore Ty Stewart kicked four first-half field goals to upset the Cornhuskers. Iowa State threw only four passes, all of them shuttle passes, and three were complete. The Cyclones ran the ball 70 times, for 399 yards.

Nebraska got off only 51 offensive snaps in the game, which took only two and a half hours.

Only once in 25 seasons did a Tom Osborne–coached team lost to an opponent that finished with a losing record. Iowa State was that opponent. The Cyclones finished 4–7 in 1992.

10 LOSSES OF NOTE IN THE MODERN ERA

1.	Hawaii	6–0	September 17, 1955
2.	Iowa State	19–10	November 14, 1992
3.	Kansas State	12–0	November 9, 1968
4.	UCLA	20–17	September 9, 1972
5.	Syracuse	17–9	September 29, 1984
6.	Arizona State	19–0	September 21, 1996
7.	Missouri	35–31	November 18, 1978
8.	Oklahoma	47–0	November 23, 1968
9.	Oklahoma	17–7	November 21, 1964
10.	Colorado	20–10	October 25, 1986

Bender's Persistence

Johnny Bender, an outstanding back at the turn of the century, is credited with having earned five varsity football letters at Nebraska from 1900 to 1904. The story goes that a young newspaper boy was passing the T Street field on which Nebraska was practicing when a football sailed over the fence.

The boy picked up the ball, stuffed it into his newspaper bag, and took off running. Bender, wearing cleated shoes, scaled the fence and sprinted after the boy, who quickly wore down—because, he said, he was observing KEEP OFF THE GRASS signs while Bender was not. The boy, hoping to escape, turned and tossed the ball back toward Bender, who fielded it on one hop and continued his pursuit.

Bender closed quickly and gave the youngster a swift kick in the seat of his pants, then returned to practice. The paper carrier said years later he considered it a point of pride that he had been kicked by Bender. Such was the admiration for Nebraska football players from the beginning.

Fat Fox

Don Bryant, who had tried out as a lineman on the freshman football team at Nebraska, met Norris Anderson in a Spanish class at the university in 1948. Anderson was working in the sports department of the *Lincoln Star* and persuaded Bryant to join him in writing about the Cornhuskers instead of playing for them. In 1954, Bryant succeeded Anderson as the newspaper's sports editor.

Bryant and Dick Becker, the sports editor of the *Lincoln Journal,* so angered Nebraska coach Bill Glassford that he nicknamed them the Bobbsey twins and once challenged them to put on gear and practice with his players. Bryant and Becker declined, claiming they had used up their eligibility.

In 1963, one year after Bob Devaney arrived from Wyoming, Bryant succeeded John Bentley as the Cornhuskers sports information director, a position he held, and defined, for 31 years.

Bentley, who also began as a Lincoln sportswriter, "showed me where the print shop was. He showed me a file cabinet and a desk. Then he left for the golf course," Bryant has said.

Bryant has been an integral part of Nebraska football for more than half a century. The "Fat Fox" is a Cornhusker institution. He was given the nickname "Fox" during a track meet at which he was competing as a student at Lincoln High School. The "Fat" was added later by the equally colorful Anderson.

Father of the Cornhuskers

Charles Sumner "Cy" Sherman was among those who braved a blinding blizzard to watch Nebraska defeat Iowa 20–18 on Thanksgiving Day, 1893. The victory was Nebraska's first in football against its neighboring state university, after a 22–0 loss in 1891 and a 10–10 tie in 1892.

The Nebraska team was referred to in newspaper accounts the next day as "bugeaters," a nickname the young Sherman considered inappropriate. Several years later, after becoming a sportswriter at the *Nebraska State Journal,* Sherman was in a position to do something about the nickname.

He suggested Nebraska's athletic teams be called "Cornhuskers," a nickname that once had been applied, derisively, to Iowa's football team by the Nebraska student newspaper following a game between the schools in 1894. "We have met the 'cornhuskers' and they are ours," the story said.

"Mr. Sherman's suggestion met with a great deal of favor on the campus," Guy Reed wrote in the university's *Semi-Centennial Anniversary Book,* published in 1917. "And Albert Watkins, Jr., then prominent in college journalism, took up the idea and firmly established the name."

In 1907, the university's student yearbook the *Sombrero* became *The Cornhusker,* and in fall 1933, Sherman was awarded a gold football and a varsity letter by the Nebraska "N" Club for giving the Cornhuskers their name. Few nonathletes have ever been honored in such a way.

By then, Sherman was sports editor of the *Lincoln Star.* He was among the best-known sportswriters of his time, along with the legendary Grantland Rice in New York City, Sec Taylor in Des Moines, Iowa, and Clyde McBride in Kansas City, among others. Sherman was a driving force in the creation of the Associated Press Top 10 national rankings, which first were published in 1936.

In 1946, the state legislature passed a bill making Nebraska the Cornhusker State. Governor Dwight Griswold gave the pen with which he signed the bill to Sherman, who died in 1951 at age 80.

Nebraska's athletic teams were referred to by various nicknames in newspaper accounts before the turn of the century. In addition to bugeaters, they were called, among other things, Old Gold Knights (old gold was the school color before scarlet and cream), Rattlesnake Boys, Antelopes, and the none-too-imaginative Nebraskans. A writer might use more than one nickname in the same story.

Although the nickname "bugeaters" sounds unflattering, the connotation was actually positive. As the story goes, a newspaper reporter from New York City was sent to Nebraska in 1875 to report on the effects of a drought. The reporter concluded, somewhat tongue-in-cheek, that because of the drought, and a grasshopper plague, Nebraskans had little left to eat except bugs.

The reporter hadn't intended to be complimentary, but those hearty pioneers to whom the term "bugeaters" applied took it as a symbol of their perseverance, their will to survive and not be driven away by unimaginable hardship. They were so tough, they would eat bugs before they would give up.

Such an image certainly fit the nature of football at that formative time.

One of the earliest references to Cornhuskers was included in the *Nebraska State Journal* account of Nebraska's 20–12 loss to mighty Minnesota at Lincoln in 1900. Near the end of the lengthy game story, the anonymous reporter wrote that "the corn huskers, failing to net gains through the line, punted again for twenty yards. The gophers brought it back 10 yards." Perhaps that reporter was Sherman.

Christians and Lions . . . or Panthers

In 1957, Coach Bill Jennings's first Nebraska team traveled to Pittsburgh to play the 20th-ranked Panthers at Pitt Stadium. Pittsburgh won 34–0. The loss was the third of nine for the Cornhuskers that season. Bill King, who did radio broadcasts of Nebraska games at the time, described it thus: "The stadium was old, very spare, Spartan, austere. They closed the gates at one end. Our poor, old football team . . . it was like closing the doors on the Christians and the lions. They re-created that scenario that day."

King, whose color commentator was former Cornhusker Tom Novak, left Nebraska and became a local celebrity in the San Francisco Bay Area, where he became a broadcaster for sports teams there and a regular at the opera and other social events, making his home on a houseboat in Sausalito.

Picture This

Owen Frank played for the Cornhuskers from 1909 to 1911 and then coached at Nebraska. He was a football assistant and served as head basketball coach for two seasons, from 1921 to 1923. Frank was among the first to take photographs when scouting opponents. He used a pocket camera, often developing the pictures and arranging them with his notes on the train ride back to Lincoln.

Notre Dame

Notre Dame's scouting report on Nebraska was prepared by Jesse Harper's assistant, Knute Rockne. Among other things, it noted that Nebraska's Guy Chamberlin always wet his fingertips when he was going to pass. Notre Dame would be alert for that when it played Nebraska in Lincoln in late October 1915.

The problem was, that particular afternoon, Chamberlin crossed them up and sometimes ran with the ball after wetting his fingertips, much to the delight of 8,000 fans at Nebraska Field. He was equally effective running, passing, and catching in the Cornhuskers' 20–19 victory against the Ramblers.

Chamberlin scored two touchdowns, the first on a 20-yard run, after teaming with Ted Riddell on a 37-yard pass play to set it up, the second on a 24-yard pass from Loren Caley, who passed 36 yards to Riddell for the third touchdown. The touchdowns, in combination with a pair of Caley extra-point conversions, were sufficient to hand Notre Dame its only loss of the season.

The game, in Jumbo Stiehm's final season as Nebraska's head coach, was the first between the Cornhuskers and Notre Dame. The teams would play 10 more times before the series was abruptly terminated by Notre Dame after the 1925 game at Memorial Stadium because of what Notre Dame officials claimed was "ill treatment and disrespectful conduct" by Nebraska fans.

Nebraska and Notre Dame didn't play again until a home-and-home series in 1947 and 1948. The Fighting Irish of Coach Frank Leahy won both games. The last of the 14 games between the tradition-rich schools was played in Miami in the 1973 Orange Bowl—Nebraska won handily, 40–6.

Notre Dame leads the series 7–6–1. Nebraska will have an opportunity to even matters when it travels to South Bend on September 9, 2000, to play the first of two more games against the Fighting Irish. Notre Dame is scheduled to play a return game at Memorial Stadium on September 8, 2001.

Although brief, the Nebraska–Notre Dame series was spirited. In addition to the 1915 game, the Cornhuskers handed Notre Dame its only losses in 1917, 1920, and 1923. Notre Dame returned the favor in 1921, defeating Coach Fred Dawson's first Nebraska team 7–0 at South Bend.

The Cornhuskers played against George Gipp and the Four Horsemen. They played Knute Rockne's first Notre Dame team as head coach to a scoreless tie in the snow at Lincoln in 1918. Rockne called Nebraska's Ed Weir as good a tackle as he had ever seen. Tom Novak twice distinguished himself in defeat against the Fighting Irish. And nearly 60 years after that first game between the schools, Johnny Rodgers almost single-handedly provided Bob Devaney with a victory in his final game as coach.

The Four Horsemen Versus the Cornhuskers

Sportswriter Grantland Rice nicknamed Notre Dame's backfield the Four Horsemen in 1924, after a 13–7 victory against Army at the Polo Grounds in New York City in October 1924.

QB—Harry Stuhldreher	5-foot-7, 151 pounds	Massillon, Ohio
LH—Jim Crowley	5-foot-11, 162 pounds	Green Bay, Wisconsin
RH—Don Miller	5-foot-11, 160 pounds	Defiance, Ohio
FB—Elmer Layden	5-foot-11, 162 pounds	Davenport, Iowa

His account of the game for the *New York Herald Tribune* began: "Outlined against a blue, gray October sky the Four Horsemen rode again. In dramatic lore they are known as famine, pestilence, destruction and death. These are only aliases. Their real names are Stuhldreher, Miller, Crowley and Layden."

A month later, Coach Fred Dawson's Cornhuskers traveled to South Bend to play against them. A crowd of 22,000 at Cartier Field looked on as Nebraska took a 6–0 lead against Notre Dame's second team. Coach Knute Rockne regularly started his number two unit, the shock troops, then substituted his first unit. Nebraska was overmatched by Rockne's first unit, which included the Horsemen. Layden plunged for Notre Dame's first and last touchdowns. Miller scored the second and third, on runs of 10 and 19 yards. And Crowley scored the fourth, on a 70-yard pass from Stuhldreher.

Quiz 4: Corraling the Four Horsemen

Stuhldreher, Crowley, Miller, and Layden played 30 games as a unit from 1922 to 1924. And they lost only twice.

To whom did they lose to and where?

The Gipper

George Gipp played against Nebraska four times. Doc Stewart's Cornhuskers defeated Gipp and Notre Dame 7–0 in 1917. It was one of only two losing games in which he played there. The teams played a scoreless tie in 1918, and Notre Dame won 14–9 in 1919 and 16–7 in 1920. Gipp rushed for 70 yards, passed for 117 yards, intercepted a pass, and scored a touchdown and two extra points in the 1920 game at Nebraska Field. He died at age 25, of complications from a throat infection in December 1920.

Notre Dame's record in the last 20 games in which Gipp played was 19–0–1. The tie, of course, was with Nebraska. Gipp was Notre Dame's first All-American. His name was included on Walter Camp's All-America team for 1920. The team was announced not long before Gipp died.

Jimmy

Jack Best arrived at Nebraska in 1888 as a night watchman and remained at the university until he died in January 1923, at age 77. Best served as Nebraska's athletic trainer for more than 30 years.

He was popular among the university students, who called him Jimmy, a reference to Jimmie Grimes, the name under which he boxed as a young man growing up in England.

Even though he was in failing health, he attended the final game at Nebraska Field, the Cornhuskers' 14–6 victory against Notre Dame. "'Tis the last game I'll ever see," Best said. "I wanted me boys to win that last one." And so they did. "His hair grew white and his body gnarled in the service of the University, but his brown eyes twinkled and his voice was merry to the last day that he sat in his old chair down in the varsity room," read a dedication in the 1923 student yearbook, *The Cornhusker.*

Answers

Quiz 1: There Were Coaches Before Devaney and Osborne

1. 1. G, 2. K, 3. C, 4. L, 5. H, 6. F, 7. A, 8. E, 9. I, 10. B, 11. J, 12. D
2. Charles Thomas, Henry Schulte, and Pete Elliott
3. 1. I, 2. E, 3. J, 4. D, 5. H, 6. A, 7. G, 8. C, 9. F, 10. B
4. Glassford's nickname was "Biff." But Nebraska had only one Biff, Biff Jones.
5. Glassford came from the University of New Hampshire.
6. D. X. Bible
7. Langdon Frothingham
8. Dana Xenophon
9. Charles Thomas, who was Nebraska's head coach for only one season.
10. W. C. "King" Cole
11. E. J. "Doc" Stewart
12. Fred Dawson
13. Elmer Ernest "Ernie" Bearg
14. D. X. Bible
15. Biff Jones was an army major. He was called back into service in World War II as a colonel.
16. Fielding Yost
17. Jumbo Stiehm. His record at Nebraska was 35–2–3.
18. Jumbo Stiehm
19. Pittsburgh, 0–6–2, and Minnesota, 0–4
20. W. C. "Bummy" Booth
21. D. X. Bible, Bob Devaney, Biff Jones, E. N. Robinson, Fielding Yost, Tom Osborne
22. Edward North Robinson, 1896–97
23. T. U. Lyman coached Nebraska for 10 days before it played Iowa.
24. Nebraska contacted Knute Rockne after the 1928 season. Rockne wasn't interested in leaving Notre Dame, but he recommended D. X. Bible. Rockne's winning percentage was .881.
25. Johnny Bender

Quiz 2: Some Things Old

1. Johnny Bender, a Nebraska football letterman from 1900 to 1904.

2. King Cole's Nebraska team defeated Haskell Indian School 119–0.

3. Nebraska defeated Kearney Normal, which is now the University of Nebraska–Kearney, 117–0.

4. Stiehm was known as Jumbo because, the student yearbook reported, his feet were "as large as an elephant's." Stiehm's given first name was Ewald—apparently, Eddie came from this.

5. Minnesota won 21–3 in 1911 and 13–0 in 1912. Both games were played in Minneapolis.

6. Owen Frank

7. Indiana hired Stiehm away from Nebraska, offering him a three-year contract. He had a gentleman's agreement to remain at Nebraska for another season. But Nebraska officials didn't try to hold him to that agreement. The business community offered to guarantee a comparable salary increase if Stiehm would remain at Nebraska. But the university faculty balked at such a suggestion. Stiehm already was making more money than anyone except the university chancellor. Stiehm said, in a prepared statement, "Had the university deemed it advisable to meet the terms offered me elsewhere, I should have gladly remained."

8. Dick Rutherford

9. Nebraska, Kansas, Missouri, Iowa, and Washington–St. Louis

10. Nebraska, Iowa State, Oklahoma, Kansas, Kansas State, Missouri

11. Colorado left the Skyline Conference to create the Big Seven in 1947. Oklahoma State was added to the conference in 1957, creating the Big Eight.

12. The University of South Dakota challenged Nebraska to a football game in 1889.

13. Ebenezer E. Mockett

14. Doane College, Nebraska Wesleyan, and Christian University, which later became Cotner College

15. Jim Thorpe was the left halfback for the Carlisle Indians. He scored a touchdown against the Cornhuskers. A newspaper headline the next day read: REDSKINS SCALP THE NEBRASKANS.

16. Nebraska defeated Oklahoma 24–0. Kansas played the Cornhuskers to a 0–0 tie in the dedication game. In 1922, Nebraska defeated Kansas 28–0 in the dedication game for its Memorial Stadium. Michigan, Ohio State, and Yale also lost games that dedicated new stadiums. "It looks like it is impossible for a team to win the game which formally opens a stadium," a newspaper account of the 1923 Kansas game said.

17. George "Potsy" Clark

18. Guy Chamberlin

19. Ed Weir

20. Henry Schulte came to Nebraska from Missouri, replacing William G. Kline in 1919.

Quiz 3: Are You Paying Attention?

Ohio State's young coach in 1955 was Woody Hayes. Paul "Bear" Bryant, Texas A&M's head coach, said after the Nebraska game in 1955, "I don't know how to say this; some people aren't going to like it. These Huskers are good kids and they hit hard. But they aren't very talented. By that I mean they aren't very fast and quick."

Quiz 4: Corraling the Four Horsemen

Both losses were against Nebraska, of course, 14–6 in 1922 and 14–7 in 1923. Both games were at Lincoln.

The Cornhuskers' loss in 1924 was certainly no disgrace. Notre Dame went 9–0 during the regular season, then defeated Stanford in the Rose Bowl, 27–10. Even though the Associated Press rankings were still a dozen years away, Notre Dame was a consensus selection as the 1924 national champion.

The program for the November 26, 1925, game against Notre Dame.
(Photo Courtesy of Author's Collection)

2

NATIONAL CHAMPIONSHIPS:
Cornhusker Style

Tom Osborne found out in the early morning hours of January 3, 1998. He was in his suite at the Sheraton Bal Harbour on Miami Beach, packing for the charter flight home in the afternoon.

The television set was tuned to the ESPN cable network. He and his family just "happened to be watching," he said with a smile at a post–Orange Bowl news conference later that morning.

When the announcement was made on ESPN, "it was kind of a surprise . . . a little bit."

Osborne was a little bit surprised to learn that his final Nebraska team had been voted the national championship in the *USA Today*/ESPN coaches' poll, moving ahead of previous number one Michigan on the strength of a 42–17 victory against number three–ranked Tennessee in the Orange Bowl game.

Michigan was voted the national championship in the Associated Press poll and had expected to earn the coaches' title as well, after defeating Washington State in the Rose Bowl game, 21–16.

"I'm really pleased for the University of Michigan, strangely enough," Osborne said at the post–Orange Bowl news conference. The Sears trophy was to his right. "Anytime somebody goes 12–0 and has the kind of year they've had, they very much deserve to be national champions. And I guess when you go 13–0 and have the kind of year we had, we hope some kind of recognition would come, also."

There was considerable doubt that would be the case, however. Nebraska had one first-place vote to the Wolverines' 69 in the AP's final regular-season poll and 8.5 of 62 first-place votes in the coaches' poll. It appeared Nebraska might be the first team to go 13–0 and not win a national championship.

The Cornhuskers lobbied hard both before and after the Orange Bowl game, asking voters to compare their performance against Tennessee to Michigan's performance against Washington State.

Scott Frost, Nebraska's quarterback, was particularly adamant that the Cornhuskers had earned at least a share of the national championship. "It's been split before," the senior from Wood River, Nebraska, said during a

Tom Osborne

(Photo Courtesy of *Huskers Illustrated*/Scott Smith)

post–Orange Bowl game interview. "It should be split, and it's up to the coaches."

Cornhusker defensive tackle Jason Peter was less generous. "If you ask me, I don't even think it should be a split title," he said. "We proved we're the best team in the country, without a doubt."

Whether the coaches who voted in the *USA Today*/ESPN poll were persuaded by such passion is unlikely. But enough were impressed by the Orange Bowl victory to change their minds. Nebraska had 32 first-place votes to Michigan's 30 in the final poll. Eight coaches split their number one votes.

As Frost indicated, there were precedents for different national champions in the two major polls. The Cornhuskers' first national title in 1970 had been shared, in fact. Texas finished number one in the coaches' poll, then sponsored by United Press International, while Nebraska was number one according to the AP.

The final UPI coaches' poll was taken before the bowl games at that time. Nebraska finished number three, behind Texas and Ohio State, both of whom were upset in New Year's Day bowl games.

Prior to 1950, when the coaches' poll was established, the AP poll was generally regarded as the means by which major college football national champions were determined. From 1950 on, the coaches' poll added a second opinion on national champions—which typically was the same.

Counting the one in 1997, there have been 10 shared national championships since 1950.

	COACHES	ASSOCIATED PRESS
1997	Nebraska	Michigan
1991	Washington	Miami
1990	Georgia Tech	Colorado
1978	USC	Alabama
1974	Alabama	Oklahoma
1973	Alabama	Notre Dame
1970	Texas	Nebraska
1965	Michigan State	Alabama
1957	Ohio State	Auburn
1954	UCLA	Ohio State

Nebraska might have won both national championships in 1997 if not for a 45–38 overtime victory at unranked Missouri in early November that cost the Cornhuskers the number one ranking in both polls.

Michigan moved from fourth to first following a 34–8 victory against number two–ranked Penn State that same day, jumping over third-ranked Florida State as well as Nebraska. Despite winning in dramatic fashion, or perhaps because of that, the Cornhuskers fell to third—with Florida State number two.

The volatility of the polls could be seen in the fact that Nebraska, which was number six in the preseason rankings, moved from second to first with a 29–0 victory against Texas Tech at Lincoln on the same afternoon that Penn State had to come from behind to beat Minnesota 16–15 at home.

The Cornhuskers were number one for three weeks before dropping. They moved back up to number two in both polls after an off week in which Florida State was defeated by Florida 32–29. Michigan completed an 11–0 regular season that Saturday by defeating Ohio State at Ann Arbor 20–14.

Nebraska's hopes of gaining on the Wolverines with impressive victories in its final two games faded in a lackluster 27–24 victory against Colorado at Boulder. Despite overwhelming Texas A&M in the Big 12 play-off 54–15 to finish the regular season, the Cornhuskers appeared locked in at number two.

Since no number one team had ever won a bowl game and dropped from the top spot, it appeared Michigan could wrap up both national championships by defeating Washington State in the Rose Bowl.

The day before that game, Osborne said, "I hope people [voters] will at least watch the games."

The national championship was Osborne's third in four seasons, something only one other school has accomplished in the modern era. Notre Dame won national titles in 1946, 1947, and 1949.

Osborne compared his three national championship teams at the post—Orange Bowl news conference. "The one in '94 was kind of held together by will and baling wire," he said. "We had [Tommie] Frazier hurt and [Brook] Berringer with a collapsed lung. . . . Matt Turman, he wasn't totally healthy."

The 13–0 1994 team had a "tremendous attitude, cohesiveness, and an improved defense," he said.

The 12–0 team in 1995 was "very, very talented on both sides of the ball, probably the most talented team I've ever coached," said Osborne. Because of much-publicized off-the-field problems, it also was "the most controversial team I've ever coached, and maybe the most unpleasant year I've ever gone through, yet, at the same time, the most pleasant year, depending which way you looked at it.

"This year's team was somewhere in between, probably a little more talented than '94, certainly not near as controversial as '95—and that was nice. So it was just kind of a nice way to go, great leadership on the part of the players, and I didn't have to do much. I had no idea it would work out this way."

Jason Peter and rush end Grant Wistrom, the Lombardi Award winner, provided the leadership to which Osborne referred. Wistrom considered bypassing his final season of eligibility and declaring for the NFL draft. The consensus was, he would have been a late first-round selection.

Peter also could have skipped the season in favor of the NFL. The fact that both returned, "I think probably put us over the hump, if not their athletic skills, their leadership," Osborne said.

"Those two guys, among some others, ramrodded that football team. They decided a year ago they were going to come back and get the thing done. Their leadership was invaluable."

Nebraska played Tennessee on the day after the Rose Bowl, so the Cornhuskers knew Michigan had won. Even so, Osborne said he thought the Cornhuskers' chances of earning at least a share of the national championship were "fifty-fifty. It wasn't like I thought it was uphill. We talked to the players after we watched the Michigan–Washington State game, got 'em together right afterward.

"I said, 'You know, that door's open at least a crack. It wasn't a thumping [in the Rose Bowl]. If Michigan had won by three or four touchdowns, we'd probably be out of it. But it's open, and we've got to take advantage of it. We've got to make sure it's wide open.' We tried to reemphasize that."

Nebraska did with a dominating 21-point third quarter against Tennessee.

After the Orange Bowl game, all the Cornhuskers could do was wait—and lobby.

Osborne didn't recall shedding any tears of joy when he got the news. "By that time, I was wrung out enough that there wasn't much emotion left," he said. "Naturally, I was very pleased."

It had been a long day, his last as Nebraska's head coach, really.

"I was thinking seriously about going to bed," he said.

Quiz 5: Top of the Hill

1. The play of the national championship season was freshman Matt Davison's diving catch of Scott Frost's deflected pass for a touchdown with no time remaining in regulation of the Missouri game. Cornhusker wingback Shevin Wiggins, the intended receiver, kept the ball alive by kicking it. Nebraska fans are familiar with Wiggins's heads-up play. A Missouri defensive back probably would have caught the ball if not for Wiggins's kick. Who was the defensive back? Did Davison catch any other passes in the game? If so, how many?

2. The Missouri game was Nebraska's first-ever overtime. The Cornhuskers scored a touchdown on their first possession in the overtime. How many plays did they run in the overtime? Who scored the winning touchdown? How long of a play was it?

Extra credit: Nebraska's defense held Missouri on four downs in the Tigers' overtime possession. What happened on Missouri's fourth and final down?

3. Nebraska recruited two Tennessee players who received a lot of media attention prior to the Orange Bowl game. Who were the two Volunteers who got away from Nebraska?

4. Tom Osborne announced the week after the Big 12 championship game that he would be stepping aside as head coach following the Orange Bowl game. Some suggested he was trying to attract votes on sentiment for the national championship. "I heard that discussed," Osborne said at an Orange Bowl news conference, adding, "You don't end your career, normally, to get a few votes." Some suggested Michigan got the sentimental vote because it hadn't won a national championship for such a long time. When was the Wolverines' last national title?

5. Two members of Nebraska's 1997 national championship team were among the three finalists for the Outland Trophy. Aaron Taylor won the award, edging teammate Jason Peter. Who was the other finalist for the award as the nation's outstanding interior lineman? From what school?

6. Nebraska's national championship teams in 1994 and 1997 were 13–0. How many other teams in Cornhusker history, if any, have won 13 games? Also identify the year or years.

7. Nebraska and Michigan had two common opponents in 1997. Who were they?

8. Tom Osborne went into the Orange Bowl game as the second-winningest active football coach by percentage in NCAA Division I-A. Who had moved ahead of Osborne on that list?

9. Tom Osborne finished his career with a record of 255–49–3, a winning percentage of .836. Which of the following Division I-A football coaches had a higher career winning percentage than Osborne: Knute Rockne, Barry Switzer, Bud Wilkinson, Bear Bryant, Woody Hayes?

10. Tom Osborne compiled more victories than any other football coach in Cornhusker history. His 255 victories represented 35.3 percent of Nebraska's total victories, all time, through the 1997 season. However, Osborne's winning percentage is not the highest in Cornhusker history. What two coaches with a minimum of five seasons have higher winning percentages?

However . . . There Was 1995

The best football team in Cornhusker history may also have been the best in major college history. Computer analyst Jeff Sagarin drew that conclusion, based on a comparison of teams dating from 1956. Coach Tom Osborne's 1995 national championship team was a clear-cut number one, with Bob Devaney's 1971 team number two, in Sagarin's post-1956 Top 25 published by USA Today in 1996.

The 1995 Cornhuskers weren't seriously challenged in the regular season, outscoring 11 opponents by an average of 39 points. They led the nation in scoring, averaging a school-record 52.4 points per game, and rushing. And they ranked second nationally in total offense, averaging 569.4 yards per game.

They capped their championship season by making short work of second-ranked Florida in the Fiesta Bowl game, scoring a bowl-record 29 points in the second quarter on the way to a 62–24 victory.

The 1995 team is among Osborne's favorites, though not only because it was a repeat national champion. "The '95 team was memorable because of the way the players hung together," Osborne has said. "They didn't allow themselves to be distracted." They maintained their focus despite negative national publicity, in large part the result of an off-the-field incident involving Lawrence Phillips.

The talented junior I-back, who had rushed for 1,722 yards and 16 touchdowns the previous season, was suspended and didn't play in six regular-season games, only two of which he started.

Phillips's absence made the offensive accomplishments even more remarkable. The key was quarterback Tommie Frazier, a dominating presence from the beginning of the season to the end. Frazier capped his extraordinary career by rushing for 199 yards and two touchdowns in the Fiesta Bowl game.

1. Lawrence Phillips started only two regular-season games in 1995. Three other I-backs started the remaining nine regular-season games. Name the three. Extra credit: Which of the three had the most starts?

2. Nebraska scored more than 70 points twice during the 1995 season. Against whom did the Cornhuskers score more than 70 points? Extra credit: What were the final scores?

Before the Polls

Charles "Cy" Sherman, a Lincoln, Nebraska, sportswriter, is known as the father of the Cornhuskers because he gave them their nickname at the turn of the century. He also was a driving force in establishing the Associated Press poll, which was the basis for their first national championship in 1970.

In 1970, the final United Press International coaches' poll was conducted before the bowl games. As a result, Texas was UPI's national champion, finishing the regular season undefeated and untied. Ohio State, also undefeated and untied, was number two. And Nebraska, with one tie, was number three.

Texas and Ohio State lost bowl games, however, while Nebraska defeated Louisiana State 17–12 in the Orange Bowl game to earn the AP version of the national championship for 1970.

Through the efforts of Sherman, sports editor of the *Lincoln Star* at the time, the AP poll was established in 1936. Nebraska was number nine in the final rankings that season. Coach Biff Jones's 1940 team, which played Stanford in the Rose Bowl, was number seven in the final AP poll, which was conducted at the end of the regular season. Nebraska wouldn't make another appearance in the AP Top 10 until 1963, when Coach Bob Devaney's second team had climbed to sixth by the end of the regular season.

Nebraska had at least one national champion prior to 1970, according to Sherman, who claimed that Coach Jumbo Stiehm's final Cornhusker team in 1915 was the nation's best. "Rating scoring power as the surest means of measuring the strength of a football team, the Cornhuskers of 1915 are the champion eleven of the nation," Sherman wrote.

Sherman supported his contention by pointing out that Nebraska had scored 282 points, second only to Cornell's 287 points. The Ivy League school had achieved that total in nine games, however, Sherman wrote, while Nebraska played only eight games. A reader responded to Sherman in a letter to the editor, noting that Vanderbilt and Rutgers also had scored more total points than Nebraska.

What the reader failed to mention, Sherman wrote in reply, was that neither Vanderbilt nor Rutgers had been undefeated and untied. Vanderbilt had lost to Auburn and Rutgers had lost to Princeton.

Nebraska's "Stiehm-rollers" had shut out five of their eight opponents. They had one close call, defeating Coach Jesse Harper's Notre Dame team 20–19 at Lincoln in late October. There was no disgrace in that, however. Notre Dame won its other seven games by a combined score of 211–9.

Drake and Iowa were the other teams that managed to cross Nebraska's goal line in 1915. The Stiehm-rollers defeated Drake 48–13 in their season opener and Iowa 52–7 in their final game.

The Iowa victory was Nebraska's 14th in a row over two seasons, a string that would reach 19 under Doc Stewart, Stiehm's successor. It also extended a Cornhusker unbeaten streak to 29 games. With the five victories to begin the 1916 season, the unbeaten streak, which began after a 13–0 loss at Minnesota on October 19, 1912, reached a school-record 34 games. Kansas ended it, 7–3, on November 18, 1916.

In an attempt to solidify Nebraska's claim as the nation's best in 1915, Stiehm contacted several eastern powers, including the Ivy League's Harvard, in hopes of scheduling a postseason game.

There were no takers. Sherman quoted an unidentified "former player and coach at Yale" as saying the Cornhuskers would defeat Harvard in "straight football" by at least two touchdowns. That opinion, no doubt, was the result of the rivalry between Yale and Harvard as much as Nebraska's strength.

"Straight football" meant without passing, which was legalized in 1906. Using the forward pass, Nebraska would have beaten Harvard by several touchdowns, according to Sherman.

Regardless of what might have happened in such an intersectional matchup, the 1915 Cornhuskers were impressive. Four of them were named to All-Western teams selected by Chicago newspapers: halfback and captain Dick Rutherford, end Guy Chamberlin, tackle Harold Corey, and guard Earl Abbott.

Chamberlin, a consensus selection, was the "most brilliant player ever developed in the annals of Missouri Valley football," Sherman wrote. Those who watched him play agreed.

The 1915 and 1902 teams were the "greatest in our history," Guy Reed wrote in a semicentennial history of the university, published in 1917. The 1902 team, coached by Bummy Booth, was even more impressive statistically than the Stiehm-rollers. Booth's Cornhuskers were 9–0, and all nine victories were shutouts, as was a season-opening exhibition victory against Lincoln High School.

Booth's 1903 team extended the shutout streak to 14, though Lincoln High managed to score in a 23–6 loss to the Cornhuskers in another preseason exhibition. Not counting the exhibition, Nebraska was 10–0 in 1903, with eight shutouts. The 19 consecutive victories in 1902 and 1903 were the heart of a 24-game winning streak that began after an 18–0 loss at Wisconsin in 1901 and ended with a 6–0 loss at Colorado in 1904. The streak held as the school record until the 1994–95 national championship seasons.

Booth, a Princeton graduate, compiled a 46–8–1 record in six seasons (not counting exhibitions), for a winning percentage of .845. Nebraska's opponent failed to score in 39 of those games.

Despite the remarkable record, Nebraska's lack of success against teams from the nationally prominent Western Conference was cause for some degree of disaffection among university students. Four of the eight losses were against Minnesota, and two were against Michigan and Wisconsin.

Among the best-known players on the 1902 team were tackle and captain John Westover, halfback and center Charles Borg, and quarterback Maurice Benedict. Borg and Benedict were freshmen.

Although it wasn't a national championship contender, Coach Ernie Bearg's 1928 Big Six championship team was in a position to attract national attention with an appearance in the Rose Bowl. The Cornhuskers won their first six games, four by shutout, then played Pittsburgh to a scoreless tie. With a victory against Army at West Point the next week, Nebraska appeared certain of receiving a Rose Bowl bid.

Led by All-American halfback Chris Cagle, however, Army won 13–3. It would be a dozen seasons and two coaching changes before the Cornhuskers would finally play in the Rose Bowl.

Nebraska rebounded from the Army loss to defeat Kansas State 8–0, shutout number five in a 7–1–1 season. The Cornhuskers dominated the all-conference team with eight selections: end Cliff Ashburn, tackles Marion Broadstone and Glen Munn, guard Dan McMullen, center Ted James, and backs Clair Sloan, Blue Howell, and Lafayette Russell. McMullen also received All-America recognition.

3. The head coach of the Army team that cost the Cornhuskers a Rose Bowl bid in 1928 took them to Pasadena for the 1941 Rose Bowl game against Stanford. Name him.

First Official Title

After Nebraska defeated Louisiana State 17–12 in the Orange Bowl game on the night of January 1, 1971, Cornhusker coach Bob Devaney was ecstatic. "Hell, yes, we're number one," he shouted in answer to a question about whether he thought his team would be first in the final Associated Press national rankings. "We're the only undefeated team. I can't see how the pope himself could vote for Notre Dame."

Though Devaney's choice of words could have been more judicious, his logic was irrefutable. Three teams had begun the day undefeated. But only Nebraska had remained that way. Number one–ranked Texas had been upset by Notre Dame in the Cotton Bowl, 24–11, leaving the national title for number two–ranked Ohio State—had the Buckeyes not been shocked in the Rose Bowl by Stanford, 27–17.

Devaney, whose team was ranked number three, was anticipating Notre

Dame coach Ara Parseghian's argument that the Fighting Irish would deserve the national championship by winning against Texas.

But Notre Dame had faltered late in the season, escaping with three-point victories at home against Georgia Tech (10–7) and LSU (3–0), then losing at traditional rival Southern Cal 38–28.

The only blemish on Nebraska's record was a 21–21 tie with those same Trojans at Los Angeles in the second game of the season. Southern Cal had been ranked number three by the Associated Press when the Cornhuskers visited the Coliseum. But Coach John McKay's team faltered.

By defeating Notre Dame, the Trojans managed to avoid a losing record. But they finished 5–4–1 and out of the rankings. Parseghian's national championship argument carried little weight.

Nebraska began the 1970 season at number nine in the AP rankings, after winning its final seven games in 1969 to finish 11th in the AP poll and 12th in United Press International's prebowl poll. The Cornhuskers moved up in the rankings, slowly but steadily, reaching number three after their next-to-last regular-season game, a 51–13 victory against number 20 Kansas State at a snow-packed Memorial Stadium. They retained the number three ranking with a 28–21 victory against unranked Oklahoma, also in Lincoln.

Devaney took the team to Miami on Christmas day to begin preparations for fifth-ranked LSU, which led the nation in defense, allowing only two rushing touchdowns all season.

Ironically, Devaney thought his Big Eight champions would be matched against Notre Dame in the 1971 Orange Bowl game. But Parseghian had opted to play top-ranked Texas in a rematch of the previous year's Cotton Bowl game, won by the national champion Longhorns 21–17. No matter. Whether Notre Dame or LSU, the Cornhuskers were all business. The players even voted to skip the Orange Bowl parade and remain at team headquarters, the Ivanhoe Hotel. There would be no distractions.

Nebraska's players and coaches watched on television at the Ivanhoe as Notre Dame upset Texas. When the Cornhuskers boarded buses for the trip to the Orange Bowl stadium, the third quarter of the Rose Bowl was coming to an end. Ohio State was clinging to a 17–13 lead over Stanford.

The tension was tangible on the ride to the stadium. At one point, with the buses stopped in traffic, Ed Periard jumped from his seat and shouted, "Get this damn thing rolling." The senior from Birch Run, Michigan, a 5-foot-9, 201-pound middle guard, was among the team's emotional leaders.

Periard's patience was further strained when the buses entered the wrong gate at the stadium and had to inch their way through the crowd. Ohio State still led in Pasadena. But there was a chance. . . .

The Cornhuskers were warming up when news came through the crowd that Stanford had taken a 20–17 lead. By the time the team went to the locker room before the kickoff, the Rose Bowl was over, and Stanford had won

27–17. The players were jubilant. "We're not number one yet," Devaney warned.

They were number one in the eyes of their fans, however. The longest telegram ever delivered by Western Union was evidence of that. The Associated Press reported that the telegram was 1,400 feet long and included more than 46,000 signatures. It said: "Congratulations and best wishes to the finest coaching staff and players in America. You are No. 1 with us. We are very proud of you. Go, Big Red."

Nebraska rode its pent-up emotion and the prospect of winning a national championship to a 10–0 first-quarter lead. But LSU, which had a rushing net of minus 45 yards in the first half, somehow battled back and took a 12–10 lead with a 31-yard touchdown pass on the final play of the third quarter.

Though he is most remembered for directing the winning touchdown drive in the 1971 "Game of the Century" against Oklahoma, quarterback Jerry Tagge took the Cornhuskers on a 14-play, 67-yard fourth-quarter drive that he capped by stretching the ball across the goal line with 8:50 remaining. LSU held on three downs from its 4-yard line but couldn't deny Tagge on the fourth. Though he was stopped short, he reached out with the ball, "one of the smartest plays I've ever seen in football," LSU coach Charlie McClendon is quoted as saying in Loran Smith's *Fifty Years on the Fifty: The Orange Bowl Story*.

Paul Rogers's extra-point kick made the score 17–12, and Nebraska's defense made the lead hold up.

The Cornhuskers were national champions for the first time.

Devaney and his wife, Phyllis, entertained the assistant coaches and their wives at the Ivanhoe into the early morning hours. Junior I-back Jeff Kinney and his wife passed the room in which the celebration was taking place. Devaney offered a glass of champagne, but Kinney declined.

"Not tonight," Kinney said. "It's been kind of a long day."

4. LSU took a 12–10 lead in the 1971 Orange Bowl game on a 31-yard touchdown pass from Buddy Lee to Al Coffee. Tigers coach Charlie McClendon replaced Lee with another, more famous quarterback with 6:10 remaining in the game. Name this quarterback.

5. Notre Dame helped Nebraska win its first national championship by unsetting top-ranked Texas in the 1971 Cotton Bowl. Name the Fighting Irish quarterback.

6. What Cornhuskers received the awards as the outstanding back and outstanding lineman in the 1971 Orange Bowl victory against LSU?

7. What Cornhuskers received the awards as the outstanding back and outstanding lineman in the 1972 Orange Bowl victory against Alabama?

Presidential Seal

Nebraska was the national champion for 1970 not only according to the Associated Press but also according to Richard Nixon, the president of the United

States. Nixon stopped in Lincoln on a trip from his California White House to Washington, D.C., to deliver a "major speech directed at the future for young people." The speech took place at the University of Nebraska Coliseum.

A crowd of 8,000 packed the Coliseum, under tight security. Nixon called Coach Bob Devaney and Cornhusker captains Jerry Murtaugh and Dan Schneiss to the podium, then presented them with a plaque that included the presidential seal and the words: "No. 1 College Football Team in the Nation."

8. Jerry Murtaugh and Dan Schneiss were the captains of the 1970 national championship team. What position did each play? Who were the captains for the other national championship teams?

Two in a Row

Nebraska's first national championship in 1970 depended to some extent on circumstance. The Cornhuskers needed help from Notre Dame and Stanford. They needed no such help to win their second national championship in 1971. They were number two in the Associated Press preseason rankings but moved up to number one after a 34–7 opening-game victory against Oregon and remained there.

They were seriously tested only once, by second-ranked Oklahoma in the Game of the Century on Thanksgiving Day at Norman, Oklahoma. Nebraska's Orange Bowl game against number two–ranked Alabama, which also was undefeated and untied, proved to be an anticlimax—as had been expected.

As he had done against Oklahoma, junior wingback Johnny Rodgers returned a punt for a touchdown to break open the Orange Bowl game. He ran 77 yards on the final play of the first quarter to increase a Nebraska lead to 14–0 and demoralize Coach Bear Bryant's Crimson Tide.

Alabama fumbled the ensuing kickoff, and Nebraska recovered at the Crimson Tide 27-yard line. Barely two minutes later, quarterback Jerry Tagge scored from one yard out and the rout was on. The Cornhuskers took a 28–0 lead to the locker room at halftime and coasted to a 38–6 victory.

Bob Devaney was confident enough his 10th Nebraska team would complete its national championship run against his old nemesis Bryant that a few days before the Orange Bowl game, he told his staff he would coach one more season before retiring to concentrate on his duties as athletic director.

He had planned to retire as coach and turn over those duties to Tom Osborne, his offensive coordinator, for the 1972 season. He was persuaded to stay on and try for a third consecutive national championship, something no major college football coach had ever done—and hasn't yet.

Even though Nebraska's 31-game unbeaten streak, which had begun with a come-from-behind 21–17 victory against Kansas in 1969, was snapped by UCLA in the 1972 opener, the Cornhuskers still managed to work themselves back into position for a shot at a third national championship.

They climbed to number three in the AP poll after a 56–0 victory against

Kansas—the third of four consecutive shutouts—and remained there until a 23–23 tie at Iowa State dropped them to fifth. A 17–14 loss to number four Oklahoma in the final game of the regular season eliminated any hope.

Devaney's final team included Rodgers, the Heisman Trophy winner; middle guard Rich Glover, the Outland Trophy and Lombardi Award winner; and defensive end Willie Harper, a two-time consensus All-American. It had an outstanding defense and an offense that averaged what was then a school-record 41.9 points per game. But the offense was erratic and, at times, self-destructive.

The 9–2–1 record in 1972 masked a team that was potentially better than the 1970 national champions according to Jeff Sagarin's 1996 computer rankings, which included Devaney's 1972 team at number 10 among all teams from 1956 on. The 1970 Nebraska team was number 24 on that list.

9. **The Game of the Century wasn't Nebraska's last in the 1971 regular season. The Cornhuskers had to play another game before beginning Orange Bowl preparations. What team did Nebraska defeat for its 12th victory in 1971? Extra credit: What was the score?**

10. **Nebraska defeated three Top 10–ranked opponents on the way to winning the national championship in 1971. Oklahoma and Alabama were both ranked number two when the Cornhuskers played them. What other Top 10 team did Nebraska defeat in 1971? Extra credit: What was the team ranked when the Cornhuskers played it? What was its final Associated Press ranking?**

11. **What Cornhusker I-back scored three touchdowns in the 34–7 opening-game victory against Oregon in 1971? Hint: He scored six touchdowns, total, during the regular season.**

Rex Lowe

Rex Lowe was from Milwaukee, Wisconsin. He was a wide receiver and a good one, according to no less an authority than Johnny Rodgers, the Heisman Trophy winner in 1972. Lowe earned letters as a sophomore and junior on Nebraska's 1969 and 1970 teams. But he was stricken with Hodgkin's disease before his senior season. Lowe was in a wheelchair on the Nebraska sideline during the Orange Bowl.

During the locker-room celebration after the game, Rodgers stood on a bench, holding the game ball and waiting to receive the award as the game's most valuable player. Lowe sat in his wheelchair at the back of the room, looking on at the celebration. Before receiving his award, Rodgers jumped down from the bench, made his way to Lowe, and presented him the game ball, "from all the guys," he said.

It was a poignant moment, one that remains vivid for Rodgers.

"Most people have forgotten about Rex," Rodgers said recently.

Almost Three

If Byron Bennett's 45-yard field goal hadn't gone wide left, Nebraska would have won the national championship for 1993. And with national titles in 1994 and 1995, Tom Osborne would have accomplished what Bob Devaney, his mentor, could not—coach three in a row.

"The '93 team was an awfully good team. I thought we played at a national championship level," Osborne has said. "I think that '93 team has to go down as one of the best."

The Cornhuskers' disappointing 18–16 loss against Florida State in the 1994 Orange Bowl game set the tone for Osborne's first national championship. The theme for 1994 was "unfinished business." And Osborne's 22nd team went about finishing the business with remarkable resolve.

Prior to the 1994 season, Osborne said a key to success would be continued good health for junior quarterback Tommie Frazier, who had been the starter since the sixth game of his freshman year. Frazier illustrated the wisdom of that assertion in the 1994 opener, a 31–0 victory against West Virginia in the Kick-off Classic. Frazier came away from the game as an early Heisman Trophy favorite.

A month later, Frazier's Heisman run ended with a blood-clot problem that surfaced during the Pacific game and kept him on the sideline until the Orange Bowl game against Miami.

Frazier took nine snaps in the Pacific game before experiencing soreness in his right knee. The problem was diagnosed as a blood clot behind the knee. Frazier was given anticoagulant medication and allowed to practice briefly. There was optimism that he might return for the Oklahoma State game.

Instead, he watched the 32–3 victory against the 16th-ranked Cowboys on television, in a hospital room, after undergoing surgery to correct the blood-clot problem. He wouldn't have played again in 1994 if the NCAA had granted his request for a hardship ruling and an extra season of eligibility.

Frazier was replaced by Brook Berringer, a redshirted junior from Goodland, Kansas, who joined Frazier briefly in the hospital with a partially collapsed lung. Because of Berringer's collapsed lung, Matt Turman, a sophomore walk-on from Wahoo, Nebraska, started the 17–6 victory at Kansas State.

Nebraska, number four in the Associated Press preseason poll, moved up to number one after the Kickoff Classic, then dropped to number two, behind preseason number one Florida, after a 42–16 victory at Texas Tech. The Tech victory proved costly for the defense, which lost starting strong safety Mike Minter for the remainder of the season to a knee injury. Minter was to the defense what Frazier was to the offense.

The Cornhuskers remained number two until the Kansas State game, after which they dropped to number three, not because of the way they were playing, probably, but rather because voters apparently didn't think they could overcome the loss of Frazier. Berringer proved they could by leading them to a 24–7 victory against Colorado, number two in the AP rankings. The next week, Nebraska was number one, overtaking Penn State, even though the Nittany Lions had defeated Indiana and also were undefeated and untied.

The Cornhuskers never relinquished the number one ranking, wrapping up Osborne's first national championship with a 24–17 victory against Miami on its home field in the Orange Bowl.

It was a fitting conclusion. The Hurricanes had been a source of frustration for Osborne. In addition to depriving Nebraska of a national championship in the 1984 Orange Bowl game, they humbled the Cornhuskers in the 1989 and 1992 Orange Bowls—the score was 23–3 in the 1989 game and 22–0 in the 1992 game.

Third-ranked Miami started off as if it would again spoil Nebraska's national championship hopes, taking a 10–0 first-quarter lead. The Cornhuskers cut the margin to 10–7 by halftime.

Osborne proved to be something of a prophet in his halftime speech, reminding the players that they were better conditioned than Miami and would wear down the Hurricanes. The Cornhuskers just needed to keep "hammering," he said. He also predicted that the Miami players would lose their composure, which would lead to a hurtful penalty, if the Cornhuskers could resist the urge to retaliate.

Three minutes into the second half, after Miami had increased its lead to 17–7, a Hurricane offensive lineman pushed Nebraska defensive tackle Christian Peter to the ground after a play had been whistled dead. Peter, not one to back down, followed Osborne's advice and didn't try to get even.

Miami was penalized back to its four-yard line, and on the next play Cornhusker defensive end Dwayne Harris pulled Hurricane quarterback Frank Costa out of the end zone for a safety.

Nebraska still trailed 17–9 going into the fourth quarter. But again, as Osborne had promised, the Hurricanes showed the effects of the constant pounding. Fullback Cory Schlesinger scored on runs of 15 and 14 yards, the second with 2:46 remaining, and the Cornhuskers were national champions. "The '94 team was particularly gratifying, because of so many injuries we sustained and then to beat Miami in Miami was memorable . . . to end up being the strongest in the fourth quarter," Osborne has said.

On the bus ride back to the team headquarters at the Sheraton Bal Harbour after the 18–16 loss to Florida State in the 1994 Orange Bowl game, Osborne told a dejected Barron Miles, "This loss doesn't mean we can't come back." Osborne pointed out to the junior cornerback that Colorado had lost to Notre Dame 21–6 in the 1990 Orange Bowl game, then came back to win the Associated Press version of the national championship by defeating the Fighting Irish in a 1991 Orange Bowl rematch 10–9.

12. Rover Mike Minter suffered a knee injury in the Texas Tech game that sidelined him for the remainder of the 1994 season. Who replaced him in the starting lineup?

13. Cornerback Tyrone Williams started every game except the Kickoff Classic in 1994. He sat out a one-game suspension. What freshman replaced him? What did they have in common?

14. Doug Colman started the first eight games at middle linebacker for the 1994 national championship team. Who started the final five games at middle linebacker?

15. Name the five members of the Cornhusker "Pipeline" in 1994 and their positions.

16. Three members of the Pipeline were from Nebraska. Name them and their hometowns. One of the five walked on at Nebraska. Which one?

17. Which member of the Pipeline had the most "pancake," or knock-down, blocks in 1994? Extra credit: Within five, how many pancake blocks did he have?

18. Which member of the Pipeline allowed only one sack in 46 games over four seasons?

19. Nebraska made a change in its offensive line for the 1995 Orange Bowl game against Miami. What was the change? Why was it made?

20. Tommie Frazier was included on the travel roster for the final regular-season game in 1994 at Oklahoma. He suited up but didn't play. He didn't wear his number 15 jersey, however. What number jersey did he wear? Why did he wear it instead of number 15?

21. What was Tommie Frazier's record as a starter at Nebraska? Easy extra credit: To what teams did the Cornhuskers lose when he started?

22. How did Nebraska score its first touchdown in the 1995 Orange Bowl victory against Miami?

23. Cory Schlesinger's two touchdowns in the fourth quarter of the 1995 Orange Bowl game were scored in the same end zone where Turner Gill's two-point conversion pass glanced off Jeff Smith's shoulder pads at the end of the 31–30 loss to Miami in the 1984 Orange Bowl game. It also was the end zone toward which Byron Bennett attempted the last-second field goal that went wide left in the 1994 Orange Bowl loss against Florida State. What end zone was it?

24. Schlesinger attended high school in Columbus, Nebraska. But that wasn't his hometown. What was?

25. Miami had lost only one of its previous 63 games in the Orange Bowl stadium prior to the 24–17 loss to Nebraska on the night of January 1, 1995. What team ended the Hurricanes' 58-game winning streak in the stadium in late September 1994?

26. Miami's hopes in the 1995 Orange Bowl game ended with a pass in-

terception. What Cornhusker made the interception? LSU's hopes in the 1971 Orange Bowl game also ended with a pass interception. What Cornhusker made that interception?

27. Dwayne Harris tackled Hurricane quarterback Frank Costa for a safety in the 1995 Orange Bowl game. The Cornhuskers also scored on a safety in the 1996 Fiesta Bowl victory against Florida. What player tackled Gators quarterback Danny Wuerffel for the safety?

28. What Cornhusker defensive starter celebrated his 23rd birthday by helping Tom Osborne get his first national championship on January 1, 1995? Hint: He was from Roselle, New Jersey.

29. What Kansas State player complained that he had been poked in the eyes following the Wildcats' 17–6 loss against Nebraska in 1994?

30. Prior to the 24–7 victory over number two–ranked Colorado at Memorial Stadium in 1994, when was the last time the Cornhuskers had defeated a higher-ranked opponent?

31. Colorado's defense seemed to ignore Nebraska's tight ends in the 1994 game. Between them, they caught nine passes for 124 yards and one touchdown. There were two. Name them.

32. Penn State was one of two teams besides Nebraska that finished the 1994 regular season undefeated and untied. The other team lost its conference championship game, however, leaving only Penn State to challenge Nebraska's claim to the national title. Name the team. Extra credit: To whom did it lose?

33. Darin Erstad handled kickoffs, punts, and long field goals for the 1994 national championship team. Who handled the extra-point kicks and the short field goals for the Cornhuskers?

Perennial Contender

In addition to winning three national championships, the Cornhuskers were in contention for the national championship more often than not during Tom Osborne's 25 seasons as coach. In the 23 non-national-championship seasons, they were ranked third or higher as late as November or December 11 times. And though their highest ranking in 1981 was a pre–Orange Bowl number four, they probably could have been national champions if they had defeated top-ranked Clemson on New Year's night.

34. Tom Osborne's teams have been ranked number one for at least one week in the Associated Press poll in seven of his 25 seasons as head coach. Two of the seasons were 1994 and 1995, when the Cornhuskers won national championships. What were the other five?

Bonus Quiz: Double Up . . .

Cornhuskers who have earned letters in both baseball and football haven't been all that uncommon. Darin Erstad was a punter and placekicker on the

1994 national championship team, before being the first player chosen in the major league baseball draft. Turner Gill, a three-time all-conference quarterback in the early 1980s, played shortstop for the baseball team. Frank Solich played the outfield for Coach Tony Sharpe's baseball team in the spring, after lugging the football for Bob Devaney's teams from 1963 to 1965. But only a handful of Cornhuskers have earned letters in football and basketball. Identify those in the following list who have done so. Be careful. Only lettermen count. And, yes, some of the possibilities predate Tom Osborne's tenure as head coach.

35. Junior Miller
36. Paul Amen
37. Keith Neubert
38. Anthony Bailous
39. Erick Strickland
40. Elmer Dohrmann
41. Jim Huge
42. Bob Antulov
43. Morgan Gregory
44. Adam Treu

Big Victories

The bowl-game victories that produced Nebraska's four national championships are arguably the greatest in Cornhusker history. Here are 10 other significant victories, chronologically.

October 18, 1913 (Lincoln) Nebraska 7, Minnesota 0

Minnesota was nationally prominent. Nebraska aspired to such prominence. The Cornhuskers had not defeated Minnesota in the previous nine games. Coach Jumbo Stiehm's team finished 8–0.

November 10, 1923 (Lincoln) Nebraska 14, Notre Dame 7

Any victory against Notre Dame would be significant. And Nebraska had its share. But this one was special because it was the only blemish on Notre Dame's record in 1923. Knute Rockne was Notre Dame's coach, and the Four Horsemen played in Notre Dame's backfield, although they didn't get their nickname from sportswriter Grantland Rice until after the Army game in 1924. Among the star players for Coach Fred Dawson's Cornhuskers that day was sophomore tackle Ed Weir.

November 18, 1939 (Pittsburgh) Nebraska 14, Pittsburgh 13

The Cornhuskers hadn't defeated powerful Pittsburgh in 12 games. The victory came two weeks after Nebraska's only loss in 1939, 27–13 at Missouri. Coach Biff Jones's team finished 7–1–1 and was ranked number 18 in the final Associated Press poll.

October 31, 1959 (Lincoln) Nebraska 25, Oklahoma 21

Coach Bill Jennings's Cornhuskers pulled probably the biggest upset in Nebraska football history, ending Oklahoma's 74-game conference unbeaten streak. The game was played on Halloween. The Sooners of Coach Bud Wilkinson had won 44 consecutive conference games.

September 17, 1960 (Austin) Nebraska 14, Texas 13

Jennings's teams were up and down. This particular night the Cornhuskers were up, defeating Texas in the season opener. The Longhorns were ranked number four in the Associated Press preseason poll. They had been 9–2 the previous season. Texas recovered to finish 7–3–1 and was ranked number 17 in the final United Press International poll. Nebraska was ranked number 12 by the Associated Press after the Texas victory. But the national prominence was short-lived. Nebraska finished the season with a 4–6 record.

September 29, 1962 (Ann Arbor) Nebraska 25, Michigan 13

When Bob Devaney arrived from Wyoming, he marked the Michigan game as the key to turning around the program. The Wolverines carried the national prominence of the Big 10 Conference. They had been good the previous season, but Devaney knew they were going to be down in 1962. If the Cornhuskers could go to Michigan and win . . . well, history has proved him right.

November 25, 1971 (Norman) Nebraska 35, Oklahoma 31

The Game of the Century. Need more be said?

January 1, 1973 (Miami) Nebraska 40, Notre Dame 6

Any victory against Notre Dame is significant. Plus, this was Devaney's final game as head coach.

September 17, 1977 (Lincoln) Nebraska 31, Alabama 24

The Cornhuskers had been upset in their opener by Washington State, 19–10. Alabama came to Memorial Stadium ranked number four by the Associated Press. Bear Bryant was the Crimson Tide coach.

November 11, 1978 (Lincoln) Nebraska 17, Oklahoma 14

This was Tom Osborne's first victory against Oklahoma, after five losses. The Sooners were undefeated, untied, and ranked number one. Nebraska had recovered from a season-opening loss at Alabama and was ranked number four. The 1978 team might have been Barry Switzer's best at Oklahoma but for the loss in Lincoln. The Sooners fumbled nine times, losing six.

Answers

Quiz 5: Top of the Hill

1. Harold Piersey, a junior free safety, probably would have intercepted the pass. But all he would have had to do was knock it down and the game would have been over. Davison had one other pass reception in the game, for a 13-yard gain. The touchdown catch was good for 12 yards, by the way.

2. Nebraska ran only three plays in overtime. I-back Ahman Green carried on the first two for gains of nine and four yards. Then quarterback Scott

Frost ran 12 yards for the touchdown. Missouri quarterback Corby Jones threw two incomplete passes and ran for three yards to leave the Tigers with a fourth down at the Nebraska 22-yard line. Jones was sacked for a six-yard loss on the game's final play. Rush ends Grant Wistrom and Mike Rucker, both of whom were from Missouri, combined on the sack.

3. Running back Jamal Lewis and quarterback Tee Martin, who was a focus of attention as Peyton Manning's backup. Manning was suffering from a knee injury, and his availability was in doubt leading up to the game. Had he been unable to play, Martin would have stepped in.

4. Michigan's last national championship before the one in 1997 came in 1948.

5. LSU's Alan Faneca, a junior offensive guard, was the other finalist.

6. Bob Devaney's second national championship team in 1971 was 13–0.

7. The Cornhuskers and Wolverines both defeated Baylor and Colorado.

8. Tennessee coach Phillip Fulmer ranked ahead of Osborne in winning percentage among active NCAA Division I-A football coaches prior to the Orange Bowl. Afterward, Osborne moved back ahead of Fulmer, but only until his retirement became official—at which point, he was no longer active.

9. Rockne, .881, and Switzer, .837, had better winning percentages as college coaches. Osborne's winning percentage is better than that of Wilkinson, .826, Bryant, .780, and Hayes, .759.

10. E. O. "Jumbo" Stiehm's teams were 35–2–3 over five seasons, a winning percentage of .913. W. C. "Bummy" Booth's teams were 46–8–1 over six seasons, a winning percentage of .845. Bob Devaney was ahead of Osborne in winning percentage, by .001, prior to the 1997 season. Devaney's teams were 101–20–2 over 11 seasons, a winning percentage of .829. Between the two of them, Devaney and Osborne coached 356 of Nebraska's 722 all-time victories, or just under half—49.3 percent.

Quiz 6: Husker Championships

1. Ahman Green, six starts; Damon Benning, two starts; Clinton Childs, one start

2. Nebraska defeated Arizona State 77–28 and Iowa State 73–14.

3. Lawrence McCeney "Biff" Jones was Army's coach in 1928.

4. Bert Jones tried, unsuccessfully, to rally the Tigers.

5. Joe Theismann

6. Quarterback Jerry Tagge and defensive end Willie Harper

7. Quarterback Jerry Tagge and middle guard Rich Glover

8. Murtaugh was a linebacker. Schneiss was a fullback. The captains in

1971 were Jerry Tagge and Jim Anderson. The captains in 1994 were Ed Stewart, Zach Wiegert, Rob Zatechka, and Terry Connealy. The captains in 1995 were Christian Peter, Aaron Graham, Phil Ellis, Tony Veland, and Mark Gilman.

9. The Cornhuskers defeated Hawaii in Honolulu 45–3.

10. Colorado was number nine when it lost to Nebraska 31–7. The Buffaloes finished number three, giving the Big Eight an unprecedented first, second, and third finish in the AP poll. Oklahoma was number two.

11. Gary Dixon got half his season's total in the opener. He also scored a touchdown in the Orange Bowl.

12. Tony Veland

13. Leslie Dennis replaced Williams in the Kickoff Classic. Both were from Bradenton, Florida.

14. Phil Ellis

15. Rob Zatechka, 6-foot-5, 315 pounds, left tackle; Joel Wilks, 6-foot-3, 280 pounds, left guard; Aaron Graham, 6-foot-3, 280 pounds, center; Brenden Stai, 6-foot-4, 300 pounds, right guard; and Zach Wiegert, 6-foot-5, 300 pounds, right tackle

16. Zatechka, Lincoln; Wilks, Hastings; Wiegert, Fremont. Wilks walked on.

17. Wilks led the Pipeline with 142 pancake blocks.

18. Wiegert

19. Stai and Wilks traded sides. Stai moved to left guard to go against the Hurricanes' Warren Sapp.

20. Frazier wore jersey number 17 during the Oklahoma game in 1994. His number 15 white road jersey was torn in the Texas Tech game and not mended because it appeared he would be lost for the season.

21. Frazier was 33–3 as a starter. The three losses he started were 19–10 to Iowa State in 1992, 27–14 to Florida State in the 1993 Orange Bowl, and 18–16 to Florida State in the 1994 Orange Bowl.

22. Brook Berringer and Mark Gilman teamed on a 19-yard pass play.

23. The east end zone, at the open end of the Orange Bowl stadium.

24. Schlesinger was from tiny Duncan, Nebraska.

25. Washington defeated the Hurricanes.

26. Kareem Moss in the 1995 Orange Bowl. Bob Terrio in the 1971 Orange Bowl.

27. Jamel Williams

28. Senior cornerback Barron Miles

29. Quarterback Chad May, who was sacked six times

30. Number six Nebraska defeated number five LSU 30–15 in the 1987 Sugar Bowl game.

31. Mark Gilman, Eric Alford

32. Alabama was 11–0 and ranked number three before losing to Florida 24–23 in the SEC play-off.

33. Tom Sieler, a walk-on from Las Vegas, Nevada

34. 1976, when Nebraska was preseason number one, 1983, 1984, 1996, and 1997

Bonus Quiz: Double Up . . .

35. Junior Miller. No. He tried out for the basketball team but didn't stay with it.

36. Paul Amen. Earned three letters in each: football, 1935–37; basketball, 1936–38.

37. Keith Neubert. Earned letters in both: football, 1987; basketball, 1984, 1986–87. By the way, that was Keith Neubert in a cameo role as a dentist in the Tom Hanks motion picture *That Thing You Do.*

38. Anthony Bailous. No. He tried out for the football team but didn't stay with it.

39. Erick Strickland. No. He went out for football after completing his basketball eligibility. He lasted one practice before calling it quits to concentrate on basketball. He's now in the NBA.

40. Elmer Dohrmann. He was a contemporary of Paul Amen and lettered in both sports the same three years. He is the all-time leading letter winner at Nebraska, finishing his career with 11. In addition to the six letters in football and basketball, he lettered three times in baseball and twice in track.

41. Jim Huge. He earned letters in both: football, 1960–62; basketball, 1961–63.

42. Bob Antulov. No. He earned one letter in basketball at Nebraska. Then he played briefly for the ill-fated semipro football team in Lincoln, Nebraska, the Comets . . . sometimes referred to as the "Comics."

43. Morgan Gregory. No. He was recruited by some major colleges out of high school in Denver, Colorado, as a basketball player, but he picked Nebraska to play football. He remained a big basketball fan, however.

44. Adam Treu. No. He was recruited by Nebraska as a walk-on, in large part because the Cornhusker coaches were impressed with his footwork when watching him in a high school basketball game.

3

THE BEST OF THE BEST:

Husker All-Americans, Award Winners, and Other Great Players

Mr. Touchdown—Bobby Reynolds

A headline on the editorial page of the August 20, 1985, *Lincoln Journal* read: SO LONG, MR. TOUCHDOWN. Bobby Reynolds had died after suffering a heart attack the morning before, at age 53.

"For Notre Dame, the legend is wrapped up in George Gipp. For Iowa, the personality and memory of Nile Kinnick fill the same mythological spot," the editorial said. "For Nebraska, the transcendent football hero always will be the man who left our company Monday morning, Bobby Reynolds."

With over a century of history as the basis, identifying a definitive Cornhusker would be as difficult as tackling Reynolds during his sophomore season in 1950, when he became "Mr. Touchdown."

Ed Weir would deserve consideration, as would Tom Novak, Johnny Rodgers, and Dave Rimington, to name a few born and raised in Nebraska, which needn't be a qualification, of course.

Even so, a solid case could be made for Reynolds, who was from Grand Island, Nebraska, where his athletic reputation was such that a football game in which he played as a high school junior was moved to Memorial Stadium in order to accommodate those eager to watch him perform.

An estimated 15,000 looked on as Grand Island High defeated Lincoln High 25–14 that afternoon in mid-November 1947. Grand Island High never lost a football game during the two and a half seasons in which Reynolds played—he missed half of his sophomore season because of a leg injury.

Reynolds, a two-time all-state halfback, was nothing short of remarkable as a high school senior. He had touchdown runs of 50, 59, and 70 yards from scrimmage. He had interception returns for touchdowns of 72 and 100 yards. And he had kickoff returns for touchdowns of 90 and 92 yards.

He also played on the Islanders' state championship basketball team and ran hurdles in track. And if that wasn't enough, he was a talented baseball player, attending a New York Yankees tryout camp at Branson, Missouri, in 1949. Another of those at the camp was Mickey Mantle from Commerce, Oklahoma.

Tommie Frazier limbers his arm at practice before the 1995 Orange Bowl game against Miami. Frazier was chosen as Nebraska's most valuable player in the game.

(Huskers Illustrated/Bob Berry)

Reynolds was a Cornhusker by birth, you could say. His father, Gil, was a reserve halfback (and Ed Weir's teammate) on Coach Fred Dawson's Nebraska team in the fall of 1923. And his mother, Blenda Olson, was captain of the senior class girls' basketball team at the university in 1925.

Reality often falls short of expectations. But Reynolds's success at Nebraska was immediate, and remarkable. The Cornhuskers opened the 1950 season at home by tying Indiana 20–20, with Reynolds scoring all of their points. He followed with two touchdowns and two extra points in a 32–26 victory at Minnesota, running 67 yards from scrimmage for one of the touchdowns.

He scored all of Nebraska's points in the next two games: a 28–19 loss at Colorado and a 19–0 victory against Penn State at Memorial Stadium. One of his touchdowns against Colorado came on an 81-yard run. Through four games, he had scored 70 points on 11 touchdowns and four extra-point kicks. He had rushed for 679 yards, averaging 8.7 yards per carry. And he had thrown two touchdown passes.

Reynolds slowed down only slightly during the second half of his sophomore season, as the Cornhuskers extended a winning streak to five going into the finale at Oklahoma. Bud Wilkinson's number one–ranked and undefeated Sooners were looking for victory number 30 in what would become an NCAA-record 47-game winning streak. Nebraska was number 16 in the Associated Press rankings.

The Cornhuskers gave a crowd of more than 53,000 some anxious moments during the first half, which ended in a tie at 21. With three minutes remaining before the intermission, however, Nebraska had rallied from a 14–0 deficit to take a 21–14 lead. And Reynolds had scored all 21 points.

The Sooners regrouped at halftime and won 49–35. But Reynolds, who kicked two extra points in the second half to finish with 23, earned Oklahoma's respect. "We'd never seen anybody as exciting as Bobby. He was probably as talented a player as ever played the game," Oklahoma's Billy Vessels recalled in an interview with Harold Keith, which is quoted in the book *Forty-seven Straight,* published in 1984.

Vessels, also a sophomore in 1950, would earn the Heisman Trophy in 1952.

The 19-year-old Reynolds might have stepped off the set of *Leave It to Beaver.* He didn't look his age, nor did he seem as big as the 5-foot-11 and 175 pounds at which he was listed. Size and age didn't matter, however, when he stepped onto the football field. His 157 points led the nation in 1950.

He scored 22 touchdowns and rushed for 1,342 yards, both modern school records. He did everything, in fact, punting and playing defense as well as running, receiving, passing, and kicking placements. And he did it all with a smile. Keith writes in *Forty-seven Straight* that after an overzealous Oklahoma defender hit him late on a punt return, Reynolds hopped up and said, "Don't worry. That's all right."

Reynolds was so self-effacing that he claimed six of his 22 touchdowns were directly attributable to automatics called at the line of scrimmage by Cornhusker quarterback Fran Nagle.

Reynolds was selected to several All-America teams, joining Ohio State's Vic Janowicz, SMU's Kyle Rote, and Notre Dame's Bob Williams in the backfield of the *Look* magazine team selected by the legendary Grantland Rice, who wrote that Reynolds "ranks with the best selected any year."

Reynolds finished eighth in voting for the Associated Press Athlete of the Year award. He and Janowicz, who was second to Philadelphia Phillies pitcher Jim Konstanty, were the only amateurs among the first 10. The others ahead of him were golfers Ben Hogan and Sam Snead, baseball player Phil Rizzuto, heavyweight boxing champion Ezzard Charles, and basketball player George Mikan.

"This fellow cannot be tied up. His changes of pace, lightning cuts, and general speed and toughness combine to make him one of the greatest running threats of the current era," New York sportswriter Stanley Woodward wrote. "The kid stands out like a neon light," Bob Broeg of the *St. Louis Post-Dispatch* wrote after watching Reynolds' performance in a 40–34 victory against Missouri in 1950.

Reynolds's picture was on the cover of several national publications prior to the 1951 season, including the *Official NCAA Football Guide,* which described him as "the sparkling University of Nebraska halfback who last season as a 19-year-old sophomore was the nation's leading scorer."

Dell publications' *Sports Album* featured Reynolds, with red jersey and red helmet, in a passing pose on its cover, beneath the headline 500 SPORTS WRITERS PICK 1951's ALL-AMERICANS.

Floyd Olds wrote in the *Illustrated Football Annual,* "With the roar of a guided missle, the young Grand Island lad shot into the nation's 1950 headlines . . . making touchdowns look easy. In no time at all this average-sized easy-going youngster became the nation's top scorer . . . the secret is tremendous starting speed, plus the most deceptive change of pace the Midwest has seen since Red Grange."

Olds continued, "There's no reason to think Bobby-Boy won't keep right on doing that again which is why championship minded Husker fans are smacking their lips for the first time since 1940."

The Cornhuskers had finished second to Oklahoma in the Big Seven Conference in 1950, with the school's first winning record in a decade. And they were number 17 in the final Associated Press poll and tied for number 20 in the United Press International rankings. Nebraska was number 12 in the preseason rankings for 1951. There was good reason for optimism. But the optimism quickly faded.

Reynolds suffered a shoulder injury during preseason practice at the ag college in Curtis, Nebraska, and was sidelined for the first four games in 1951. He never regained his sophomore form because he was never again completely healthy. Before he finished at Nebraska, he suffered another shoulder injury, a severe ankle injury, and an eye injury caused by the lime used to line the football field.

He played in only 10 games as a junior and senior, scoring a combined 43 points. He never quit, however, contributing in any way he could. After Nebraska lost at Missouri 35–19 in 1951, Norris Anderson, the sports editor of the *Lincoln Star,* wrote, "He became a defensive giant, time and again slamming Missouri carriers to the ground with vicious shoulder-against-knee tackles."

Despite missing half of his junior season, Reynolds still led the Cornhuskers in rushing in 1951, gaining 424 yards on 87 carries. He rushed for only one touchdown, however.

His ill fortune continued after the football season of his senior year when he suffered a broken leg playing baseball. Despite the injury problems, he was drafted by the NFL's Los Angeles Rams, but he opted for professional baseball, playing briefly with the minor league Lincoln Chiefs.

When healthy, Reynolds was "a poet in motion, a Doak Walker type of highly intuitive runner who fakes them out of their shoes," Francis Wallace wrote for the preseason preview in the September 15, 1951, issue of *Collier's* magazine. Reynolds, "'the torso with the two-way twist,' was fabulous."

Quiz 7: Remembering Reynolds

We'll begin with easy questions, but we won't finish that way.

1. Reynolds looked young enough as a 19-year-old sophomore that his jersey number might have been mistaken for his age. What was his jersey number? Extra credit: Two other Devaney-Osborne era Cornhusker All-Americans wore that number. Who were they?

2. Reynolds's success as a sophomore earned him consideration for the Heisman Trophy. Where did he finish in the Heisman balloting? Extra credit: Who was the Heisman Trophy winner in 1950? Hint: Like Reynolds, he also was an outstanding baseball player.

3. Nebraska's coach during Reynolds's career was a stern taskmaster who had once been an assistant at Pittsburgh under the legendary Jock Sutherland. Who was he?

4. With Reynolds sidelined by a shoulder injury at the start of the 1951 season, the Cornhuskers lost five of their first six games and could never get on track, finishing with a 1–8–1 record. The team with which they tied subsequently forfeited, giving them a 2–8 record. With whom did they tie? Hint: It was a member of the Big Seven, and the Big Six before that. Extra credit: What score went in the record book for forfeited games at that time?

5. Nebraska had a winning record again when Reynolds was a senior in 1952. A Cornhusker tackle earned All-America honors in 1952. He was from Cambridge, Nebraska. Name him.

6. Did Reynolds play right halfback or left halfback? You've got a fifty-fifty chance.

Now for some tough questions, faniacs!

7. Reynolds was a cocaptain as a senior in 1952. There were two other cocaptains, both linemen. One was from Omaha; the other was from Ogallala, Nebraska. Name them.

8. The optimism prior to the 1951 season was in part the result of the presence of a halfback who was expected to take some of the ball-carrying pressure off Reynolds—not that he needed the help, according to one preseason college football publication. The new halfback was described as the Cornhuskers' first recruit from Boys Town, Nebraska. He was originally from Los Angeles, and he would have been among the first African-Americans to compete in athletics at Nebraska since the early 1900s. He didn't make it to the start of the season, however. Name him.

9. Reynolds set the modern school rushing record in 1950, with 1,342 yards. The problem is, Nebraska's rushing records are inexact prior to 1946, so the record he broke was set in 1949. The previous mark was 559 yards. The player who set it was a senior in 1950. Name him. Hint: If it helps, the player in question was from Omaha and earned four football letters.

10. A measure of how remarkable Reynolds was in 1950 can be seen in the fact that his rushing touchdowns still rank second on Nebraska's all-time list. How many of his 22 touchdowns in 1950 were by rushing? Who holds the single-season record for rushing touchdowns?

11. Even though he missed half of the 1951 season because of a shoulder injury, Reynolds led the Cornhuskers in total offense as well as rushing. He passed for 200 yards, second behind quarterback John Bordogna's 431 yards. Who was Nebraska's leading receiver in 1951, as well as in 1949 and 1950? Hint: He was from Burchard, Nebraska, and he was first-team all-conference.

12. Perhaps Reynolds's most memorable performance came in a 40–34 victory against Missouri at Memorial Stadium in 1950. He scored 22 points and rushed for 175 yards. Nebraska's other halfback rushed for 129 yards, and the fullback rushed for 91 yards in the game. Name the halfback, who was from Ravenna, Nebraska, and the fullback, who was from Chicago.

"Rampant Robert's Peerless Jaunt"

Bobby Reynolds scored three touchdowns against Missouri in 1950. That was a typical performance for him in 1950. But the last of those three was the stuff of legend. He was credited with a 33-yard touchdown run, but he ran more than 100 yards before crossing the goal line to clinch the victory.

The Cornhuskers lined up fourth-and-three at the Missouri 33-yard line with six minutes remaining. Reynolds took the snap from center—Nebraska often ran from a single-wing formation—and dropped back as if to pass. Under pressure from four Missouri defenders, he ran to his left, giving ground as he went. He dropped inside his own 45 before reversing field and starting back toward the goal.

He reversed his field again and sprinted down the west sideline, untouched, to score as his teammates cleared a path with their blocks. Lincoln sportswriter Norris Anderson described the touchdown run in the Sunday *Journal and Star* as requiring "microscopic study before it can be believed."

Early in the run, the Cornhuskers' Charles Toogood, a six-foot, 220-pound all-conference tackle from North Platte, Nebraska, knocked down a would-be tackler and wouldn't let him up.

"Reynolds has already gone by," the Missouri player complained.

"He might be back," Toogood explained.

Anderson called it "rampant Robert's peerless jaunt." It was witnessed by a Homecoming crowd of some 38,000 at Memorial Stadium. All of them agreed with Anderson's assessment.

Mr. Touchdown II—Mike Rozier

Despite the injury problems that plagued him as a junior and senior, Bobby Reynolds finished his career at Nebraska with 28 touchdowns. Mike Rozier scored one more than that—as a senior in 1983. Rozier scored 52 touchdowns during his three seasons as a Cornhusker, a total even more remarkable considering that only six of the 52 came during his sophomore season.

Rozier arrived at Nebraska by a circuitous route that included a season's stop at Coffeyville Community College in Kansas, where he rushed for 1,100 yards despite missing two games because of a shoulder injury. Coffeyville ran from a wishbone offense. "If we'd have run out of the I formation, he probably would have rushed for 2,500 yards," Coffeyville coach Dick Foster said after the season.

Rozier went to Coffeyville to get his grades in order. He was a fraction of a point below the NCAA minimum for freshman eligibility. Part of the problem was that a teachers' strike delayed the start of classes at Woodrow Wilson High School in Camden, New Jersey, when Rozier was a senior.

The eligibility issue caused some major programs to back off Rozier out of high school. But there could be no doubt about his ability. He rushed for 258 yards on 24 carries and scored three touchdowns in the East-West Holly Bowl high school all-star game at Glassboro, New Jersey, in the summer following his graduation. He ran 62 yards to score on the game's first play from scrimmage.

Nebraska encouraged him to attend Coffeyville Community College, and he remained loyal to the Cornhuskers, even though he could have gone just about anywhere after a season there.

Rozier's problems in getting to Nebraska weren't finished, however. He arrived in Lincoln for fall practice as a sophomore after a 34-hour bus ride from Camden. The bus pulled into the Greyhound depot at 2 A.M. He didn't fly because of an air traffic controllers' strike. His mom discouraged him from flying, "and I wasn't crazy about it either," Rozier said at the time. "I didn't want to risk a crash."

Quiz 8: Mike Rozier

1. Official NCAA statistics don't include bowl games. Rozier scored 52 regular-season touchdowns during his Cornhusker career. He played in three bowl games. Did he score any touchdowns in the bowl games? If so, how many and in which bowl games?

2. Rozier played a significant role in the first touchdown scored in the Cornhuskers' 22–15 loss to Clemson in the 1982 Orange Bowl game. How was he involved?

3. Rozier is Nebraska's career rushing leader. He rushed for 100 or more yards in 26 games. Did he ever rush for 100 or more yards in a bowl game? If so, in which one(s)?

4. Rozier's brother also came to Nebraska in fall 1981, as a freshman scholarship recruit. What was his brother's name? What position did he play?

5. Rozier's 52 touchdowns are the most in Cornhusker history. Who is number two on the list?

USC, Would You Believe?—Johnny Rodgers

Johnny Rodgers was Nebraska's first Heisman Trophy winner in 1972. But if things had worked out the way he hoped, he wouldn't have been the Cornhuskers' first Heisman Trophy winner. Rather, he would have been Southern California's third Heisman Trophy winner, following Trojan tailbacks Mike Garrett in 1965 and O. J. Simpson in 1968—when Rodgers was a senior at Omaha Technical High School.

Rodgers wanted to play for Coach John McKay's Trojans, who were national champions according to both major wire services in 1967 and the UPI national title runners-up in 1968. "Southern Cal was like what Nebraska is now," Rodgers said as the Cornhuskers prepared for the 1996 Fiesta Bowl. "Back then, it would have been like trying to talk me out of going to Nebraska in order to go to Southern Cal now. There wouldn't have been much Coach Devaney could have said."

As it turned out, all Devaney had to say to Rodgers was "Want a scholarship?" Southern California backed off from him because of his size and didn't offer him a scholarship. In addition, Devaney got some recruiting help from two of his Cornhuskers, Mike Green and Dick Davis. Green, like Rodgers, was an Omaha Tech graduate. Davis had come to Nebraska from North High in Omaha.

"Mike Green and Dick Davis persuaded me to come to Nebraska," said Rodgers.

Quiz 9: Heisman Who-Am-I

1. I was an All-America fullback for Nebraska in 1936 and finished second to Yale's Larry Kelley in voting for the Heisman Trophy that season. I also competed in the shot put in the Olympic Games in Berlin, during the summer of 1936. Who am I? Where was my home?

2. I was an I-back who transferred to Nebraska from Oregon State. I finished eighth in the Heisman Trophy voting in 1980. Who am I? Where was my home? Extra credit: What running back won the Heisman Trophy in 1980? For what school did he play?

3. I finished ninth in the Heisman Trophy voting as a senior. We led the

nation in both total defense and passing yardage defense that season. I played middle guard and was a two-time consensus All-American. Like Bob Devaney, I was from Michigan. Who am I?

4. I played on Nebraska's "Scoring Explosion" team in 1983 and finished fourth in the voting for the Heisman Trophy. I might have gotten a few more first-place votes if it hadn't been for the fact that my Cornhusker teammate, Mike Rozier, was the Heisman Trophy winner. Who am I?

5. I was the first Cornhusker quarterback to finish in the top 10 in voting for the Heisman Trophy. I was seventh the year that Auburn's Pat Sullivan won the award. Tom Osborne was my position coach, and I was a Nebraska cocaptain. Who am I?

6. We finished fifth and 10th, respectively, in the Heisman Trophy voting the year that Georgia's Herschel Walker won the award. One of us finished in the Heisman voting top 10 twice. We both played offense, and one of us was a lineman. Who are we?

7. We finished eighth and ninth in the Heisman voting the year Colorado's Rashaan Salaam won the award. We both played offense, and one of us was a lineman. Who are we?

8. I am one of only two Cornhuskers to finish second in voting for the Heisman Trophy. The first is the subject of number 1 above. I was runner-up to a player from Ohio State. Who am I?

9. I am one of four Nebraska quarterbacks who have finished in the top 10 in voting for the Heisman. I finished fifth the year Ohio State's Archie Griffin won the first of his two Heisman Trophies. Bob Devaney and Tom Osborne both coached me. Who am I?

10. I finished higher than any other Cornhusker lineman in voting for the Heisman Trophy. I was third my senior year. One of my teammates also finished in the top 10 that year. I made a lot of tackles in a memorable game against Oklahoma. Who am I?

"I Want Ed Weir"

After Nebraska lost to Notre Dame 34–6 at South Bend in 1924, Knute Rockne visited the Cornhusker locker room. "I want Ed Weir," the legendary coach said as he entered the room.

Henry Schulte, who coached Nebraska's linemen, wondered if Weir had done something to offend Rockne. Before he had time to respond, however, Rockne had located Weir.

According to Weir, in a newspaper interview many years later, Rockne said, "Weir, I want to say to your face that you're the greatest tackle and the cleanest player I have ever watched. It takes a real football player to shine on a team that is being beaten, and you outdid everyone on the field today."

Rockne expressed the same opinion in his nationally syndicated newspaper column, making Weir a college football luminary as bright as Rockne's famed

Four Horsemen and Illinois's "Galloping Ghost," Red Grange. Weir's "playing was so respected, opposing elevens frequently delegated two players to oppose the Cornhusker captain," wrote Walter Eckersall, a prominent All-America selector.

The six-foot, 191-pound Weir was Nebraska's first two-time All-American. He was a consensus selection in 1924 and 1925, when he was included on all of the prominent teams.

Weir was among the first "red-dogging" defenders, setting up as much as two yards off the line of scrimmage and then charging across when the ball was snapped. If trap plays had been commonplace in the early 1920s, his charge would have left the defense vulnerable. But they didn't "mousetrap so much in those days," he often said. Plus, he had support from linebacker Harold Hutchinson. Weir would signal Hutchinson by snapping his fingers behind his leg when he planned to red dog.

Weir's most memorable performances were against Notre Dame, if for no other reason than Rockne's teams were the most famous in the Midwest. But Weir also held his own against Grange.

Weir led a Nebraska defense that limited Grange to 57 yards rushing on 13 carries to open the 1924 season at Memorial Stadium. But Illinois left Lincoln with a 9–6 victory, its second in a row against the Cornhuskers. Illinois won at Champaign in 1923, when Weir was a sophomore, 24–7.

Nebraska finally defeated Illinois in 1925, 14–0 in the rain and mud at Champaign. Again the Cornhuskers shut down Grange, who gained only 62 yards on 19 carries before leaving early in the fourth quarter, in tears of frustration and with the pain of a sprained wrist. Grantland Rice wrote, "Thousands turned out to see Red Grange, but in the Nebraska line was another gentleman, known in his hometown as Ed Weir . . . and though it might sound presumptuous to say that Mr. Grange had met his match, it can be said safely that when Mr. Grange had gone five yards he had made his run."

Weir also played in three games against Notre Dame, including two victories in Lincoln: 14–7 in 1923 and 17–0 in 1925. The 1923 game was Notre Dame's only loss. The 1925 game was Weir's last as a Cornhusker as well as the last in the Nebraska–Notre Dame series until 1947 and 1948.

Notre Dame officials terminated the series as a result of what they considered rude treatment on the part of Cornhusker fans. Interest in the Thanksgiving Day game in 1925 was such that Memorial Stadium was filled, though a newspaper estimate of a crowd of some 45,000 was almost certainly inflated, considering seating capacity at the stadium, which opened in 1923, was only 31,000.

Late in the game, Weir recalled years later, he looked at the Notre Dame sideline and "all of a sudden Rockne saw me and broke into his contagious grin. He gave me a big wink . . . no one else could know what he meant, but I understood. We had some great games, and we had each other's respect."

As with the questions regarding Reynolds, these start out easy and get more difficult.

1. Weir was a Nebraskan. What was his hometown?

2. Weir's brother lettered at Nebraska from 1924 to 1926. What was his name?

3. The final season for Notre Dame's Four Horsemen was 1924, which also was the year Grantland Rice gave them their nickname. They became the Four Horsemen following a 13–7 victory against Army at the Polo Grounds in New York City a month before they played Nebraska. Name them. Extra credit: Which one of the four was not a consensus All-American?

4. Ed Weir was Nebraska's first two-time All-American. The Cornhuskers wouldn't have another for more than 40 years, after Bob Devaney arrived. Who was Nebraska's second two-time All-American? What position did he play? Extra credit: Where was he from?

5. Nebraska's 14–0 victory against Illinois to open the 1925 season also marked the debut of a Cornhusker head coach who had worked previously with Red Grange as a Fighting Illini assistant. Name this coach, and name the coach he replaced at Nebraska.

6. There was little consistency in jersey numbers in the early 1920s, but Weir wore jersey number 35 for his final game as a Cornhusker. Grange, however, was known by his jersey number. Weir was a lineman with a number that a back would wear now. Grange was a back who wore what now would be a lineman's number. What was Grange's jersey number?

7. Here's a tough one. If you can answer this question correctly, go to the head of the class: Weir's aggressive defensive play caused Notre Dame's Rockne to change the way his players wore their equipment, specifically their hip pads. Explain the change and why it came about.

8. In addition to picking All-America teams, Walter Eckersall was involved in college football in another way. What did he do during the season to qualify as an expert on players?

9. Weir played three seasons in the National Football League before returning to Nebraska to coach. He was enticed into playing professional football by a player-coach who is one of only two former Cornhuskers in the NFL Hall of Fame. For what early NFL team did Weir play? Who was the player-coach who convinced him to play professionally? Who is the other former Cornhusker enshrined in the NFL Hall of Fame? He also was a Nebraska assistant from 1936 to 1941.

10. Ed Weir was a Cornhusker football assistant from 1928 to 1937 and again in 1943, when Nebraska's athletic business manager—a former Cornhusker letterman—served as head coach. The business manager–football

coach also coached the basketball team and the baseball team. Who was this popular former Cornhusker? What other sport did Weir coach at Nebraska?

Quiz 11: Outlandish and All

1. Nebraska has produced more Outland Trophy winners than any other program since the award was first presented to Notre Dame's George Connor in 1946. Seven Cornhuskers have earned eight Outlands. What two schools are tied for second behind Nebraska with four winners each? One is in the Big 12, the other in the Big Ten. Extra credit: Have any schools besides Nebraska had back-to-back winners?

2. Which Cornhusker Outland Trophy winners also won the Lombardi Award in the same season? Hint: You should be able to identify three.

3. Match the Cornhusker Outland Trophy winner with his hometown.

1. Larry Jacobson	A. Omaha
2. Rich Glover	B. Jersey City, New Jersey
3. Dave Rimington	C. Fremont, Nebraska
4. Dean Steinkuhler	D. Lawton, Oklahoma
5. Will Shields	E. Burr, Nebraska
6. Zach Wiegert	F. Sioux Falls, South Dakota
7. Aaron Taylor	G. Wichita Falls, Texas

4. Three Cornhusker All-Americans each have worn the following jersey numbers: 12, 66, 75, and 96. Identify the three for each of the numbers.

5. The jerseys of 11 Cornhuskers had been retired through the 1996 season. Two of the 11 have the same number on them. What is the number? Who were the players who wore it? Extra credit: Identify the numbers on the other retired jerseys and the players who wore them.

6. What is the lowest jersey number worn by a Cornhusker who earned All-America recognition? What is the highest number worn by a Cornhusker All-American?

7. Seven Cornhuskers have earned back-to-back consensus All-America honors. The key word is "consensus." Name the seven, three of whom played for Bob Devaney and three of whom played for Tom Osborne. The seventh played for neither.

8. Match the Cornhusker consensus All-American with his hometown. You will have to use some hometowns more than once.

1. Guy Chamberlin	A. Toledo, Ohio
2. Ed Weir	B. Superior, Nebraska
3. George Sauer	C. Lincoln, Nebraska
4. Danny Noonan	D. Bellevue, Nebraska
5. Bob Brown	E. Cleveland, Ohio

6.	Larry Kramer	F.	Austin, Minnesota
7.	Freeman White	G.	Mount Holly, New Jersey
8.	Walt Barnes	H.	Chicago, Illinois
9.	Ed Stewart	I.	Davenport, Iowa
10.	LaVerne Allers	J.	Midland, Texas
11.	Bob Newton	K.	Blue Springs, Nebraska
12.	Willie Harper	L.	Yorba Linda, California
13.	Marvin Crenshaw	M.	La Mirada, California
14.	Rik Bonness	N.	Palmetto, Florida
15.	Mark Traynowicz	O.	Cedar Falls, Iowa
16.	Junior Miller	P.	Wichita Falls, Texas
17.	Jake Young	Q.	Odessa, Texas
18.	Kelvin Clark	R.	Houston, Texas
19.	Trev Alberts	S.	Detroit, Michigan
20.	Aaron Taylor	T.	Webb City, Missouri
21.	Grant Wistrom		
22.	Broderick Thomas		
23.	Irving Fryar		
24.	Brenden Stai		
25.	Tommie Frazier		

Train Wreck—Tom Novak

A more rugged player than Tom Novak never wore a Nebraska football jersey.

After Nebraska played Notre Dame at South Bend in 1947, a *Chicago Tribune* sportswriter described the Cornhuskers as a "tough and stubborn bunch of roughnecks . . . big, brutal, and, at times, they performed with murder in their hearts." And that was after Nebraska had lost 31–0.

Novak qualified on about all counts except "big." He stood just a shade over 5-foot-10 and weighed 205 pounds. But he played with such ferocity that he seemed much bigger to those in his way.

Novak weighed 226 pounds when he enrolled for his freshman year and began football practice at Nebraska in fall 1946. "In three weeks, I weighed 198," he once recalled. He was 21 years old and just out of military service, with the GI Bill to help defray his educational expenses.

Novak, like Ed Weir two decades earlier, earned the respect of Notre Dame players and fans. Notre Dame quarterback Johnny Lujack, the Heisman Trophy winner in 1947, called Novak the toughest linebacker he had ever seen, and the Fighting Irish fans gave Novak a standing ovation.

He was a one-man assault team that afternoon in mid-October 1947. During one stretch of 21 plays on two Notre Dame possessions, he was involved in 17 tackles. He even intercepted a Lujack pass and returned the ball to the Fighting Irish 37-yard line in the first quarter—but to no avail.

Notre Dame, which had a line anchored by two-time consensus All-America tackle and 1946 Outland Trophy winner George Connor, could not block the Cornhusker sophomore in jersey number 68. A Lincoln newspaper headline the next day said: CONNOR ALL-AMERICAN? GIVE US NOVAK!

In his account of the game for the *Sunday Journal and Star,* Walt Dobbins wrote, "From a Nebraska standpoint, the game is a story about one player." And that player was Novak.

Interest in Notre Dame was such that the Cornhuskers were met and applauded by a crowd of students who assembled at the Burlington Railroad station in Lincoln on the Monday morning after the game. The crowd called for a speech by Novak, who had been a game captain at Notre Dame. So before he joined his teammates in an open-topped convertible for a parade down O Street and back to campus, Novak addressed the students. "They weren't as tough as I thought they'd be," he said.

Nebraska had been a 40-point underdog against Notre Dame, which would finish the 1947 season undefeated and untied and the Associated Press national champion. After the season, the Fighting Irish picked an all-opponent team, a common practice at the time, and Novak was the center.

Novak played all but 30 minutes total of the 1947 season. NCAA rules were liberalized to allow for substitutions until 1949, Novak once explained. "When you went out, you couldn't go back in. There were only 44 men on the squad, and it took 75 minutes to get a letter," he said. "You figure it out."

Novak was a four-time first-team all-conference selection, the only Cornhusker football player ever to be so honored. He was an All–Big Six fullback in 1946, an All–Big Six center in 1947, an All–Big Seven center in 1948, and an All–Big Seven center and linebacker in 1949. He earned such recognition despite playing for teams that had a combined 11–26 record during his four seasons.

Novak played nearly every down of the College All-Star game in 1950. The game, sponsored by the *Chicago Tribune* as a charity benefit, was played annually at Soldier Field in Chicago. It matched a team of college players who had completed their eligibility the previous fall against the reigning National Football League champion. The All-Stars upset the Philadelphia Eagles 17–7 in the 1950 game.

The NFL draft wasn't constituted as it is now, and Novak had opportunities to sign with three NFL teams. But he turned them all down because they didn't offer enough money.

In November 1976, on the night before the Nebraska–Iowa State game at Ames, Iowa, Novak fell at his brother's house in Omaha and suffered a spinal injury, which left him confined to a wheelchair. In characteristic fashion, Novak never lamented his situation. "I've lived my crazy life," he once said. "I'm not mad at myself about being paralyzed. I don't push the handicap liability on anyone else."

The biggest problem was, "I lost my balance, my ability to play handball," he said.

Quiz 12: Sorting Through the (Train) Wreckage

1. What Omaha high school did Novak attend?

2. Novak played for three coaches in his four seasons at Nebraska. Name them.

3. Identify who said, "My eyes have never seen Tom Novak's equal at any position. As football players go, the Good Lord made Tom Novak, then threw away the mold."

4. Novak was an avid handball player before his fall. He regularly played handball against Nebraska's veteran grounds manager. Name the grounds manager. Hint: This is a giveaway, but the grounds manager has always worn a distinctive red-and-white polka-dot cap.

5. The head coach at Notre Dame when the Cornhuskers played the Fighting Irish in 1947 and 1948 was from Nebraska. Name him and the Nebraska town from which he came.

6. A consensus All-America halfback at Notre Dame in 1948 (and also in 1949) considered enrolling at Nebraska in 1946. But he was discouraged from doing so after being told the Cornhuskers already had an abundance of backs. Name him. Yes, this is tough.

7. Novak's jersey number was the first ever to be retired at Nebraska, and it is the only jersey number still retired. Because of a numbers crunch, Nebraska put all other retired numbers back into service and now retires only a player's jersey. What is Novak's retired jersey number? Extra credit: He wore two other jersey numbers during his career. What were they? Why did his number remain retired while the rest were brought out of retirement?

8. Nebraska was 0–4 against its perennial Big Ten nemesis Minnesota during Novak's four seasons. Novak held his own against two big Golden Gopher linemen who were consensus All-Americans in 1949. One was a center and a unanimous All-America selection. The other, a tackle, also was a consensus All-American in 1948 and later played in 197 consecutive professional games with the San Francisco 49ers. His nickname was "the Lion." Name them.

9. Two of Novak's Cornhusker teammates became professional wrestlers, and Novak promoted matches in the mid-1950s. One was from Ravenna, Nebraska. His father was a pro wrestler also. His father's nickname was "Tiger John." The other was from Omaha. His son followed him in wrestling, performing for a time under the name "the Million Dollar Man."

10. Novak had two sons who were basketball lettermen at Nebraska. Name them.

11. Novak also earned two letters at Nebraska in another sport. What was it?

12. Novak had a brother who earned three football letters at Nebraska. What was his name?

Driven to Succeed

Tom Novak enjoyed the attention that came with being an outstanding football player. The desire to be noticed contributed to his success. One of the first times he could remember his picture being in an Omaha newspaper was in 1941, when he was a high school football player, he once said.

The photograph showed him chasing a ball carrier from Benson High. He decided then, "my picture or my name was going to be in the paper," he said. "I drove myself into the scrapbook."

His high school coach told him to "play for your folks," which was one of the reasons he played at Nebraska. "They could drive the 60 miles to see me play," he said. His coach also told him "to stay out of pool halls, stay out of the movies, and don't buy a car." Because of that last bit of advice, Novak regularly hitch-hiked from Lincoln to Omaha and back on weekend visits during the off-season.

Finding a ride was never difficult. "I'd wear my Nebraska letter sweater," he explained.

Quiz 13: Heisman Blitz

The following questions refer to Heisman Trophy winners who have played against Nebraska. They will test your knowledge of college football in general.

1. A sophomore halfback on the Texas A&M team that defeated Nebraska 27–0 at Memorial Stadium in 1955 won the Heisman Trophy in 1957. Name him.

2. A junior end on the Notre Dame team that defeated the Cornhuskers 44–13 at Memorial Stadium in 1948 won the Heisman Trophy in 1949. Name him.

3. A sophomore back on the Iowa team that Nebraska defeated 28–0 at Memorial Stadium in 1937 won the Heisman Trophy as a senior in 1939. The Cornhuskers also shut out his Hawkeye team at Iowa City in 1938, 14–0. Nebraska and Iowa didn't play each other in 1939. Nebraska fans, no doubt, took particular delight in the two shutout victories because the Iowa player in question was a graduate of Benson High School in Omaha. He died in 1943 when the fighter plane he was piloting crashed into the Caribbean Sea, near a U.S. aircraft carrier. Name him.

4. A halfback on the Syracuse team that defeated Nebraska 28–6 at Memorial Stadium in 1961 won the Heisman Trophy that season. He was the first African-American to win the award as the nation's best collegiate football player. He died of leukemia at age 23. Who was he?

5. Through the 1997 season, Nebraska had played against five of the previous 10 Heisman Trophy winners, including three in the season in which they won the award. Name the five.

6. Johnny Rodgers was only the third player from a school in the former Big Eight Conference to win the Heisman Trophy. Who were the first two? Mike Rozier was the fifth player from a school in the former Big Eight to win the Heisman. Who was the fourth?

7. Minnesota was the Associated Press national champion in 1941. But the Golden Gophers had problems with a Nebraska team that finished with a 4–5 record. The Cornhuskers lost 9–0 at Minneapolis. A Minnesota halfback won the Heisman Trophy that season. Name him.

8. The first Heisman Trophy winner in 1935 played at Memorial Stadium. Name him.

Three Times Charmed—Zach Wiegert

Zach Wiegert redshirted his first season at Nebraska in 1990. That meant he spent practice on the scout team, running the offense of upcoming opponents. Scout-team duty is thankless and often discouraging. More than one young scout-team player has considered giving up.

That wasn't Wiegert's problem, however. By his own admission, he just wasn't motivated to give a good effort. "When you're on the scout team next year, you'd better be giving a better effort," Jack Pierce, an assistant coach at the time, warned him as the season drew to a close.

"I'm not going to be on the scout team ever again," said Wiegert, who worked hard in spring practice and earned a backup's job at tackle in 1991. He played in all but the Washington and Colorado games in 1991 and became a starter in 1992 as a redshirted sophomore. He started 36 consecutive games. He was first-team All–Big Eight three times. And he capped his career by winning the Outland Trophy.

Quiz 14: A Family Enterprise

1. Zach Wiegert's brother was a three-year letterman (1989–91) at offensive guard, earning first-team all-conference recognition as a senior. What was his name?

2. The Wiegert brothers' uncle was a Cornhusker football letterman in 1965 and 1966. He was a reserve quarterback from Hastings, Nebraska. Who is their uncle?

1. Tom Novak is the only Cornhusker in history to be first-team all-conference four times. And fewer than two dozen Cornhuskers have ever been first-team all-conference three times. Three other offensive linemen have been so honored during Tom Osborne's tenure as head coach. Name them. Only one quarterback has been first-team all-conference three times. Name him. Tough extra credit: Name Nebraska's first three-time all-conference honoree. Hint: As if this is going to help, he was a back who played for Jumbo Stiehm from 1912 to 1914.

2. Have you been paying attention? How many Heisman Trophies have been won by players from Nebraska high schools? Name them. How many of the Cornhuskers' eight Outland Trophies through the 1997 season had been won by Nebraska natives? Name them.

3. Zach Wiegert was a Cornhusker cocaptain as a senior in 1994. Erik Wiegert was a Cornhusker cocaptain as a senior in 1991. What other brother combinations have been Cornhusker captains? Hint: There have been two others, both under Osborne.

Warning: The final question in this chapter is for informational purposes only.

4. For a tough finish, try this one. At certain times during its football history, Nebraska's captains have been appointed on a game-to-game basis. Osborne had three season's captains plus one named on a game-by-game basis in 1986. During the Devaney-Osborne era, captains have always been seniors. But prior to 1962, there was no such restriction. As a result, a player could be a captain for more than one season. What Cornhuskers have been captains more than once? Hint: Since the team wasn't called Cornhuskers until around 1900, anyone before that wouldn't qualify. There have been only three, in 1901–1902, 1924–25, and 1950–51.

Answers

Quiz 7: Remembering Reynolds

1. Reynolds wore jersey number 12. Quarterback David Humm and I-back Jarvis Redwine also wore number 12 jerseys, as did quarterback Turner Gill. Surprisingly enough, Gill never earned first-team All-America honors. He was a first-team All–Big Eight selection three times, however.

2. Reynolds finished fifth in the voting for the Heisman Trophy in 1950. The Heisman Trophy winner that season was Ohio State's Vic Janowicz, who played briefly with the Pittsburgh Pirates.

3. Bill Glassford, whose record for seven seasons was 31–35–3.

4. Nebraska and Kansas State tied 6–6 at Manhattan. The Wildcats

were forced to forfeit that game as well as a 14–12 victory against Missouri. The score is 1–0 in the record book.

5. Jerry Minnick earned All-America recognition as a junior in 1952.

6. Reynolds played left halfback.

7. Carl Brasee was from Omaha. Ed Hussman was from Ogallala.

8. Tom Carodine. He had "tremendous speed," according to one publication.

9. Bill Mueller rushed for 559 yards and two touchdowns on 142 carries in 1949.

10. Reynolds rushed for 19 touchdowns in 1950. Mike Rozier rushed for 29 touchdowns in 1983.

11. Frank Simon caught 21 passes for 339 yards and one touchdown in 1951. Note: This question is included not only because Simon was a good player but also because of author privilege. Simon's wife was among the author's elementary-school teachers in York, Nebraska.

12. Halfback Ron Clark rushed for 129 yards. Fullback Nick Adduci rushed for 91 yards.

Quiz 8: Mike Rozier

1. Rozier didn't score any touchdowns in bowl games.

2. Rozier threw a touchdown pass to wingback Anthony Steels.

3. Rozier rushed for 118 yards on 26 carries in the 1983 Orange Bowl game against LSU and 147 yards on 25 carries in the 1984 Orange Bowl game against Miami. He had 75 yards on 15 carries in the 1982 Orange Bowl game against Clemson. His bowl totals were 340 yards on 66 carries.

4. Guy Rozier was a monster back, earning letters in 1983 and 1985.

5. Johnny Rodgers is second, with 45 touchdowns.

Quiz 9: Heisman Who-Am-I

1. Sam Francis, who was from Oberlin, Kansas

2. Jarvis Redwine, who was from Inglewood, California. George Rogers, South Carolina

3. Wayne Meylan, who was from Bay City, Michigan

4. Turner Gill

5. Jerry Tagge

6. Center Dave Rimington was fifth in 1982. I-back Mike Rozier was 10th. Rozier also finished in the top 10 the next year. He was first, becoming the Cornhuskers' second Heisman winner.

7. I-back Lawrence Phillips was eighth in 1994. Tackle Zach Wiegert was ninth.

8. Tommie Frazier was second to Ohio State tailback Eddie George in 1995.

9. Dave Humm

10. Rich Glover was third in Heisman voting in 1972, the year Johnny Rodgers won it.

Quiz 10: What about Weir?

1. Superior

2. Joe Weir "is developing into a real end," the game program in 1925 said.

3. Harry Stuhldreher, Jim Crowley, Elmer Layden, and Don Miller, who was not a consensus All-American

4. Wayne Meylan was an All-American middle guard in 1966 and 1967. He was from Bay City, Michigan.

5. Ernie Bearg came to Nebraska from Illinois, succeeding Fred Dawson.

6. Illinois's triple-threat "Galloping Ghost" wore jersey number 77.

7. Notre Dame players typically wore their hip pads outside their jerseys. After watching Weir grab the hip pads and use them to pull down the Irish ball carriers, Rockne told them to wear their hip pads beneath their jerseys.

8. Eckersall officiated games. He worked the 1925 Nebraska–Notre Dame game, in fact.

9. Weir played for the Frankford Yellowjackets. Frankford was a suburb of Philadelphia. Former Cornhusker Guy Chamberlin convinced Weir to play professional football for $350 a game. William Roy "Link" Lyman and Chamberlin are in the NFL Hall of Fame. Lyman and Chamberlin were teammates in Frankford in 1925. Weir and Chamberlin were teammates there in 1926. Weir's younger brother Joe spent the 1927 season with the Yellowjackets. The 1927 season was Ed's last as a professional.

10. Because of the economic concerns caused by World War II, A. J. Lewandowski was responsible for just about everything in the Cornhusker athletic department for a brief time. Weir also served as Nebraska's track-and-field coach. The Cornhuskers' outdoor track is named in his honor.

Quiz 11: Outlandish and All

1. Oklahoma and Ohio State. Oklahoma's are Jim Weatherall, 1951; J. D. Roberts, 1953; Lee Roy Selmon, 1975; and Greg Roberts, 1978. Ohio State's are Jim Parker, 1956; Jim Stillwagon, 1970; John Hicks, 1973; and Orlando Pace, 1996. No other school has had back-to-back winners.

2. Rich Glover, 1972; Dave Rimington, 1982; and Dean Steinkuhler, 1983

3. 1. F, 2. B, 3. A, 4. E, 5. D, 6. C, 7. G

4. Number 12: Bobby Reynolds, Dave Humm, and Jarvis Redwine.

Turner Gill did not earn All-America honors. Number 66: Dan McMullen, Wayne Meylan, and Brenden Stai. Number 75: Larry Kramer, Larry Jacobson, and Will Shields. Number 96: George Andrews, Jimmy Williams, and Jim Skow

5. The number 75 jerseys of Larry Jacobson and Will Shields have been retired. Number 15, Tommie Frazier; number 20, Johnny Rodgers; number 30, Mike Rozier; number 34, Trev Alberts; number 50, Dave Rimington; number 60, Tom Novak; number 71, Dean Steinkuhler; number 72, Zach Wiegert; and number 79, Rich Glover

6. Quarterback Steve Taylor wore number 9. Defensive tackle Neil Smith wore number 99.

7. Ed Weir, 1924–25; Wayne Meylan, 1966–67; Johnny Rodgers, 1971–72; Willie Harper, 1971–72; Dave Rimington, 1981–82; Mike Rozier, 1982–83; and Jake Young, 1988–89

8. 1. K, 2. B, 3. C, 4. C, 5. E, 6. F, 7. S, 8. H, 9. H, 10. I, 11. M, 12. A, 13. A, 14. D, 15. D, 16. J, 17. J, 18. Q, 19. O, 20. P, 21. T, 22. R, 23. G, 24. L, 25. N

Quiz 12: Sorting Through the (Train) Wreckage

1. South High

2. Bernie Masterson, 1946 and 1947; Potsy Clark, 1948; and Bill Glassford, 1949

3. Longtime radio broadcaster, and a legend in his own right, Lyell Bremser

4. Bill Shepard, who is "a fine player," Novak said. "But his knees are a problem now."

5. Frank Leahy was from O'Neill, Nebraska.

6. Emil Sitko

7. Novak's number 60 is retired. He wore number 68 as a freshman and sophomore and number 61 as a junior. His number 60 jersey was retired in 1950 by the "N" Club. The other numbers were retired by the athletic department, which would not have the authority to reverse the letterman's club.

8. Clayton Tonnemaker was the center. Leo Nomellini was the tackle.

9. Jack Pesek and Mike DiBiase were Novak's teammates. Tiger John Pesek was a nationally known professional wrestler at a time when that involved less showmanship than it does now. Iron Mike DiBiase's son, Ted, was formerly known as "the Million Dollar Man."

10. Tom Novak Jr. lettered from 1972 to 1974. Terry Novak lettered from 1975 to 1977.

11. He was a baseball letterman in 1949 and 1950.

12. Ray Novak lettered for the Cornhuskers in 1951, 1952, and 1953.

Quiz 13: Heisman Blitz

1. John David Crow
2. Leon Hart
3. Nile Kinnick
4. Ernie Davis
5. Barry Sanders, Oklahoma State, 1988; Gino Torretta, Miami, 1992; Charlie Ward, Florida State, 1993; Rashaan Salaam, Colorado, 1994; and Danny Wuerffel, Florida, 1996. Nebraska played against Torretta and Wuerffel in bowl games at the end of the seasons before they won the Heisman Trophy.
6. Oklahoma's Billy Vessels won the Heisman Trophy in 1952, when the conference was the Big Seven, and the Sooners' Steve Owens won it in 1969. Oklahoma's Billy Sims was the fourth, in 1978.
7. Bruce Smith
8. Jay Berwanger of the University of Chicago, which lost to Nebraska 28–7 to open the season.

Quiz 14: A Family Enterprise

1. Erik Wiegert, who played one season at Nebraska with his little brother Zach
2. Wayne Weber

Quiz 15: Fade-out

1. Three-time first-team all-conference offensive linemen under Osborne have been Dave Rimington, 1980–82; Will Shields, 1990–92; and Aaron Taylor, 1995–97. The only Cornhusker quarterback to be a three-time first-team all-conference selection was Turner Gill, 1981–83. Vic Halligan was the first.
2. Two. Nebraska's Johnny Rodgers in 1972 and Iowa's Nile Kinnick in 1939. Both went to high school in Omaha: Tech for Rodgers and Benson for Kinnick. Four of the Cornhuskers' Outland Trophies have been earned by Nebraska natives Zach Wiegert, Dean Steinkuhler, and Dave Rimington, who won two.
3. Mike Keeler, 1983, and Andy Keeler, 1988. Christian Peter, 1995, and Jason Peter, 1997
4. John Westover, 1901–1902; Ed Weir, 1924–25; and Robert Mullen, 1950–51. Prior to 1900, the only one was James H. Johnston, 1891–92. If you got any but Weir right, you need to write the next book.

4

THE BIG RED MACHINE:
Offense

Bob Devaney liked to tell the story about the time he was coaching at Wyoming and the Cowboys returned to Laramie after a game in which they had played poorly, particularly on offense, and had lost. As he got off the train (many of his stories involved getting off the train), he bumped into a little old lady (many of his stories also involved bumping into little old ladies).

Devaney: "Excuse me, Ma'am."
Little old lady: "Where do you think you're going?"
Devaney: "Nowhere."
Little old lady: "Oh . . . another Wyoming running back."

The More Things Change . . .

Amos Foster coached only one football season at Nebraska. His 1906 team went 6–4. The most decisive of the losses was against the University of Chicago, in Chicago, 38–5.

Foster, who was replaced by W. C. "King" Cole, was criticized in the 1907 student yearbook, *The Cornhusker*, because his offense "relied too firmly on befooling the enemy out of victory." The plays on which his "childish" offense depended were "of the tricky variety," the yearbook said.

The yearbook also described what was expected of Nebraska's quarterback. He had to be able to "run fast, to dodge and twist [his] way through a broken field."

Nearly a century later, the same criteria apply.

Tom Osborne placed a premium on quarterbacks who can run in developing his option offense. "We want to be able to run enough option football for people to have to prepare for it," he said. "It complicates the defensive preparation if the option is a threat."

Prior to Nebraska's winning national championships in 1994, 1995, and 1997, Osborne was occasionally criticized for having an unimaginative, run-oriented offense. However, with the right players, including quarterback Tommie Frazier, Osborne's option offense seemed to be transformed.

"To defensive coaches preparing for Nebraska, he's very imaginative, very

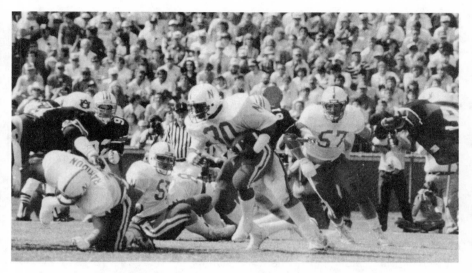

Mike Rozier, the 1983 Heisman Trophy winner, carries against Auburn in 1982. Scott Raridon is making a block. Mark Traynowicz (57) played tackle that season as a sophomore and later earned All-American honors at center.
(Photo Courtesy of *Huskers Illustrated*/Randy Hampton)

creative," Cornhusker receivers coach Ron Brown said. Osborne's offense is "well-planned, very thoroughly planned. All of the bases are covered. We try to get all 11 [defenders] knocked down. For some teams, if they can get the front five going the other way, that's okay. But we're thinking touchdown on every play."

As a result, everyone, including the quarterback, is expected to block for the ball carrier.

"That's the thoroughness, the attention to detail," said Brown. "Tom's a very nice, very gentle man. But he's also very demanding. We are very demanding of our players. Everybody's got to do it.

"There are no shortcuts: pursuit on defense; everybody blocks on offense."

That philosophy has made Nebraska "the best big-play running team in the country," Brown said.

That and quarterbacks who could run with the ball. "The idea was not necessarily to recruit sprinters at quarterback, but speed. If a guy could pass on top of that, it was a plus," Osborne said. "But we wanted to make sure he could run. As we got those quarterbacks, we tended to run more options."

Osborne began emphasizing speed at quarterback in the mid-1970s. The first quarterback recruited with that in mind was Jeff Quinn, who came to Nebraska in 1976. Quinn, who was from Ord, Nebraska, consistently ran the 40-yard dash in 4.7 seconds. At 6-foot-3 and 190 pounds, he also had good size.

Quinn shared the starting job with Tim Hager in 1979, as a junior. From that point on, with only a few exceptions, the Cornhusker quarterbacks were as much runners as passers.

Nate Mason arrived in 1979, and Turner Gill was a member of the 1980 recruiting class, which formed the foundation of the "Scoring Explosion" team in 1983. Gill set the standard by which Nebraska's quarterbacks were measured until the arrival of Frazier from Palmetto, Florida, in 1992.

Frazier was the definitive quarterback for Osborne's option offense.

In many ways, Nebraska's offense has gone full circle since 1962, when Bob Devaney arrived. Devaney's first teams used an offense with an unbalanced line and a full-house backfield, "somewhat similar to a wishbone setup," Osborne wrote in his autobiography, *More Than Winning*.

The majority of Devaney's early quarterbacks were more apt to run than throw. After enduring 6–4 seasons in 1967 and 1968, Devaney decided he needed to change his offense. And he gave Osborne the primary responsibility for making that change. Osborne was coaching the receivers. In 1969, he also began meeting with the quarterbacks and calling plays from the press box on game day.

Osborne patterned the new offense on Oklahoma's. The Sooners had been successful against Nebraska running from the I formation. They had won three in a row from the Cornhuskers, including a 47–0 embarrassment at Norman, Oklahoma, in 1968 that Devaney called his worst loss ever.

Osborne figured the best way to beat Oklahoma was to play the way Oklahoma played. So he reshaped Nebraska's offense and encouraged Devaney to recruit linemen from California junior colleges to make the new system work. A year later, Devaney got the first of his back-to-back national titles.

When Osborne succeeded Devaney in 1973, the offense had become pass-oriented. Beginning with Jerry Tagge and Van Brownson, the Cornhusker quarterbacks were more likely to drop back and pass than to take off running. Osborne's early quarterbacks included David Humm and Vince Ferragamo, neither of whom was much of a runner. Ferragamo ran the 40-yard dash in 4.7 seconds—which was about the same as Tagge. And "Dave Humm probably wasn't that fast," Osborne has said.

"We ran a little bit of option football [then], but that was just to keep people honest. We had pretty good I-backs, though we didn't have great ones. And we threw the ball a lot."

Nebraska was successful with such an offense until it played Oklahoma. The Sooners had gone away from the I-formation offense in favor of the option-oriented wishbone, which head coach Barry Switzer copied from archrival Texas while he was Oklahoma's offensive coordinator.

Osborne's teams lost five in row to Oklahoma before finally winning at Memorial Stadium in 1978. Osborne concluded that the offense was a big part of the problem. "We always had good throwers," he said. "But we'd seem to get Oklahoma on the ropes and they'd have a quarterback with great option ability who would make a play to win. We had a hard time beating anyone with speed at quarterback.

"Certainly, we didn't need to go to the wishbone. But we felt we needed to get more speed at quarterback." Again, the best way to beat the Sooners was to play the way they played.

In addition to recruiting quarterbacks with speed, Osborne placed a premium on offensive linemen who could run block, fullbacks who were willing to block, and running backs who were exceptional.

"We probably have had better running backs since about 1978 or 1979," he has said.

Quiz 16: California Connection

Osborne recruited California for Devaney and was instrumental in attracting some junior college players who made significant contributions to the national championship teams in 1970 and 1971. Three California junior college transfers came to Nebraska in 1969: Bob Newton, an offensive tackle from Cerritos Junior College; Dale Didur, a wide receiver from Long Beach City College; and Bob Terrio, a fullback from Fullerton Junior College who was moved to linebacker at Nebraska.

Newton played in 1969 and 1970. Didur was bothered by injuries and earned only one letter, on the 1971 national championship team. Terrio was a key player in both 1970 and 1971.

Question: The Cornhuskers recruited three more junior college offensive linemen in 1970, all of whom played on the national championship teams. Two were from California junior colleges, and the other was from Phoenix Junior College in Arizona. Who were the three linemen?

Quiz 17: The Scoring Explosion—1983

The Nebraska sports information office organizes its annual football media guides around themes. The theme for the 1983 season was "the Scoring Explosion." Nearly every game in 1983 provided evidence of the accuracy of that designation. The Cornhuskers scored 60 or more points five times, with a high of 84 against Minnesota—they had a sense of symmetry, scoring 21 points in each quarter.

Perhaps the most dramatic indication of Nebraska's offensive explosiveness in 1983 was the third quarter of a 69–19 victory against Colorado at Memorial Stadium on October 22. The Cornhuskers scored 48 points during the quarter, including 41 in a span of 9:10. The possession time to score those 41 points was only 2:55, an NCAA Division I-A record for most points scored in a brief period of time.

The scoring explosion went like this:

14:25 remaining—Irving Fryar, 54-yard run and Scott Livingston kick
13:07—Mike Rozier, 13-yard run and Livingston kick
12:36—Turner Gill, 17-yard run and Livingston kick
9:40—Fryar, 34-yard pass from Gill and Livingston kick
5:58—Rozier, 18-yard run but kick failed
5:15—Jeff Smith, 12-yard run and Dave Schneider kick
2:47—Shane Swanson, 1-yard pass from Nate Mason and Schneider kick.

The 48 points were unanswered, though Colorado finished off the 55-point quarter by covering 80 yards on six plays for a touchdown. The Buffaloes had trailed only 14–12 at halftime.

Afterward, Tom Osborne told reporters, "I was amazed the way the game broke open. As a result, I suppose we'll have to deal with the 'running up the score' charge again."

Osborne had been criticized in the national media for running up the score in the 84–13 victory at Minnesota. Because it was a road game, however, he was limited in the number of players he could take to Minneapolis, and as the score mounted against Minnesota, which blitzed on nearly every down, Osborne didn't have the option of putting in lower-unit players, the way he would have at a home game. Osborne used a sixth-string tight end and fullback and numerous fifth-string players in the Colorado game.

1. Colorado's head coach was an enthusiastic former Big Eight football player in only his second season as the Buffaloes' head coach. He designated Nebraska as Colorado's rival. Who was he? Whom did he follow at Colorado? At what Big Eight school did he play football?

2. While he was an assistant at Nebraska, Osborne applied for the head coaching job at South Dakota. He was not offered the job, however. The coach who got the job at South Dakota was the coach of the Minnesota team the Cornhuskers defeated 84–13. Who was he?

3. The coach referred to in the previous question was replaced after the 1983 season. Based on the score, anyway, Minnesota showed significant improvement in 1984, losing to number one–ranked Nebraska in Lincoln 38–7. Who was the Gophers' new head coach in 1984?

Quiz 18: The Scoring Explosion II—1995

As potent as Nebraska's offense was in 1983, it was slightly better in 1995. Consider the comparisons:

First Downs/Game
1983—26.5
1995—27.1

Total Offense/Game
1983—546.7
1995—556.3

Rushing Yards/Game
1983—401.7
1995—399.8

Passing Yards/Game
1983—145.0
1995—156.5

Points/Game
1983—52.0
1995—52.4

1. Name the following for the 1983 and 1995 teams, including their statistics for extra credit: the rushing leader, the pass-receiving leader, and the total offense leader.

2. Nebraska led the nation in two of the team categories listed above in both 1983 and 1995. They were the same categories. Which two were they?

3. Nebraska has led the nation in total offense twice since 1946. What were the seasons, and who was the starting quarterback in each of those seasons?

Quiz 19: Centers of Attention

Nebraska's offensive success has depended on outstanding linemen. Six of the Cornhuskers' eight Outland Trophies have been won by offensive linemen, and 16 Nebraska interior offensive linemen (counting double winners) have earned consensus All-America honors. Six of those consensus All-Americans have played center. In all, 14 Cornhusker centers have earned All-America recognition, including three double winners.

1. Name the 14 centers—you must come up with only 11 names because of the double winners. Identify the double winners, and identify the consensus All-America centers.

Extra credit: Three Cornhusker centers have been unanimous consensus All-Americans, including one who was twice honored that way. Who were they, and in what seasons were they honored?

2. Name the other nine Cornhusker offensive interior linemen who have earned consensus All-America honors. They all played for either Devaney or Osborne. Two of the nine were teammates, which is extremely rare according to the NCAA record book.

3. The 1994 offensive line was among the best in Cornhusker history. It was nicknamed the Pipeline. Name the starters from tackle to tackle. Which of the five walked on?

Quiz 20: Great Glenn from Gilead

Glenn Presnell ranks among the greatest running backs in Cornhusker history. But because he played at Nebraska from 1925 to 1927, his accomplishments often are overlooked.

The records kept before the "modern era," somewhat arbitrarily defined as post–World War II or post-1950, are sometimes difficult to interpret. For example, a statistician might not have been careful in differentiating scrimmage runs from punt and kickoff returns, or even pass receptions.

According to some sources, Presnell led the nation's colleges in rushing in 1927, gaining 1,446 yards in eight games. Those sources indicate he gained 259 of those yards in a 7–6 loss at Missouri—which underscores the problem. How does a player rush for that many yards in a 7–6 game?

Nebraska's records show one thing. Missouri's show another.

Whatever the truth statistically, Presnell was an outstanding running back. Lawrence Perry, a well-known sportswriter of that time, included Presnell on his 1927 All-America team for the Consolidated Press Association. Perry compared Presnell to Red Grange of Illinois. "Some teams stopped Grange cold, but no one stopped Presnell," Perry wrote.

Presnell was born in tiny Gilead, Nebraska, and attended high school in nearby DeWitt. He played semipro football for three seasons with the Ironton Tanks, and he played six seasons in the young National Football League with the Detroit Lions and their predecessors, the Portsmouth Spartans.

He also coached at Nebraska, first as an assistant and then as head coach in 1942.

Jock Sutherland, the legendary coach at Pittsburgh, told the *New York Times* many years later that Presnell was "as good a football player as I ever saw in my entire career."

Sutherland said Notre Dame coach Knute Rockne had tipped him off to Presnell's greatness. Presnell was a sophomore when Nebraska defeated Notre Dame 17–0 at Memorial Stadium in 1925.

Sutherland, whose team defeated Nebraska 21–13 in 1927, quoted Rockne on Presnell: "Unless you can stop him behind the line of scrimmage, he'll average seven yards a try on you."

1. Another of Nebraska's great pre–modern era running backs played in the mid-1930s. He stood 6-foot-3, weighed 200 pounds, and earned the nickname "Wild Hoss." He was born in Republic City, Kansas, but grew up in

Seward, Nebraska. He also was an outstanding track-and-field athlete. Who was he? And who was the famous fullback who helped open holes for him?

2. The position distinctions we now take for granted didn't apply in college football's early years. One of Nebraska's great early ball carriers was designated an end, which more accurately describes the position he played on defense. He was from Blue Springs, Nebraska, and was persuaded to transfer to Nebraska from Nebraska Wesleyan. His nickname was "the Champ." Who was he? And who was the halfback who blocked for him in 1914 and 1915?

Quiz 21: Heavier Than He Looks—Frank Solich

Frank Solich, Nebraska's new head coach, admits he once taped weights inside in his sweat clothes. However, he often has said, "I hate to talk about it."

Solich hid the five pounds' worth of weights beneath an oversize gray T-shirt in hopes of avoiding the dubious distinction of being the lightest Cornhusker. He weighed about 150 pounds when he was recruited by Bob Devaney in 1962. Teammate Larry Wachholtz also weighed about 150 pounds.

Solich has always maintained the idea was Paul Schneider's, not his. Schneider was Nebraska's trainer at the time, and a certified character. Without a doubt, he was capable of suggesting such a ruse. "It happened only one time," said Solich. "It's not something I look back on. . . ."

Solich's size became an issue when Devaney moved him from running back to fullback—a 5-foot-8, 158-pound (his official weight as a senior in 1965) fullback was as much of a curiosity then as it would be now. Most fans at the time knew Solich was major college football's smallest fullback, thanks to Dan Jenkins, who wrote about him, and the five-pound weight incident, in *Sports Illustrated*.

Solich's picture was on the cover of the magazine's September 20, 1965, issue.

Devaney recruited Solich out of Holy Name High School in Cleveland, Ohio, with the intention of using him as a kick returner. But his abilities were such that those plans quickly changed.

Nebraska ran a lot of plays from a spread formation at the time, so the fullback position wasn't the same as it is now. Solich ran draws and spread options, plays that were quick-hitting.

He never lacked for respect. After the Cornhuskers' 39–28 loss against Alabama in the 1966 Orange Bowl game, Crimson Tide coach Bear Bryant came across the field to compliment Solich, even though the Nebraska senior had been sidelined by an injury during the third quarter.

In 1965, Solich set Nebraska's single-game rushing record by gaining 204 yards in a 27–17 victory against the Air Force Academy. He scored touchdowns on runs of 80, 21, and 41 yards.

Solich still regrets the hidden weights. And even with them, he was lighter than Wachholtz.

1. Solich's single-game rushing record against Air Force in 1965 held for more than 10 seasons. Who broke it? How many yards did he gain? Against what team?

2. For the real Cornhusker fanatics, Nebraska became interested in Solich while it was recruiting one of his high school teammates—a fullback, by the way. The teammate also came to Nebraska and earned a letter in 1965. Who was he? And who was the Cornhusker assistant coach responsible for recruiting them? Hint: He later was an assistant at Notre Dame.

Quiz 22: School Record, and Then Some

Mike Rozier needed only three seasons to set Nebraska's career rushing record. With more and more players, particularly those at the skill positions, opting to turn professional before completing their eligibility, Rozier's 4,780 yards may remain at the top of the list for a long time.

If the truth be known, Rozier's career total ought to be 4,812. In his final regular-season game as a sophomore, he gained 32 yards after catching a lateral pass from quarterback Mark Mauer. The official statistics credited Rozier with 32 receiving yards on the play. But films of the game showed that the pass was a lateral, which means the 32 yards should have been included in his rushing total.

On the Monday after the game—played in Norman, Oklahoma—the Oklahoma sports information office indicated that it would amend the statistics. The host school has the final say in such matters. The correction was never made, however, and Rozier finished with 943 rushing yards in 1981.

Did Rozier lead the Cornhuskers in rushing as a sophomore? If not, who did?

Quiz 23: Kansas—Wrong Place, Wrong Time

Nebraska scored a touchdown to take a 33–0 lead against Kansas with 40 seconds remaining in the first half of the 1980 game at Lawrence, Kansas. Because the extra-point kick after the Cornhuskers' previous touchdown had failed, Tom Osborne called for a two-point conversion attempt.

Osborne was criticized after the game for his decision to go for the two points when his team already led by 33. But he was always consistent in his commitment to scoring as many points as possible during the first half of a game. "The greatest disrespect you can show an opponent is to assume the game is over before the half," Osborne told reporters that afternoon. "If I'd kicked the extra point and they had come back to beat us 35–34, what do you think I'd have heard from our fans?"

The two-point conversion attempt failed. But Kansas didn't come back. The final score was 52–0. More often than not, it has turned out that way when Osborne's teams played Kansas.

The Jayhawks have provided the opposition (but not much resistance) for many remarkable performances by Nebraska players during Osborne's tenure as head coach.

Craig Johnson was one such Cornhusker. An I-back from Westside High School in Omaha, Johnson earned letters at Nebraska in 1978, 1979, and 1980, primarily as a top backup. In three games against Kansas, however, he played as if he were a Heisman Trophy winner.

Kansas was among the schools that recruited Johnson, adding insult to injury he inflicted. He got his first crack at the Jayhawks as a sophomore in 1978. He was a third-string I-back that week, but those ahead of him, Rick Berns and Tim Wurth, were slowed by injuries early in the game at Lawrence.

Johnson ran 64 yards for a touchdown on his first carry. He ran 78 yards for a touchdown after catching a screen pass from quarterback Tim Hager the third time he touched the ball. And he bolted 60 yards for a touchdown on his fifth carry, leaving Kansas defenders clutching bits of his tearaway jersey.

He finished with 192 rushing yards on 10 carries, and the three touchdowns. His average of 19.2 yards per carry is a Cornhusker single-game record—with a minimum of 10 carries.

Nebraska gained 799 yards, a Big Eight record at the time, in winning 63–21.

The Cornhuskers scored 35 points in the second quarter, with quarterback Tom Sorley directly involved in four of the five touchdowns. He scored the first on a one-yard sneak, then threw touchdown passes for 44 yards to Junior Miller, 17 yards to Tim Smith, and 44 yards again to Miller.

In 1979, Johnson again came off the bench against Kansas and made the most of limited opportunities, carrying nine times for 138 yards and two touchdowns. The second came on a 94-yard run to establish the Cornhusker record for a run from scrimmage. The record was subsequently tied.

Nebraska shut out Kansas in the 1979 game, 42–0.

In 1980, Johnson went easy on the Jayhawks—relatively speaking. He started at I-back, carrying 17 times for 109 yards and two first-quarter touchdowns in the 52–0 victory mentioned earlier.

Johnson's combined statistics against Kansas in three seasons included 36 carries for 439 yards, an average of 12.2 per carry, and seven touchdowns, six of them by rushing.

1. As remarkable as Johnson's statistics were against Kansas, they didn't quite match those of another Osborne-era running back who also wore jersey number 30. Who was he?

2. Nebraska's single-game rushing record was set against Kansas. Who set it, how many yards did he gain, and in what season did he gain them?

3. One of three players who share Nebraska's single-game record for

touchdowns did it against Kansas. Name all three, one of whom did it twice. How many touchdowns did they score? Against whom did they score the touchdowns and when?

4. As good as the Scoring Explosion team and the 1995 team were, they didn't set the school single-game scoring record. What are Nebraska's two highest-scoring games?

5. According to Osborne, the quality of Nebraska's running backs began to improve in the late 1970s. But chance played a part. One of the running backs to whom Osborne referred borrowed money from his girlfriend to buy a plane ticket so he could walk on. Another transferred to Nebraska from Oregon State. Who were these two I-backs?

6. As mentioned earlier, Craig Johnson shares the Cornhusker record for the longest run from scrimmage—94 yards against Kansas in 1979. Who else has run 94 yards? Against whom did he make the run? Who holds the Nebraska record for the longest run from scrimmage without scoring a touchdown? How long was the run? Against whom was the run and when?

7. How many times did Mike Rozier rush for 200 or more yards in a game?

Quiz 24: Raising Minnesota

Dennis Claridge, who had been the starter as a sophomore in 1961, was Bob Devaney's first quarterback at Nebraska. He also was the best, Devaney said on several occasions.

Claridge was from Robbinsdale, Minnesota, and because of him, the University of Minnesota threatened to suspend a series with Nebraska that dated to 1900. He was set to attend Minnesota in 1959, but while watching the Cornhuskers win in Minneapolis in the second game in 1959, he changed his mind.

Classes had yet to begin at Minnesota, so he never enrolled. Minnesota claimed that Claridge had become a student when he registered for classes. Nebraska disagreed. The NCAA investigated the matter and ruled in Nebraska's favor. So Claridge became a Cornhusker, and in July 1960, Minnesota notified Nebraska athletic director Bill Orwig that it would no longer compete against the Cornhuskers.

Orwig responded, "If Minnesota decides not to meet us in football, it certainly is a selfish reaction and an indirect attempt to keep us from further recruiting in Minnesota. We feel that we have the privilege, as any other school has, of recruiting in any section of the country where we please. If Minnesota wishes to recruit in Nebraska, and they have, they are perfectly free to do so."

Minnesota athletic officials relented, and after a two-year break (in 1965 and 1966), the schools resumed playing against each other on an annual basis from 1967 through 1974.

Claridge was the All–Big Eight quarterback in 1962 and 1963, as well as an

Academic All-American in 1963. His best season, statistically, was Devaney's first at Nebraska. He completed 56 of 128 passes for 829 yards and four touchdowns, and he was the team's second-leading rusher, with 370 yards. He also led the team in scoring, with 10 touchdowns and a pair of two-point conversions.

Claridge rewrote the passing section of the Cornhusker record book, finishing with 125 of 298 completions for 1,733 yards and eight touchdowns, with 14 interceptions.

Johnny Bordogna, who played quarterback for Coach Bill Glassford from 1951 through 1953, held Nebraska's career passing records before Claridge. Bordogna passed for 1,618 yards and six touchdowns during his three seasons. But the teams on which he played were run-oriented.

"We were a ground-attack team, and we figured if we could get three or four yards on each play, we could beat most clubs," Bordogna once said. The problem was getting those "three or four" yards. The Cornhuskers didn't beat most clubs during those three seasons. Their record was 10–18–2.

Even so, Bordogna established himself as one of Nebraska's best quarterbacks during the pre–Devaney and Osborne era. In addition to setting the passing record, he finished as the career rushing leader among Cornhusker quarterbacks, with 782 yards. "Running was one of my specialties," he said.

Glassford's offense was a "modified T," with a wingback lining up outside one of the ends. It was a power-running offense, much like the single wing from which it evolved. "We might have two guards or a guard and a tackle pulling, so that we had four men out in front of our ball carrier. Back then, you felt you were a running back as much as anybody else in the backfield," said Bordogna. "When the quarterback comes out for that option play, the defense has to be aware that this guy can run as well as pass."

He was speaking of the early 1950s. But his remarks apply to Nebraska's quarterbacks in the 1990s as well.

1. Bordogna set Nebraska's single-game rushing record for a quarterback in 1952, when he ran 25 times for 143 yards against Iowa State. That record held for more than 30 years. What Osborne-era quarterback broke Bordogna's record? Against whom? In what season?

2. Through the 1997 season, what was Nebraska's single-game rushing record by a quarterback? Who set it? Against whom did he set it? In what season?

3. Who holds Nebraska's career rushing record for a quarterback? Who holds the Cornhuskers' single-season rushing record by a quarterback?

Quiz 25: No Place Like Home

Fred Duda was a quarterback in Devaney's first recruiting class. He came from Chicago and picked the Cornhuskers in part because they ran an option offense that was identical to the one he directed in high school. Adjusting to Nebraska's offense was easy, "like falling out of bed," Duda once said.

Getting accustomed to small-town life might have been more difficult. "I had to look at a map," Duda recalled. "Lincoln was right in the middle, when I opened up the map, on a crease."

By the time he graduated, however, Lincoln had become a second home, he said.

What are the hometowns of these Cornhusker quarterbacks? Some are mentioned elsewhere in this book. But you'll have to depend on your own knowledge for most.

1. Johnny Bordogna (1951–53)
2. Bob Churchich (1964–66)
3. Frank Patrick (1967–69)
4. Fran Nagle (1949–50)
5. Jerry Tagge (1969–71)
6. David Humm (1972–74)
7. Vince Ferragamo (1975–76)
8. Turner Gill (1980–83)
9. Tom Sorley (1976–78)
10. Mickey Joseph (1988–91)
11. Keithen McCant (1989–91)
12. Ernie Sigler (1967–68)
13. Brook Berringer (1992–95)
14. Steve Taylor (1985–88)
15. Van Brownson (1969–71)
16. Terry Luck (1974–75)
17. Steve Runty (1972–73)
18. Dennis Claridge (1961–63)

No Passing Fancy

Tom Osborne's offense became primarily ground-bound by design rather than by default. Osborne has more than a passing knowledge of . . . well, the passing game. In fact, Osborne's "command of the passing game is tremendous," former Cornhusker quarterback Vince Ferragamo has said.

But the Cornhuskers have "so much success running, it's hard to fault it."

Quiz 26: Cornhusker Quarterback Quiz

The following questions will test your knowledge of Nebraska's quarterbacks. This section also provides an opportunity to use the alliteration "Quarterback Quiz."

1. What is the longest pass play in Cornhusker history? Who threw the pass? Who caught it? How long was the play? What year was it? And against whom?

2. What is the longest nontouchdown pass play in Cornhusker history? Give the particulars.

3. Two Nebraska quarterbacks have passed for 290 or more yards in a game. One of the two did it twice. Name them, their totals, and the games in which they passed for those totals.

4. At 6-foot-7 and 225 pounds, Frank Patrick was the biggest quarterback in Cornhusker history. He earned letters in 1967, 1968, and 1969. But

he didn't play quarterback in 1969. Sophomores Jerry Tagge and Van Brownson did. To what position was Patrick moved for his senior season?

5. Only one Cornhusker quarterback has thrown five touchdown passes in a game. Who was the quarterback? Against whom did he throw for five touchdowns?

6. Three Cornhusker quarterbacks have passed for 2,000 or more yards in one season. Who were they? What were their passing-yardage totals? In what season did they achieve those totals?

7. Nebraska has led the conference in passing yardage six times since 1946, but only once under Tom Osborne. What was the season under Osborne? Who was the regular quarterback?

Extra Credit: What were the other five seasons, and who were the regular quarterbacks?

8. Nebraska has ranked in the Top 10 in the nation in passing yardage only once since 1946. What was the season? Who was the regular quarterback? For how many yards did he pass?

9. Five Nebraska quarterbacks have passed for 3,000 or more yards during their careers. Name the five, and for extra credit, include their yardage totals within 10 yards.

10. Six Cornhusker quarterbacks have thrown 30 or more career touchdown passes. Name the six and their totals. Which of the six holds the single-season record for touchdown passes?

Quiz 27: Curiouser and Curiouser

As Tom Osborne often has pointed out, the quarterback gets too much praise when a team is successful and too much blame when it is not. But that wasn't a problem for Coach E. J. "Doc" Stewart's Cornhusker teams in 1916 and 1917 . . . because they didn't utilize a quarterback.

Stewart, a native of Steubenville, Ohio, came to Nebraska from Oregon State after Jumbo Stiehm's departure and brought with him a unique offensive philosophy that replaced the quarterback with a second fullback. The center called the signals and passed the ball directly to the carrier.

Stewart's center also departed from standard practice. Instead of snapping the ball back through his legs, the center stood next to the ball and tossed it sideways to the running back.

The no-quarterback offense worked well. Stewart's teams were a combined 11–4 and won two Missouri Valley Conference titles. In 1917, his Cornhuskers overwhelmed Nebraska Wesleyan 100–0.

They also played good defense. Eight of the 11 victories were by shutout. Stewart's tenure at Nebraska was brief because of World War I.

1. Steubenville, Ohio, provided Nebraska with an outstanding running back in the mid-1960s. He scored the Cornhuskers' lone touchdown in a

10–7 loss against Arkansas in the 1965 Cotton Bowl. Can you name this big halfback whose nickname was "Lighthorse"?

Bill Jennings, Bob Devaney's immediate predecessor as Cornhusker head coach, went the opposite direction from Stewart regarding the importance of a quarterback. Jennings concluded that if one quarterback was good, two would be even better . . . maybe twice as good.

Jennings took the two-quarterback concept beyond theory. In spring 1959, he began preparing his two-quarterback alignment. The preparation was clandestine. Only the players directly involved—the center, the quarterback, and selected running backs—were privy to the plan.

The alignment, a "tandem T," was a variation of the T formation. The difference was that one of the halfbacks lined up alongside the quarterback, directly behind the center. The idea was that defenders wouldn't know whether the ball was snapped to the quarterback or to the halfback. And then, to further confuse the issue, and the defense, one player ran right and the other ran left after the center snap.

Jennings continued to work with select players in fall 1959 as Nebraska prepared for its season-opener against Texas. Coach Darrell Royal's team was number 17 in the Associated Press preseason poll. Nebraska, a combined 4–16 in Jennings's first two seasons, had no national aspirations.

That the Cornhuskers wouldn't upset Texas was apparent almost from the opening kickoff. The Longhorns' defensive alignment confused Nebraska. The first chance he had, the Cornhusker quarterback got on the phone and asked an assistant in the press box, "What are they doing [defensively]?"

"I don't know," the assistant replied.

Going into the fourth quarter, Nebraska trailed 20–0. It was time for the tandem T.

The Cornhuskers pulled the surprise during a drive from their own 29-yard line to the Texas 40, where the Longhorns finally forced a fourth down and a punt. As soon as Nebraska lined up in the tandem T, Royal and his assistant began yelling "illegal" from the Texas sideline.

Cliff Ogden, the game's referee as well as the head of officials for the Big Seven Conference, said afterward that he was "dumbfounded" by the alignment. As he moved down the field, past Jennings on the sideline, Ogden told the Cornhusker coach that the formation almost certainly was illegal.

Immediately after the game, Ogden consulted a rule book, discovered he was right, and went to the locker room to notify Jennings. The two got into an argument, during which Jennings vented his frustrations regarding a clipping penalty that had nullified a 92-yard punt return for a touchdown.

The next week, as he prepared his team to play Minnesota, Jennings told reporters he wasn't abandoning the tandem T. But the Cornhuskers never ran another play from the illegal formation.

2. The quarterback in the tandem T was a transfer who suffered an

Achilles injury in the Minnesota game and played barely enough to earn a letter in his only season at Nebraska. Who was this quarterback—who would have transferred to Oklahoma instead of Nebraska if Sooner coach Bud Wilkinson had been interested? From what four-year school did he transfer?

3. The other "quarterback" in Jennings's tandem T for the Texas game was actually the left halfback, who carried once out of the formation for a 12-yard gain. He also returned the punt 92 yards for a touchdown, only to have it called back because of the clipping penalty. He was the youngest of four brothers who earned football letters at Nebraska, and he had a long and outstanding NFL career as a defensive back. Who was he?

Quiz 28: Enough of Offense

Before moving on to something else, here are some final offense-oriented questions. They get harder as you go along—at least, that's the intention. You may be a connoisseur of Cornhusker offensive facts and figures. And even if you're not, there's a chance for more alliteration.

Also, we need to acknowledge Nebraska's pass receivers, who often get overlooked because of the Cornhuskers' well-established reputation for running the ball. Recruiting outstanding receivers is difficult but certainly not impossible, as Nebraska's record book shows.

The Cornhuskers' all-time best receiver, Heisman Trophy winner Johnny Rodgers, is discussed at length elsewhere in this book. But there have been many others who deserve mention.

1. Johnny Rodgers is Nebraska's all-time leading pass receiver. That's a no-brainer. But who are the next four, in order, on the Cornhuskers' career receptions list? For extra credit, include their career totals for receptions and yards. Rodgers caught 143 passes for 2,479 yards.

2. Mike Rozier led the nation in rushing in 1983. He's the only Cornhusker to do so during the modern era. However, Cornhuskers have ranked among the nation's top five rushers in six other seasons since 1946. Rozier was fourth in 1982. Who were the other five? Where did they rank?

3. Only two modern-era Cornhuskers rushed for 1,000 yards in a season prior to Tom Osborne's becoming head coach. Who were they? Who was the first 1,000-yard rusher under Osborne?

4. Roger Craig was an outstanding pass receiver as an NFL running back. How many passes did he catch at Nebraska? Tom Rathman also proved to be a versatile back in the NFL, catching passes as well as running and blocking. How many passes did he catch at Nebraska?

5. Vince Ferragamo, Jimmy Burrow, Dean Gissler, and Ray Phillips all had to be held out of Nebraska's 1975 season-opener against Louisiana State. Why?

6. Steve Taylor broke his San Diego high school's total offense record. What future NFL Hall of Fame running back held the record Taylor broke? Talyor also broke the school's pass completion percentage record, held by the running back's brother. What was the brother's name?

7. Who's the Heisman Trophy winner here? On his way to winning the Heisman Trophy in 1988, Oklahoma State's Barry Sanders rushed for 189 yards and four touchdowns in a 63–42 Cowboy loss at Memorial Stadium. Nebraska scored 35 points in the first quarter and led 42–0 just over three minutes into the second. Sanders was overshadowed by a Cornhusker running back that afternoon. Who was the running back? How many yards did he gain? And how many touchdowns did he score? Another Cornhusker also had impressive stats. Who was he?

8. Seven Cornhuskers have amassed 4,000 or more yards of total offense (passing and rushing yards) during their careers. Identify the seven. Extra credit: Include their total yardage, within 10 yards.

9. Only five Cornhuskers have amassed 2,000 or more yards of total offense in a season. Identify them. Extra credit: Include their yardage, within 10 yards.

10. Only five Cornhuskers have caught three touchdown passes in one game. Johnny Rodgers did it once, against Minnesota in 1971. Who were the other four?

11. Only five Cornhuskers have ever caught 35 or more passes in a season. Johnny Rodgers did it in each of his varsity seasons, catching 55 in 1972, 53 in 1971, and 35 in 1970. Who were the other four? How many passes did they catch? In what season?

12. What Cornhusker receiver shares the NCAA Division I-A record for consecutive pass receptions for touchdowns? The record is six, and LSU's Carlos Carson shares it.

Answers

Quiz 16: California Connection

Dick Rupert came from Harbor Junior College, Keith Wortman came from Rio Hondo Junior College, and Carl Johnson came from Phoenix Junior College. All three were starters in 1971. Rupert also started in 1970, when Wortman and Johnson were top backups.

Quiz 17: The Scoring Explosion—1983

1. Bill McCartney was Colorado's coach. He replaced Chuck Fairbanks. He played at Missouri.

2. Joe Salem, who probably wished he were still at South Dakota that night in 1983

3. Lou Holtz

Quiz 18: The Scoring Explosion II—1995

1. Mike Rozier was the Cornhuskers' leading rusher in 1983, with a school-record 2,148 yards. Ahman Green was the leading rusher in 1995, with a school freshman–record 1,086 yards. Irving Fryar was the leading receiver in 1983, with 40 catches for 780 yards. Clester Johnson was the leading receiver in 1995, with 22 catches for 367 yards. Rozier was the total offense leader in 1983, with 2,148 yards. Tommie Frazier was the total offense leader in 1995, with 1,966 yards.

2. The Cornhuskers led the nation in rushing and scoring in both 1983 and 1995. Despite their impressive offensive yardage totals, they were second nationally both years.

3. In 1978, the Cornhuskers averaged 501.4 yards per game. Tom Sorley was the quarterback. In 1982, the Cornhuskers averaged 518.6 yards per game. Turner Gill was the quarterback.

Quiz 19: Centers of Attention

1. Lawrence Ely, 1932; Charles Brock, 1938; Tom Novak, 1949; Rik Bonness, 1974 and 1975; Tom Davis, 1977; Dave Rimington, 1981 and 1982; Mark Traynowicz, 1984; Bill Lewis, 1985; Jake Young, 1988 and 1989; Aaron Graham, 1995; and Aaron Taylor, 1996. The two-time All-Americans were Bonness, Rimington, and Young. The consensus picks were Bonness in 1975, Rimington in 1981 and 1982, Traynowicz in 1984, and Young in 1988 and 1989. Taylor was a two-time All-American but he earned the honor as a guard in 1994.

The unanimous consensus picks were Bonness in 1975, Rimington in 1981 and 1982, and Traynowicz in 1984. A unanimous selection is one who received first-team votes from all the major selectors.

2. LaVerne Allers, guard, 1966; Bob Newton, tackle, 1970; Marvin Crenshaw, tackle, 1974; Kelvin Clark, tackle, 1978; Randy Schleusener, guard, 1980; Dean Steinkuhler, guard, 1983; Will Shields, guard, 1992; Zach Wiegert, tackle, 1994; and Brenden Stai, guard, 1994

3. From left to right: tackle Rob Zatechka, guard Joel Wilks, center Aaron Graham, guard Brenden Stai, tackle Zach Wiegert. Wilks was the only one of the five who walked on.

Quiz 20: Great Glenn from Gilead

1. Lloyd Cardwell was given the nickname "Wild Hoss" by Frederick Ware, sports editor of the *Omaha World-Herald* and a legendary figure in his own right—or write. Ware explained, "It's his roaring, tearing, gay, freebooting way that reminds me of the defiant, joyous, speeding wild horse

that loves to run with the winds on the plain." Sam Francis was the fullback who led Cardwell on his way.

2. Guy Chamberlin was a consensus All-American end in 1915. Those who had seen them both play compared Cardwell to him. Dick Rutherford helped to provide the 180-pound Chamberlin with room to run, as this quote from Guy Reed, writing in an early history of the University of Nebraska, indicates: "Rutherford's blocking, with Chamberlin's marvelous dodging, kept the largest number of people that ever witnessed a football game on Nebraska Field continually on their feet."

Quiz 21: Heavier Than He Looks—Frank Solich

1. Isaiah Hipp carried 28 times for 254 yards against Indiana as a sophomore in 1977. Hipp rushed for 207 yards a week later against Kansas State, on his way to 1,301 rushing yards for the season.

2. Solich's high school teammate was Mike Worley. George Kelly recruited them.

Quiz 22: School Record, and Then Some

Roger Craig, a junior, was Nebraska's leading rusher in 1981, with 1,060 yards.

Quiz 23: Kansas—Wrong Place, Wrong Time

1. Mike Rozier rushed for 587 yards and also scored seven touchdowns in three games against Kansas. Rozier gained 285 of those yards in the 1983 game to set what was then the school record.

2. Calvin Jones came off the bench to rush for 294 yards against the Jayhawks in Lawrence in 1991. Derek Brown, Nebraska's starting I-back for that game, was forced to the sideline after being poked in the eye. Jones rushed for more career yards than Rozier did against Kansas, 596 in three games.

3. Calvin Jones scored six touchdowns against the Jayhawks in the 1991 game, a 59–23 victory. Harvey Rathbone scored six touchdowns against both Peru State and Haskell Institute in 1910. Bill Chaloupka scored six touchdowns against Doane College in 1907. Chaloupka, who was from Wilber, Nebraska, was listed as Nebraska's right tackle. Position designations didn't have the same meaning back then. Nebraska won the Doane game 85–0. The Cornhuskers set a school scoring record in the 1910 Haskell game.

4. Nebraska defeated Haskell 119–0 in 1910, to avenge a 16–5 loss in 1909, and Kearney State 117–0 in 1911. The 1910 game was the last of the season, as well as the last for Coach King Cole. And the 1911 game was the first of the season, as well as the first for Coach Jumbo Stiehm.

5. Isaiah Hipp came from South Carolina as a walk-on. Jarvis Redwine transferred from Oregon State.

6. Roger Craig ran 94 yards for a touchdown against Florida State in 1981. Craig was a junior that season. He and Johnson were teammates in 1980. The longest run from scrimmage without scoring a touchdown was 73 yards by Hipp against Indiana in 1977. Hipp was a sophomore.

7. Rozer rushed for 200 or more yards in seven games, including a school-record four in a row in 1983. He gained 227 against Kansas State, 212 against Iowa State, 285 against Kansas, and 205 against Oklahoma. He rushed for 212 yards against Colorado and 204 yards against Kansas State in back-to-back games in 1982. He also rushed for 251 yards against Oklahoma State in 1982.

Quiz 24: Raising Minnesota

1. Steve Taylor rushed for 157 yards against Utah State in 1987.

2. Gerry Gdowski rushed for 174 yards on 17 carries against Iowa State in 1989.

3. Taylor holds the career rushing record for a quarterback, gaining 2,125 yards from 1985 through 1988. Scott Frost holds the single-season record, with 1,095 yards in 1997.

Quiz 25: No Place Like Home

1. Turtle Creek, Pennsylvania
2. Omaha, Nebraska
3. Derry, Pennsylvania
4. West Lynn, Massachusetts
5. Green Bay, Wisconsin
6. Las Vegas, Nevada
7. Los Angeles, California
8. Fort Worth, Texas
9. Big Spring, Texas
10. Marrero, Louisiana
11. Grand Prairie, Texas
12. Dallas, Texas
13. Goodland, Kansas
14. Spring Valley or Fresno, California. Taylor grew up in Fresno but moved to Spring Valley, in suburban San Diego, for his final two years of high school. Whenever he went back to Fresno, his friends reminded him that his home was Fresno, not Spring Valley. So either is right.
15. Shenandoah, Iowa
16. Fayetteville, North Carolina
17. Ogallala, Nevada

18. Robbinsdale, Minnesota. Just checking to see if you're paying attention.

Quiz 26: Cornhusker Quarterback Quiz

1. Fred Duda passed to Freeman White for 95 yards and a touchdown against Colorado in 1965.

2. Steve Taylor and Todd Millikan teamed up on a 73-yard pass against South Carolina in 1986.

3. David Humm, 297 yards against Wisconsin and 292 yards against Missouri, both in 1973; Frank Patrick, 290 yards against Oklahoma in 1967. Only the Wisconsin game was a victory, by the way.

4. Tight end. He caught three passes for 40 yards.

5. Steve Taylor threw for five touchdowns against UCLA in 1987.

6. David Humm, 2,074 yards in 1972; Vince Ferragamo, 2,071 in 1976; and Jerry Tagge, 2,019 in 1971.

7. The Cornhuskers led the Big Eight in passing yardage in 1976. Ferragamo was the quarterback.

The Cornhuskers led the Big Eight in passing yardage in four of Bob Devaney's 11 seasons: 1964, Bob Churchich; 1967, Frank Patrick; 1971, Jerry Tagge; and 1972, David Humm. Nebraska also led the conference in passing in 1948. Kenny Fischer was the regular quarterback.

8. David Humm passed for 2,074 yards in 1972. Nebraska ranked number eight nationally.

9. David Humm, 1972–74, 5,035 yards; Jerry Tagge, 1969–71, 4,704 yards; Tommie Frazier, 1992–95, 3,521 yards; Turner Gill, 1980–83, 3,317 yards; and Vince Ferragamo, 1975–76, 3,224 yards.

10. Tommie Frazier, 43; David Humm, 41; Turner Gill, 34; Jerry Tagge, 32; Vince Ferragamo, 32; and Steve Taylor, 30. Ferragamo threw 20 touchdown passes in 1976.

Quiz 27: Curiouser and Curiouser

1. Harry Wilson

2. Tom Kramer transferred to Nebraska from the University of California–Berkeley. He was referred to Oklahoma by California coach Pete Elliott. Curiously enough, Elliott preceded Jennings as head coach at Nebraska. Jennings was an assistant on Elliott's staff. Elliott, who spent only one season in charge of the Cornhuskers, and Jennings both had been assistants to Wilkinson at Oklahoma.

3. Pat Fischer

Much decorated Cornhusker center Dave Rimington, who won the Out-land Trophy in 1981 and 1982 and the Lombardi Award in 1982, in addi-tion to being a two-time All-American.

(Photo courtesy of *Huskers Illustrated*/Randy Hampton)

Quiz 28: Enough of Offense

1. Jeff Kinney, 1969–71, 82 receptions, 864 yards; Guy Ingles, 1968–70, 74 receptions, 1,157 yards; Tim Smith, 1977–79, 72 receptions, 1,089 yards; and Irving Fryar, 1981–83, 67 receptions, 1,196 yards.

2. Bobby Reynolds was number two in 1950, 1,342 yards; Jarvis Red-wine was number five in 1980, 1,119 yards; Ken Clark was number five in

1988, 1,497 yards; Lawrence Phillips was number three in 1994, 1,722 yards; and Ahman Green was number two in 1997, 1,877 yards.

3. Bobby Reynolds, 1,342 yards in 1950, and Jeff Kinney, 1,037 yards in 1971, were the pre-Osborne 1,000-yard rushers. Tony Davis, 1,008 yards in 1973, was Osborne's first.

4. Craig caught 16 passes for 102 yards during his three seasons at Nebraska. Rathman caught five passes for 70 yards and one touchdown during four seasons as a Cornhusker.

5. They had made bowl trips as redshirts, which was illegal under NCAA rules at the time.

6. Marcus Allen, Damon Allen. The school was San Diego Lincoln High.

7. Ken Clark rushed for 256 yards and scored three touchdowns, the first on a 73-yard run 1:05 into the game. Quarterback Steve Taylor ran for three touchdowns and passed for two.

8. Tommie Frazier, 1992–95, 5,476 yards; Jerry Tagge, 1969–71, 5,283 yards; David Humm, 1972–74, 5,027 yards; Steve Taylor, 1985–88, 4,940 yards; Mike Rozier, 1981–83, 4,780 yards; Turner Gill, 1980–83, 4,634 yards; and Scott Frost, 1996–97, 4,210 yards. Rozier is the only nonquarterback. His yardage was all by rushing.

9. Jerry Tagge, 1971, 2,333 yards; Scott Frost, 1997, 2,332 yards; Gerry Gdowski, 1989, 2,251 yards; Mike Rozier, 1983, 2,148 yards; and Keithen McCant, 1991, 2,108 yards. Gdowski needed only 76 more rushing yards to become the first Cornhusker in modern history to rush and pass for 1,000 yards in a season.

10. Clarence Swanson, 1921, Colorado State; Frosty Anderson, 1973, Minnesota; Don Westbrook, 1974, Kansas; and Tom Banderas, 1987, Missouri

11. Jeff Kinney, 41 in 1969; Irving Fryar, 40, 1983; Bob Revelle, 38, 1972; and Dennis Richnafsky, 36, 1967

12. Tight end Gerald Armstrong caught six consecutive passes for touchdowns as a junior in 1992. They were spread over five games, from September 5 to November 7, when he completed the streak with two touchdown catches against Kansas. He finished the season with eight receptions, seven of which were for touchdowns. Armstrong, a walk-on from Ponca, Nebraska, caught 19 passes during his career, 12 for touchdowns.

5

BLACKSHIRTS RULE:

Defense

Here's another of Bob Devaney's stories about getting off a train while he was coaching at Wyoming and being confronted by a little old lady who also happened to be an unhappy Cowboy fan.

The team had just returned to Laramie after a particularly poor performance. Devaney accidentally bumped into the little old lady and said, "Excuse me, ma'am. I meant no offense."

The little old lady replied, in disgust, "Your defense stinks, too."

Often Overlooked

Nebraska came to be characterized by run-oriented offense during Tom Osborne's tenure as head coach. When he was being recruited by the Cornhuskers as a high school senior in Highland Springs, Virginia, Brian Washington said, "People back home told me Nebraska was an offensive-minded school."

Washington was a *Parade* magazine high school All-America defensive back in 1984. Nevertheless, he accepted the Cornhuskers' scholarship offer and earned four letters as a strong safety. "I'm not saying I can change it totally, but I can help change it," he said of Nebraska's offensive image.

The Cornhuskers have never ignored defense. Their first two Outland Trophy winners were defensive linemen: Larry Jacobson in 1971 and Rich Glover in 1972. And they've had their share of consensus All-America defensive players since the mid-1960s, when NCAA rules allowed two-platoon play.

Osborne served as his own offensive coordinator. Although he met regularly with the defensive coaches, he rarely interfered. "Tom lets us do what we want," defensive coordinator Charlie McBride has said. "He likes to know our thoughts, and he might say, 'You've got to be careful because you're putting in too much.' There's discussion. We'll go through all the stuff.

"But if we really believe in something, he'll argue but he won't say no."

Osborne's knowledge of offense and his penchant for studying game film provided him with valuable insights into defensive philosophy. But he left the strategy decisions to the defensive coaches, for good reason. "I can remember him calling only a couple of defenses, a couple of weeks in a row," McBride

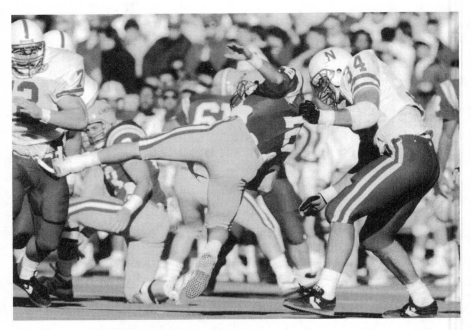

Trev Albert, the 1993 Butkus Award winner and Nebraska's career sacks leader, pulls down Iowa State's quarterback.
(Photo courtesy of *Huskers Illustrated*/William Lauer)

said. "We were going, 'No. No.' But we ran them . . . and they were both touchdowns."

Osborne always had a defensive coordinator, beginning with Monte Kiffin, a carryover from Bob Devaney's staff of assistants. Kiffin, a Cornhusker letterman from 1961 through 1963, was succeeded by Lance Van Zandt in 1977, and McBride succeeded Van Zandt in 1982.

Nebraska has consistently ranked among the nation's leaders in most major defensive categories in recent seasons. "When we've not been very good on defense, we've tried to do too much," said McBride, who also coaches the defensive tackles. "But Tom has never come up and said, 'Hey, I don't want you to do that.' I remember only one occasion when he said, 'I don't ever want you to run that defense again.'

"And I wasn't the defensive coordinator then. Lance Van Zandt was."

Blackshirts Forever

The week before the opening game of the season, Nebraska's first-team defensive players are given black practice jerseys. If two players are listed on the depth chart as sharing the number one position, each is given one of the black mesh jerseys. Second-team defenders wear yellow practice jerseys.

The practice jerseys are left in the players' lockers. Opening a locker and finding a black jersey is an emotional experience for most Cornhuskers, and particularly those from Nebraska.

"It's a lot more than a black jersey," said Chad Kelsay, who earned one as a sophomore in 1996.

Kelsay grew up in Auburn, Nebraska, a community of 3,500 in the southeast corner of the state, and played immediately, without sitting out a redshirt season. "You grow up as a kid and you hear this thing called a 'Blackshirt.' You grow up loving Nebraska football, and then you finally . . . see that Blackshirt. A lot of guys would rather have a Blackshirt jersey than a game jersey because it means so much."

Even those who aren't familiar with the Blackshirt tradition before they get to Nebraska quickly gain an appreciation for it. "Guys cherish it a lot," said Ed Stewart, a four-year Cornhusker letterman and consensus All-American linebacker in 1994 who was recruited from Chicago.

"I don't know if it's as big as it was three, four, or five years ago," Stewart said when he was a senior. "But it's still a big deal, definitely. I always knew I wanted to get one of those."

Barron Miles, a first-team All–Big Eight cornerback in 1993 and 1994, came to Nebraska from Roselle, New Jersey. "The Blackshirt is the top," he once said. "You don't want to be at practice with a white or a yellow jersey, for that matter." The scout squad players wear white practice jerseys.

"It's a good tradition a lot of schools don't have," Cornhusker defensive coordinator Charlie McBride has said. "One high school coach in New Jersey calls his defense the Blackshirts.

"It's something a lot of people in the country know about now. They've picked up on the tradition and started wearing T-shirts and hats (promoting the Blackshirts). Some people just like defense. They'll say, 'The Blackshirts did a good job.' Or: 'The Blackshirts did a bad job.'

"They'll use it as a starting point to talk about the defense. The thing that's good about it is, it entails the whole defense. In general, everybody on the defense is a Blackshirt in some ways."

The "Blackshirts" nickname provides an identity. "It's not just the present, it's the past. It gives them a title rather than just 'the defense.' It's a goal for a lot of players," said McBride.

Nebraska's Blackshirt tradition quickly evolved from a modest beginning. No one seems to know exactly when the concept was formed. But its roots can be traced to George Kelly, the defensive line coach for Bob Devaney's teams from 1962 to 1968. Kelly was the first to assign black pullovers to the top defensive unit during practice. The pullovers were distributed by trainer Paul Schneider.

Second-team defenders were given yellow pullovers, and third-team defenders wore green ones. Now green pullovers are used for quarterbacks who aren't to be tackled in scrimmages.

Even the black pullovers were special, according to Adrian Fiala, who came from Bishop Ryan High School in Omaha and lettered at linebacker for the Cornhuskers from 1967 to 1969.

Getting a black pullover from Schneider before practice was "huge," said Fiala, a color commentator on the Cornhusker radio network. "That was the best thing that ever happened to you here. As long as you were there at number one on the depth chart, you had one. We had our own ways of wearing it. I took mine and cut it down the middle so it was a lot easier to get on, like a vest. Then I would just tie it."

Kelly might have settled on the Blackshirt concept to give Nebraska's defense the kind of distinction Paul Dietzel's "Chinese Bandits" defense at Louisiana State enjoyed, according to Fiala.

The Blackshirt image flourished under Kiffin, whom Osborne made defensive coordinator in 1973. Devaney's staff didn't have a designated defensive or offensive coordinator.

The Blackshirts have no idea of how or when the tradition began. All they know is, they want to be a part of it. "It's a black practice jersey with white numbers on it. But boy, it's a whole lot more than that," said Kelsay. "The thing could be a rag, and you'd still look at it like a shrine."

Best of the Best

The 1984 defense was among the best, statistically, in Cornhusker history. The Blackshirts ranked number one in total defense (203.3 yards per game) and scoring defense (9.5 points per game), and they ranked number four in rushing defense (78.8) and number five in passing defense (124.5).

Eight starters returned from an oft-maligned 1983 defense. The difference was, "they just had more maturity," Mark Traynowicz, an All-America center, said in defense of his teammates.

1984 BLACKSHIRTS

Left end—Bill Weber, 6-2, 210, senior, Lincoln, Nebraska
Left tackle—Chris Spachman, 6-5, 250, sophomore, Kansas City, Missouri
Middle guard—Ken Graeber, 6-3, 245, senior, Minneapolis, Minnesota
Right tackle—Rob Stuckey, 6-3, 245, senior, Lexington, Nebraska
Right end—Scott Strasburger, 6-1, 210, senior, Holdrege, Nebraska
Strongside linebacker—Mark Daum, 6-3, 235, senior, Dix, Nebraska
Weakside linebacker—Marc Munford, 6-2, 230, sophomore, Littleton, Colorado
Left cornerback—Dave Burke, 5-10, 190, senior, Layton, Utah
Right cornerback—Neil Harris, 6-0, 190, senior, Kansas City, Kansas
Monster—Mike McCashland, 6-1, 200, senior, Lincoln, Nebraska
Safety—Bret Clark, 6-3, 200, senior, Nebraska City, Nebraska

1. Four of the starters in 1984 came to Nebraska as walk-ons. Name them.

2. One of the starters was an I-back on the freshman team. Name him.

3. One of the starters was a four-year letterman. Name him.

4. One of the starters played eight-man football in high school. Name him.

5. A ninth defender who would have been a returning starter in 1984 suffered a knee injury in the Spring Game and sat out as a medical redshirt before returning in 1985. Name him.

6. Two of the starters were two-time Academic All-Americans. Name them.

7. A future All-American middle guard was a sophomore backup at left tackle in 1984. Name him.

8. A future All-American was a junior backup at right tackle in 1984. Name him.

9. The brother of one starter also was a Nebraska football letterman. Name him.

10. Nebraska has led the nation in total defense in one other season. Which was it?

Best of Broderick

And now, heeeeeere's Broderick . . .

"I believe no one else is like Broderick Thomas," Broderick Thomas said. Thomas came from Houston's Madison High School and played defensive end, or outside linebacker, for Nebraska from 1985 through 1988. He was a three-year starter, a three-time first-team all-conference selection, and a two-time All-American, including a consensus selection in 1988.

He was a cocaptain as a senior, and he was a favorite of reporters throughout his career because he was almost always good for a quote, particularly early on. He was constantly compared to Oklahoma's Brian Bosworth, "the Boz." He was the first to refer to Memorial Stadium as "Our House"—beginning with a 30–10 victory against Oklahoma State there in 1986. And he proclaimed the 1987 season the Cornhuskers' "Hell-Raisin' Tour" following a victory against LSU in the 1987 Sugar Bowl.

By the time he was a senior, Thomas was more reserved in his comments. He told a reporter in 1988, "It was like: 'Well, he's just going to be quiet for a while. He'll come out and say something.' It's kind of hilarious. Sometimes I have to say it three or four times to the same guy: 'No comment.'

"He might even go away, reword the question, and come back. But I still tell

Broderick "the Sandman" Thomas
(Photo Courtesy of *Huskers Illustrated*/William Lauer)

him: 'No comment.' If the media has something to say, then let the media say it. I'll let my Bike [helmet] do my talking."

Before his senior season, however, Thomas was a master of words and frankness.

On his nickname, which he earned in high school because, he said, he put ball carriers to sleep when he tackled them: "I'm 'the Sandman.' I happen to like it. As far as I'm concerned, it'll always be Broderick 'the Sandman' Thomas. It'll never be just Broderick Thomas again if I have to write it.

"Whenever I look up in the sky and see the name 'Broderick Thomas,' I'll always open it up and put 'the Sandman' in there, too. There's not another 'Sandman' in the world."

On comparisons to Bosworth: "I'm not Bosworth. He talks a lot, but he also talks in a negative way. I don't want people to think I'm just a loudmouth because I'm not. He's wild. You don't know what type of person he is. His mind might go off sometime. I'm not wild. When I'm on the field, the fun is knocking somebody around. That's football. But I'm a gentle guy off the field, friendly, you know."

On players who talk trash: "I call 'em perpetrators. Guys who talk noise to me don't bother me. I'm the master of the talking game. I'm the master of the physical game. I'm the master of disaster."

On trash-talking in general: "My father always told me: 'Unless you're right, keep your mouth shut. If you're wrong, keep quiet.' If I'm not confident enough to do my job, I'll keep my mouth shut. Talking doesn't win ball games. You have to go out there and execute, do things well."

On playing football: "I'm going to raise hell 'til I can't raise hell no more. I want to be great. I want people to remember me."

On his junior season, and Alabama's Cornelius Bennett, a three-time All-American and the Lombardi Award winner in 1986: "If he's what they call great, I want to see what they say this year. I'm working to be the best, to be able to dominate a game. I might not achieve that goal. But I'm trying."

On I-back Doug DuBose, whose Cornhusker career ended after the 1985 season because of a knee injury. Thomas was speaking after the 1986 season, in which Nebraska was 10–2: "If Doug had played, we'd be sitting here now, waiting for the [national championship] rings."

On "Our House," Memorial Stadium, after Oklahoma quarterback Jamelle Holieway suggested that the Sooners had a key. Oklahoma defeated Nebraska there in 1986 and 1987: "There's no way any keys can be made. I have the only key. I'd just hate for him [Holieway] to be caught in my house."

More on "Our House," before the 1987 Oklahoma game. After the Sooners' dramatic, come-from-behind 20–17 victory at Memorial Stadium in 1986, Oklahoma coach Barry Switzer began referring to "Sooner Magic" in games against Nebraska: "Houdini is not allowed in 'Our House,' so there's not going to be any fourth-quarter magic around here . . . unless we're doing it."

Note: Thomas was partly right. The 1987 game was billed as the "Game of the Century II," matching number one–ranked Nebraska against number two–ranked Oklahoma, just as it had been in the first "Game of the Century" in 1971 at Norman, Oklahoma. The Sooners dominated the 1987 game, even though the final score was only 17–7. But as Thomas said, there wasn't any fourth-quarter magic, on either side.

On his sophomore season: "People ran right at me. They thought: 'He's not going to stop us.' But I stopped the best they had to offer. I made the fourth-and-one plays because they brought 'em at me."

On what would happen if he intercepted a pass: "They might think it's Eric Dickerson running."

On South Carolina receiver Sterling Sharpe before the teams played in 1987. Nebraska defeated the Gamecocks 30–21 at Memorial Stadium: "I can stop anybody walking. We're going to match our talents against each other. I'll be 'manning up' on him a little, and I'm going to show him what the Big Eight's all about. I intend to display what I can do. It's going to be 'the Sandman' again."

On why he didn't go to Oklahoma. Switzer aggressively recruited him as a defensive tackle, but Thomas was determined to play defensive end: "It was just a matter of him telling me I could play defensive end. But he said I couldn't play defensive end for them, so I didn't want to talk to him no more."

Beneficiary of Circumstance

The Blackshirts came up big on the bitterly cold afternoon in 1978 when Nebraska defeated Oklahoma for the first time during Tom Osborne's tenure as head coach. And none played better than Bruce Dunning, a walk-on linebacker from Arvada, Colorado, who waited three years for his opportunity.

Dunning's experience as a walk-on was both typical and unique. He grew up in Colorado and planned to attend either Colorado or Wyoming, depending on which school offered him a scholarship.

Wyoming offered a football scholarship. Colorado did not. "But I wanted to play in the Big Eight, so my dad told me I should go to Colorado and walk on," Dunning said, several years later.

Walking on at Colorado was easier said than done, however. Bill Mallory, the Buffaloes' head coach, wasn't the least bit interested, according to Dunning. "Colorado wouldn't even talk to us."

After Dunning's senior year at Arvada West High School in suburban Denver, his father, Roger, had taken a job in Nebraska. One of Roger's associates in Lincoln was a neighbor of Paul Schneider, the Cornhuskers' head trainer. "Schnitzy got things rolling," Dunning said.

With encouragement from Schneider, Dunning sent film to Tom Osborne, who had just completed his second season as head coach. Osborne was willing to let Dunning walk on.

"It was a great opportunity, but I'll say this, nothing was given to me but an opportunity," said Dunning. "Nobody had anything given to them there, not even the scholarship guys."

When Dunning arrived as an eager freshman in 1975, he found himself among 100 other walk-ons who were just as eager. There wasn't enough space in the freshman locker room in Schulte Fieldhouse to accommodate all of them. Dunning considered himself fortunate, however, because Glen Abbott, the freshman equipment manager at the time, "took a liking to me." Though he wasn't assigned a locker, Dunning was allowed to keep his things in a special place in the equipment room.

It was easy to become discouraged under such conditions. But "if you made it through your freshman year and spring practice, you pretty much knew you were okay," Dunning said.

Dunning made it through his freshman year and a redshirt season, spent on the scout team, though not without some struggle. At one point, he became so discouraged, he considered transferring to San Jose State. Monte Kiffin, the Cornhuskers' defensive coordinator, was "instrumental" in his staying.

"He told me: 'You can play here if you hang around and work,'" said Dunning.

With regular encouragement from Kiffin, he improved. But Kiffin left after Dunning's sophomore season, and Lance Van Zandt was hired as defensive coordinator. "I really thought: 'Aw man, this is the end for me.' But Coach Van Zandt was another guy who gave me a chance," Dunning said.

Dunning played enough to earn a letter in 1977. But he was primarily a special-teams player and spent practice on the scout team. It wasn't until 1978, his fourth and final year, that he became a starter. He finished second on the team in tackles, with 113 in 12 games, including the Orange Bowl.

Despite the frustrations, Dunning has a special affection for Nebraska and the Cornhuskers. "I still live, breathe . . . and cuss 'em," he said. "People in Nebraska treated me well, a lot of people."

Quiz 30: Quick Hitters

1. Dunning was the starting weakside linebacker in 1978. The starting strongside linebacker that season was from Golden, Colorado—he played the weakside previously. Name him.

2. The starting strongside linebacker in 1978 was a two-sport letterman at Nebraska. In what other sport did he letter? Be as specific as possible.

3. The Cornhuskers refer to the weakside linebacker as "Will," the strongside linebacker as "Sam," and the middle linebacker as "Mike." When Dunning played, however, in a "50" defense, women's names often were used for the weakside and strongside linebackers. What women's names were commonly used? Why wasn't there a woman's name for a middle linebacker?

4. When he played linebacker at Oklahoma, Brian Bosworth said no matter what he did on the field, one Cornhusker I-back would always get up after being tackled and cheerfully extend a hand to help him up. Such behavior could be as infuriating as it was surprising. Name the I-back.

5. In addition to serving as defensive coordinator from 1973 to 1976, Monte Kiffin coached a position. What was the position? Who replaced him as coach for that position? Lance Van Zandt succeeded Kiffin as defensive coordinator. He also coached a position. What was that position, and who coached it previously? From what Big Eight school did Van Zandt come?

6. From 1965, when NCAA rules were changed to allow two-platoon play, through 1982, Nebraska had only two captains each season, one from the offense and the other from the defense. During that time, six of the de-

fensive captains played linebacker. Identify the linebacker cocaptain from each of the seasons: 1965, 1970, 1974, 1976, 1977, and 1982. Extra credit: Two of the six were from Omaha. Which two and from what high schools?

7. This Cornhusker linebacker was a three-time all-conference selection and a cocaptain in 1986. He was from Littleton, Colorado, but his father was from Lincoln and was an outstanding basketball player at Nebraska Wesleyan University. Name the linebacker.

8. As in 1978, Nebraska's starting linebackers in 1985 were both from Colorado. The weakside linebacker is identified in the previous question. Name the strongside linebacker. Extra credit: What was his hometown? Hint: He missed the 1984 season with a knee injury.

9. During Bob Devaney's 11 seasons as coach, one Nebraska linebacker earned All-America honors. Although he wasn't a consensus selection, he was first-team according to the Associated Press, the *Football News,* and the Walter Camp Foundation. Name him and the year.

10. Nebraska's first two Outland Trophy winners were defensive players. Name them, the years in which they earned the trophy, and the position each played.

11. Through the 1996 season, three Tom Osborne–era outside linebackers had been first-round selections in the National Football League draft. Name them and the years in which they were chosen. Extra credit: Identify the teams that selected each player.

12. Through the 1996 season, three other Osborne-era Cornhuskers had been first-round NFL draft picks as linebackers. Two of the three were listed as defensive ends at Nebraska, however. Name the three. Extra credit: Name the teams that drafted them. Hint: All three were defensive captains. Their senior seasons were 1973, 1978, and 1981.

Dumb and Dumber

Charlie McBride was in his first season as offensive line coach at Wisconsin under John Jardine, and the Badgers were playing Ohio State at Columbus, Ohio, in 1970. When McBride came onto the field for pregame warm-ups, he passed Hayes, who was leaning against a goalpost.

A couple of years earlier, McBride had written a letter to Ohio State coach Woody Hayes, asking about a graduate assistant's job. McBride's father and Hayes had been freshman roommates at Denison College in Granville, Ohio, so McBride figured Ohio State would be a good place to begin. After two years at Fenger High School in his native Chicago, he wanted to move to the next level.

Hayes's response to McBride's inquiry was, well, succinct.

"Dear Charlie," the letter began. "No." Signed, "Woody."

"There wasn't any explanation, just 'No,'" McBride said.

Hayes acknowledged him as he walked past that afternoon in 1970. "Hey,

McBride, are you as dumb as your old man was?" Hayes, the Hall of Fame coach-to-be, asked the young assistant.

"I was kind of intimidated because I didn't know what to say back to him," said McBride.

The game began, and Wisconsin quickly scored a touchdown. Across the field, Hayes was ranting and raving, "yelling at everybody on the team, tearing his hat up and doing all kinds of stuff."

The Badgers' lead was short-lived, however. Ohio State came back to win 56–7, McBride said.

No sooner had the final gun sounded than Hayes charged across the field to the Wisconsin sideline, ignoring Jardine and the coaches' postgame handshake and going right to McBride.

"I just want you to know one thing; you are as dumb as your old man was," Hayes said.

McBride laughs when he tells the story. He was a youngster when he first met Hayes at a college reunion his parents were attending. "Woody was always good to me in coaching," said McBride. "He'd always make it a point when we'd be at coaches' conventions to come over and say hello, and ask how my folks were. He was really a nice person in that. Actually, for as tough of an old guy as he was, he probably was one of the most thoughtful people because he was always concerned about my folks."

Time-out

The Atlanta, Georgia, Quarterback Club selected Tom Osborne to receive its Bobby Dodd Coach of the Year Award for 1978. When Osborne was in Atlanta for the award presentation, Furman Bisher, noted sports editor of the *Atlanta Journal,* aptly described him as a "walk-on" coach.

Osborne wasn't paid when he joined Bob Devaney's staff as a graduate assistant in 1962.

Osborne is "the only academic counselor I ever knew who became head coach of a team in the main channel of big-time football," Bisher wrote, referring to the fact that Osborne served as academic adviser for the football team under Devaney. Ursula Walsh succeeded Osborne in the position.

From Odd to Even

Nebraska's defensive success in recent seasons is a result of a well-documented change in philosophy. In the early 1990s, the Cornhuskers scrapped their familiar odd-front 50 defense and replaced it with an even-front, 4–3 base alignment. Instead of reading and reacting, they began attacking.

The defensive evolution came about over time. But one game in particular convinced Tom Osborne and his defensive assistants that the more aggressive approach was the way to go.

The final step in the change was born of "desperation," Osborne has said. Nebraska was playing Oklahoma at Norman in 1992 and having serious defensive difficulties. Though the Cornhuskers led 10–9 at halftime, Oklahoma had nearly 200 yards in total offense. The Sooners' Cale Gundy had completed 8 of 14 passes for 92 of the yards. If not for one critical mistake, Oklahoma would have led.

Late in the first quarter, Nebraska linebacker Ed Stewart had intercepted a Gundy pass and returned it 50 yards for the game's only touchdown. But that was one of the few bright moments for the Blackshirts. Their dilemma was how to stop Gundy without leaving themselves vulnerable to the run.

Oklahoma had rushed for 101 yards on 26 carries during the first half. The concern was that if Nebraska went to its "dime" defense exclusively in the second half, the Sooners would be able to run even more effectively. In the dime, defensive backs replaced linebackers, trading size for speed.

"We always felt the dime defense was predicated on passing," said Osborne. The defensive back–type linebackers matched up better in pass coverage. But they were more susceptible to the run.

That proved to be a misconception at Norman in 1992, however. Even though the Cornhuskers played the second half with their dime package, they were able to stop both the pass and the run. Gundy completed only one of six passes for six yards. And Oklahoma averaged barely two yards per rush.

Nebraska got its offense on track and won going away, 33–9. Afterward evaluating films of the game, the Cornhusker defensive coach decided the 4–3 could be sound enough against the run. And because practicing both the 50 and the dime was so time-consuming, they settled on the latter. "We were teaching two packages, and you can't do that," said defensive coordinator Charlie McBride.

"It took a huge amount of time to practice a 50 front and a four–three," Osborne said.

So instead of entering the game in apparent passing situations, players such as Ed Stewart were kept on the field all the time. Stewart stood 6-foot-1 and weighed 215 pounds as a senior. He would have been a strong safety in Nebraska's 50 defense—in fact, that's the position at which he was listed when he arrived as a scholarship recruit in 1990. But he was immediately moved to weakside linebacker, where he earned consensus All-America honors on the national championship team in 1994.

Troy Dumas, the starting strongside linebacker in 1994, played free safety his first three seasons at Nebraska, starting four games in the secondary as a junior before moving to linebacker. At 6-foot-4 and 220 pounds, Dumas was a good size for a defensive back. But he was light for a linebacker.

The change to the four–three required a recruiting emphasis on defensive backs with speed and the ability to cover receivers man-to-man. "When I first came here, we played a lot of zone [coverage]," McBride said of the secondary. "We always had good hitters, tough kids, walk-ons who could hit.

"When we were playing zone, we didn't look for speed. We looked for guys who would hit you. In zone [coverage], it was: Come up, hit them, and hope the ball comes out. You can play tight zone coverage and it looks like man-to-man. But a good passing team will eat up a zone."

Nebraska was facing good warm-weather passing teams in bowl games. And the more sophisticated the passing, the more difficulty the Cornhuskers had playing zone coverage.

McBride was regularly criticized by fans for not blitzing more, as if the blitz were a cure-all strategy that hadn't occurred to him. "The general public was aware of it," McBride said of the obvious deficiencies in zone pass coverage. "And we knew it. But we had to get the kids who could run first.

"If you don't have them, you're really in trouble in man-to-man. It was hard to get rid of the zone until the one-back sets. Then it really got ugly . . . and we got corners who could cover man-to-man."

McBride's response to such criticism in October 1991 underscored the dilemma. "You've got to rush the passer, but you've also got to watch for the draw play. You've got to watch out for the matchup that put a 4.4 (in the 40) receiver on a 4.7 linebacker. You can't just blitz," he said.

Another impetus for the switch to a 4–3 was a desire to take full advantage of the skills of players such as Trev Alberts, whose strength and quickness made him an outstanding pass rusher. In the 50 defense, outside linebackers (Alberts's position) rushed but also dropped off the line in pass coverage.

In the 4–3, players who had been outside linebackers became rush ends and were freed up to go after the quarterback. Alberts earned the Butkus Award as the nation's best collegiate linebacker as the defense evolved. He dominated in a way few Nebraska defenders ever had as a senior in 1993.

Broderick Thomas, a two-time All-America outside linebacker, was a Butkus Award finalist, even though "we probably wasted him some because he was dropping and rushing," Osborne said.

The change in philosophy "wasn't a stroke of genius," he said. "It was just more that we fell into it. You always evolve with the personnel you have and what's happening in football."

For nearly 20 years under Osborne, Nebraska's defensive philosophy was bend but don't break. Now the philosophy is to attack, with six defensive backs, two of whom are called outside linebackers

Quiz 31: From Odd to Even

1. Nebraska has led the nation in passing yardage defense three times, including twice under Tom Osborne. In 1967, the Cornhuskers allowed an

average of 90.1 yards passing per game. In 1981, they allowed an average of 100.1 yards per game. The other seasons in which they led the nation in passing yardage defense, they allowed only 39.9 yards per game. What season was it?

2. The Cornhusker record for pass interceptions in a season, seven, is shared by three players. Name them. Hint: The seasons were 1966, 1969, and 1970.

3. Nebraska's career leader in pass interceptions was a Cornhusker co-captain in 1969. Name him. Hint: He was from Lincoln, Nebraska, where he played at Pius X High School. Extra credit: How many passes did he intercept during his three seasons?

4. Rich Glover holds the Cornhusker single-game record for tackles. He made 22 in the 1971 Game of the Century against Oklahoma. Nebraska's single-game record for unassisted tackles also was against Oklahoma, in the 1987 game, which didn't live up to its billing as the Game of the Century II. What Cornhusker had 13 unassisted tackles in that 17–7 loss? Hint: He was a junior strongside linebacker.

5. The Nebraska single-season record for tackles by a defensive back, 87, was set in 1991 by a junior strong safety from Wahoo, Nebraska. Name him.

6. A different player holds the career record for tackles by a defensive back, with 209 in four seasons from 1989 to 1992. Hint: He was a free safety from Chandler, Arizona.

7. Here's a toughie. What defensive tackle holds the Cornhusker career record for fumble recoveries? He was an offensive lineman as a freshman. He missed the 1975 season because of a broken ankle, coming back for his senior season in 1976. He was from Compton, California.

8. Here's another toughie. The Nebraska career record for pass breakups, 19, is shared by five players, all of whom played only three seasons. Their careers spanned 1965–67, 1969–71, 1982–84, 1986–88, and 1992–94. If you can name more than two, go to the head of the class. If you can name all five, go directly to the final quiz for true Cornhusker fanatics at the end of this book. Hint: Three of the five were cocaptains. Two were from Nebraska.

Taking the good with the bad . . . from here on out, the bad.

9. Nebraska has allowed 48 or more points in a game 10 times in its history. Not surprisingly, the opponent in four of those games was Oklahoma. What Big Ten team was the opponent in three of those games? What are the most points ever scored against Nebraska? By what team? Hint: The Cornhusker coach was Potsy Clark. Extra credit: What was Clark's real first name?

10. What are the most points ever scored against Nebraska in one half? By what team? In what season? Hint: Tom Osborne was the coach.

11. Two teams have rushed for more than 500 yards in a game against Nebraska. The record is 506 against Pete Elliott's team in 1956. What team set the record? Hint: Elliott was a former assistant coach at the school. The second-most rushing yards came against Potsy Clark's team in 1948. Name the opponent. Hint: It won national titles in 1946, 1947, and 1949, but not in 1948.

12. Two opponents have passed for more than 400 yards against Nebraska. Both games were played in the 1990s, one at home and one on the road. The Cornhuskers won them both. Identify the teams, the seasons, and the quarterbacks. You needn't identify the passing yardage.

13. Three teams have gained more than 600 yards in a game against Nebraska. One of those three games was against a Tom Osborne–coached team. Identify the opponent and the year. Extra credit: What was the final score? Where was the game played?

Neil, for Real

Neil Smith would have been a rush end extraordinaire had Nebraska's base defense been a 4–3 in the mid-1980s. He was an outstanding pass rusher, "one of the finest we've had here," Tom Osborne once said. Also, Smith "probably made as much improvement as anyone we've had around here."

The Cornhuskers took a chance on Smith because they were short on young defensive linemen in 1984. "We had to take him," said defensive coordinator Charlie McBride, who also coaches the linemen. "We thought: 'We've got to take this guy and hope he grows.' Then he becomes Superman."

Nebraska discovered Smith in New Orleans. "Chanced upon him" is more accurate. The Cornhuskers were watching film of a quarterback at another Louisiana high school when they spotted Smith, a gangly 6-foot-6, 200-pound defensive end whom the quarterback seemed to be wearing.

Smith had attracted recruiting attention from small black colleges, most prominently Grambling, Southern, and Florida A&M. LSU and Tulane were the only other NCAA Division I-A schools besides Nebraska interested in Smith—and they weren't interested until Nebraska came calling.

Smith was the first Louisiana high school football player to whom Nebraska ever offered a scholarship, and he seemed a long shot, at best. "We felt we were taking a chance," Osborne said.

Although he reportedly ran the 40-yard dash in 4.7, Smith was timed at 5.09 the first time he tested as a freshman. In addition, he weighed only 208 pounds, not the 230 at which he was listed.

His best qualities, it appeared, were a sincere enthusiasm that bordered on naïveté and a seven-foot, one-and-a-half-inch arm span that was cause for hope. If he could get stronger and faster . . . whoa.

By the first freshman-junior varsity game in 1984, Smith weighed 224 pounds. By his senior season, his weight had increased to 261 pounds. His vertical jump—a measure of explosiveness—had increased to 35 inches, and his 40-yard dash time had dropped to 4.63, electronically measured.

Smith was a dominating presence as a senior, leading the Cornhuskers' defensive linemen in total tackles and unassisted tackles, and he was credited with 7.5 quarterback sacks for 50 yards in losses. He also was a cocaptain and a first-team All-American, according to the *Football News*.

Quiz 32: Mr. Smith Goes to the NFL and Other Matters

1. Neil Smith was a first-round pick in the 1988 National Football League draft. What team drafted him? He was not the first player chosen in the draft. What pick was he? Extra credit: Name the first player drafted in 1988. From what college was he? Who drafted him?

2. Smith's New Orleans high school had a unique name. What was it? Did Smith get to play against Louisiana State while he was at Nebraska? Explain.

3. Even though Smith was an outstanding pass rusher, he didn't lead the Cornhuskers in sacks as a senior—or in any of his three seasons, for that matter. Name the sack leader in 1987. Hint: He came to Nebraska as a walk-on and left as a fourth-round draft pick of the Los Angeles Raiders. Extra credit: From what Nebraska high school did he come?

4. The player to whom question number 3 refers was described in the 1987 media guide as possibly the "best second-string defensive lineman in the country." He earned the starting job, however, forcing the previous year's starter into a backup role. Name that player. Hint: He was undersized for the position, but like Smith, he was exceptionally fast, with 4.7 speed in the 40.

5. A senior defensive tackle on Bob Devaney's final team in 1972 logged more minutes than anyone on offense or defense, yet he wasn't a starter. He was never a starter at Nebraska, in fact, but he earned three letters and was selected in the second round of the 1973 draft by the Oakland Raiders, for whom he played eight seasons. Name this player, who definitely would have qualified as the best second-string collegiate defensive lineman in the country. Extra credit: Whom did he back up at left tackle in 1972? And who was the starting right defensive tackle?

6. An undersized (he was generously listed at 250 pounds), myopic defensive tackle from Omaha holds or shares several of Nebraska's records for sacks and tackles for loss. He was credited with 44 tackles for losses totaling a school career–record 288 yards during his three seasons. Name him. Extra credit: From what Omaha high school did he come?

7. Even with four-year lettermen becoming more commonplace, the top three on Nebraska's career tackles list all played only three seasons.

Name them, in order. Extra credit: The career leader also holds the single-season record for unassisted tackles. But he does not hold the single-season record for total tackles—unassisted and assisted. Who does?

8. Not surprisingly, a significant majority of the Cornhuskers' career tackle leaders were linebackers. What nonlinebacker ranks the highest on the career-tackles list?

9. Nebraska's single-season record for blocked kicks by a lineman is also the position career record. What late-1960s middle guard and defensive tackle holds these records? How many kicks did he block? Hint: His daughter also has been an athletic letter-winner at Nebraska.

10. Nebraska's all-time leader in assisted tackles is Steve Damkroger, who was involved in 157 tackles during the four seasons in which he earned letters (1979–82). In 1982, another Steve started at linebacker alongside Damkroger. The other Steve, also a senior in 1982, underwent three knee operations while he was at Nebraska. He was from Fairfield, Iowa. Name him.

11. The player who started at linebacker alongside Damkroger in 1981 was from Chesterfield, Missouri. He played fullback on the Cornhusker freshman team in 1978, then switched to defense. He came off the bench to set up what proved to be the winning touchdown against Missouri, his home-state university, in 1982. He returned the interception to the Tiger 16-yard line with 3:48 remaining and Nebraska leading 16–13. The final score was 23–19. Name him.

12. Pat Larsen walked on at Nebraska and earned three letters as a safety from 1980 to 1982. Larsen was from Fullerton, Nebraska, and returned there to coach another Cornhusker who earned three letters after walking on. Who was the player Larsen coached at Fullerton High?

Little Big Man

Barron Miles holds Nebraska's career record for blocked kicks regardless of position with seven in three seasons. Miles, a cornerback, stood only 5-foot-8 and weighed no more than 165 pounds. But he played a big role on Nebraska's national championship team as a senior in 1994.

He was "tremendous," Cornhusker defensive coordinator Charlie McBride said. "People didn't give him enough credit. He helped us some in every phase of the game. When something bad happened, he never got down. Barron understood probably more than anybody I've been around his ability, what he could do and what he couldn't do. He knew how far off to play when he was in man [-to-man] coverage. He just had great football instincts and knew his capabilities. He wasn't a big holler guy. But he was a leader."

Miles's blocked punt in the 1993 Oklahoma State game was pivotal in providing Tom Osborne with his 200th victory as head coach. Miles recovered his punt block in the end zone for a touchdown with the score tied at 13 early in the fourth quarter at Stillwater, Oklahoma. Nebraska went on to win 27–13.

Everyone remembers the dramatic performances of walk-on quarterback Matt Turman and I-back Lawrence Phillips in Nebraska's 17–6 victory at Kansas State in 1994. With Tommie Frazier sidelined by a blood clot and Brook Berringer recovering from a partially collapsed lung, Turman started the game. And despite the pain of a severely sprained thumb, Phillips carried 31 times for 117 yards. But Miles "was probably the major factor in us winning," said McBride.

Miles broke up what was at the time a school-record six passes and made five tackles, including four unassisted, to earn recognition as the Big Eight Defensive Player of the Week.

Three Plus Four Is Seven

Oklahoma State's Thurman Thomas was leading the nation in rushing when the Cowboys played Nebraska in mid-October of 1987. Oklahoma State fans were excited about playing the number two-ranked Cornhuskers at Stillwater. The Cowboys were 5–0 and ranked number 12 in the Associated Press poll. A crowd of 54,440 was on hand at Lewis Field for the game, which was televised nationally.

Emotions were high. The night before, players from the teams exchanged unpleasantries outside of a Stillwater theater complex. Thomas was among those involved in the brief exchange.

Later, several Nebraska players claimed Thomas had boasted that the Cornhusker defense wouldn't be able to stop him. If he really said that, he came to regret his words the next day. He carried only nine times before leaving the game in the third quarter of a 35–0 loss to Nebraska.

On three of his carries, Thomas was tackled for losses totaling five yards. Neil Smith was involved in two of those tackles, along with Lawrence Pete and LeRoy Etienne. Steve Forch made the other. Thomas's longest run was four yards, and he finished with a net of seven, prompting Cornhusker cornerback Charles Fryar to remark afterward, "What's his number, 34? Well, three plus four is seven."

Thomas, whose number 34 jersey has been retired by Oklahoma State, is the Cowboys' career rushing leader. He finished the 1987 season with 1,613 yards on 251 carries. He rushed for 100 or more yards in 10 of 12 games, including a 35–33 victory against West Virginia in the Sun Bowl game.

If not for Nebraska, he almost certainly would have led NCAA Division I-A in rushing. Instead, Ickey Woods of Nevada Las Vegas led the nation with 1,658 yards on 259 carries.

The Blackshirts kept Thomas from making a serious run at the Heisman Trophy, just as earlier in the season, they put an end to the Heisman Trophy candidacy of UCLA's Gaston Green.

When the Bruins came to Lincoln, Green was being promoted for the Heisman. He had rushed for 100 or more yards in eight consecutive games, dating to the previous season. When he left the field at Memorial Stadium that afternoon, he had added only 46 yards (on 19 carries) to his season's rushing total.

Cornhusker defensive tackle Tim Rother was chosen as the Big Eight Defensive Player of the Week for his performance against Green and the Bruins—11 tackles and three quarterback sacks.

Quiz 33: Some Succeeded, Some Did Not

1. Nebraska's defensive effort against Oklahoma State in 1987 was impressive not only because Thomas was shut down but also because the Cowboys were shut out. In addition to Thomas, Oklahoma State had the Big Eight's leading passer and leading receiver. Name them.

2. Thomas was replaced at tailback in the third quarter and didn't return for the remainder of the game. His replacement gained 60 yards on only seven carries. Name his replacement.

Note: If the first two questions seemed too easy, the next few shouldn't.

3. Nebraska opened the 1955 season, Bill Glassford's last as head coach, with a 6–0 loss against Hawaii in Lincoln. A week later, the Cornhuskers regained some measure of respect against a Big Ten team that included the running back who would win the 1955 Heisman Trophy. Even though Nebraska lost the road game, the score was a respectable 28–20. The Heisman Trophy winner-to-be rushed for 170 yards on 21 carries. Name him, the team for which he played, and the coach of the team. Hint: The nickname of the player in question was "Hopalong."

4. Jay Berwanger, the first Heisman Trophy winner in 1935, played in Lincoln that season. Nebraska's defense held him in check. The Chicago University halfback scored a touchdown on an 18-yard run early in the second quarter. But Coach Clark Shaughnessy's Maroons had little else to celebrate in a 28–7 loss. A Cornhusker returned the ensuing kickoff 86 yards for a touchdown, one of three he scored that afternoon to take the spotlight. Name him.

Linked to Lyman

Wilfrid Smith of the *Chicago Tribune* wrote that Nebraska's kickoff return, a reverse that began with a Henry Bauer handoff, was a "hoary trick play which has been worked many times, and none other than Roy [Link] Lyman, one time Nebraska star, later a member of the Chicago Bears and now line coach at his alma mater, may well have dug this one out of the book. Back in Lyman's university days, a Notre Dame team scored on the Cornhuskers in the first 30 seconds of play by the same trick, a touchdown that eventually brought victory for the [Knute] Rockne troops."

5. Jim Pillen was a "monster." Mike Minter was a "rover." Essentially, however, both Pillen and Minter played the same position. What is another name for the position they played?

6. Nebraska's switch to the 4-3 defense occurred at the end of the 1992 season. Players listed as middle guards in 1992 became nose tackles in 1993, reflecting the change. The Cornhuskers opened the 1993 Orange Bowl game against Florida State in their dime defense, which meant the player who had been the starting middle guard throughout the season was on the sideline. Name the last Cornhusker who started at middle guard. Name the player who replaced him in the dime. Hint: The replacement played eight-man football in high school.

7. At 6-foot-4 and 260 pounds, he was one of Nebraska's biggest middle guards, particularly at the time he played. He was from Huntsville, Alabama, and he made nine tackles, including two sacks, in his first start as a junior in the 34–14 victory against Florida State in 1981. Name him.

8. Nebraska's outstanding defender in the 1981 Florida State game came off the bench to return a fumble on a kickoff 13 yards for a touchdown. He also made six tackles, one of which was a quarterback sack, to earn Big Eight Defensive Player of the Week honors. He was a walk-on defensive end, who played quarterback at Omaha Central High School. He relied on speed and quickness to record 14 sacks in his final two seasons. Name him.

9. What Cornhusker was pictured on the cover of the *Official Collegiate Football Record Book* published by the NCAA in 1967? Hint: He was chosen because he was the nation's only returning consensus All-American on defense. He also was a consensus All-American in 1967.

10. Bill Kosch returned a pass interception 95 yards for a touchdown in Nebraska's 34–7 victory against Texas A&M in 1971 to tie the school record for longest interception return. The record was set in a 37–30 victory against Colorado in 1955. Who was the first Cornhusker to return an interception 95 yards for a touchdown? Extra credit: Where was he from? Truly tough extra credit: The longest interception return against Nebraska was a 99-yarder in the 1969 Minnesota game. What Gopher made the interception? Who threw the pass?

11. The Nebraska record for pass interceptions in a game, three, is shared by three players. Name at least one of those three players. Hint: The games in which the three-interception performances occurred were: 1969 against Colorado, 1970 against Kansas State, and 1979 against Kansas State. The three who share the record were defensive backs.

12. Name the Cornhusker who blocked three punts and recovered two of them for touchdowns in 1966. Hint: He was a lineman.

By Any Other Name . . .

In 1995, Jared Tomich and Grant Wistrom were listed as "outside linebackers." In 1996, they were listed as "rush ends." The position they played didn't change, only the terminology.

You might say it was a matter of truth in advertising. The position names aren't interchangeable.

"If 'outside linebacker' is used to refer to 'rush end,' it's really a misnomer," Cornhusker defensive backs coach George Darlington has said. Darlington coached Nebraska's defensive ends from 1973 to 1985. But they weren't really traditional defensive ends. They were outside linebackers.

"If someone coached the position I coached [from 1973 to 1985] now, he would be working with only one player," said Darlington. That player would be the strongside linebacker. Confused?

Nebraska's 50 defense had two ends. They stood up at the line of scrimmage instead of getting down in a three-point stance. They dropped in pass coverage. And they blitzed. The "eagle" end lined up on a tackle, and the other end lined up on the strong side, across from the tight end.

The eagle designation could change from left end to right end, depending on where the strong side of the offensive formation was. Or one end could be designated as the eagle, which meant he would line up sometimes on the right and sometimes on the left. Nebraska did it both ways.

Based on the terminology, the Cornhuskers' "weak eagle" defense had two ends, two tackles, a middle guard, two linebackers—strongside and weakside—and four defensive backs. In truth, however, there were three defensive down linemen and four stand-up linebackers.

The correlation isn't exact, however, because of the pass coverage in the secondary. In the 50 defense, the ends dropped in zones rather than matching up man-to-man—as Nebraska does now.

Nebraska began using the term "outside linebacker" to placate Broderick Thomas, who considered himself a linebacker not a down lineman, which the designation "defensive end" implied. When Thomas was a senior in 1988, the Cornhuskers began experimenting with a 4–3 defense when it inserted a "nickel back" in apparent passing situations. Thomas became a rush end, in a three-point stance then, as did Jeff Mills, the other outside linebacker. Mike Croel, the nickel back, was like an outside linebacker.

As Nebraska's defense evolved from an odd to an even front, the terminology again lagged. Donta Jones and Dwayne Harris, the starting outside linebackers on the 1994 national championship team, were really rush ends, as was Trev Alberts, the Butkus Award winner in 1993. "Those guys were on the edge of it," said defensive coordinator Charlie McBride. "By Trev's junior year, they were rush ends."

It wasn't until 1996, however, that the terminology caught up with the position.

All-America defensive ends Willie Harper, George Andrews, Derrie Nelson, Jimmy Williams, and Broderick Thomas—a defensive end at the beginning of his Cornhusker career—often are grouped with recent players such as Alberts, Tomich, and Wistrom. But the positions are different.

"A lot of them had the same physical characteristics of the rush ends now," McBride said. "That's kind of what we've stayed with. We haven't gone with the big 4–3 type rush ends that a lot of teams have. We've stayed more with speed guys so we could get that quick pressure from the outside."

Harper was 6-foot-2 and 207 pounds, more like an outsider linebacker now. Andrews was 6-foot-4 and 225 pounds. Williams was 6-foot-3 and 215 pounds. In contrast, Alberts was 6-foot-4 and 240 pounds, Tomich was 6-foot-2 and 260 pounds, and Wistrom was 6-foot-5 and 255 pounds.

The size of players has increased over the last decade or so, which accounts for some of the difference. But the primary reason is that the positions are substantially different.

Quiz 34: Who Am I?

1. My name would be in the NCAA record book under the heading "Most Touchdowns Scored on Interception Returns (Season)," except that enough players have done it that only the most recent are listed. I returned three interceptions for touchdowns in 1971. Even so, I was the only starter in the secondary who didn't earn first-team All–Big Eight recognition that season. I lettered as a split end in 1969, then redshirted in 1970. Who am I?

2. I was the strongest Cornhusker as a senior in 1976. I lined up at defensive back late in the fourth quarter of the 1976 Hawaii game, which we won 68–3. But I was a 6-foot-5, 275-pound defensive tackle. Tom Osborne wasn't amused. I was a three-year starter, following John Dutton, and earned first-team All-America honors from United Press International, the *Football News*, *The Sporting News*, and the Walter Camp Foundation in 1976. I grew up a Cornhusker fan in Lincoln, Nebraska, and was the state high school shot put champion. Who am I?

3. My home was Decatur, Alabama, but I went to high school in Boys Town, Nebraska, where I was a multisport athlete. I walked on and spent five seasons at Nebraska, mostly on the scout team, earning a letter as a senior in 1978. My nickname was "Dollar Bill," and I was among the most popular Cornhuskers. I almost always had a smile on my face. Who am I?

4. When Correll Buckhalter was recruited from Mount Olive, Mississippi, in 1997, he was described as Nebraska's first scholarship recruit from Mississippi. But we were recruited from Mississippi in 1972 and earned five letters between us from 1973 to 1976. One of us was from Louisville and played linebacker. The other was from Amory and played middle guard.

Who are we? Also during that time, there was another Mississippi athlete on the team, from Amory, though he played on the freshman team at the University of Mississippi before transferring to Nebraska. He was a defensive back. His son was in Nebraska's 1997 scholarship recruiting class. Who was he?

5. Oklahoma's Randy Hughes and I shared the award as Big Eight Athlete of the Year in 1974. I was a linebacker from Bloomington, Minnesota. Monte Johnson and Bruce Hauge also were from Bloomington, but none of us came from the same high school. I was from Jefferson, Johnson was from Lincoln, and Hauge was from Kennedy. I was a two-time Academic All–Big Eight honoree and a first-round NFL draft pick. I played in the Senior Bowl and the College All-Star Game. My brother also lettered as a linebacker at Nebraska. Who am I?

6. I was a four-year letterman when that was still rare under Tom Osborne. I came from Sacramento, California, and sat out a medical redshirt as a freshman in 1974. I began my Cornhusker career as a linebacker but ended up as a safety. I put the hit on Oklahoma's Billy Sims near the goal line to force the final fumble that preserved our 17–14 victory against the Sooners in 1978, when I received all-conference honorable mention. I became the starter in the latter half of the 1978 season, after Russell Gary was sidelined by a knee injury. Who am I?

7. I was recruited specifically as a defensive back, at a time when Nebraska usually waited until freshmen reported before deciding whether they would play offense or defense. I was a *Parade* magazine high school All-American from Highland Springs, Virginia, a suburb of Richmond. I was a four-year letterman, from 1984 to 1987, beginning as a cornerback but soon moving to monster. I was stretching in the north field house after a preseason freshman scrimmage when Coach Osborne came down to tell me he was promoting me to the varsity. Who am I?

8. In the second quarter of our 41–17 loss to Florida State in the 1990 Fiesta Bowl game, the Seminole offensive linemen were penalized for holding on three consecutive downs. Each time, I was the Cornhusker being held. Because of my quickness, they had trouble handling me any other way. Tom Osborne called me "possibly the best pass rusher in the country." I was a 6-foot-4, 230-pound defensive tackle, with 4.78 speed in the 40-yard dash. I was small for a defensive tackle and would probably have been even better as a linebacker. But I couldn't play that position.

I came from Crane, Texas. I scheduled recruiting trips to Baylor, Texas, and Oklahoma, but I canceled them after visiting Nebraska because I realized it had the best support program for me.

I played in both the National Football League and the Canadian Football League, and returned to Nebraska to complete a bachelor's degree with an art major. Who am I?

Quiz 29: Blitz 1984

1. Graeber, Strasburger, Daum, and McCashland
2. Burke
3. Weber was the only four-year letterman among the starters.
4. Daum played eight-man at Dix High School. His brother Mitch played 11-man at Kimball High.
5. Mike Knox, a linebacker
6. Strasburger and Stuckey
7. Danny Noonan alternated with Spachman.
8. Jim Skow alternated with Stuckey in 1984 and 1983.
9. Strasburger's brother Matt earned a letter in 1985.
10. Despite finishing 6–4, the 1967 Cornhuskers ranked number one in the nation in defense.

Quiz 30: Quick Hitters

1. Lee Kunz, a three-year letterman
2. Lee Kunz lettered as a discus thrower on the Cornhusker track-and-field team.
3. The weakside linebacker was regularly referred to as "Wanda" and the strongside linebacker was called "Sara" when Dunning played. There was no middle linebacker in the "50" defense.
4. Doug DuBose was the Nebraska I-back to whom Bosworth referred.
5. Kiffin coached the defensive line. His successor was Charlie McBride. Van Zandt coached the defensive backs. Prior to that, Warren Powers coached them. Van Zandt came from Kansas.
6. Mike Kennedy, 1965, Omaha South; Jerry Murtaugh, 1970, Omaha North; Tom Ruud, 1974; Clete Pillen, 1976; Jeff Carpenter, 1977; and Steve Damkroger, 1982
7. Marc Munford's dad, Jim, was a small-college basketball star.
8. Mike Knox was the strongside linebacker. He was from Castle Rock, Colorado.
9. Jerry Murtaugh was an All-America linebacker in 1970.
10. Defensive tackle Larry Jacobson won the Outland Trophy on the 1971 national championship team. Middle guard Rich Glover succeeded Jacobson in winning the Outland Trophy in 1972.
11. Broderick Thomas, 1989, Tampa Bay; Mike Croel, 1991, Denver; and Trev Alberts, 1994, Indianapolis
12. Tom Ruud, 1974, Buffalo; George Andrews, 1979, Los Angeles Rams; and Jimmy Williams, 1982, Detroit. Andrews and Williams were identified as defensive ends at Nebraska.

Quiz 31: From Odd to Even

1. Osborne's first team in 1973 allowed only 39.9 passing yards per game to rank number one in the nation.

2. Larry Wachholtz, 1966; Dana Stephenson, 1969; and Bill Kosch, 1970

3. Dana Stephenson intercepted 14 passes from 1967 to 1969.

4. LeRoy Etienne

5. Steve Carmer, who was a three-year letterman from 1990 to 1992

6. Tyrone Byrd

7. Ron Pruitt

8. Marv Mueller, 1965–67; Jim Anderson, 1969–71; Bret Clark, 1982–84; Charles Fryar, 1986–88; and Barron Miles, 1992–94. Mueller, Anderson, and Clark were captains. Mueller and Clark were Nebraskans, from Columbus and Nebraska City, respectively.

9. Indiana was the opponent in three of the games. Minnesota, the opponent in two of the games, defeated Clark's 1945 Nebraska team 61–7. Clark's first name was George.

10. UCLA scored 38 points in the first half of a 41–28 victory in 1988.

11. Oklahoma rushed for 506 yards against Nebraska in a 54–6 victory at Norman, Oklahoma, in 1956. Elliott was a Sooner assistant before coming to Nebraska for that one season. Notre Dame rushed for 502 yards against Clark's Cornhuskers in a 44–13 victory at Memorial Stadium in 1948.

12. Kansas State's Chad May completed 30 of 52 passes for 489 yards in a 45–28 loss to Nebraska at Memorial Stadium in 1993. Missouri's Jeff Handy completed 29 of 44 for 424 yards in a 34–24 loss to the Cornhuskers at Columbia, Missouri, in 1992. Each quarterback was intercepted twice.

13. Washington gained 618 yards in its 36–21 victory against the Cornhuskers at Memorial Stadium in 1991. The record for total yardage against Nebraska is 656 by Oklahoma in 1956. Second on the list are the 620 yards Notre Dame gained in defeating the Cornhuskers 44–13 in 1948.

Quiz 32: Mr. Smith Goes to the NFL and Other Matters

1. The Kansas City Chiefs took Smith with the second pick in the first round of the 1988 draft. The Atlanta Falcons made Auburn's Aundray Bruce the number one pick in 1988.

2. Smith was a graduate of McDonogh 35 High School. He played against LSU once, in the 1986 Sugar Bowl game. He had five tackles, including one sack, in the 30–15 victory. The Cornhuskers also defeated LSU in the 1985 Sugar Bowl game. But Smith was a freshman and didn't get to play.

3. Tim Rother was the Cornhuskers' sack leader in 1987, with 10 for 84 yards in losses. Rother came from Bellevue East High School. He began his career at Nebraska as an offensive lineman.

4. Rother replaced 245-pound Lee Jones as the starting right tackle in 1987.

5. Monte Johnson backed up Bill Janssen. John Dutton was the starting right tackle.

6. Jim Skow came from Roncalli High School in Omaha.

7. Jerry Murtaugh, 1968–70, 342 tackles; Lee Kunz, 1976–78, 276 tackles; and Clete Pillen, 1974–76, 273 tackles. Murtaugh made 71 unassisted tackles in 1970. Kunz was in on 141 tackles in 1977.

8. Wayne Meylan, a middle guard from 1965 to 1967, was credited with 238 tackles during his career.

9. Bill Hornbacher blocked his career total of six kicks as a junior in 1968. His daughter Rebecca was the number one goalkeeper for Coach John Walker's Husker soccer team in 1996 and 1997.

10. Steve McWhirter, the strongside linebacker, earned four letters despite the injuries.

11. Brent Evans was the starting strongside linebacker in 1981, when McWhirter was slowed by injury. Evans made a career-high 19 tackles in a 30–15 victory against Kansas.

12. Larsen coached Brian Schuster, who lettered as a fullback from 1994 to 1996.

Quiz 33: Some Succeeded, Some Did Not

1. Quarterback Mike Gundy and wide receiver Hart Lee Dykes

2. Duh . . . Barry Sanders. Thought you'd get this one.

3. Howard Cassady was the running back. Ohio State was the team. Woody Hayes was the coach. When the team returned to Lincoln and was greeted by a couple of hundred people, one Cornhusker, who wasn't identified, was quoted in the Lincoln newspaper: "Gee, you mean they don't hate us anymore?"

4. Lloyd Cardwell, about whom legendary *Lincoln Journal* sports editor Walter Dobbins wrote, "Call him what you may—The Wild Horse of the Plains; The Scarlet Express; The Cornhusker Thunderbolt—Lloyd Cardwell is one of the greatest halfbacks in the country today."

5. "Monster" and "rover" are names Nebraska uses for the strong safety.

6. David Noonan was the starting middle guard in 1992. He became a nose tackle in 1993. Terry Connealy replaced Noonan in the dime defense in 1992 and started the 1993 Orange Bowl game. Connealy played eight-man football at Hyannis High School in Nebraska.

7. Jeff Merrell, a three-year letterman from 1980 to 1982

8. Tony Felici, a three-year letterman from 1980 to 1982

9. Nebraska middle guard Wayne Meylan is pictured on the cover.

10. Willie Greenlaw was from Portland, Maine. Minnesota's Gary Hohmann intercepted Jeff Kinney's halfback pass and returned it 99 yards

for a touchdown that led to a 14–7 Gopher lead with just under nine minutes remaining in the first half of a 42–14 Nebraska victory. The Cornhuskers' first touchdown came on a 12-yard pass from Kinney, a high school quarterback, to Guy Ingles.

11. Dana Stephenson, 1969; Joe Blahak, 1970; and Ric Lindquist, 1979

12. Middle guard Wayne Meylan

Quiz 34: Who Am I?

1. Dave Mason was the starting monster back. Cornerbacks Jim Anderson and Joe Blahak and safety Bill Kosch all earned first-team all-conference honors in 1971. Mason's interception returns for touchdowns were 53 yards in a 42–6 victory against Utah State, 28 yards in a 41–13 victory against Oklahoma State, and 25 yards in a 45–3 victory against Hawaii. He had six interceptions total.

2. Mike Fultz

3. Bill Bryant

4. Percy Eichelberger was the linebacker. Willie Thornton was the middle guard. Jimmy Burrow, whose son Jamie was a freshman redshirt in 1997

5. Tom Ruud. His brother John also was a Cornhusker letterman.

6. Jeff Hansen

7. Brian Washington

8. Kenny Walker was deaf from the age of two, after suffering from spinal meningitis. Because of that, he would have had difficulty playing linebacker. He could read lips and got signals in the huddle from the strongside linebacker that way. At the line of scrimmage, the middle guard used hand signals to communicate with him. He lettered in 1989 and 1990, earning first-team all-conference and All-America recognition as a senior. He was a popular player and an inspiration to those with disabilities.

6

VERY SPECIAL TEAMS:

The Cornhusker Hit Parade

His pep talks to the first football team he coached at Big Beaver High School in Birmingham, Michigan, included the same game-opening strategy, Bob Devaney always said. If his team won the coin toss and elected to receive the opening kickoff, "let's see who can recover our fumble."

And if his team lost the toss and had to kick off to start the game, he said, he always encouraged his players to "line up quickly and see if we can block their try for the extra point."

Devaney was joking, of course. He was serious about kickoffs and punt returns. And Tom Osborne followed that lead, placing even more emphasis on special teams than his Hall of Fame predecessor. In fact, Osborne didn't use the term "special teams." They were the "kicking teams."

The kicking teams handle and receive kickoffs, handle and receive punts, and attempt field goals and extra-point kicks. "They're not teams where you take a bunch of guys who are on the bench and give them an opportunity to play. These are the best players we've got to do the job," Osborne has said. "Our philosophy here has been, basically, to put the best possible players on the kicking teams."

Jon Hesse, the Cornhuskers' All–Big 12 middle linebacker as a senior in 1996, continued to play on most of the kicking teams—which had provided him his first opportunity as a young player. When they become starters, particularly as seniors, players often try to avoid the kicking teams.

Not Hesse, who pestered defensive coordinator Charlie McBride for a chance on the kickoff team when he was a sophomore. "I was so frustrated my sophomore year," Hesse once said. "I still didn't have anything because I didn't get to play in every game (as a linebacker). I had accepted the fact that I was a third-string guy. But I had to get on the field somehow. The kickoff team is what saved me."

Hesse made the most of his first opportunity, making a big hit on a kickoff during Nebraska's 32–3 victory against Oklahoma State in 1994. The next week he was a fixture on the kickoff team.

Osborne works on the kicking game in the middle of practice instead of at the end, the way many coaches do. "We want them [the players] to feel it's an

Nebraska's Johnny Rodgers is tackled by a host of Oklahoma Sooners as he runs the opening kickoff back for 20 yards in first-quarter action of college football's Game of the Century in 1971. The No. 1-ranked Cornhuskers defeated the home team, 35–31.

(Photo Courtesy of UPI/CORBIS-BETTMANN)

important part of the game," he has said. How important? "You're going to win two or three games [a season] with the kicking game."

Johnny the Jet

The kicking game was a significant factor in one of the most memorable games in Cornhusker history: the 35–31 victory against Oklahoma at Norman, Oklahoma, in the "Game of the Century." Less than four minutes into the game, Johnny Rodgers returned a punt 72 yards for a touchdown.

Rodgers's return on Thanksgiving Day of 1971 might be the best-known play in Nebraska football history. It also was "essentially the difference" in the game, according to Tom Osborne, who was an assistant and Rodgers's position coach at the time. "Oklahoma didn't have that."

Nebraska's 1971 team is considered among the best in college football history. Jeff Sagarin, whose computer rankings regularly appear in *USA Today*, analyzed teams from 1958 to 1995 and determined that the 1971 Cornhuskers were second-best during that time—behind the 1995 Cornhuskers.

However, "as great as that [1971] team was, take Johnny Rodgers out of there on kickoff and punt returns, and it probably wouldn't have gone 13–0," Osborne has said.

Rodgers, a junior, returned three punts and one kickoff for touchdowns during the 1971 regular season, then capped Nebraska's national championship run with a 77-yard punt return for a touchdown in the 38–6 victory against second-ranked Alabama in the 1972 Orange Bowl game. In addition, Rodgers provided the Cornhusker offense with outstanding field position, averaging 16.6 yards on punt returns and 30.4 yards on kickoff returns to rank among the nation's leaders in both categories.

Rodgers holds nearly all of Nebraska's punt return records. His success depended on instinct rather than design. After his sophomore season in 1970, he was exempt from following the principles that ordinarily apply to returning kicks. For example, coaches usually encourage punt returners to signal for a fair catch or simply let the ball go, depending on where they are in relation to their own goal line.

But Clete Fischer, who worked with the kicking teams at the time, "gave me the green light to do whatever I wanted to do after a year of successfully doing it," Rodgers has said.

What he wanted to do was make something happen, and he couldn't do that if he made a fair catch and allowed the ball to bounce into the end zone for a touchback. So he fielded every kick he could. "Having the green light on returns meant everything to me," he said. "When the ball bounces, the first thing a coach tells you is to get away from it. But I'd try my best to figure out how I was going to get the ball.

"If you don't follow the program, there's not a set script. I wasn't into that visualization stuff, but I could imagine I was going to score. The question was how. If I couldn't imagine how [in advance], the defense wasn't going to be able to, either. So the script was: There was no script."

That meant Rodgers might not follow his blockers during a return. "When you run away from your blockers, that's taking a chance," said Rodgers. "But we had it down pretty good." And because of his unpredictability, "a lot of times, they [defenders] would hit me before I got it. They have no idea what you're thinking because you don't know what you're going to do until you do it."

Had he followed conventional wisdom instead of trying to return every punt, the Game of the Century might have turned out differently. "I probably should have made a fair catch," Rodgers said.

Rodgers developed his kick-returning skill while he was a student at Horace Mann Junior High in Omaha. He was regularly challenged by neighborhood toughs on his way home from school. His athletic success made him a target, he has said. "They were upset because I was known. That's all I can think of. They would hurt you, try to beat you up. But nobody ever shot anybody."

Rodgers used to walk in the street on the way home. That way he was less apt to be caught by surprise. Plus, he had more room to run and escape, which he often did. "I was tougher than they thought, but it wasn't just one or two guys; several were jumping on me. So I had to get up and run." By comparison, eluding a few tacklers on a punt or kickoff return "was no big deal," he said.

Quiz 35: Johnny R, Superstar—20 Questions

1. Osborne said the difference in the Game of the Century was Rodgers's punt return for a touchdown. Did Rodgers return any other punts in the game? How many did Oklahoma return? Extra credit: How much punt return yardage, within five yards, did the Sooners have?

2. Who was the Oklahoma punter in the Game of the Century? He was a starter, though he didn't start that game because of an injury. What position did he play?

3. What Cornhusker threw the final block on Rodgers's punt return touchdown in the 1971 Oklahoma game? What position did he play? What was his jersey number? Oklahoma fans claim the block should have been ruled a clip. What Sooner was it made against? Hint: He played split end and caught four passes for 115 yards and two touchdowns in the game. He also was a high school teammate of Oklahoma's quarterback. Name the quarterback as well.

4. How many times did Nebraska punt in the Game of the Century, and who was the Cornhusker punter? What was his position? Where was he from?

5. Rodgers holds the Cornhusker career record for touchdowns on punt returns. How many punts did he return for touchdowns? Bowl game statistics are not included in school records, so don't count the punt return for a touchdown in the 1972 Orange Bowl.

6. Through the 1996 season, Rodgers shared the NCAA Division I-A record for punt return touchdowns in a career. With whom did he share the record? This is a toughie, but not impossible for Nebraska fans with a good grasp of conference history. The player with whom Rodgers shared the record was an All-America quarterback at Oklahoma in the late 1940s (lettered 1946–48), and he was the head football coach at Kansas from 1958 to 1966.

7. How many punts, if any, did Rodgers return for touchdowns when playing on Nebraska's freshman team in 1969? The Cornhusker freshmen were 3–1 in 1969. Extra credit: Who was the leading rusher for the freshman team in 1969? Who was the freshman head coach?

8. Did Rodgers return punts for touchdowns in any other bowl games? His final game as a Cornhusker was against Notre Dame in the 1973 Orange Bowl. His performance was remarkable. How many punts did he return in that game? For how many yards, within five?

9. Rodgers averaged 23.8 yards on kickoff returns during his career at

Nebraska. How many kickoffs, if any, did he return for touchdowns? Be as specific as possible.

10. Rodgers holds the Cornhusker record for average yards per punt return during a career (15.46). However, he does not hold the single-season record—with a minimum of 10 returns. Who holds the single-season record? In what season did he set it? Extra credit: Within two yards, what is Nebraska's single-season record for average yards per punt return?

11. Rodgers holds the Nebraska record for longest punt return for a touchdown. How long was the return? Against whom? In what season? Who holds the Cornhusker record for the longest punt return that didn't produce a touchdown? How long? Against whom? When?

12. Rodgers returned punts for touchdowns against five of the former Big Eight teams. Against what three former Big Eight teams did he not return punts for touchdowns? He returned two punts for touchdowns against one of the former Big Eight teams. Which one?

13. Who held the Cornhusker record for longest punt return prior to Rodgers? How long was the return? Against whom? Hint: It was a conference team, barely.

14. Through the 1996 season, Rodgers held Nebraska records for punt return yardage in a season (618) and in a career (1,515). However, he did not hold the Cornhusker record for punt return yards in a game. What Bob Devaney–era player held the record? How many yards did he gain on punt returns, within 10? Against whom? When? Hint: He led the nation in punt return yardage until the final game of the previous season, when he was a junior, finishing second to Notre Dame's Nick Rassos by only seven yards. He also was a placekicker.

15. Through the 1996 season, Rodgers held Nebraska records for punt returns in a season (39) and in a career (98). However, he did not hold the Cornhusker record for punt returns in a game. What Devaney-era player held the record? How many punts did he return? Against whom? When? Hint: He also was a punter and held the school record, through 1996, for punts in a season. Extra credit: What is the record for punts in a season and in what season?

16. Who holds the record for the longest kickoff return in Cornhusker history? How long? Against whom? In what season? Who holds the record for the longest kickoff return in modern (post-1946) Cornhusker history? How long? Against whom? In what season?

17. Rodgers was Nebraska's first Heisman Trophy winner. Mike Rozier was the second. Rozier had a forgettable kickoff return during his distinguished career. Explain.

18. Rodgers had a personal rivalry with another Big Eight punt returner in 1970 and 1971. In 1970, Rodgers finished second in the conference to

this player. But in 1971, he finished first, edging the player 16.6 yards per return to 16.3. Who was this player? For what conference school did he play? Hint: The player continued his career with the NFL's Oakland Raiders.

19. Rodgers played high school football in Omaha. The high school has since closed its doors. What was his high school? And who was his high school football coach?

20. In case these questions have caused some frustration, here's an easy one with which to conclude. Rodgers's jersey number was retired after the 1972 season, along with the jersey number of middle guard Rich Glover. Their jerseys are still retired, but not the numbers. What was Rodgers's jersey number? What was Glover's? How many other Cornhusker jersey numbers had been retired at that time? What were the numbers? And whose numbers where they?

The Last Word on Rodgers

Jim Walden was a Cornhusker assistant coach before moving on to be a head coach at Washington State and Iowa State. He was Nebraska's defensive ends coach in 1971 and 1972. Twenty years later, when he was at Iowa State, Walden still had not seen Rodgers's equal as a punt returner.

"Once you've been around a Johnny Rodgers, it's all kind of downhill after that in my lifetime," Walden told the Associated Press. "I spent time at Nebraska with the greatest punt returning athlete in the history of the game, in my opinion. John could break a punt that didn't have a block."

Quiz 36: Husker Special Teams Fact

Nebraska went 24 seasons during the Devaney-Osborne era without allowing a punt return for a touchdown. UCLA's Darryl Henley ended the streak, which began after Billy Crockett returned a punt 80 yards for a touchdown in the Cornhuskers' 26–21 victory at Minnesota in 1964. Henley returned a punt 75 yards to score in the Bruins' 41–28 victory at the Rose Bowl in Pasadena, California, in 1988.

During the streak of 284 games, Nebraska returned 35 punts for touchdowns, including five that were blocked and recovered in the end zone or returned only a short distance:

Wayne Meylan recovered his own block against Wisconsin, 1966.
Meylan recovered his own block against Kansas State, 1966.
Kent Smith recovered a block against Missouri, 1976.
Larry Young recovered a block by Randy Rick against Baylor, 1977.
Bruce Dunning recovered a block against Indiana, 1978.

1. Meylan blocked two points and then turned them into touchdowns in 1966. But he doesn't hold the Cornhusker single-season record for blocked kicks by a Cornhusker middle guard. Who does? In what season? Hint: His season total was also his career total.

2. Nebraska had three middle guards from Michigan who earned letters in the late 1960s. Name them. Extra credit: Identify their hometowns.

Quiz 37: Little Big Man

Barron Miles stood 5-foot-8 and weighed 160 pounds—at least, his weight was listed at 160. That may have been generous. But he came up big blocking kicks. Miles set the Cornhusker career record for blocked kicks with seven during his three seasons, 1992 through 1994.

Miles's most significant block contributed to Tom Osborne's 200th coaching victory. On a fourth-and-25 early in the fourth quarter of the 1993 Oklahoma State game at Stillwater, Oklahoma, with the score tied at 13 and the Cowboys at their own two-yard line, Miles made the block and recovered the ball for a touchdown. He faked to the outside, then cut inside and went to the punter untouched.

Miles was "one of those few guys, and there aren't very many, who will look right at the football and put their face on it," Osborne said of Miles's knack for knocking down kicks.

1. Miles did more than block kicks. He was one of the best players in Cornhusker history at his regular position. What was that position? Also, he was tried at another position in 1994. The trial was brief, during one practice. What was that position and why? Extra credit: What was Miles's hometown?

2. Miles's punt block against Oklahoma State in 1993 was set up by a third-down sack for a nine-yard loss. Who sacked Cowboy quarterback Toné Jones? Who was the Cowboy punter?

3. What was the final score of Osborne's 200th coaching victory?

Kicks Just Keep Getting Harder to Find

Okay. So this isn't what Paul Revere and the Raiders had in mind with their late-1960s hit song "Kicks." But Cornhusker fans get a kick out of recalling what Dale Klein did on October 19, 1985. And kicks equal to Klein's that afternoon in Columbia, Missouri, have been hard to find in NCAA Division I-A.

Klein set an NCAA Division I-A record (Best Perfect Record of Field Goals Made) by kicking seven field goals in seven attempts in the Cornhuskers' 28–20 victory against Missouri. The seven field goals tied the record for field goals in a game. Western Michigan's Mike Prindle kicked seven field goals against Marshall the previous season. Prindle, however, needed nine attempts.

Klein kicked five of the seven field goals in the first half to set an NCAA Division I-A record. New Mexico State's Dat Ly tied Klein's record of five field goals in a half in 1988.

Klein's kicks against Missouri, 1985:

1. 32 yards, 7:27 remaining first quarter
2. 22 yards, 3:52, first quarter
3. 43 yards, 12:30, second quarter
4. 44 yards, 8:29, second quarter
5. 29 yards, 1:35, second quarter
6. 43 yards, :25, third quarter
7. 43 yards, 4:16, fourth quarter

Klein, a junior who had come to Nebraska as a walk-on, also kicked an extra point in the Missouri game to finish with a Cornhusker-record 22 points by kicking. Afterward, he told reporters, "A lot of people didn't think I was a good kicker. I was happy when I could show them I could kick."

Klein might not have been at Faurot Field to kick the seven field goals if Craig Schnitzler had been healthy. Schnitzler had competed for the number one job in fall camp and had kicked a 35-yard field goal in the second game of the season against Illinois. But a sore leg was keeping him on the sideline.

Klein had been struggling since the final game of the 1984 regular season, a 17–7 loss against Oklahoma in which he had missed on two field goal attempts, from 49 and 23 yards. After the game, he stayed in his dorm room for the better part of a week, even skipping some classes—which was rare. Klein was a two-time academic all-conference selection and an Academic All-American in 1986.

He recovered from the frustration of the Oklahoma game to kick four extra points in the Cornhuskers' 28–10 victory against Louisiana State in the 1985 Sugar Bowl game. But he missed an extra-point kick in the 1985 opener, a 17–13 loss against Florida State, and was replaced by Schnitzler.

Klein regained the number one placekicking job because of Schnitzler's sore leg, but he missed his first three field goal attempts in 1985 (from 31, 30, and 27 yards) to increase the string that had begun the previous season to five going into the conference opener at Oklahoma State.

Because of travel roster restrictions, Tom Osborne considered taking only one placekicker to Stillwater, Oklahoma, and that one probably would have been Chris Drennan, a true freshman who had kicked a 42-yard field goal in the final nonconference game against New Mexico to move ahead of Klein on the depth chart. Osborne relented, however, and decided to take both Drennan and Klein.

Drennan missed a 47-yard field goal early in the Oklahoma State game, pulling it to the right. Drennan's right foot was bothering him, but he hadn't said anything to the coaches because he kicked with his left foot, and besides, he wasn't about to miss the chance to travel to the Oklahoma State game. It wasn't until after the game that he learned a rupture in his right arch had caused some internal bleeding.

The injury occurred when he planted his foot to kick during warm-ups before the New Mexico game. The discomfort grew worse the next week, but Drennan remained silent. He limited his warm-ups before the Oklahoma State game, thinking that might help. It did not. As a result, he deferred to Klein when the Cornhuskers had a second field goal opportunity with 23 seconds remaining in the first half.

Clete Fischer, who coached the kickers, called for Drennan, who turned to Klein and said, "You take it." Two seasons later, Drennan would describe his decision as "a not very smart move on my part."

The move may not have been smart, but it was right for the team. Klein kicked the 40-yard field goal and added another 40-yard field goal in the third quarter to win back the number one job.

Drennan wasn't included on the travel roster for the Missouri game the next week, and he sat out the 1986 season as a redshirt before becoming the Cornhuskers' regular placekicker in 1987.

Klein was an unlikely candidate to kick seven field goals in a game. He was among a dozen walk-on placekickers in 1982. His goal was to make the team, "so I could say I did it." He had played split end and defensive back in high school in addition to kicking. He had kicked a 42-yard field goal as a junior. But his high school coach told him his best chance at Nebraska probably would be as a punter.

He had never attended a kicking school. He had learned to kick with four other brothers, none of whom played high school football. The high school football field was near their house, and "we liked to kick the ball around," Klein once said. He kicked for fun. He went out at Nebraska to have a good time.

Quiz 38: Just Kicking Around

1. Klein's five field goals gave the Cornhuskers a 15–7 halftime lead at Missouri in 1985. As Klein ran to the locker room at the intermission, the holder for placekicks told him he might have to kick seven or eight field goals if Nebraska was going to win against the fired-up Tigers. The holder, a sophomore quarterback, also told him he was capable of kicking that many. Klein justified the backup quarterback's confidence. Who was Klein's holder?

2. Klein's five first-half field goals tied the Big Eight record for field

goals in a game, shared by two players, one of whom had done it twice, including once against Nebraska. Name the two. Hint: One played for Oklahoma State and the other played for Kansas.

3. Klein's 22 points were enough to defeat Missouri. But the Cornhuskers scored a touchdown midway through the fourth quarter to take a 25–13 lead. The touchdown, on a 22-yard run, was set up by a fumble recovery at the Tigers' 39-yard line. Who recovered the fumble? He was a linebacker. And who scored Nebraska's touchdown? He was an I-back.

4. Including the seven-for-seven field goals against Missouri, how many in a row did Klein kick before missing? Against whom did he finally miss to end the string? In what season?

5. Klein once said when people recognized him as a Nebraska football player, he often replied, "No, I don't play football; I kick footballs." Did he kick them straightaway or soccer style?

6. Klein's coach his senior year in high school suggested he walk on at Nebraska as a punter. Did he ever punt in a varsity game for the Cornhuskers? And, by the way, where did he attend high school? Extra credit: Who was the high school football coach his senior year?

7. Two players handled the placekicking for the Cornhuskers' "Scoring Explosion" team in 1983. Who was the number one placekicker at the start of the season? Who finished the season as the number one placekicker? Between them, how many field goals did they attempt? How many did they make? If Tom Osborne had decided to kick the extra point instead of attempting the two-point conversion pass in the 1984 Orange Bowl game, who would have kicked it?

8. This is a tough one. Who holds the Nebraska record for extra-point conversions in a game? Hint: He played for Coach W. C. "King" Cole and set the record in 1910.

9. Three players share Nebraska's record for longest field goal. What was the distance? Who were the kickers? Extra credit: Against whom did they kick the field goals? In what seasons? Hint: Two were from the Osborne era, one from the Devaney era.

10. What is the Cornhusker record for consecutive extra-point kicks made? Who made them? Hint: The record was set over four seasons.

11. Who holds the Nebraska record for most extra points in a season without missing? Where is he from, and what high school did he attend?

12. Who holds the Cornhusker record for extra-point kicks in a season? How many? What season? Who holds the record for field goals in a season? How many? What season?

13. Who holds the Nebraska career record for highest percentage of extra-point kicks made?

14. From 1962, Devaney's first season, through 1997, three Cornhuskers

have earned first-team all-conference honors as placekickers. Who were they? In what seasons were they selected?

Proper Perspective

Success didn't spoil Klein, who scored 196 points during his Cornhusker career. After his record-setting performance against Missouri, he said, "Everybody called me 'Mr. NCAA Record.' But I just blew that off. I could have just as easily gone out the next week and missed seven in a row. I said: 'Hey, if that was in the Orange Bowl and I kicked seven for seven, I'd be sky-high, really happy.'"

Doink, Doink . . .

Byron Bennett was Nebraska's career scoring leader by kicking through the 1996 season. He scored 222 regular-season points, making 150 of 156 extra-point kicks and 24 of 39 field goal attempts. He would just as soon forget a couple of his games as a Cornhusker, however.

One would be the 1994 Orange Bowl game, which Nebraska lost 18–16 when Bennett's 45-yard field goal attempt with one second remaining sailed wide left. With 1:16 left in the game, Bennett had given the Cornhuskers a 16–15 lead by kicking a 27-yard field goal. They couldn't hold it, however.

Another probably would be the Cornhuskers' 18–9 victory at Arizona State in 1991. Bennett was one of five on field goal attempts against the Sun Devils, hitting a 28-yarder with 6:18 remaining in the third quarter. He missed on two attempts after turnovers gave Nebraska the ball deep in Arizona State territory. The first, from 31 yards, hit the right upright. The second, from 23 yards, hit the left upright.

Those misses were only two minutes apart. Bennett's other field goal attempts, from 52 and 30 yards, were blocked. And to complete the evening's frustration, Bennett's first extra-point kick was blocked. Fortunately for Nebraska, William Washington got the ball in the end zone for two points.

Tandem Kickers, Double Trouble in 1994

Tom Sieler was a four-year letterman kicker from 1991 through 1994. "I've got the heart of a linebacker. But I don't have the tools," he once said. "I want to hit people. If I were a linebacker, I would hate kickers because it looks like we're just wasting time [during practice]."

Sieler was 6-foot-5, but at 205 pounds, he would have been light for a linebacker. He also lacked the speed to play defense. He handled kickoffs and was Byron Bennett's backup in 1993, and he shared the placekicking duties with Darin Erstad in the 1994 national championship season.

Erstad, the first player selected in the 1995 major league baseball draft, also was the Cornhuskers' punter in 1994. He averaged 41.2 yards on 50 punts. If Erstad had returned for the 1995 season, he could have established himself among the best punters in Nebraska history, according to Dan Young, the Cornhuskers' kicking coach. "He had a tremendously strong leg," Young said.

Quiz 39: Quick Kicks

1. In general, how were the placekicking responsibilities divided between Erstad and Sieler in 1994? In other words, when was Erstad used and when was Sieler used?

2. Sieler was a walk-on. What was his hometown? Erstad came to Nebraska on a baseball scholarship. What was his hometown? The 1971 national championship team included players from Sieler's hometown and Erstad's home state. One of the two was a junior starter in 1971. The other was a sophomore redshirt. Both were starters on Bob Devaney's final team in 1972. Identify them and the hometown of the one from Erstad's home state.

3. Mike Stigge averaged 41.75 yards per punt from 1989 through 1992. Through the 1996 season, that was the Cornhusker career record. Stigge punted 167 times during his career. He also set the record for the longest punt in Nebraska history in 1992. How long was the punt? Against whom?

4. Who held Nebraska's record for career punting average before Stigge? Hint: He played in 1946 and 1947 and went on to become a professional wrestler—or rassler.

5. In 1996, Jesse Kosch broke the Cornhusker single-season record by averaging 44.7 yards per punt. The previous record was 43.36 yards per punt. Who held it? In what season? Who held the record, at 42.7 yards per punt, before that? In what season?

6. Stigge was a walk-on who played running back and quarterback in high school. The latter experience served him well in the 1990 Fiesta Bowl game against Florida State. Four plays into the game, instead of punting, he completed a pass for a 41-yard gain to the Seminoles' 22-yard line. Who caught the pass? Also, where did Stigge go to high school?

7. Stigge was the All–Big Eight punter as a junior in 1991, averaging 42 yards on 39 punts. Typically, punters on Tom Osborne's teams haven't gotten as much game experience as their counterparts at other schools, as the 1991 season illustrates: Stigge didn't punt in either of the first two games, against Utah State and Colorado State. He also earned Academic All–Big Eight honors in 1991. In all, how many times was he an academic all-conference honoree?

8. What Cornhusker punter besides Stigge has earned Academic All-America honors. Hint: He did it in 1988. What Cornhusker placekicker has earned Academic All-America honors?

9. After the ball is kicked, the punt team still has to cover and prevent a long return. A pair of punt returns were Nebraska's undoing in its only regular-season loss in 1989. To whom did the Cornhuskers lose? The punt returns, of 47 and 57 yards, were by the same player. Who was he?

10. On the strength of Erstad's kicking, Nebraska ranked second in the nation in net punting in 1994. But the Cornhuskers also have ranked first in the nation in net punting during the last decade. In what season was Nebraska number one in net punting? Who was the punter?

Anybody Get the License Plate Number?

Tom Osborne's first coaching victory against Oklahoma came in dramatic fashion at Memorial Stadium on November 11, 1978, when the Cornhuskers upset the number one–ranked Sooners 17–14. In his autobiography, *Bootlegger's Boy*, Barry Switzer called the 1978 team possibly his best at Oklahoma.

Jim Pillen's recovery of a Billy Sims fumble at the Nebraska three-yard line with 3:27 remaining in the game preserved the victory. What was for many fans of both teams an even more memorable play that frigid afternoon, however, occurred on a Cornhusker kickoff early in the fourth quarter.

Billy Todd initiated the play by kicking off after his 24-yard field goal had broken a tie at 14. Kelly Phelps, a backup quarterback, fielded the kick inside his own 10-yard line. Phelps's momentum as he went after the ball nearly carried him out of bounds at the nine. He would have been better off had that happened. But he regained his balance and cut back at an angle, toward the middle of the field.

Phelps was almost to the 20-yard line, near the hash mark, when Nebraska's John Ruud hit him, going full speed, shoulder high. The ball went bouncing back toward the Oklahoma goal line. And Phelps went to the turf with a separated shoulder. The Cornhuskers' Dan Lindstrom recovered inside the 15.

Inexplicably, the officials ruled Phelps was down before he fumbled the ball, which meant Oklahoma retained possession near its 20-yard line. The officials' ruling was "as bad of a call as you'll ever see," said Frank Broyles, the color commentator for ABC television that afternoon.

"I do not believe that he was down," ABC's Keith Jackson said.

The videotaped replay clearly showed Phelps was not down before the fumble. There wasn't a shred of doubt. George Darlington, a Nebraska assistant coach, has described the play as one of the "biggest snafus" he has ever seen. "The game shouldn't have been that close," he has said.

Ruud, a backup linebacker, set the standard by which subsequent kickoff-team play at Nebraska was, and is, measured. "It was a good hit," he said during an interview nearly 20 years later.

1. A future Cornhusker walk-on, who established himself on the kicking teams, was 14 years old and watching on television when Ruud put the hit on Phelps. The Cornhusker-to-be earned the nickname "Maniac" for his play on special teams. He often wore a T-shirt with a skull and the words "Seek and Destroy" on the front. He was elected a cocaptain as a senior, primarily for his contributions on special teams, though he also played linebacker. Who was he?

2. Jon Marco was 12 years old and sitting in the South Stadium end zone the day of the Oklahoma game in 1978. He not only saw Ruud's hit, he "heard it." Marco also walked on at Nebraska and first made a name for himself on the kickoff team. He was an L-1 wedge breaker. From what high school did Marco come? What regular position did he play?

3. Ruud was remembered for the big hit on Phelps. In the early 1990s, another kickoff team regular became a fan favorite for a series of big hits and collisions running down the field. He wore jersey number 91 as a sophomore and junior outside linebacker and jersey number 29 as a senior, when he was tried at fullback. He put one of his biggest hits on Arizona State's Mario Bates in the Cornhuskers' 45–24 victory in 1992. "I was on a full sprint to the ball carrier and hit him with a full head of steam—there was nothing like it," he said afterward. Who was he?

4. The wedge breaker extraordinaire in 1990 whom the player described in question number 3 succeeded went on to become Nebraska's first Butkus Award winner. Who was he?

5. Two brothers who came from Jacksonville, Florida, to walk on at Nebraska established reputations for their reckless abandon on the kickoff teams. Who were they?

6. As with many notable wedge breakers, this one walked on and volunteered. His small-town Nebraska background was unique. He lived in the Clearwater school district. He had a Neligh telephone listing. And his address was in Elgin. Who is he?

7. The wedge breakers often become fan favorites because they are involved in violent collisions. But kicking game success depends on players with many skills. Adam Treu and Aaron Graham have been outstanding deep snappers in recent seasons, and Tom Osborne singled out a player during a news conference in 1996 for his contributions as a "double bumper." Osborne explained, "Almost any punt protection scheme that you devise, you can take care of everybody man-on-man. But eventually, somebody's got to block two people, with the right configuration. And that's hard to do when they're flying at you." The player responsible for blocking two people is the double bumper. Who was the double bumper Osborne was praising?

8. If not for the punt coverage team, Nebraska's 1994 national champi-

onship run might well have been derailed by Wyoming in the fifth game of the season—at Memorial Stadium, no less. Nebraska was forced to punt late in the fourth quarter, after the pesky and emotional Cowboys had driven 86 yards on 13 plays to score and cut Nebraska's lead to 35–32. The Cornhuskers avoided a dramatic finish, however. Wyoming's Je'Nay Jackson fumbled the Darin Erstad punt and Nebraska recovered at the Cowboy eight-yard line. On first down, Lawrence Phillips ran eight yards for the clinching touchdown. What Cornhusker recovered Jackson's fumble?

9. Talk about situational substitutions . . . the Cornhuskers had an extremely specialized special teams player in 1978. He was used in situations when a fake punt was anticipated. The first-team defense remained in the game except for this player, who was inserted as a deep safety. If there was a punt, he was instructed to make a fair catch. The player in question came to Nebraska as a wrestler but immediately turned his attention to football. He stood 5-foot-8 and weighed 165 pounds. He played defensive back. And he was from Central City, Nebraska. Who was he?

10. The value of national television exposure to a major college football program is inestimable. The Cornhuskers' nationally televised 44–6 victory against Penn State in the 1983 Kickoff Classic was among the factors that influenced a player from Atlantic City, New Jersey, to walk on at Nebraska. He was impressed that two players from New Jersey, Mike Rozier and Irving Fryar, were part of the Scoring Explosion team in 1983. The player in question was a significant contributor to Nebraska's kicking teams. Who was he? Hint: He had a jewel of a first name.

Making a Big Hit on the Kicking Teams

Here are some final words of wisdom from a couple of notable Cornhusker kicking team players from the Tom Osborne era on how to be successful in covering kicks.

Doug Welniak, 1985–87: Maintain your balance. "You've got to keep your feet. That's the key. You can be going full speed and wipe out, take yourself right out of the play."

Jon Marco, 1986–88: Be running faster than your opponent at impact. "You learn it after you get hit once by somebody who's going faster and harder than you are. You've got to keep running. A lot of people have a tendency to slow down, but you've got to keep running as fast as you can."

Billy Legate, 1995–present: Use the element of surprise whenever possible and, above all, never be timid. "You see guys pulling up. That's when I'm grinning."

For What It's Worth

Even though he claimed he was only estimating, Tom Osborne never left anything to chance. He knew the percentages exactly, and he said this about field position after the NCAA moved kickoffs from the 40-yard line back to the 35: "If we start out on our own 20-yard line, we probably will score maybe a fourth or a fifth of the time. If we start out on our own 40-yard line, we would probably score about 50 percent of the time. The difference between [starting at] the 20- and the 40-yard line, statistically for us, would probably reflect a 50 percent difference in the opportunity to score."

When There Was Solace in Small Victories

You probably would have heard Tommy Edwards singing "It's All in the Game" on the car radio during the drive to Memorial Stadium. The song was working its way to the top of the *Billboard* chart, where it would remain for six weeks . . . if you weren't listening to a pregame show, of course.

If you had lost interest in Nebraska football in the wake of the Cornhuskers' 1–9 record the previous season, you may have been driving downtown to see Paul Newman and Elizabeth Taylor in the motion picture version of Tennessee Williams' play *Cat on a Hot Tin Roof*—in its "record third week" at the Stuart Theater. If you already had been to see *Cat on a Hot Tin Roof*, there was always Williams's *A Streetcar Named Desire* with Marlon Brando and Vivien Leigh showing at the Lincoln Theater.

And, well, *The Fiend Who Walked the West* starring Hugh O'Brian (really) was being shown at the Nebraska Theater if you'd had enough of culture and Cornhusker football. You could take in a matinee, dine with the football crowd at the Cotner Terrace Restaurant, where a fried "spring chicken dinner" was only $1.35, and then go dancing to the sounds of Mickey Kull at the Turnpike Ballroom.

The date was September 20, 1958, a Saturday. And if you weren't among the 25,000 or so who were curious enough to show up at Memorial Stadium to see if Coach Bill Jennings's second Nebraska team was likely to be more successful than his first, you missed a monumental upset, as well as the memorable varsity debut of a 5-foot-9, 163-pound halfback out of Westside High in Omaha named Pat Fischer.

The 14–7 upset of traditional eastern power Penn State and the debut of Fischer—number 40 in your 25-cent official program—were intertwined in such a way as to be inseparable.

After Coach Rip Engle's Nittany Lions had taken a 7–0 lead and appeared poised to finally dismiss the inexperienced and undersized Cornhuskers, Fischer, a sophomore following older brothers Clete, Ken, and Rex as a Nebraska football letterman, returned the ensuing kickoff 92 yards for a touchdown.

He fielded the ball eight yards from the north end zone and started up the middle of the field, then angled to his left, running along the east sideline. He was close enough that the players standing in front of the Penn State bench could have reached out and stopped him. For an instant, it appeared he might be forced out of bounds as he crossed his own 40-yard line. But he managed to keep just enough to the right of the chalk line to stay inbounds, and from that point on, he began pulling away, though only slightly.

Three stubborn defenders, including big Andy Stynchula, refused to give up the pursuit, which was little more than form during the final yards. Fischer crossed the goal line on his feet.

Stynchula, a 6-foot-3, 224-pound tackle who had used an angle to stay in the race, finally conceded the six points as Fischer approached the Nittany Lions' 10-yard line. Fischer's kickoff return was the turning point, according to Engle. "That gave them a lift," he told reporters after the game.

Fischer's punt return and the stirring victory to which it contributed were, no doubt, topics of much discussion at the Cotner Terrace Restaurant and wherever else Cornhusker fans congregated that night. But the excitement didn't last through the middle of October. By the time Nebraska upset 14th-ranked Pittsburgh 14–6 in the last home game of the season, Jennings had been hanged in effigy.

The Cornhuskers might have been perfect against Pennsylvania, and even unofficial champions of the state. But Nebraska fans were more concerned that their team had posted only one other victory in 10 games, defeating Iowa State 7–6 in the third week of the season—also at Memorial Stadium.

Though he never returned another kickoff for a touchdown at Nebraska, Fischer established two Cornhusker kickoff return records that have yet to be broken. He averaged a season-record 33.71 yards on seven returns in 1958, and he averaged a career-record 25.35 yards per return.

Quiz 41: Finishing with a Touchdown—and the Extra Point

1. During Bob Devaney's 11 seasons as coach, Nebraska returned three kickoffs for touchdowns. Each of the three was by a different player, and you should be familiar with two of the three players even if you're too young to remember them from having watched them play. Hint: The Cornhuskers' first kickoff return for a touchdown during the Devaney years came in the 1962 Gotham Bowl. The second was in 1964. The third, and longest, was in 1971.

2. How many kickoff return touchdowns did Devaney's Nebraska teams allow?

3. Florida's Reidel Anthony returned a kickoff 93 yards for a touchdown late in the fourth quarter against the Cornhuskers to complete the scoring in the 1996 Fiesta Bowl game. Prior to Anthony's kickoff return for a touchdown, how many had Tom Osborne's teams allowed? Two of them were by the same player, in consecutive seasons. Who was he? For whom did he play?

4. Nebraska's final touchdown in its 73–21 humiliation of old rival Okla-

homa in 1996 was scored on a kickoff return with 28 seconds remaining. Who returned the kickoff? How long was the return? How many kickoff returns for touchdowns had Osborne-coached teams managed before that one? Who returned them? And which one was the longest?

5. One of Nebraska's all-time best kick returners stood 5-foot-9 and weighed 170 pounds. He was fearless, however, and fast—he ran the 40-yard dash in 4.39 seconds. He refused to fair catch punts. "If I have two yards, I'm good, even if the guy is right there," he once said. "I try to return everything." Who was this kick returner? Extra credit: What was his nickname?

6. The player to whom question number 5 refers was followed by another kick returner who wore the same jersey number and had a similar nickname. He led the Big Eight and ranked seventh in the nation in punt returns as a redshirted freshman in 1989. Who was he? What was the jersey number he shared with his friend and predecessor? And what was his nickname?

7. Where were the players described in questions number 5 and number 6 from? Extra credit (and this is tough): The high school football coach of the player described in question number 6 was a Cornhusker in the early 1970s, but he never earned a letter. What is his name?

Rodgers Redux

Returning punts requires more than speed. "You need someone who can catch the ball, someone who has maneuverability, and someone who has a running instinct," Tom Osborne has said.

Johnny Rodgers was such a someone, on every count.

Answers

Quiz 35: Johnny R, Superstar—20 Questions

1. Rodgers returned one other punt, for eight yards. Oklahoma had one punt return, for seven yards.

2. Halfback Joe Wylie was the Sooners' punter. He carried three times for 11 yards.

3. Cornhusker cornerback Joe Blahak, number 27, made the final block for Rodgers. The Sooner he blocked was Jon Harrison, whose high school teammate, Jack Mildren, was the quarterback.

4. Nebraska's Jeff Hughes punted five times in the game and averaged 36.4 yards per punt. Hughes was a wingback, the same position as Rodgers. He was from Burlington, Vermont.

5. Rodgers returned seven punts for touchdowns in three varsity seasons.

6. Jack Mitchell returned seven punts for touchdowns during his career at Oklahoma.

7. Rodgers returned one punt for a touchdown on the freshman team. He also was the team's leading rusher, with 310 yards on 57 carries. Jim Ross was the freshman team's coach.

8. No. Rodgers returned only the one punt for a touchdown in a bowl game. In the 1973 Orange Bowl game, the Cornhuskers' greatest kick returner had one punt return for a minus three yards.

9. Rodgers returned one kickoff for a touchdown, 98 yards against Texas A&M in 1971.

10. Rod Smith holds the single-season record, averaging 18.92 yards on 12 returns in 1986.

11. Rodgers's 92-yard punt return for a touchdown against Oklahoma State in 1971 is the record. Corey Dixon returned a punt 68 yards but didn't score in the 1993 Colorado game.

12. Obviously, Rodgers never returned a punt for a touchdown against Nebraska. He also didn't have a punt return touchdown against Kansas or Colorado. He returned two for scores against Oklahoma State.

The Rodgers punt-return-for-touchdown file:

1970	48 yards, Missouri
	66 yards, Oklahoma State
1971	92 yards, Oklahoma State
	62 yards, Iowa State
	72 yards, Oklahoma
	77 yards, Alabama, 1972 Orange Bowl
1972	64 yards, Minnesota
	52 yards, Kansas State

13. Pat Fischer returned a punt 84 yards for a touchdown against Oklahoma State in 1960. The Cowboys joined what had been the Big Seven Conference in 1960, to form the Big Eight.

14. Larry Wachholtz returned three punts for a total of 133 yards against Utah State in 1966.

15. Dana Stephenson returned nine punts in a 29–0 victory against Texas Christian in 1967. Stephenson also punted a record 69 times during the 1967 season, averaging 35.1 yards per punt.

16. Owen Frank returned a kickoff 105 yards in 1911. Ron Clark returned a kickoff 100 yards in 1949. Both were in victories against Kansas State: 59–0 in 1911 and 13–6 in 1949.

17. Rozier fielded the opening kickoff, stepped back into the end zone, and downed the ball for a safety against Kansas State in 1983. After spotting the Wildcats two points six seconds into the game, Rozier went to work, rushing for 227 yards and three touchdowns on only 23 carries in a 51–25 victory.

18. Colorado's Cliff Branch led Big Eight punt returners in 1970 and was second in 1971.

19. Rodgers went to Omaha Tech. His football coach there was Dick Christie.

20. Rodgers's jersey number was 20—this is question number 20, right? Glover's jersey number was 79. Only one other jersey number had been retired at that time, Tom Novak's number 60.

Quiz 36: Husker Special Teams Fact

1. Bill Hornbacher was credited with six blocked kicks in 1968.

2. Meylan was from Bay City. Hornbacher was from Rogers City. Ed Periard was from Saginaw.

Quiz 37: Little Big Man

1. Miles was an outstanding man-to-man coverage cornerback, one of the best, according to defensive backs coach George Darlington. He was an option quarterback in high school and took some snaps at quarterback in 1994 because of the depth problems there. His hometown was Roselle, New Jersey.

2. Trev Alberts sacked Jones. The Cowboy punter was Scott Tyner.

3. The score was 27–13. Osborne reached 200 victories in his 21st season, quicker than any football coach in NCAA Division I-A history. At age 56, he also was the youngest to reach 200.

Quiz 38: Just Kicking Around

1. Clete Blakeman offered the encouragement-prediction.

2. Oklahoma State's Larry Roach and Kansas's Bruce Kallmeyer. Kallmeyer kicked five field goals against Nebraska in 1981 to account for all of the Jayhawks' points in a 31–15 loss.

3. Mike Knox recovered the fumble. Doug DuBose scored the touchdown. DuBose finished the game with 199 rushing yards. The Cornhuskers gained 320 yards on the ground. However, they lost one fumble and had two passes intercepted—one fewer than their completions in 15 attempts.

4. With the two field goals against Oklahoma State, Klein kicked nine in a row. He missed on his first attempt, a 46-yarder against Colorado, the week after the Missouri game.

5. Klein kicked soccer style, even though he never played organized soccer.

6. Klein punted twice in 1985 and once in 1986. His average was 34.7 yards per punt. He attended Seward High School, in Nebraska, where the football coach his senior year was Bob Starr.

7. Dave Schneider began the 1983 season as the Cornhuskers' number

one placekicker. Scott Livingston finished the season as the number one placekicker. Nebraska was four of five on field goal attempts that season. Livingston was two of three in the regular season and made a 34-yarder in the Orange Bowl. Schneider was of one, hitting a 34-yarder against Penn State in the Kickoff Classic. Livingston would have attempted the extra-point kick in the Orange Bowl. Counting three in the bowl game, he was 38 of 40 on extra-point kicks, meaning Osborne passed up a 95 percent chance of a tie to play for the victory.

8. Owen Frank had 17 point-after conversions in the 119–0 victory against Haskell.

9. The distance was 55 yards. Paul Rogers kicked one against Kansas in 1969. Billy Todd kicked one against Kansas in 1977. And Chris Drennan kicked one against Northern Illinois in 1989.

10. Gregg Barrios was successful on 83 extra-point kicks from October 19, 1986, to September 9, 1990.

11. Kris Brown kicked 62 of 62 extra points in 1997. He is from Carroll High School in Southlake, Texas.

12. Brown's 62 extra-point kicks in 1997 are the school single-season record, as are his 18 field goals in 21 attempts in 1997.

13. If you didn't know but guessed Barrios, you were right. He was 127 of 129 on extra-point kicks during his four-year career from 1986 through 1990. He sat out the 1987 season as a redshirt.

14. Paul Rogers in 1970, Dean Sukup in 1979, and Dale Klein in 1985

Quiz 39: Quick Kicks

1. Erstad kicked off and handled field goals of 40 yards or longer. Sieler kicked extra points—he was 40 of 42 in 1994 and 56 of 59 for his career—and field goals shorter than 40 yards. Erstad was three for eight on field goal attempts. His longest was 48 yards. Sieler was four for six. His longest was 35 yards.

2. Sieler was from Las Vegas, Nevada. Erstad was from Jamestown, North Dakota. Quarterback David Humm, who also was from Las Vegas, sat out the 1971 season as a redshirt. Bill Janssen alternated at defensive tackle in 1971, after missing the 1970 season with a broken arm. He was from Grand Forks, North Dakota.

3. Stigge had an 87-yard punt against Oklahoma State.

4. Jack Pesek held the record Stigge broke: 41.5 yards per punt.

5. Kosch broke Grant Campbell's record, set in 1981. Campbell broke Pesek's record, set in 1947.

6. Stigge, who went to high school in Washington, Kansas, threw the pass to Mark Dowse.

7. Stigge was an academic all-conference honoree in each of his four

seasons at Nebraska. He and Rob Zatechka are the only Cornhuskers who have been four-time academic all-conference selections. Also like Zatechka, Stigge was a two-time Academic All-American.

8. Punter John Kroeker was an Academic All-American in 1988. Place-kicker Dale Klein was an Academic All-American in 1986. Klein was a two-time academic all-conference honoree.

9. Nebraska's only regular-season loss in 1989 was at Colorado, 27–21. The Buffaloes' Jeff Campbell returned the two punts, to the Cornhusker four- and 19-yard lines, respectively.

10. The Cornhuskers led the nation in net punting in 1992. Stigge was the punter.

Quiz 40: Whoa Nellie, the Hitmen, and Others

1. Doug Welniak, who earned letters in 1985, 1986, and 1987, was an L-2 wedge breaker on the kickoff team. The "L-2" meant he was the second player to the left of the kickoff man. At 5-foot-11 and 220 pounds, he wasn't particularly big. But he packed a wallop. And he had the proper mind-set. "I just want to have one of those John Ruud hits," he once said.

2. Marco came from West High School, in Bellevue, Nebraska. He was a 6-foot-1, 230-pound defensive end. Throughout his career, he said, he was driven "to have a hit like John Ruud."

3. Lance Gray, a walk-on from Owego, New York, ranks with Nebraska's most fearless wedge breakers in recent seasons. "I'm looking for the guy with the ball or the guy in front of me, and I'm looking to knock him out every time," Gray once said in explaining his philosophy of covering kickoffs.

4. Trev Alberts was a wedge breaker as a redshirted freshman in 1990. "Nobody knew much about Trev then," former Cornhusker assistant coach Kevin Steele once said. Steele worked with the kicking teams. By season's end, however, everyone knew about Alberts, who was chosen as the Big Eight's Defensive Freshman of the Year. He became a regular in 1991 . . . and Gray became a wedge breaker.

5. Matt Penland earned letters in 1990 and 1992. He missed the 1991 season because of knee surgery. Aaron Penland earned letters from 1992 through 1995. Both were fearless on the kickoff team.

6. The kicking teams offered Billy Legate an opportunity to get on the field. He wasn't one to shy away from contact. Among other things, he was an R-1 wedge breaker, which means he was the first player lined up to the right of the kickoff man—the terminology is pretty much self-explanatory. "You've got to be a person who's not afraid to go into contact," he has said. "You've got to be a little crazy. It's a lot of fun. When the game starts, you want to set a tone. If you can get in on a special team, you feel like you're doing a lot. You can make a big difference."

7. Wingback Jon Vedral, a walk-on from Gregory, South Dakota, was the double bumper.

8. Damon Benning, a sophomore I-back who volunteered for kicking team duties throughout his career at Nebraska, recovered the fumble to set up the Phillips touchdown.

9. Dave Liegl was a three-year letterman who saw his first action on kicking teams. He got in his first varsity game as an end on the punt return team in 1978. He was asked if he could block a punt, and he replied, "Sure, anything to play." That's also how he became a punt returner. Lance Van Zandt, the Cornhuskers' defensive coordinator at the time, told all of the punt returners to go with him one afternoon during spring practice. Liegl decided he might as well be a punt returner. So he went.

10. Cartier Walker was impressed when he saw Rozier and Fryar playing for the Cornhuskers. One of his best performances came in Nebraska's 42–33 victory against UCLA in 1987. He blocked a punt to set up the Cornhuskers' first touchdown and recovered a Bruin fumble on a botched field goal attempt in the third quarter. UCLA was ranked number three, and Nebraska was ranked number two. The game was televised nationally on the ESPN cable network.

Quiz 41: Finishing with a Touchdown—and the Extra Point

1. Willie Ross had a 92-yard touchdown return in the Gotham Bowl. Frank Solich returned a kickoff 89 yards for a touchdown against Oklahoma State in 1964. And Johnny Rodgers—you knew he had to be one of the three—ran back a kickoff 98 yards to score against Texas A&M in 1971.

2. Four, as follows: North Carolina State's Joe Scarpati, 91 yards in 1962; Kansas's Vince O'Neill, 96 yards in 1970; Oklahoma State's Dick Graham, 98 yards in 1970; and Texas A&M's Hugh McElroy, 94 yards in 1971. McElroy and Nebraska's Rodgers traded kickoff return touchdowns.

3. Nebraska had allowed four touchdowns on kickoff returns under Osborne before Anthony's in the Fiesta Bowl, as follows: Wisconsin's Selvie Washington, 96 yards in 1973; Iowa State's Luther Blue, 95 yards in 1976; and Colorado's Howard Ballage, 98 yards in 1977 and 100 yards in 1978. Both of the Ballage returns followed field goals by Nebraska's Billy Todd. And both produced 7–3 leads.

4. Kenny Cheatham returned the kickoff against Oklahoma, 85 yards. His was the fourth under Osborne. The other three were as follows: Mike Rozier, 93 yards against Oklahoma State in 1981; Keith Jones, 98 yards against Kansas in 1985; and Tyrone Hughes, 99 yards against Kansas State in 1991.

5. Dana Brinson, whose nickname was "D-Rock," was a flashy dresser as well as a flashy player. In addition to returning kicks, he played wingback.

Kickoff returns were less challenging than punt returns, he said, explaining, "On kickoffs, you've got time to let your blockers set up the wall. And after you catch the ball, you normally have about 10 yards to run before contact. But on punt returns, as soon as you catch the ball, you've got to start faking people out because they're right on top of you."

6. Tyrone Hughes, whose nickname was "Baby Rock," wore the number 33 jersey Brinson had worn. Hughes supposedly got the jersey number by default. Brinson had taken a vicious hit in the UCLA game in 1988, and as a result, no one else wanted number 33. Athletes can be superstitious about jersey numbers. Osborne once said Hughes ranked among the best kick returners during his time at Nebraska, as an assistant as well as a head coach. The top two, of course, were Johnny Rodgers and Irving Fryar.

7. Brinson was from Valdosta, Georgia. Hughes was from St. Augustine High School in New Orleans, where his football coach was Burton Burns, whose career at Nebraska was cut short by a knee injury. Burns was a fullback on the 1971 Cornhusker freshman team, which finished 4–0. Former Cornhuskers David White and Vincent Hawkins also were coached by Burns for parts of their careers at St. Augustine.

7

GAMES OF THE CENTURY:

The Husker-Sooner Rivalry

The Nebraska and Oklahoma football teams won't play each other in the regular season in 1998. They could meet in the Big 12 championship game. Otherwise they will go their separate ways for two seasons under the conference's system of interdivisional play, something that last happened in 1927.

Nebraska and Oklahoma were conference rivals in 1927. But the Missouri Valley Intercollegiate Athletic Association, like the Big 12 now, had more members than could be accommodated on eight-game schedules. Oklahoma A&M had dropped out of the Southwest Conference to become the Missouri Valley's 10th team. In 1928, Nebraska, Missouri, Oklahoma, Iowa State, Kansas, and Kansas State broke away to form their own conference. Officially, it was still the Missouri Valley Intercollegiate Athletic Association. But it came to be known by its numerical designation, the Big Six.

Nebraska dominated the series early on. The Cornhuskers were 16–3–3 from the teams' first meting in 1912 through 1942. From 1943 until 1968, however, Oklahoma held the upper hand, winning 22 of 26 games, including a streak of 16 in a row that ended with Nebraska's dramatic upset in 1959.

Oklahoma was the Cornhuskers' opponent in the first game ever played in Memorial Stadium. Nebraska won it 24–0 on October 13, 1923. And the Sooners were indirectly responsible for Nebraska's being forced to withdraw from the Missouri Valley Conference in 1919, the year before Oklahoma joined. But neither of those occurrences was a sufficient foundation for what has become a notable rivalry.

As with any tradition, there is no exact beginning. For the sake of argument, however, October 31, 1959, might suffice in this case. "In a way, though other people might not agree, I thought we kind of got the whole thing started," Bill Jennings once said. Jennings was Nebraska's coach in 1959. You probably know the story if you're a Cornhusker or Sooner fan. If not, read on. But first . . .

Bob Devaney discusses strategy with QB Jerry Tagge during the 1971 game versus Oklahoma.

(Photo Courtesy of UPI/CORBIS-BETTMANN)

Quiz 42: Pregame Stretching

1. In 1925, Oklahoma A&M joined the Missouri Valley Intercollegiate Athletic Association, bringing the membership to 10. Name the other nine. Hint: Since you know Nebraska was one of the nine, and five others are identified in the preceding section, you only have to come up with three. By the way, none of the three have NCAA Division I-A football programs now.

2. Though its official name remained the MVIAA, the conference expanded to seven schools to become the Big Seven in 1947. What school joined in 1947? Extra credit: The new member came from a conference in which Bob Devaney once coached. What was the conference?

3. In 1957, the Big Seven became the Big Eight when a former conference member rejoined. What school was added? Extra credit: In what year did the MVIAA officially become the Big Eight?

4. Nebraska and Oklahoma played for the first time in 1912, at Lincoln. The Cornhuskers won 12–0, on the way to posting a 7–1 record under what second-year head coach? Extra credit: Who was Oklahoma's coach? Hint: Did you know Oklahoma's home is Memorial Stadium?

5. Oklahoma has handed the Cornhuskers their only regular-season loss

five times: in 1964, 1966, 1975, 1979, and 1987. Nebraska has handed the Sooners their only regular-season loss twice. In what seasons did that occur? Extra credit: Who were the teams' coaches in those seasons?

6. The Associated Press national rankings were established in 1936. How many times have Nebraska and Oklahoma been number one and number two in the AP rankings when they played each other? In what season or seasons has that occurred? What was the result?

7. If you can't lick 'em, join 'em. After his Oklahoma teams suffered back-to-back shutout losses against Nebraska, what head coach was hired by the Cornhuskers? Hint: He replaced D. X. Bible and compiled a 28–14–4 (.652) record in five seasons as head coach at Nebraska. Extra credit: He was retired from the military. What rank did he achieve in the army? What was his nickname?

8. Two Heisman Trophy winners have played for Nebraska: Johnny Rodgers and Mike Rozier. Three Heisman Trophy winners have played for Oklahoma. Name them. Extra credit: Two of the three Sooner Heisman Trophy winners were from Oklahoma. Which one was not?

Independent Cornhuskers

Nebraska was without a conference affiliation from 1918 to 1920, in part because of Oklahoma. The Missouri Valley Intercollegiate Athletic Association suspended operations in 1918 because of World War I, but it was back in business in 1919 without the Cornhuskers. Under pressure from alums in Omaha, as well as from some university students, Nebraska athletic officials were persuaded to play a nonconference home game against the Sooners in Omaha, even though MVIAA rules prohibited member institutions from scheduling games off campus. Rather than face conference sanctions, Nebraska withdrew from the MVIAA prior to the start of the 1919–20 school year.

Coach Henry Schulte's Cornhuskers played Oklahoma as the second half of a football doubleheader in Omaha on October 25, 1919. The other game matched Creighton and Marquette.

The doubleheader was less than successful for Nebraska, which had promoted the event in hopes of turning a profit as well as pacifying the Omaha alums. The Cornhuskers and the Sooners played to a 7–7 tie, and Nebraska made barely $2,000 after expenses, which included $2,000 to Creighton and Marquette for their participation. That despite the fact that gate receipts totaled approximately $12,000.

With Nebraska out of the MVIAA, Oklahoma was added to the conference in 1920. Kansas was the only MVIAA school willing to play the Cornhuskers in 1920, so they had to look elsewhere. Apparently, they had no problem in finding opponents. They played nine games instead of the typical eight, including Rutgers at the Polo Grounds in New York City and Penn State at State College,

Pennsylvania, in a four-day span in early December. Five of the nine games were played in Lincoln, and Nebraska finished 5–3–1.

Nebraska officials sought membership in the powerful Western Conference, now the Big Ten, without success. So Chancellor Samuel Avery headed a committee responsible for getting the Cornhuskers back into the MVIAA. That was accomplished in time for the 1921–22 school year.

Halloween Homecoming

On October 31, 1959, the Cornhuskers of Coach Bill Jennings produced arguably the greatest upset in Nebraska football history, defeating Oklahoma 25–21 at Memorial Stadium.

Although the Sooners of Coach Bud Wilkinson had already lost games against Northwestern and Texas and were only 19th in the Associated Press rankings, they were still the scourge of the conference. It was just two years earlier that their NCAA-record 47-game winning streak had ended.

The winning streak began in 1953 and included national championships in 1955 and 1956. But Oklahoma's dominance of the conference, as well as the nation, was established before that. The Sooners shared the final two Big Six championships in 1946 and 1947. They won every Big Seven championship (1948 through 1957) outright. And they won the first two Big Eight championships outright.

Despite the loss to Nebraska, they were conference champs in 1959, for the 14th season in a row. All but the first of those 14 came under the direction of the legendary Wilkinson.

Oklahoma hadn't lost a conference game since 1946, the year before Wilkinson succeeded Jim Tatum as coach. The Sooners' conference unbeaten streak had reached 74 games, the last 36 of which were victories. They had been tied twice during the streak—by Kansas in 1947 and by Colorado in 1952. They hadn't lost to Nebraska since 1942, when the Cornhuskers left Norman with a 7–0 victory. Oklahoma had won 16 in a row against the Cornhuskers, beginning in 1943, by a combined score of 313–47.

Nebraska seemed an unlikely candidate to snap Oklahoma's remarkable streak. The Cornhuskers had won only six of 26 games in Jennings's two-plus seasons as head coach. They had lost to Oklahoma by scores of 32–7 in 1957 and 40–7 in 1958. And they hadn't exactly distinguished themselves in their first six games in 1959. They were 2–4 and had scored a touchdown or less in five of those games.

They had scored only 10 points total in three consecutive losses following victories against Minnesota (32–12) and Iowa State (7–6). The Minnesota victory, at Minneapolis, followed a 20–0 opening-game loss to Texas and was cause for optimism, but only briefly.

A less than amicable relationship between Wilkinson and Jennings was the basis for a significant subplot to the game. Jennings, an Oklahoma native, had been a football end at Norman High School under Coach Dewey "Snorter" Luster, who later coached the Sooners from 1941 to 1945. Jennings went on to play end and wingback for Coach Tom Stidham at Oklahoma, earning letters in 1938, 1939, and 1940.

After serving in the Marine Corps, Jennings returned to his alma mater in 1946 as a graduate assistant under Tatum, and when Wilkinson succeeded Tatum in 1947, Jennings was made a full-time assistant. In addition to coaching, Jennings handled recruiting for Wilkinson, making visits to high school players. Soft-spoken and straightforward, Jennings was an excellent recruiter, a quality that was later apparent when he left Nebraska with the players responsible for a dramatic turnaround in 1962.

Jennings spent seven seasons as Wilkinson's backfield coach, working with numerous All-Americans, among them Eddie Crowder, Billy Vessels, Buck McPhail, Leon Heath, Darrell Royal, and Jack Mitchell. He left Oklahoma after the 1953 season to take a job with an oil company in Fort Worth, Texas.

The year after Jennings left, the NCAA investigated alleged recruiting improprieties at Oklahoma. Jennings maintained there was no correlation between his resignation and the investigation. "I had resigned at the University of Oklahoma prior to knowledge of any NCAA investigation," he told the *Lincoln Journal* several years later. Nevertheless, he ended up in the middle of the controversy.

The NCAA uncovered relatively minor infractions and placed Oklahoma on two years' probation, beginning in April 1955. The problems didn't end with that, however. The NCAA handed the Sooners another probation in January 1960 for what it said was a special fund to bring prospective athletes to campus. Again, Jennings had to defend himself. "If I'm the only one that knew about it, why don't they go ahead and reveal the books on it? It would only affect me," he told the *Lincoln Journal*.

By then, Jennings was Nebraska's coach. Pete Elliott had hired him as the Cornhuskers' backfield coach in 1956, and when Elliott left after one season to coach at California, Jennings moved up.

Jennings immediately found himself at odds with Wilkinson again, and not just because the teams were conference rivals. Jennings was upset that Wilkinson had tried to recruit Monte Kiffin, a multisport athlete at Lexington High School in Nebraska. Jennings said Wilkinson was violating his own policy against recruiting an out-of-state athlete before the athlete had announced that he wasn't interested in attending his home-state university. Kiffin had made no such announcement, according to Jennings.

Oklahoma responded by complaining about Jennings's recruitment of a player from Wichita, Kansas. Wilkinson, the athletic director as well as head football coach, also protested the eligibility of two Nebraska freshman players. Faculty representatives were drawn into the controversy, and Jennings suggested that both schools present their complaints to the NCAA. Oklahoma declined.

"This is a pretty rough game," Jennings told the *Lincoln Journal,* in reflecting on the controversy two years later. "I recruited hard for Oklahoma, and now I'm recruiting hard for Nebraska."

Even though Wilkinson and Crowder, who had become an assistant, had made a trip to Lexington to try to persuade him to attend Oklahoma, Kiffin picked Nebraska, announcing his decision after the state high school track-and-field championships in spring 1958. Because of a back operation, however, Kiffin didn't begin his Cornhusker career until fall 1960. He was a three-year letterman, from 1961 through 1963, then served as an assistant under both Bob Devaney and Tom Osborne.

Despite the strained relations, Jennings and Wilkinson were both gentlemen. Jennings was carried off the field by jubilant players and students after the Cornhuskers' upset victory in 1959. Wilkinson had to follow the crowd in order to shake Jennings's hand, after Jennings was finally set down.

Jennings's coaching tenure at Nebraska was a roller coaster of dramatic upsets and disappointing losses, against opponents often considered to be no more talented than the Cornhuskers. Jennings was allowed a one-season grace period—his first team in 1957 finished with a 1–9 record—before the criticism that contributed to the resignation of Bill Glassford after the 1955 season began anew.

The 1958 season was typical of what Jennings faced. The Cornhuskers opened with a 14–7 upset of Penn State, lost at Purdue 28–0, then edged Iowa State 7–6 in their conference opener in Lincoln. They lost their next five in a row. After the fourth of those losses, 31–0 to Missouri in their Homecoming game, Jennings was hanged in effigy on campus by angry and unforgiving students.

Two weeks later, students were applauding Jennings, after Nebraska upset Pittsburgh 14–6 at Memorial Stadium. The Panthers had come to town ranked 14th nationally by the Associated Press. The next week, the season came to an inauspicious end with a 40–7 loss to Oklahoma in Norman.

The 1959 season was almost a carbon copy of the 1958 season to that point. The Cornhuskers again went to their Homecoming game with a 2–4 record and a three-game losing streak. They had even won their third game 7–6 at home, although it was against Oregon State instead of Iowa State.

THE 1959 NEBRASKA OFFENSIVE LINEUP

Left end	**Dick McDaniel**	6-3, 196, sophomore, Port Arthur, Texas
	John Bond	6-0, 188, junior, Missouri Valley, Iowa

Left tackle	**Gregory Haney**	6-1, 188, sophomore, East Point, Georgia
	Duane Mongerson	6-4, 210, senior, Omaha, Nebraska
Left guard	**Don Olson**	6-3, 213, junior, Grand Island, Nebraska
	John Ponsiego	5-9, 189, junior, Chicago, Illinois
Center	**Jim Moore**	6-0, 192, senior, Omaha, Nebraska
	Darrell Cooper	5-11, 217, junior, Fort Worth, Texas
Right guard	**Dick Kosier**	5-10, 183, junior, Watertown, South Dakota
	LeRoy Zentic	5-11, 197, senior, Rock Island, Illinois
Right tackle	**Roland McDole**	6-3, 232, junior, Toledo, Ohio
	Joe Gacusana	6-2, 204, junior, Lincoln, Nebraska
Right end	**Max Martz**	6-2, 184, senior, Beatrice, Nebraska
	Don Purcell	6-1, 202, sophomore, Omaha, Nebraska
Quarterback	**Harry Tolly**	6-1, 198, senior, North Platte, Nebraska
	Ron Meade	6-0, 168, sophomore, Canby, Minnesota
Left halfback	**Pat Fischer**	5-9, 166, junior, Omaha, Nebraska
	Dallas Dyer	5-10, 180, sophomore, Lexington, Nebraska
Right halfback	**Clay White**	5-9, 178, junior, Toledo, Ohio
	Carroll Zaruba	5-9, 201, senior, Fullerton, Nebraska
Fullback	**Don Fricke**	6-0, 187, junior, Hastings, Nebraska
	Noel Martin	5-11, 191, sophomore, Clay Center, Nebraska

Oklahoma took a 7–0 lead in the first quarter, which came as no surprise to a crowd of 32,765. Nebraska countered with a touchdown early in the second quarter, on a pass from quarterback Harry Tolly to end Dick McDaniel. But the Sooners retained the lead when a two-point conversion pass failed. Long-suffering Cornhusker fans had seen this before. They didn't anticipate what was to come.

A few minutes later, Oklahoma's Bob Cornell tried to catch the defense by surprise, dropping back for a quick kick on second down. Under pressure from Nebraska's Jim Moore, however, Cornell shanked the kick. The Cornhuskers' Lee Zentic, a game captain, picked up the ball and returned it 36 yards for a touchdown. Moore threw a key block for Zentic at the Oklahoma 25-yard line.

Ron Meade's extra-point kick missed. But Nebraska had the lead, 12–7.

Oklahoma regained the lead by halftime and held it until Meade's 22-yard field goal late in the third quarter made the score 15–14. Wilkinson and Jennings both played for field position throughout the game, as a curious sequence that began on the final play of the third quarter illustrated.

Jennings called a time-out with one second remaining in the quarter so Tolly could punt with a gentle breeze at his back on second down. Oklahoma started the fourth quarter by punting the ball back to Nebraska on first down. The Cornhuskers couldn't pick up a first down, despite good field position, and punted to the Oklahoma four-yard line. The Sooners ran one play, then punted again.

Pat Fischer, a diminutive junior from Omaha, fielded the 54-yard punt at his own 36-yard line. Fischer showed no signs of the knee sprain he had suffered during the first half. He ran through Oklahoma's punt coverage and continued inside the Sooner four-yard line before being knocked off his feet.

On third down, Tolly got the ball across the goal line. Dallas Dyer handled a poor center snap, and Meade kicked the extra point. With 9:16 remaining in the game, Nebraska led 22–14.

Two plays after the ensuing kickoff, the Cornhuskers had the ball back, after Don Olson recovered a fumble at the Oklahoma 43-yard line. The Sooners regrouped to keep Nebraska out of the end zone, but Meade came on to kick his second field goal and boost the Cornhuskers' lead to 25–14.

Oklahoma refused to concede the victory and its 74-game conference unbeaten streak, however, driving 67 yards on nine plays to make the score 25–21. The Sooners then forced a punt and drove to the Nebraska 30-yard line, where they had a first-and-10 with 1:13 remaining.

Oklahoma went to the air. The Cornhuskers' Don Fricke broke up a first-down pass, and Dyer and Carroll Zaruba knocked down a second-down pass in the end zone. Oklahoma went to the end zone again on third down, but Meade intercepted to end the suspense. The Sooners headed for the locker room with seconds still showing on the north field house clock, and the celebration began.

Even though the steel goalposts were set in concrete, they were pulled down by celebrants and carried across campus. Pieces of the goalposts were later sold as paperweights, commemorating the victory. University classes were canceled on the Monday after the game. And the governor announced that he would make "every Cornhusker football player an admiral in the Great Navy of Nebraska." Accounts of the upset were beamed to Japan, Israel, and Germany by the university's shortwave radio club.

Long after the celebration, Jennings, his wife, Mary, and their daughter, Jan, walked to the parking lot beneath the viaduct behind the north field house. As they crossed the street, a carload of young men drove past.

"What was the score?" one of them yelled.

The Jennings family shouted in unison, "25–21."

The car slowed where the street curves. "Who won?"

"Nebraska," came the reply.

The car seemed to swerve just a little before picking up speed.

1. Nebraska fans were familiar with Oklahoma's Wilkinson before he became a head coach. He played quarterback and guard as a collegian for a school that was 3–0 against the Cornhuskers during his career there. At what school did Wilkinson play?

2. Nebraska won the recruiting battle with Oklahoma for Monte Kiffin. Two of Kiffin's senior teammates at Lexington High School were three-year Cornhusker lettermen. Name them. Hint: One of the two went on to play 17 seasons in the National Football League.

3. A sophomore halfback on the 1959 Oklahoma team was an assistant coach on Tom Osborne's staff at Nebraska in 1980 and 1981. Name him. Hint: He also was the recruiting coordinator.

4. The Big 12 conference associate commissioner for academic services and life skills played in the 1959 Oklahoma-Nebraska game. He was a fullback. Name him.

5. A veteran member of Nebraska's medical staff was a sophomore halfback on the 1959 Cornhusker team. He was one of the Cornhuskers' first two Academic All-Americans. Name him. Extra credit: The other of Nebraska's first two Academic All-Americans was a junior fullback on the 1959 Cornhusker team. He is now a Lincoln dentist. Name him.

6. A sophomore end for the 1959 Cornhuskers was a high school teammate of actor Nick Nolte. Name him. Hint: They were teammates at Benson High School in Omaha.

7. A sophomore tackle for the 1959 Cornhuskers became a well-known professional wrestler. He called himself the Baron and claimed to be from Germany, but he was from Omaha, Nebraska. He never lettered in football at Nebraska, but he was a conference heavyweight wrestling champion for the Cornhuskers. Name him. Extra credit: Where did he go to high school?

8. A sophomore halfback for the 1959 Cornhuskers later coached a pair of upset victories against Nebraska at Memorial Stadium. Name him and the team(s) he coached.

9. A senior end on the 1959 Cornhuskers had a son who was a four-year letterman on the Cornhusker basketball team from 1984 through 1987. Name the end. Name his son.

10. Jennings assisted with the football team of Castle Rock High School in Colorado in the early 1980s and coached a Cornhusker linebacker-to-be there. Name the linebacker.

Two and One Half in a Row

Nebraska went to Norman in 1960 and defeated Oklahoma again, 17–14. The Cornhuskers rallied from a 14–0 halftime deficit for the victory. With the score 14–8 in the fourth quarter, Nebraska fullback Bill "Thunder" Thornton ran 68 yards for a touchdown on a trap play to tie the score at 14.

Ron Meade, whose extra-point attempt after Thornton's touchdown was blocked, came back to kick the winning field goal from 22 yards—the same distance as each of his two field goals in 1959.

Oklahoma fans blamed Jennings for giving information to the NCAA about the recruiting slush fund, which led to the Sooners' probation. Passions were so high in 1960 as a result that Jennings received threats, and police officers were stationed on the Cornhusker sideline during the game.

The Cornhuskers led Oklahoma 14–0 at halftime of the 1961 game at Memorial Stadium and appeared to be well on their way to a third consecutive victory against Wilkinson's Sooners. Nebraska could have scored as many as 28 first-half points if a pair of passes by sophomore quarterback Dennis Claridge hadn't been dropped. One, on a fake field goal, was dropped in the end zone. The other was dropped at the Oklahoma 10-yard line. Even so, it appeared the Cornhuskers were in control.

Oklahoma pulled out the victory, however, scoring three second-half touchdowns, the last late in the game on a 98-yard drive that followed a 70-yard Claridge punt to the Sooner two-yard line.

Harold Keith wrote in *Forty-seven Straight: The Wilkinson Era at Oklahoma,* published by the University of Oklahoma Press in 1984, that Bill Jennings told him years later, "I used to say that we beat OU two and one-half years in a row because we led 14–0 at the half" of the 1961 game.

The 1961 game against Oklahoma was Jennings's last as Nebraska's coach. He was fired, not only because his record for five seasons was 15–34–1 but also because he had alienated people in the state with remarks he made to an Omaha booster club in 1960. "I don't think this state can ever be great in anything," he said. "There are so few people in this state." He subsequently apologized.

The student newspaper was not to be appeased, however. An editorial offered the opinion that Jennings had "bought a one-way ticket back to private business, unless any other school wants him."

In December 1961, Jennings was told by Chancellor Clifford Hardin that his contract would not be renewed. "We can't feed the ego of the state of Nebraska with the football team," Jennings said.

Jennings was hardworking and sincere, a good man in a difficult situation, created in part by his own honesty. He wasn't making excuses. He really believed what he had told Hardin and the booster club in Omaha a year earlier. Ironically, it was through his recruiting efforts that Bob Devaney was able to accomplish a dramatic turnaround in the program in 1962. During the transition, the two coaches met briefly in the football offices, which were located on the second floor of the NU Coliseum. "With the bunch of kids you have left here, if you'd stay another year, you'd win," Devaney told him.

That choice wasn't Jennings's to make, however. Despite the losing record, the upsets alone were sufficient to earn Jennings induction in the Nebraska Football Hall of Fame in 1996.

Even if Nebraska had held on to its halftime lead in 1961 to win for a third time in a row against Oklahoma, Jennings probably would have been gone. But "I talked to the chancellor afterward, and he said he thought it might have been tough to sell people on firing a guy who had just beat Oklahoma," said Clete Fischer, one of two Jennings assistants who was retained on staff by Devaney.

Fischer, who also coached under Tom Osborne, provides perspective on Jennings's brief tenure as the Cornhuskers' head coach. "Bill was a bright guy. He was a little bit like Tom Osborne, really," Fischer said. "When Bill took over, the cupboard was bare. When Bob [Devaney] came here, there were a lot of good players. Bob admitted that. It was just a matter of getting things turned around."

The Game of the Century

Nebraska's four-point victory against Oklahoma in 1959 was arguably the most memorable upset in Cornhusker football history. The most memorable victory in school history also came at the expense of Oklahoma—and the margin of victory also was four points, for whatever that's worth.

The game was played at Norman, Oklahoma, on November 25, 1971, Thanksgiving Day. It was televised nationally by ABC. Kickoff was 1:50 P.M., Central Standard Time. The announced attendance was 61,826.

Starting Lineups

NEBRASKA OFFENSE

Split end	**Woody Cox**	5-9, 167, senior
Left tackle	**Darryl White**	6-4, 238, sophomore
Left guard	**Dick Rupert**	6-2, 221, senior
Center	**Doug Dumler**	6-3, 237, junior
Right guard	**Keith Wortman**	6-3, 238, senior
Right tackle	**Al Austin**	6-5, 222, sophomore
Tight end	**Jerry List**	6-1, 218, junior
Quarterback	**Jerry Tagge**	6-2, 215, senior
I-back	**Jeff Kinney**	6-2, 210, senior
Wingback	**Johnny Rodgers**	5-10, 171, junior
Fullback	**Bill Olds**	6-1, 215, junior

NEBRASKA DEFENSE

Left end	**John Adkins**	6-3, 221, senior
Left tackle	**Larry Jacobson**	6-6, 250, senior
Middle guard	**Rich Glover**	6-1, 234, junior

Right tackle	**Bill Janssen**	6-3, 228, junior
Right end	**Willie Harper**	6-3, 207, junior
Linebacker	**Bob Terrio**	6-2, 209, senior
Linebacker	**Jim Branch**	5-9, 203, junior
Left corner	**Joe Blahak**	5-10, 184, junior
Right corner	**Jim Anderson**	6-0, 180, senior
Monster	**Dave Mason**	6-0, 199, junior
Safety	**Bill Kosch**	6-0, 176, senior

OKLAHOMA OFFENSE

Split end	**Jon Harrison**	5-9, 157, senior
Left tackle	**Dean Unruh**	6-3, 235, junior
Left guard	**Darryl Emmert**	6-2, 218, senior
Center	**Tom Brahaney**	6-2, 231, junior
Right guard	**Ken Jones**	6-4, 236, junior
Right tackle	**Robert Jensen**	6-5, 244, junior
Tight end	**Albert Chandler**	6-3, 234, junior
Quarterback	**Jack Mildren**	6-0, 199, senior
Left halfback	**Roy Bell**	5-11, 205, senior
Right halfback	**Greg Pruitt**	5-9, 176, junior
Fullback	**Leon Crosswhite**	6-2, 203, junior

OKLAHOMA DEFENSE

Left end	**Raymond Hamilton**	6-1, 237, junior
Left tackle	**Lucious Selmon**	6-1, 221, sophomore
Right tackle	**Derland Moore**	6-4, 252, junior
Right end	**Lionell Day**	6-0, 236, senior
Linebacker	**Albert Qualls**	6-3, 222, senior
Linebacker	**Steve Aycock**	6-2, 205, senior
Linebacker	**Mark Driscoll**	6-0, 208, senior
Left corner	**Kenith Pope**	6-0, 205, sophomore
Right corner	**Steve O'Shaughnessy**	5-11, 180, senior
Strong safety	**Larry Roach**	6-0, 181, junior
Safety	**John Shelley**	6-0, 195, senior

Quiz 44: No Place Like Home, and Other Matters

1. Oklahoma's starting lineups on offense and defense for the Game of the Century included only three players who weren't from either Oklahoma or Texas. One of those three was a graduate of a high school in Nebraska. Which Sooner was he? Of what high school was he a graduate? Hint: He was from Omaha, if that helps. No? Okay. He was a lineman.

2. As indicated in question number 1, 19 of Oklahoma's 22 starters were from either Texas or Oklahoma. Were more of the Sooner starters from Oklahoma or Texas?

3. Lucious Selmon was the first of three brothers to play for the Sooners. Who were the other two? What was their hometown? Did all three play together at Oklahoma?

4. Jack Mildren threw passes to Jon Harrison for two of the Sooner touchdowns in the 1971 game. They were high school teammates. What was their hometown?

5. Tom Brahaney, Oklahoma's All-America center in 1971, was from the same hometown as a two-time All-America center at Nebraska in the 1980s. Who was the Cornhusker center? Extra credit: What was the hometown they shared?

Game of the Century Scoring

FIRST QUARTER

Nebraska   Johnny Rodgers 72-yard punt return (Rich Sanger kick), 11:28 remaining
Oklahoma   John Carroll 30-yard field goal, 5:53 remaining

SECOND QUARTER

Nebraska   Jeff Kinney one-yard run (Sanger kick), 11:08 remaining
Oklahoma   Jack Mildren two-yard run (Carroll kick), 5:10 remaining
Oklahoma   Jon Harrison 24-yard pass from Mildren (Carroll kick), :28 remaining

THIRD QUARTER

Nebraska   Kinney three-yard run (Sanger kick), 8:54 remaining
Nebraska   Kinney one-yard run (Sanger kick), 3:38 remaining
Oklahoma   Mildren three-yard run (Carroll kick), :28 remaining

FOURTH QUARTER

Oklahoma   Harrison 16-yard pass from Mildren (Carroll kick), 7:10 remaining
Nebraska   Kinney two-yard run (Sanger kick), 1:38 remaining

6. Brahaney earned consensus All-America honors in 1971. But he had his hands full with Cornhusker middle guard Rich Glover. How many tackles did Glover make?

7. Roy Bell started at left halfback for Oklahoma in the Game of the Century because the Sooners' regular left halfback was slowed by a sore ankle. He played. He just didn't start. He was a junior and had been Oklahoma's leading rusher and scorer in 1970. Name him. Hint: He scored two touchdowns in the Sooners' 28–21 loss to Nebraska in 1970.

8. Al Austin started and played the entire game for Nebraska at right offensive tackle. The Cornhuskers' regular right tackle, a first-team All–Big Eight honoree, missed the game because of a knee strain. Who was Nebraska's regular right tackle? Extra credit: Austin was one of only five Cornhuskers from Nebraska to start the Game of the Century. Where was he from? At what high school did he play? What former Cornhusker was his high school coach?

9. Name the other four in-state players who started for Nebraska in the Game of the Century. Extra credit: Identify their high schools. Hint: Two of the four were high school teammates.

10. The Game of the Century featured five players who earned consensus All-America recognition in 1971. Tom Brahaney was one of the five. Name the other four. Remember, they were consensus All-Americans in 1971. Don't include those who may have been consensus All-Americans in another season. Hint: Three of the other four were Cornhuskers. Extra credit: Three other Nebraska players earned All-America honors in 1971. Name them.

11. Nebraska wasn't ranked number one in the Associated Press preseason poll in 1971. But the Cornhuskers moved up to number one after their opening victory. Where was Nebraska ranked in the AP preseason poll? Whom did Nebraska defeat in its opener in 1971? What current television sports reporter–commentator played for the team the Cornhuskers defeated in their opener? Hint: He is a close friend of Michael Jordan.

12. The Game of the Century was not the last one in the regular season for either Nebraska or Oklahoma. Each team played one more game before making bowl preparations. What teams did Nebraska and Oklahoma play after playing each other? Both had to play on the road.

13. Oklahoma fans, of course, still maintain that the Cornhuskers' Joe Blahak should have been penalized for clipping near the end of Johnny Rodgers's 72-yard punt return for a touchdown in the Game of the Century. Whom did Blahak block on the play?

14. Oklahoma's 31 points were easily the most scored against Nebraska, which ranked third in the nation in scoring defense in 1971. Nebraska allowed more than one touchdown in only two other games. What team scored the second-most points against the Cornhuskers? How many did that team score? What team managed the second-lowest margin of defeat against Nebraska in 1971? What was the Cornhuskers' lowest point total of the 1971 season? Extra credit: Nebraska posted three shutouts in 1971. Against whom were they?

15. Three coaches on Oklahoma's staff for the Game of the Century later were head coaches in the National Football League. Name the three.

16. Three Sooner assistant coaches in 1971 later were head coaches at schools in the former Big Eight Conference. Name them and the Big Eight schools at which they coached.

17. Five Nebraska assistant coaches in 1971 later were major college head coaches. Name them and the schools at which they were head coaches.

18. One of Oklahoma's assistants in 1971 was a captain on Arkansas's 1964 national championship team, which defeated the Cornhuskers in the Cotton Bowl 10–7. Name him.

19. Oklahoma set the NCAA Division I-A rushing record in 1971. The Sooners averaged 472.4 rushing yards per game. Within 10 yards, how many rushing yards did they have against Nebraska? Extra credit: Oklahoma's Greg Pruitt was the nation's leading rusher going into the Game of the Century. Within 10 yards, how many did he gain against Nebraska?

20. Nebraska changed its coverage in the secondary for the Oklahoma game in 1971. The change involved the way the Cornhuskers played Sooner wide receiver Jon Harrison. What did Nebraska do differently in dealing with Harrison? Who was the Cornhuskers' secondary coach?

First-and-10

Johnny Rodgers's first-quarter punt return has come to represent the Game of the Century. But Rodgers was involved in an equally crucial yet often overlooked play during Nebraska's game-winning drive late in the fourth quarter—the drive required 12 plays and covered 74 yards.

The Cornhuskers faced third-and-eight at the Oklahoma 46-yard line. Rodgers was one of four receivers who were to run hook patterns on the play. On the previous down, quarterback Jerry Tagge had attempted a pass to Rodgers that was incomplete. Rodgers was supposed to go 15 yards before hooking. But when he looked back and saw Tagge under pressure and about to run, he cut the route short.

Tagge saw Rodgers's number 20 jersey and released the ball, which was low to the ground. Rodgers went down to catch it. The gain was 11 yards and kept the drive alive with 4:37 remaining on the clock.

From there, the sequence of plays went like this:

first-and-10, OU 35-yard line—Jeff Kinney, 13 yards off left tackle (4:08)
first-and-10, OU 22-yard line—Rodgers, wingback reverse for seven yards
second-and-three, OU 15-yard line—Kinney, seven yards over left tackle (3:15)
first-and-goal, OU eight-yard line—Kinney, two yards pitch right

second-and-goal, OU six-yard line—Kinney, four yards over left tackle
third-and-goal, OU two-yard line—Kinney, two yards over left tackle

TOUCHDOWN!

21. After Jeff Kinney scored the winning touchdown with 1:38 remaining, Oklahoma ran four plays. On third-and-six from his own 23-yard line, Sooner quarterback Jack Mildren was sacked for an eight-yard loss. On fourth-and-14 from his 15-yard line, his desperation pass was knocked down. Who sacked Mildren on the third-down play? Who knocked down Mildren's final pass with 1:10 remaining? Extra credit: Kinney carried on the final play of the game for a three-yard gain. Officially, at what yard line did the Game of the Century end?

22. Nebraska had 59 rushing plays, with Jeff Kinney carrying on 31 of them. Kinney was the game's leading rusher. For how many yards did he rush, within 10?

23. Only one other Cornhusker carried more than four times during the game. He was Nebraska's second-leading rusher behind Jeff Kinney. Who was he?

24. Nebraska completed only six passes in 13 attempts during the Game of the Century. Johnny Rodgers caught five of the passes. Who caught the other pass?

25. Jerry Tagge threw 12 of Nebraska's 13 passes in the game. Who threw the 13th pass?

26. The Cornhuskers used one other I-back besides Jeff Kinney in the Game of the Century. He carried once for a two-yard gain. Name Nebraska's second-string I-back.

27. Oklahoma lost three fumbles in the game. All were forced by the same Cornhusker. Who was the Cornhusker? How many, if any, of the fumble recoveries preceded touchdowns?

28. How many fumbles, if any, did the Cornhuskers lose in the Game of the Century?

29. Nebraska punted five times in the game, for an average of 36.4 yards per punt. Who was the Cornhusker punter? Extra credit: What position did he play?

30. Last but not least—Nebraska ran the first play from scrimmage in the Game of the Century. It produced an eight-yard gain. What was that first play? Be specific.

Sooner Magic

Oklahoma was a source of considerable consternation for Tom Osborne early in his tenure as head coach. Osborne's teams lost their first five games and eight of their first nine against Barry Switzer's Sooners. In addition, Osborne's first coaching victory against Switzer in 1978 was offset by the fact that Nebraska had to play the Sooners again in a rare Orange Bowl rematch—and lost.

Several of the Oklahoma losses were even more frustrating because Nebraska appeared to be on its way to victory. In 1976, the Sooners scored with 38 seconds remaining to win 20–17. In 1980, they scored with 56 seconds remaining to win 21–17. And in 1986, they scored with six seconds remaining to win 20–17. After the 1986 game, in particular, there was much talk of "Sooner Magic."

Oklahoma's success against Nebraska had more to do with talented players than it did with magic, however. By the late 1980s, Osborne's Cornhuskers had broken Oklahoma's spell. Nebraska has won the last seven and nine of the last 10 games between the schools, which are in opposite divisions of the Big 12 Conference and won't play again during the regular season until the year 2000.

Quiz 45: No Illusions Here

1. In Nebraska's 20–17 loss to Oklahoma in 1976, all three of the Sooner touchdowns were scored by the same player. Who was that "proud" player with the famous first name?

2. In the 1976 game, Oklahoma began the winning drive at its own 16-yard line, trailing 17–13. The Cornhuskers had already begun talking of representing the Big Eight Conference in the Orange Bowl game. Oklahoma crossed midfield on one 47-yard halfback pass play. Name the halfback who threw the pass and the receiver who caught it.

3. The winning touchdown in 1976 was set up by a razzle-dazzle pass play known as the "hook-and-lateral." After catching the pass, the receiver pitched the ball to a teammate, who carried it to the Nebraska three-yard line. Who threw the pass? Who caught it? To whom did he pitch?

4. Nebraska began the 1976 season ranked number one by the Associated Press. But the Cornhuskers immediately dropped to number eight after being tied in their opener. The tie was one of only three during Tom Osborne's tenure as head coach. By whom was Nebraska tied to open the 1976 season? What were the other two ties under Osborne?

5. In Nebraska's 21–17 loss to Oklahoma in 1980 at Memorial Stadium in Lincoln, the winning touchdown was scored by a Sooner freshman running back from Miami, Florida. He later played wide receiver. Name him. Hint: His first name was George, but he was known by a nickname.

6. Nebraska's first touchdown in the 1980 game came on an 89-yard run, just over six minutes into the first quarter. As he finished off the run, this player turned and pointed at the Oklahoma defenders chasing him. Who made the run and taunted the Sooners?

7. The Cornhuskers had worked their way back to number four in the

Associated Press rankings before playing number nine Oklahoma in 1980. Nebraska had been as high as number three until an 18–14 loss in its final nonconference game at Memorial Stadium. To whom had the Cornhuskers lost earlier?

8. The week before the Oklahoma game in 1981, Turner Gill, the Cornhuskers' sophomore quarterback, suffered a lower-leg injury in a 31–7 victory against Iowa State. He was replaced by a senior who directed Nebraska to a 37–14 victory at Norman, Oklahoma. Who was this senior quarterback? Extra credit: Where was his hometown?

9. Nebraska made it two in a row against Oklahoma in 1982, winning at Memorial Stadium 28–24. The Sooners' attempt to work their magic failed. With less than a minute to go, a Sooner screen pass was intercepted and returned to the Oklahoma one-yard line, setting off a near riot with 26 seconds still showing on the clock. Who intercepted the pass? Who threw the pass?

It Ain't Over till It's Over

After the 28–24 victory against Oklahoma in 1982, Tom Osborne said, "I hope this win will help our fans get over their Oklahoma hang-up. I admit it's become a minor irritant to me, but I keep reading and hearing about how our players tighten up when they play Oklahoma. That's just not true. In the middle '70s, Oklahoma probably had the better overall talent. But that has changed since then."

Minor irritant? It was more than that. Nebraska's lack of success against Oklahoma in Osborne's first five seasons as head coach contributed to his serious consideration of Colorado athletic director Eddie Crowder's offer in December of 1978 of the job as head coach of the Buffaloes. Osborne would have to deal with more Sooner irritation from 1984 through 1987 before finally getting the upper hand.

10. The epitome of Sooner Magic occurred at Memorial Stadium in 1986, when number three–ranked Oklahoma avoided being upset, or tied, by number five Nebraska. The finish had to be seen to be believed. The Sooners tied the game at 17 on a 17-yard touchdown pass and extra-point kick with 1:22 remaining. Who threw the touchdown pass? Who caught it?

11. Oklahoma got the ball back but faced a third-and-12 at its own 45-yard line with 18 seconds remaining. The Sooners gained 41 yards on a pass play, for a first down at the Nebraska 14-yard line with nine seconds remaining. Who threw the pass? Who caught the pass? What Cornhusker had primary responsibility for covering the receiver in that situation?

12. Who kicked the winning 31-yard field goal for Oklahoma in 1986?

13. After the 1986 game, an Oklahoma defender said, "I don't think it was a comeback. It was just a matter of destiny. . . . I understood why we went for the tie. But tying in a war is no fun. A minute to go, we

had plenty of time." Identify this well-known Sooner, a two-time consensus All-American. Hint: After the NCAA prohibited him from playing in the 1987 Orange Bowl game, he wore a T-shirt on the sideline that said "National Communists Against Athletes." Extra credit: What was this controversial player's jersey number?

14. Oklahoma's success against Nebraska was a distant memory in the 1990s. The Cornhuskers won 37–0 in Lincoln in 1995, on their way to a second consecutive national championship. But they defeated Oklahoma even more decisively at Norman, Oklahoma, in 1996. What was that score?

Not Just Another Game

Mark Traynowicz was a three-year letterman and consensus All-America center at Nebraska in 1984. The Oklahoma game was special, he has said, even for Coach Tom Osborne. "He wouldn't let on that it meant more, but it went unsaid, I guess. It was always more tense. There was more anxiety on the coaching staff before the Oklahoma game," said Traynowicz, who was from Bellevue, Nebraska.

"As a kid growing up in Nebraska, it meant a lot to me," he said.

Osborne's first victory as head coach against the Sooners also ranks among the most memorable in Nebraska history. In his 1990 autobiography, *Bootlegger's Boy,* Barry Switzer writes that the 1978 team might well have been his best at Oklahoma and that the number one–ranked Sooners' 17–14 loss to Nebraska at Lincoln in mid-November "clearly cost us the national championship for that season."

Switzer coached the Sooners from 1973 to 1988. During those 16 seasons, his record was 157–29–4, a winning percentage of .837. That ranks fourth all-time among collegiate football coaches, behind Knute Rockne (.881), Frank Leahy (.864), and George Woodruff (.846). Switzer coached Oklahoma to three national championships and 12 Big Eight championships. And in games decided by three points or fewer, his record at Oklahoma was 17–1. Nebraska was responsible for that one.

Prior to the 1978 game, Osborne admitted his frustration in losing to Oklahoma five consecutive times. "Oklahoma wins because it has better players," he said. "But the obsession with Oklahoma is getting to me. It's getting pretty hard around here for fans to appreciate a good year without beating Oklahoma."

Quiz 46: "That Sand Sifting Through My Toes"

1. The victory against Oklahoma in 1978 earned Nebraska the right to represent the Big Eight in the Orange Bowl. Unfortunately for the Cornhuskers, they had to play Oklahoma again. The day of the 17–14 upset, however, no one knew that would happen. "When I saw that 1:16 left on the

clock and no more time-outs for Oklahoma, I could start to feel that sand sifting through my toes," said a jubilant Cornhusker defender. Who was the defender? Hint: He played monster back.

2. Name the players in Oklahoma's starting backfield in 1978. Which of the Sooner backs were from Texas? Extra credit: Identify the hometowns of the backs from Texas.

3. Although they all had recorded similar times in the 40-yard dash, which Sooner back was considered the fastest? Which one was considered the slowest?

4. Two of the starters in Nebraska's backfield were from Texas. Name them and their hometowns. Who were the Cornhuskers' other backfield starters? Where were they from?

5. How many times did Oklahoma fumble in the 1978 game? How many of the fumbles were lost?

6. The Sooners' final fumble came at the Nebraska three-yard line with 3:27 remaining in the game. What Oklahoma player fumbled? Who was credited with the tackle that forced the fumble? Who recovered the fumble? How many other fumbles did he recover in the game?

7. The player who made the tackle that forced the fumble was a fifth-year senior who started for only the third time in his Cornhusker career. He was told he would start at safety on the Thursday before the game because the regular starter was injured. Who was Nebraska's regular starting safety in 1978? He did not see action in the Oklahoma game.

8. Nebraska's leading tackler in the 1978 game was a walk-on linebacker from Arvada, Colorado. The Cornhuskers' defensive game plan was to be physical, and this linebacker was that. He was involved in 19 tackles. Afterward, he said of the Sooners, "As fast as they are, you better out-hit 'em because you sure as heck aren't going to out-quick 'em." Who was he?

9. Nebraska hadn't scored in the fourth quarter of a game against Oklahoma since the 1971 Game of the Century. The streak ended just over three minutes into the fourth quarter in 1978 when the Cornhuskers got their game-winning 24-yard field goal. Who kicked the field goal? Extra credit: What was the hometown of Nebraska's field goal kicker in 1978?

10. Even though this is discussed elsewhere, any mention of the 1978 Nebraska-Oklahoma game wouldn't be complete without mention of John Ruud's hit on Sooner punt returner Kelly Phelps. So consider this a mention. And by the way, what was Ruud's jersey number?

11. What Sooner said, prophetically, before the 1978 Nebraska game, "Ain't nobody going to stop us unless we stop ourselves." Hint: He scored both Oklahoma touchdowns in the game.

12. Senior Rick Berns scored Nebraska's first touchdown on a five-yard run. He led the Cornhuskers in rushing with 113 yards. He didn't score Nebraska's second touchdown, however. Who did? Extra credit: Berns may not

have been superstitious, but he did something before the 1978 Oklahoma game that could have been interpreted as superstitious. What did he do? Why?

13. Prior to the 1978 game, Oklahoma Coach Barry Switzer said of a player, "When he's not in there, it's like being in the Indy 500 with one of those high-powered A. J. Foyt cars and then halfway around the track switching to one of those mopeds." About whom was he talking?

14. On the Friday before the 1978 Nebraska-Oklahoma game, Cornhusker athletic director Bob Devaney was honored in a unique way. How was Devaney honored? Extra credit: What was Deveney's record as head coach in games against Oklahoma?

15. Nebraska assistant coach George Darlington said about one of the players he coached, he "would never harm a flea off the field. He'd never do anything illegal either, but you better not ever get in his way because he'll come at you with both barrels blazing." The player had a key role in the 1978 Oklahoma game. He was a senior in eligibility but a graduate student at the university. He almost always had a smile on his face, except in games. Name him.

16. "I hope it's this year, but if we don't beat them [the Sooners], we go across the field, shake their hands, and hope we don't get lynched come next Monday." Who made that tongue-in-cheek (sort of) statement before the 1978 Oklahoma game?

17. In the celebration that followed the 17–14 victory against Oklahoma in 1978, the goalposts at Memorial Stadium were torn down. When was the last time the goalposts at Memorial Stadium had been pulled down following a Cornhusker upset victory?

Answers

Quiz 42: Pregame Stretching

1. Drake, Grinnell, and Washington, Missouri, which was an original member of the MVIAA

2. Colorado left the Skyline Conference to join the MVIAA and make it the Big Seven.

3. Oklahoma State returned to the conference in 1957. In 1968, the official name became the Big Eight.

4. Jumbo Stiehm. The Sooner coach was Bennie Owen. The field at Memorial Stadium in Norman, Oklahoma, is named in his honor. Owen Field is probably more familiar to Nebraska fans.

5. Nebraska handed Oklahoma its only regular-season loss in 1971 and in 1978. The head coaches were Bob Devaney and Chuck Fairbanks in 1971

and Tom Osborne and Barry Switzer in 1978. And yes, Osborne and Switzer were assistant coaches at their respective schools in 1971.

6. Nebraska was number one and Oklahoma was number two in 1971, when Nebraska won 35–31 at Norman. Also, Nebraska was number one and Oklahoma was number two in 1987, when Oklahoma won 17–7 at Lincoln.

7. Lawrence McCeney Jones came from Oklahoma to replace Bible and direct the Cornhuskers to the 1941 Rose Bowl game. Jones was an army major. His nickname was "Biff."

8. Billy Vessels, 1952; Steve Owens, 1969; and Billy Sims, 1978. Sims was from Hooks, Texas; Vessels was from Cleveland, Oklahoma; and Owens was from Miami, Oklahoma.

Quiz 43: Check Your OQ (Oklahoma Quotient)

1. Minnesota

2. Dallas Dyer and Mick Tingelhoff were Kiffin's teammates at Lexington High School. Dyer and Tingelhoff lettered at Nebraska from 1959 through 1961. Tingelhoff played 17 NFL seasons.

3. Jerry Pettibone

4. Prentice Gautt was a Sooner senior in 1959.

5. Pat Clare is the chief of Nebraska's medical staff. He and Don Fricke earned Academic All-America honors in 1960, the first Cornhusker football players to be so honored.

6. Don Purcell and Nolte were teammates at Benson. Nolte finished at Omaha Westside High.

7. Jim Raschke became Baron von Raschke. He used the dreaded "claw" to subdue opponents.

8. Warren Powers coached Washington State and Missouri to upsets of Nebraska.

9. Max Martz's son Mike played basketball at Nebraska.

10. Mike Knox

Quiz 44: No Place Like Home, and Other Matters

1. Ken Jones, Oklahoma's starting right offensive guard, was from Burke High School in Omaha, where his football coach was Henry Amend. I mention Amend because he was my football coach, and English teacher, in high school. Since I'm writing this, I can include that information.

2. Eleven Oklahoma starters in the Game of the Century were from in-state: Emmert, Jensen, Bell, Crosswhite, Chandler, Hamilton, Selmon, Driscoll, Pope, Roach, and Shelly.

3. Lucious Selmon was followed by brothers Lee Roy and Dewey. They

were from Eufala, Oklahoma. Yes. Lucious lettered from 1971 to 1973. Lee Roy and Dewey lettered from 1972 to 1975.

4. Mildren and Harrison were teammates at Cooper High School in Abilene, Texas.

5. Jake Young, an All-American in 1988 and 1989, and Brahaney were both from Midland, Texas.

6. Glover, who won the Outland Trophy the next season as a senior, was in on 22 tackles.

7. Bell started in place of Joe Wylie.

8. Austin replaced injured senior Carl Johnson for the 1971 Oklahoma game. Austin was from Lincoln, where he played for Frank Solich at Southeast High School.

9. Jeff Kinney, McCook High School. Johnny Rodgers, Omaha Technical High School. Joe Blahak and Bill Kosch were teammates at Columbus Scotus High School.

10. The other consensus All-Americans in the 1971 game were Oklahoma's Greg Pruitt and Nebraska's Willie Harper, Larry Jacobson, and Johnny Rodgers. Rich Glover, Jeff Kinney, and Jerry Tagge also earned All-America honors in 1971. They were not consensus selections, however.

11. Nebraska was number two in the AP preseason rankings in 1971. But the Cornhuskers moved up to number one and stayed there after defeating Oregon 34–7 in their opener at Memorial Stadium. The Ducks' touchdown was scored by Bobby Moore on a seven-yard run. Moore's name is now Ahmad Rashad.

12. Nebraska won at Hawaii, 45–3. Oklahoma won at Oklahoma State, 58–14.

13. Jon Harrison

14. Kansas State scored 17 points, to Nebraska's 44, in the game immediately before the Oklahoma game. Other than Oklahoma, Colorado came the closest to the Cornhuskers in 1971, losing by 24 points, 31–7. The 31 points were the fewest by Nebraska in 1971. Nebraska shut out Missouri and Kansas back to back, 36–0 and 55–0, respectively. The Cornhuskers also shut out Iowa State, 37–0.

15. Sooner head coach Chuck Fairbanks and assistants Barry Switzer and Jimmy Johnson

16. Barry Switzer, Oklahoma; Jimmy Johnson, Oklahoma State; and Jim Dickey, Kansas State

17. Tom Osborne, Nebraska; Carl Selmer, Miami; Monte Kiffin, North Carolina State; Jim Walden, Washington State and Iowa State; and Warren Powers, Washington State and Missouri

18. Jimmy Johnson was a Razorback captain in 1964.

19. The Sooners rushed for 279 yards against Nebraska, their lowest to-

tal of the season. Pruitt was limited to 53 yards rushing. Cornell's Ed Marinaro finished the season as the nation's leading rusher.

20. Safety Bill Kosch, who normally played zone coverage, was assigned to cover Harrison man-to-man. In effect, Kosch was a cornerback during the game. Warren Powers was the secondary coach.

21. Larry Jacobson sacked Mildren on third down. Rich Glover deflected Mildren's final pass. Kinney carried for three yards on the final play of the game to the Sooner three-yard line.

22. Kinney rushed for 174 yards on his 31 carries, an average of 5.6 yards per carry.

23. Quarterback Jerry Tagge rushed for 49 yards on 17 carries.

24. I-back Jeff Kinney caught one pass.

25. Johnny Rodgers threw a pass intended for split end Woody Cox in the second quarter. It was incomplete.

26. Gary Dixon

27. Joe Blahak forced the fumbles, which were recovered, in order, by Jim Anderson at the NU 46-yard line; Rich Glover at the NU 27-yard line; and Bill Kosch at the NU 47-yard line. The fumbles recovered by Anderson and Kosch preceded Cornhusker touchdown drives in the first and third quarters.

28. Nebraska lost one fumble. Jerry Tagge fumbled and Lucious Selmon recovered at the OU 31-yard line with 11:47 remaining in the game. The Sooners drove 69 yards on 12 plays to take a 31–28 lead.

29. Senior Jeff Hughes, wingback or slot back

30. The first play from scrimmage was a pass from Jerry Tagge to Johnny Rodgers.

Quiz 45: No Illusions Here

1. Elvis Peacock scored the touchdowns, on runs of one, 50, and two yards.

2. Freshman Steve Rhodes made an outstanding catch of a Woodie Shepard pass.

3. Quarterback Dean Blevins threw the pass to Steve Rhodes, who pitched the ball to Elvis Peacock.

4. Unranked Louisiana State tied Nebraska 6–6 in Baton Rouge, Louisiana, to open the 1976 season. Osborne's first team in 1973 was tied by Oklahoma State at Stillwater, Oklahoma, 17–17. The number nine–ranked Cornhuskers and number 15–ranked Colorado played to a 19–19 tie at Boulder, Colorado, in 1991.

5. Buster Rhymes scored the touchdown. He described himself as "Buster, the man with luster."

6. Jarvis Redwine, who was disciplined by running backs coach Mike

Corgan during practice the next week for his indiscretion on the touchdown run. Iron Mike wouldn't tolerate such nonsense.

7. Bobby Bowden brought Florida State to Lincoln for the first time and won 18–14.

8. Mark Mauer directed the victory, completing 11 of 16 passes for 148 yards and one touchdown to earn Big Eight Offensive Player of the Week honors. He was from St. Paul, Minnesota.

9. Cornhusker defensive end Scott Strasburger intercepted the pass, thrown by Oklahoma's Kelly Phelps. Nebraska was assessed a 15-yard penalty for the behavior of its fans.

10. Quarterback Jamelle Holieway threw the pass to tight end Keith Jackson.

11. Again, the pass was from Jamelle Holieway to Keith Jackson. Nebraska's Broderick Thomas was covering Jackson. The coverage was good. But Jackson made a one-handed catch.

12. Tim Lashar

13. Linebacker Brian Bosworth wore jersey number 44.

14. Nebraska defeated the Sooners 73–21 in 1996.

Quiz 46: "That Sand Sifting Through My Toes"

1. Senior Jim Pillen

2. They all were from Texas. Quarterback Thomas Lott was from San Antonio. Halfbacks Billy Sims and David Overstreet were from Hooks and Big Sandy. And fullback Kenny King was from Clarendon.

3. Fullback Kenny King was considered the fastest. Quarterback Thomas Lott was considered the slowest. Lott's 40-yard dash time was listed at 4.5 seconds. King's was listed at 4.4 seconds.

4. Quarterback Tom Sorley was from Big Spring, and I-back Rick Berns was from Wichita Falls. Wingback Kenny Brown was from Cincinnati, Ohio. Fullback Andra Franklin was from Anniston, Alabama.

5. The Sooners fumbled nine times, six of which Nebraska recovered.

6. Billy Sims fumbled. It was his second lost fumble in the fourth quarter of the game. Cornhusker safety Jeff Hansen made the hit on Sims, along with cornerback Andy Means. Monster back Jim Pillen recovered the fumble. Pillen also recovered an earlier Sooner fumble.

7. Russell Gary missed the game. Jeff Hansen replaced him.

8. Bruce Dunning

9. Billy Todd, who was from Chandler, Arizona

10. John Ruud wore jersey number 46.

11. Billy Sims made the statement and scored on touchdown runs of 44 and 30 yards.

12. Isaiah Hipp scored the Cornhuskers' second touchdown, on an eight-

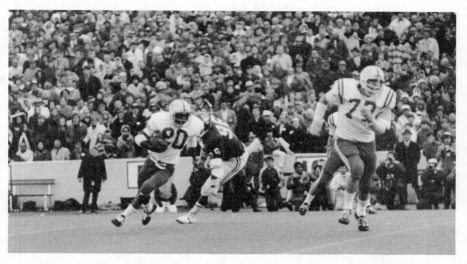

Johnny Rodgers runs away from Ray Hamilton as Dick Rupert prepares to block upfield.

(Photo Courtesy of UPI/CORBIS-BETTMANN)

yard run in the third quarter. Berns shaved off his mustache before the game. He had worn a mustache in two previous Oklahoma games, and Nebraska had lost those games. The 1976 loss was particularly frustrating, Berns said.

13. Switzer was talking about Sooner quarterback Thomas Lott. Switzer considered Lott the key to the success of Oklahoma's wishbone offense. In the Sooners' 38–7 victory against Nebraska at Norman, Oklahoma, in 1977, Lott rushed for 143 yards on 22 carries.

14. On the Friday before the game, the Nebraska legislature voted to change the name of the Nebraska Sports Complex to the Bob Devaney Sports Center. Devaney's record against Oklahoma was 5–6.

15. George Darlington coached the defensive ends in 1978. George Andrews was the player to whom Darlington referred. Andrews's nickname was "the Smiling Assassin."

16. Tom Osborne made the statement at the weekly meeting of the Extra Point Club.

17. The last time they had been torn down was after the 1959 upset of Oklahoma, ending the Sooners' 74-game conference unbeaten streak. That prompted Nebraska athletic director Bob Devaney to remark, "We ought to be able to afford new goalposts once every 20 years."

8

ALWAYS IN THE HUNT:

The Postseason Bowl Games

Bob Devaney once said, tongue in cheek, he didn't learn that Nebraska had lost the 1941 Rose Bowl game until well into his first season as head coach. His point was, Cornhusker fans had such reverence for the Rose Bowl experience that the 21–13 loss to Stanford was a secondary consideration.

The Rose Bowl was Nebraska's first. And when the bid was accepted, United Press International described it as the "biggest moment since the territory of Nebraska became one of the 48 states."

Acceptance of the bid, and its approval by the Athletic Board, the University Board of Regents, and the Big Six Conference, was front-page news in Nebraska, of course. The story even pushed a wire service report of Joseph Kennedy's resignation as United States ambassador to England to an inside page of the *Omaha World-Herald*. The celebration in Lincoln lasted the better part of 24 hours. The bid was accepted on a Sunday night, and Chancellor Chauncey Boucher canceled university classes the next day.

Then, as now, fans followed the Cornhuskers. Nebraska's allotment of 5,000 tickets quickly sold out. Nebraskans took pride in the state university's football program, which had endured only three losing seasons in its first 50 years—the 1940 season was number 51. The Rose Bowl certified that success.

Lawrence McCeney "Biff" Jones was in his fourth season as coach, after succeeding the popular D. X. Bible, who left after the 1936 season to become coach and athletic director at Texas. Though he was gone, Bible helped the Cornhuskers get to the Rose Bowl by coaching the Longhorns to a 7–0 victory against rival Texas A&M on Thanksgiving Day. Texas A&M had been undefeated and untied and among the candidates to play the Pacific Coast Conference champion in Pasadena on New Year's Day. Defeating A&M was "one of my most satisfying victories because it helped Nebraska," Bible said.

Minnesota, number one in the final Associated Press national poll, would have been the logical opponent for Stanford, which was ranked number two. But the Big Nine Conference, of which Minnesota was a member, didn't allow postseason play. Pennsylvania, the Ivy League champion, also was a possibility but reportedly wasn't interested and declined a bid. Stanford, as PCC cham-

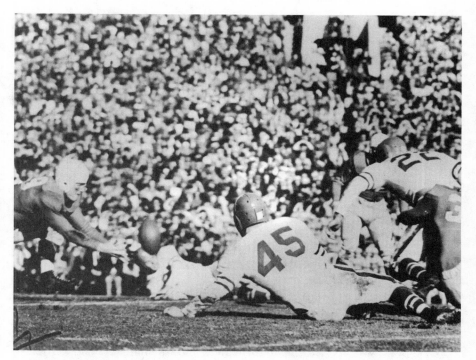

Rose Bowl 1941

(Photo courtesy of UPI/CORBIS-BETTMANN)

pion, participated in the process. Norm Standlee, the Indians' starting full-back, was a member of the selection committee.

Michigan and Tennessee were also ranked higher than Nebraska. But Michigan, like Minnesota, was prohibited from playing by the Big Nine Conference, and Tennessee had been unimpressive as the number two–ranked team in losing to Southern California 14–0 in the previous year's Rose Bowl game.

Nebraska, ranked number seven and the Big Six champion, had posted eight consecutive victories after an opening-game 13–7 loss at top-ranked Minnesota. The Cornhuskers had enjoyed national prominence since the Associated Press established its rankings in 1936, finishing number nine that first year, number 11 the second, and number 18 the fourth. They were as high as number six in both 1936 and 1937.

The lone exception was Jones's second season as head coach, 1938, when Nebraska suffered through the second-worst season in school history. Despite a 3–5–1 record, Roy "Link" Lyman, the Cornhuskers' line coach, predicted that Nebraska would be good enough to contend for a Rose Bowl berth by the time the sophomores in 1938 became seniors. Among the players to whom he referred were Roy Petsch, Harry Hopp, Royal Kahler, Robert Burress, Warren Alfson, Forrest Behm, and Ray Prochaska.

Nebraska traveled by train to Phoenix and set up headquarters at the Camelback Inn resort two weeks before the game to prepare for an undefeated and untied Stanford team that had made a dramatic turnaround under first-year head coach Clark Shaughnessy. The Indians, 1–7–1 the previous season, befuddled opponents with the help of Shaughnessy's innovative T-formation offense.

Shaughnessy had been the coach at the University of Chicago, which disbanded its football program after the 1939 season. He had developed his T-formation offense in discussions with George Halas of the Chicago Bears, who showed how devastating the offense could be in defeating the Washington Redskins 73–0 in the National Football League championship game in early December 1940.

Lyman and W. H. Browne, another Nebraska assistant, traveled to Chicago to learn what they could about the T formation by watching the Bears before the Cornhuskers left for Phoenix.

Glenn "Pop" Warner had predicted that Shaughnessy, the "Father of the Modern T Formation," would have difficulty winning at Stanford with the T formation. The offense just wasn't suited to the college game, according to Warner. Shaughnessy proved the legendary coach wrong.

Deception was a key to the T formation, and Shaughnessy had a 5-foot-9, 170-pound magician he could put in charge of it. Frankie Albert, a junior from Glendale, California, was the perfect T-formation quarterback. Albert was a two-time consensus All-American, and he finished in the top four in voting for the Heisman Trophy in both 1940 and 1941. He was fourth in the balloting in 1940 and third in 1941.

Based on the reports of Lyman and Browne following their trip to Chicago, the Cornhuskers developed a defensive plan that involved a five-man front with three linebackers, two halfbacks, and a safety. Warren Alfson, a guard on offense, dropped off the line of scrimmage and became a third linebacker on defense. Robert Cooper, a 6-foot, 176-pound freshman from Omaha, was "Frankie Albert" on the scout team.

Alfson was one of the first Cornhuskers to sit out a redshirt season. He played on the freshman team in 1936, then asked to be held out of the 1937 season because of the number of experienced players at his position. He lettered in 1938, 1939, and 1940, when he earned All-America recognition.

At age 25, Alfson was "older and wiser than the average," UPI reported. He had worked for three years following graduation from Wisner High School before enrolling at Nebraska.

The game was promoted as a battle between Nebraska's "muscle" and Stanford's "dexterity," even though the Indians had a slight weight advantage in their starting line. "Like most of the clubs in this section [of the country], where the temperature is too unpredictable to build a passing game, Nebraska depends chiefly on a savage ground game," a Nebraska newspaper reporter wrote before the game. "The Cornhuskers rely on power through the middle and the tackles for most of their gains."

Some things don't change. Nearly 60 years later, Nebraska coach Tom Osborne often echoed that in discussing his affinity for the run-oriented option offense that served his program so well.

Nebraska's travel roster included only one out-of-state player, a reserve, while Stanford's roster, which was larger, featured players from seven states besides California. Five of the 11 starters were from out of state, including end Fred Meyer and guard Dick Palmer, who were from Oklahoma City. Hugh Gallarneau, the Indians' 6-foot, 190-pound senior halfback, was from Chicago.

In addition, Nebraska didn't provide its athletes with any form of financial aid. "Times haven't been too good in Nebraska (the state hasn't had a real crop in 10 years)," a Lincoln newspaper reported. As a result, "more than half the players are working their way through school."

The Cornhuskers, who arrived in Los Angeles on the day before the game and made their headquarters at the Vista Del Arroyo Hotel, were given little chance against Stanford.

Nebraska's Rose Bowl Starters

Jones's first two units were regarded as being fairly equal in ability, and he used them interchangeably throughout the season. Harry Hopp was the team's leading rusher during the regular season, gaining 531 yards on 142 carries. Herm Rohrig alternated with him and was the team's leading passer, completing 23 of 46 with four interceptions. Walter Luther had the best rushing average, 5.51 yards per carry. He gained 369 yards on 67 carries. Vike Francis carried 75 times for 321 yards, a 4.28-yards-per-carry average.

The Cornhuskers' starting lineup included seven players from the group that Lyman had predicted two years before would be the basis for a Rose Bowl–contending team.

Left end	**Fred Preston**	6-3, 191, junior, Fairbury
Left tackle	**Royal Kahler**	6-3, 220, senior, Grand Island
Left guard	**Ed Schwartzkopf**	5-9½, 175, junior, Lincoln
Center	**Robert Burress**	5-10½, 188, senior, Omaha
Right guard	**Warren Alfson**	6-0½, 188, senior, Wisner
Right tackle	**Forrest Behm**	6-4, 200, senior, Lincoln
Right end	**Ray Prochaska**	6-3, 198, senior, Ulysses
Quarterback	**Roy Petsch**	6-1, 175, senior, Scottsbluff
Left halfback	**Harry Hopp**	5-11, 198, senior, Hastings
Right halfback	**Walter Luther**	6-0, 180, senior, Cambridge
Fullback	**Vike Francis**	6-2, 201, junior, Lincoln

The Game: Not So Rosy, 21–13

A crowd of some 92,000, the largest ever to watch a Nebraska game, was on hand at the Rose Bowl. The temperature was in the 90s. The Cornhuskers started quickly. Francis returned the opening kickoff 28 yards to the Nebraska 47-yard line and, six plays later, scored a touchdown from two yards out. He also added the extra-point kick, and the Cornhuskers led 7–0 before the late-arrivers were seated.

Stanford tied the score late in the first quarter on Gallarneau's nine-yard touchdown run and Albert's extra-point kick, but Nebraska's number two unit regained the lead in the second quarter on a 33-yard touchdown pass from Herm Rohrig to Al Zikmund. The extra-point kick was blocked, leaving the score at 13–7.

The touchdown was set up by Zikmund, who recovered an Albert fumble on the Stanford 33.

Again Stanford countered, on a 41-yard pass play from Albert to Gallarneau. Albert's extra-point kick made the score 14–13 at halftime. The Indians had all the points they would need to win.

Stanford's T-formation offense forced Nebraska's defense to spread out more than it had during the regular season. The Cornhuskers bent, allowing 277 yards rushing, but they refused to break. In the third quarter, Stanford drove to a first-and-goal at the Nebraska two-yard line and couldn't score.

After four plays, the Indians were still inches short of the end zone, and Nebraska took possession. Hopp punted out of trouble to Pete Kmetovic, who fielded the ball near the Cornhusker 39-yard line and, with the aid of several key blocks, scored an insurance touchdown. Nebraska also lost Francis for the remainder of the game as a result of the punt return. Francis suffered a hip injury somersaulting over a blocker in his attempt to stop Kmetovic. No one questioned the Cornhuskers' effort that day.

Quiz 47: It Must Have Been the Roses

1. Warren Alfson was one of two Cornhuskers who earned All-America honors in 1940. The other was inducted in the National Football Foundation Hall of Fame in 1988. Name him.

2. Stanford quarterback Frankie Albert's jersey number was distinctive. It was also the number Roy Petsch, Nebraska's starting quarterback, wore. What was Albert's jersey number?

3. Here's a toughie, just to see if you really know your Nebraska football history. As indicated earlier, Nebraska had only three losing records in its first 50 seasons. The Cornhuskers were 3–5–1 in 1938 and they were 2–3–1 under coach William G. Kline in 1918. What was Nebraska's other losing season to that time? What was the record? Who was the coach?

4. Identify the following Cornhuskers on the 1940 Rose Bowl team using their nicknames: a. the Senator, b. Hippity, c. Cowboy, d. Butch, e. King Kong.

5. The 1941 Rose Bowl game was played with the specter of World War II on the horizon. One of the Cornhuskers was killed in action during the war. Name him. Extra credit: Because of the war, the 1942 Rose Bowl wasn't played in Pasadena, California. Where was it played?

6. On the day after the Rose Bowl game, the Cornhuskers toured a movie studio. They were guests of a well-known actor of the time. The actor was from Filley, Nebraska, and was a graduate of Beatrice High School. Name this actor. Extra credit: What was the actor's real name?

7. Stanford coach Clark Shaughnessy played against Nebraska as a collegian. The team for which he played was a longtime Cornhusker nemesis. Jumbo Stiehm's first two teams in 1911 and 1912 lost only two games, one each season. And both were against the team for which Shaughnessy played. Name this team, which Nebraska last played in 1990. Hint: The Cornhuskers have a losing record against this team, despite winning the last 14 games between the schools.

8. One of the Cornhuskers who played in the 1941 Rose Bowl game had an older brother who was a Nebraska All-American and finished second in the Heisman Trophy voting in 1936. Name the Cornhusker on the Rose Bowl team and his brother. Hint: They played the same position.

9. In addition to the Rose Bowl, Nebraska has played in four other bowl games only once. Name the four bowls in which the Cornhuskers have made only one appearance. Extra credit: What was the year of each bowl? Who did Nebraska play? What was the score?

10. Nebraska has played in two bowl games in the same calendar year three times. Identify the years and the bowl games. Extra credit: Identify the opponents and the scores.

The Forgotten Bowl

Through the 1997 season, Nebraska had played in 17 Orange Bowl games, far and away the most of any bowls. The Cornhuskers' first trip to Miami was the most forgettable, coming as it did at the end of a 6–4 season in which they lost two of their final three games by a combined score of 76–14.

The season was Bill Glassford's next-to-last as the Cornhuskers' coach— 1954. Nebraska lost two of its first three games, then won four in a row before falling to Pittsburgh 21–7 in the Homecoming game and 55–7 to Oklahoma at Norman, Oklahoma. The Sooners were ranked number three nationally by the Associated Press, and they were Big Seven Conference champions. But the conference prohibited teams from participating in bowl games in consecutive seasons, so the runner-up got the bid.

Oklahoma had played in the 1954 Orange Bowl, defeating Maryland 7–0. So that meant the Big Seven runner-up got to represent the conference in Miami on New Year's Day. And Nebraska, which had completed the regular season with a 50–0 victory at Hawaii, was the runner-up.

The Cornhuskers were matched against a Duke team that was 7–2–1 and had edged out Maryland for the Atlantic Coast Conference championship. The Blue Devils were two-touchdown favorites, not only because of comparative records but also because of Nebraska's 48-point loss at Oklahoma.

Glassford tried his best to explain the loss at the Orange Bowl's kickoff luncheon at Miami's Bayfront Auditorium. "We played our best football of the year the first half; then it was like a bottle of olives," he told the audience. "After you get the first two out, the others come pretty fast."

Something more substantial than olives cascaded onto Nebraska at Norman, Oklahoma. The Cornhuskers came away bruised and battered. Dennis Korinek, a 5-foot-10½, 170-pound senior from Ulysses, Nebraska, suffered a broken jaw in a collision with Bo Burris, Oklahoma's All-America halfback.

In Nebraska's defense, Bud Wilkinson's Sooners were doing the same thing to every other opponent. Their victory against Nebraska was the 18th in what would become an NCAA-record 47 in a row. They shut out four of their 10 opponents in 1954 and never allowed more than two touchdowns.

Glassford's team may have lacked firepower. But it didn't lack heart. Despite the broken jaw, Korinek came back for the Orange Bowl. "I watched Nebraska train for the Rose Bowl game with Stanford in 1940," said Frank Johnson, a regent-elect from Lexington, Nebraska. "This squad has even more spirit."

The spirit didn't carry the Cornhuskers very far, however. Duke scored 14 points in the second quarter to take charge. Nebraska managed to cut the deficit to 14–7. But, as expected, it was no match for the Blue Devils. The final score was 34–7. Dick Becker wrote in the Lincoln *Sunday Journal and Star*, "Bowl pacts which won't allow a team to attend two years in a row were probably set back 10 years by this debacle which saw fans leaving at the start of the fourth quarter."

Despite the less-than-glamorous matchup, the game attracted what was then an Orange Bowl record crowd of 68,750. What that meant was, there were a lot of people leaving early. A headline in the Lincoln newspaper the next day read: UNWANTED HUSKERS DRAW FEW ORANGE BOWL CHEERS.

The game was expected to match a Nebraska offense that ranked in the nation's top 20 in rushing against a Duke passing attack. But the Blue Devils had little need to throw. They rushed for 288 yards while holding Nebraska to 84 yards on the ground and 110 yards total. Duke was seven of 13 passing for 82 yards and two touchdowns. Nebraska completed one of nine passes, with two interceptions.

"By today's standards, we weren't very good. But we were proud of what we did," Don Comstock said many years later. Comstock scored the Cornhuskers' lone touchdown in the game.

No Luck, for Starters

Willie Greenlaw, Nebraska's starting right halfback in the 1955 Orange Bowl game, was from Portland, Maine. The Junior Chamber of Commerce in Greenlaw's hometown announced that he was the first football player from Maine ever to compete in a college bowl game. The Portland Jaycees raised money to send Greenlaw's father to Miami for the game, and they sent a telegram to Greenlaw, wishing him luck.

The telegram included 2,800 signatures and was reportedly 100 yards long. Greenlaw suffered a hip injury on the second play of the game and was unable to return. That's how it went.

Nebraska opened the game this way:

Left end	**Andy Loehr**	5-11, 180, senior, Turtle Creek, Pennsylvania
Left tackle	**Bill Holloran**	5-11, 220, senior, Schuyler, Nebraska
Left guard	**Charles Bryant**	6-0, 175, senior, Omaha, Nebraska
Center	**Bob Oberlin**	6-1, 205, senior, West Allis, Wisconsin
Right guard	**Bob Wagner**	6-0, 190, senior, Lincoln, Nebraska
Right tackle	**Don Glantz**	6-0, 220, senior, Central City, Nebraska
Right end	**Jon McWilliams**	6-0, 180, junior, Sidney, Nebraska
Quarterback	**Dan Brown**	6-1, 173, senior, Sioux Falls, South Dakota
Left halfback	**Don Comstock**	6-0, 185, sophomore, Scottsbluff, Nebraska
Right halfback	**Willie Greenlaw**	5-11, 190, sophomore, Portland, Maine
Fullback	**Bob Smith**	5-10, 195, senior, Grand Island, Nebraska

Quiz 48: Maybe You Do Remember

1. A backup quarterback for Duke got in the 1955 Orange Bowl game and threw one pass, which was incomplete. He later played 18 seasons in the National Football League for the Philadelphia Eagles and Washington Redskins and was selected to the Pro Bowl five times. Name him.

2. Nebraska stayed at the Flamingo Hotel rather than the more exclusive hotels on Miami Beach, which discriminated against African-Americans. Three of the Cornhuskers who made the trip to Miami were African-American. Name them. Hint: Two of the three were starters.

3. Greenlaw started in place of the regular right halfback, who suffered a severe ankle sprain stepping off a curb in Lincoln not long before the team left on a six-hour charter flight for Miami. The player in question also was in the backfield with Bobby Reynolds as a junior in 1950. He returned to Nebraska to complete his eligibility after serving in the military. Name him.

4. One of the Cornhusker regulars in 1954 transferred to Alabama in 1955. He played two seasons for the Crimson Tide. "I tell people I helped

get [Bear] Bryant his job," the player joked years later. Bryant was hired by Alabama in 1958 and proceeded to turn around the program there. Name the player. Extra credit: His younger brother earned three football letters at Nebraska and was a starter as a senior on Bob Devaney's first team in 1962. Name the brother.

5. The Nebraska players elected cocaptains for the 1955 Orange Bowl game. Name them.

It Was the Socks

The Duke players suffered from blisters after their first practice in Miami. The Blue Devil trainers determined that the problem was socks. They had packed wool socks. University of Miami coach Andy Gustafson loaned Duke cotton socks, and the blisters disappeared.

Nebraska would get even with Gustafson for his kindness toward the opposition at the end of the 1962 season when it defeated his Hurricanes in the second, and last, Gotham Bowl 36–34.

The Cornhuskers also had some problems with socks during the bowl trip. Their equipment room was burglarized, and socks were stolen along with three helmets and five jerseys. As a result of the burglary, Nebraska's Rex Fischer wore argyle socks in practice until more athletic socks could be purchased.

6. Among those in the Orange Bowl record crowd of 68,750 was the vice president of the United States. Name him. Hint: He would become popular among Cornhusker fans.

7. On New Year's night, Omaha University defeated Eastern Kentucky 7–6 in the Tangerine Bowl in Orlando. Some Nebraskans left Miami immediately after the Orange Bowl game and went to Orlando for the Tangerine Bowl. Both head coaches in that game were former Cornhusker running backs. Name them. Extra credit: The Tangerine Bowl evolved into another bowl, in which Nebraska has played. What is the bowl? Whom did Nebraska play in it?

8. This is to see if you're paying attention. Where is Duke University located?

9. Andy Loehr, the Cornhuskers' starting left end in the 1955 Orange Bowl game, was from Turtle Creek, Pennsylvania. Two other Nebraska lettermen during Bill Glassford's tenure as head coach were from Turtle Creek. One was a quarterback, who lettered in 1951, 1952, and 1953. The other was a fullback, who lettered in 1951, 1952, 1955, and 1957. Name the two players. Extra credit: The high school coach of Loehr and the other two lettermen from Turtle Creek was a Cornhusker assistant for Glassford from 1950 to 1952. Name him.

10. Glassford played against Nebraska in the early 1930s for a nationally prominent eastern power. The Cornhuskers last played the school, against

Irving Fryar after the Cornhuskers' 31–30 loss to Miami in the 1984 Orange Bowl game. Tom Osborne elected to go for two points and the victory instead of settling for a tie. Fryar, a consensus All-American, was also the first player picked in the NFL draft.
(Photo Courtesy of *Huskers Illustrated*/Randy Hampton)

which they are 4–15–3 all-time, in 1958. Name the school at which Glassford played. Extra credit: Name his legendary coach there.

Playing to Win

During a news conference on the day before the 1984 Orange Bowl game, Tom Osborne was asked if he would play for a tie the following night against Miami if it meant winning a national championship. The consensus of opinion was, a tie might be sufficient to earn the title for Nebraska.

The Cornhuskers had, after all, been ranked number one throughout the season, and they might still have the nation's best record even with a tie—depending on what happened in the other major bowls.

"I suppose if it was fourth-and-20 with no time left and it was a question of doing nothing more than throwing a Hail Mary pass, I might try to kick a field goal," Osborne said after brief consideration. "But if it came down to a two-pointer or if I were inside their 10-yard line, I'd have to go for it."

He paused, than added, "That's a one-in-a-hundred question."

Whatever the odds, the situation arose the next night. And Osborne went for the two-point conversion, just as he said he would. Danny Noonan, a consensus All-American for Osborne in 1986, watched the drama unfold as a freshman. "I was standing pretty close to him, and there was no hesitation at all. He was just like: 'Okay, two-point conversion,'" Noonan would recall a dozen years later.

"There was no talking on the headphones to somebody in the press box, thinking: 'Let's discuss this.' Coach Osborne knew we were going for two, and everybody else did, all the players."

Mark Traynowicz, the Cornhuskers' junior center in 1983, snapped the ball on the play Osborne hoped would be successful. Quarterback Turner Gill's pass, intended for I-back Jeff Smith, was tipped by the Hurricanes' strong safety, and the ball glanced off Smith's shoulder pads, falling incomplete.

"We had practiced that play just about all season . . . there was no doubt about it," said Traynowicz. "Sure we were going for two. I'd do the same again. We went down there to win."

Given the circumstances, Osborne probably wouldn't have been criticized for accepting an almost certain tie. Nebraska had rallied from a 31–17 deficit in the fourth quarter, putting itself in a position to tie or win with a six-play, 74-yard drive that began with 1:47 remaining in the game. Smith capped the drive with a 24-yard touchdown run on fourth-and-eight, with only 48 seconds on the clock.

"I was just so tunneled into winning the game that it never occurred to me to kick the point," Osborne told reporters afterward. The next day, when the Associated Press and United Press International rankings were announced, Nebraska, as expected, was second behind Miami. But the Cornhuskers received four and a half first-place votes in the AP media poll and six first-place votes in the UPI coaches poll.

Dramatis Personae (Nebraska)

The Cornhuskers averaged 52 points per game in 1983, the second-highest single-season average in major college history at the time. It now ranks third. Nebraska's offense was nicknamed "the Scoring Explosion," and it featured three consensus All-Americans. The starters:

OFFENSE

Split end	**Ricky Simmons**	5-10, 175, senior, Greenville, Texas
Left tackle	**John Sherlock**	6-1, 260, senior, Omaha, Nebraska
Left guard	**Harry Grimminger**	6-3, 260, junior, Grand Island, Nebraska
Center	**Mark Traynowicz**	6-6, 260, junior, Bellevue, Nebraska
Right guard	**Dean Steinkuhler**	6-3, 270, senior, Burr, Nebraska
Right tackle	**Scott Raridon**	6-3, 280, senior, Mason City, Iowa

Tight end	**Monte Engebritson**	6-1, 220, senior, Hastings, Nebraska
Quarterback	**Turner Gill**	6-0, 190, senior, Fort Worth, Texas
Fullback	**Mark Schellen**	5-10, 225, senior, Waterloo, Nebraska
I-back	**Mike Rozier**	5-11, 210, senior, Camden, New Jersey
Wingback	**Irving Fryar**	6-0, 200, senior, Mount Holly, New Jersey

DEFENSE

Left end	**Bill Weber**	6-1, 210, junior, Lincoln, Nebraska
Left tackle	**Mike Keeler**	6-4, 245, senior, Omaha, Nebraska
Middle guard	**Mike Tranmer**	5-11, 230, senior, Craig, Nebraska
Right tackle	**Rob Stuckey**	6-3, 250, junior, Lexington, Nebraska
Right end	**Scott Strasburger**	6-1, 205, junior, Holdrege, Nebraska
Linebacker	**Mark Daum**	6-3, 230, junior, Dix, Nebraska
Linebacker	**Mike Knox**	6-3, 235, junior, Castle Rock, Colorado
Left cornerback	**Neil Harris**	6-1, 195, junior, Kansas City, Kansas
Right cornerback	**Dave Burke**	5-10, 195, junior, Layton, Utah
Monster	**Mike McCashland**	6-1, 195, junior, Lincoln, Nebraska
Safety	**Bret Clark**	6-2, 200, junior, Nebraska City, Nebraska

Quiz 49: The Unforgettable Finish

We'll start with some easy questions and work our way up.

1. Turner Gill's two-point conversion pass was deflected by the Hurricanes' rover, or strong safety. Name him. Extra credit: His jersey number was significant. What was it?

2. Miami's quarterback was a redshirted freshman. He was among a handful of Hurricanes who were not from Florida. Name him and his hometown. Extra credit: What was his jersey number?

3. Who was the Hurricanes' number two quarterback for the 1984 Orange Bowl game?

4. Miami head coach Howard Schnellenberger caused a stir with the manner in which he arrived at the Orange Bowl stadium for media day. How did he arrive?

5. How many consecutive games had Nebraska won before losing to Miami? What was the last team to defeat the Cornhuskers? What was the score?

6. Nebraska scored its first touchdown against Miami in the second quarter in an unconventional manner. How was the touchdown scored? Who scored it?

7. A senior player on Miami's roster for the 1984 Orange Bowl game was

a Cornhusker scholarship recruit and played for the freshman-junior varsity in 1979. He subsequently transferred in order to be close to home. He didn't play in the game. Name him.

8. Two Cornhusker defenders switched jerseys for the Orange Bowl game. Name them. Extra credit: What were their jersey numbers? Why did they switch jerseys?

9. Miami's first two touchdowns came on passes to the tight end. Name him. Extra credit: Name the players who scored the Hurricanes' other two touchdowns.

10. Nebraska trailed at halftime of the Orange Bowl 17–14. The Cornhuskers had trailed at halftime only once during the regular season. Against whom? What was the score?

What about Mike?

Mike Rozier carried 21 times for 138 yards in the first half of the 1984 Orange Bowl game. But the Cornhuskers' Heisman Trophy winner suffered a severe ankle sprain that sent him to the sideline after only four carries in the second half. He finished with 147 yards rushing.

"I wanted to win that game," Rozier said a dozen years later. "I've heard people say I threw the game, that Irving [Fryar] threw the game. What would I get out of throwing the game?"

Those who questioned Rozier and Fryar, who couldn't hold a potential touchdown pass, didn't know either player very well. Both were intense competitors. As was the case during the season, Fryar was Nebraska's leading receiver in the Orange Bowl game, with five catches for 61 yards.

Rozier had proven beyond the shadow of a doubt his ability to play with pain. There has never been a tougher running back at Nebraska than "Michael Heisman." The ankle injury that sidelined him for the second half didn't completely heal until his second professional season.

"People don't understand," he said. "I liked to compete, and win."

Jeff Smith, a junior from Wichita, Kansas, picked up the slack, rushing for 99 yards and two touchdowns on only nine carries in the second half. Smith redeemed himself, after losing a fumble inside the Miami five-yard line late in the third quarter. The Hurricanes recovered at their own one-yard line.

11. Rozier was the number one pick in the second United States Football League draft, two days after the 1984 Orange Bowl game. What USFL expansion team drafted him?

12. Although he didn't sign with the USFL, Fryar also was selected in the "open phase" of the short-lived league's second draft. What USFL team drafted Fryar?

13. Miami went into the 1984 Orange Bowl game ranked number four by UPI and number five by the AP. If not for at least one bowl game upset, and possibly two, the Hurricanes almost certainly wouldn't have been voted na-

tional champions. Only one team besides Nebraska was undefeated and un-tied going into the bowl games. That team was number two in both polls, and it lost. Name the team, the bowl game in which it lost, and the team to which it lost. Extra credit: What was the score?

14. Miami rode a 10-game winning streak into the Orange Bowl. The Hurricanes lost their season opener. To whom did they lose? Extra credit: What was the score of their loss?

15. Nebraska had serious fumble problems in the Orange Bowl game. How many times did the Cornhuskers fumble? How many of the fumbles did they lose?

16. If Osborne had opted to attempt an extra-point kick and settle for the tie, who would have made the attempt? He was not the number one place-kicker at the beginning of the season. Who was?

17. I-back Jeff Smith was the intended receiver on the two-point conver-sion attempt. Did Smith catch any passes during the 1983 season? Did he catch any passes in the Orange Bowl game?

18. Miami mounted an outstanding defensive effort against the Corn-huskers, who were second in the nation in total offense. Which team fin-ished the game with more total yards of offense?

19. The Orange Bowl celebrated its 50th anniversary with the 1984 game. How many times had Nebraska played in the Orange Bowl game prior to that?

20. When was Nebraska's first Orange Bowl victory? Against whom? What was the score?

We're Number One

Miami middle guard Tony Fitzpatrick, a 6-foot, 240-pound senior from St. Petersburg, Florida, missed most of the season because of an injury, but he re-turned to play in the Orange Bowl game against Nebraska. Fitzpatrick's com-ments the week before the game were insulting to the Cornhuskers, particularly the offensive linemen. After the failed two-point conversion, Fitz-patrick and Nebraska center Mark Traynowicz were face-to-face. Fitzpatrick raised his index finger, signifying number one. Traynowicz raised his middle finger, signifying, well . . . "I was so disgusted, I flipped him off," Traynowicz said several years later, recalling the scene, which was captured by a newspa-per photographer.

"I saw a flash out of the corner of my eye and thought: 'Oh no, that's going to be on the front page of the paper tomorrow.'" A print of the photograph now hangs in Traynowicz's office.

A Bowl by Any Name Would Smell As Sweet

Coach Bob Devaney and his assistants tried to persuade the players to vote against accepting a bid to play in the Gotham Bowl following the 1962 season.

Senior I-back Jay Sims proclaims Nebraska national champion in advance of the final *USA Today*/ESPN coaches' poll.

(Photo Courtesy of *Huskers Illustrated*/Scott Smith)

The bid wasn't extended until December 4, just 11 days before the game, which was to be played at Yankee Stadium in New York City.

The Gotham Bowl could hardly be described as prestigious. Its history extended only to the previous season, when the first game was played at the Polo Grounds in New York City. And it didn't have the feel of a postseason bowl game. Bowls were supposed to be played in warm weather.

Still, it represented a reward for the players, many of whom had endured a 3–6–1 record under Deveney's predecessor, Bill Jennings, in 1961. They were eager to play in a bowl game, regardless of its reputation or where it was held. They deliberated less than a minute before voting to accept.

Miami, their opponent, had already accepted a bid, after inexplicably turning down an opportunity to play in the more established (and warmer) Gator Bowl in Jacksonville, Florida. The Hurricanes were led by quarterback George Mira, a 5-foot-11, 182-pound junior from Key West, described by Lincoln sportswriter Dick Becker as "a magnificent moleskin matador."

Nebraska's trip to the Gotham Bowl was far from typical of what a bowl experience is now. The Cornhuskers didn't leave for New York City until the day before the game, and only then after waiting at the Lincoln Municipal Airport for Gotham Bowl officials to place a check in escrow to cover the team's travel expenses. If the check hadn't been deposited, Nebraska would not have made the trip.

The Cornhuskers were supposed to receive $35,000 for participating in the Gotham Bowl, which was a charitable event to benefit the March of Dimes— had there been a profit after expenses.

ABC paid a reported $15,000 for the right to telecast a delayed, abbreviated version of the game on its *Wide World of Sports* program later in the afternoon. The ABC affiliate in Omaha was able to reach an agreement to telecast the game live and in its entirety, but that covered only a limited area.

The game began at 11 A.M. local time so as not to conflict with the 2 P.M. kickoff of an American Football League play-off game between the New York Titans and the Houston Oilers at the Polo Grounds. Yankee Stadium, in the Bronx, and the Polo Grounds, in upper Manhattan, were located just across the Harlem River from each other. Gotham Bowl officials hoped fans might attend both games.

Neither had the benefit of much pregame publicity because of a strike that involved New York City's four largest newspapers. The Gotham Bowl optimistically predicted it would attract 30,000 fans, or twice the attendance for the previous year's game. Yankee Stadium would have been about half-full had the prediction come true. Youngsters were to be given free admission to the bleacher sections.

The paid attendance was 6,166, though that may have been inflated, in part because of the weather. The temperature, driven by a raw wind, never got above 20 degrees. The field was frozen, and by the second half, most of the players were wearing tennis shoes to avoid slipping.

Before the game, Devaney compared the situation to back-alley fights in which he was involved as a youngster growing up in Saginaw, Michigan. "There wouldn't be anyone watching there, either," he told the Cornhuskers. "But pride was still the most important thing in the world."

Whether or not Devaney's speech had an effect, Nebraska played for pride and produced the first bowl game victory in school history, 36–34. The scoring went like this:

First Quarter

NU—Bill Thornton one-yard run (run failed), 6:04 remaining   6–0

UM—Ben Rizzo 10-yard pass from George Mira (kick failed)   6–6

Second Quarter

UM—Nick Spinelli 30-yard pass from Mira (pass failed)   6–12
NU—Willie Ross 92-yard kickoff return (Rudy Johnson kick)   13–12
UM—Nick Ryder one-yard run (Ryder pass from Mira)   13–20
NU—Mike Eger six-yard pass from Dennis Claridge (Johnson kick) 20–20

Third Quarter

UM—John Bennett three-yard run (Bobby Wilson kick)   20–27
NU—Thornton one-yard run (Claridge run)   28–27

Fourth Quarter

NU—Ross one-yard run (Thornton run)   36–27
UM—Ryder one-yard run (Wilson kick)   36–34

Quiz 50: A Little Test on Bob and His Bowls

1. Nebraska played in the second, and last, Gotham Bowl game. What teams played in the first Gotham Bowl at the Polo Grounds in 1961? Who won? What was the final score?

2. George Mira completed 24 of 46 passes for 321 yards and two touchdowns against Nebraska in the Gotham Bowl. But he also threw two interceptions, the second at the Cornhusker 43-yard line with 1:09 remaining in the game. What Nebraska All-American intercepted that Mira pass?

3. Nebraska's first interception also came in the fourth quarter and set up what proved to be the winning touchdown. Who made that interception? Hint: The Cornhusker in question had played only offense on a regular basis until the final regular-season game against Oklahoma.

4. The Gotham Bowl ended in a curious way, by current standards. Cornhusker quarterback Dennis Claridge was involved in the game's final play. What was the play?

5. Nebraska was one of three Big Eight teams to play in bowl games after the 1962 season. It was the first time in conference history for three teams to do so. What other Big Eight teams played in bowls? Extra credit: In what bowls did they play? Whom did they play? What were the scores?

Like Father, Like Son—Sort Of

George Mira's son, George Mira Jr., was a freshman redshirt on the Miami team that defeated Nebraska 31–30 in the 1984 Orange Bowl game. The young Mira did not play quarterback, however. He was a 6-foot, 219-pound linebacker and earned four letters from 1984 through 1987.

6. Nebraska and Miami have played football against each other nine times, including four times during the regular season. In how many of those four games was Tom Osborne been Nebraska's coach? What was Osborne's record against the Hurricanes? Extra credit: Who was the Miami coach in each of the games Osborne coached against Miami?

7. Who was Miami's head coach the first three times the Hurricanes played Nebraska? Hint: He coached the Hurricanes in the Gotham Bowl game.

8. George Mira was the first in a long line of outstanding Miami quarterbacks. Mira was from Florida, but most of the great Hurricane quarterbacks have come from other states. Name the hometown of each of the following Miami quarterbacks: a. Jim Kelly, b. Bernie Kosar, c. Vinny Testaverde, d. Steve Walsh, e. Craig Erickson, f. Gino Torretta. Which have played against Nebraska?

9. What was Bob Devaney's record as a head coach in bowl games?

10. How many consecutive bowl-game victories did Devaney coach?

11. Devaney's first Orange Bowl victory came against Auburn, 13–7, after the 1963 season. Who scored the Cornhuskers' only touchdown, on an Orange Bowl–record run from scrimmage? How long was the run? Who kicked two field goals for Nebraska in the 1964 Orange Bowl game? Extra credit: The field goals were both record distances. How long was each field goal?

12. The outcome of the 1964 Orange Bowl game was in doubt until the final minutes. Auburn's quarterback passed the Tigers to a first down at the Nebraska 18-yard line. Nebraska held and took over on downs, however. John Kirby, Dick Callahan, and Bruce Smith all made big defensive plays for the Cornhuskers. Name Auburn's quarterback in the 1964 Orange Bowl game.

13. The finish might not have been so exciting if an 80-yard punt return for an apparent touchdown hadn't been nullified by an official's ruling that the returner had nicked the out-of-bounds line at the Nebraska 42-yard line. What Cornhusker returned the punt? Hint: He was a sophomore fullback from Cleveland, Ohio.

One of Devaney's Best

If Nebraska had won the 1966 Orange Bowl game, the Cornhuskers would have been the Associated Press national champions. They were undefeated and untied in 10 games during the regular season and took a number three ranking in both the AP and United Press International polls to Miami.

UPI's final poll was conducted before the bowl games, which meant Michigan State was its national champion. The AP national champion wasn't determined until after the bowls, however.

On New Year's Day of 1966, number one–ranked Michigan State lost to UCLA in the Rose Bowl, 14–12, and number two–ranked Arkansas lost to LSU in the Cotton Bowl, 14–7, leaving the top spot open for the winner of the Orange Bowl game between Nebraska and number four–ranked Alabama.

An estimated 13,000 Cornhusker fans among the 74,214 watched in disbelief as the smaller but quicker Crimson Tide broke out to a 24–7 halftime lead. The game was more lopsided than the 39–28 final score indicated. Alabama was the AP national champion despite an early-season loss and tie.

14. Alabama's first two plays from scrimmage set Nebraska's defense back on its heels. The Crimson Tide completed tackle-eligible passes for gains of 10 and 17 yards. The Alabama tackle who caught the passes was a converted halfback. What was his name?

15. The Alabama quarterback completed 20 of 28 passes in the game for an Orange Bowl–record 296 yards and two touchdowns. The 20 completions also were a record. Identify the Crimson Tide quarterback. Extra credit: He also started the 1965 Orange Bowl against Texas, but was replaced after Alabama fell behind 14–0. The replacement rallied the Crimson Tide with a pair of touchdown passes. But Texas won 21–17. Name the replacement quarterback.

16. Nebraska's quarterback in the 1966 Orange Bowl game tied a record by throwing three touchdown passes, two of them to the same receiver, which also tied a record. Name the Cornhusker quarterback and receiver. Extra credit: An Alabama receiver caught two touchdown passes as well. His totals for the game were nine catches for a record 159 yards. Name him.

17. Nebraska and Alabama played a rematch in the 1967 Sugar Bowl. The Crimson Tide led 24–0 at halftime and 27–0 after three quarters on the way to a 34–7 victory. Again, Alabama used the forward pass to befuddle the Cornhuskers. The Crimson Tide's first play from scrimmage was a 45-yard pass that carried to the Nebraska 27-yard line. Who threw the pass? Who caught it?

18. Nebraska's quarterback in the 1967 Sugar Bowl completed 21 of 34 passes for 201 yards and one touchdown. Name him. Extra credit: The uncle of a Cornhusker Outland Trophy winner came off the bench to play quarterback late in the 1967 Sugar Bowl. Name him and his nephew.

19. After two seasons of staying home from bowl games, Nebraska played Georgia in the 1969 Sun Bowl. The Cornhuskers took an 18–0 first-quarter lead on the strength of four field goals. Name the placekicker who made the four field goals, from distances of 50, 32, 42, and 37 yards.

20. Nebraska defeated Notre Dame 40–6 in the 1973 Orange Bowl game, Bob Devaney's last as head coach. Johnny Rodgers played I-back in the game and set Orange Bowl records for touchdowns and points. How many touchdowns and how many points did Rodgers score?

21. Rodgers also threw a touchdown pass in the 1973 Orange Bowl game. To whom did he throw the I-back pass? Extra credit: How long was the pass play?

22. Name Notre Dame's quarterback in the 1973 Orange Bowl game.

23. Nebraska surprised the Fighting Irish with its first play from scrimmage. What was the play?

24. The Cornhuskers gained 560 yards against Notre Dame. The interior offensive line often is overlooked in such performances. Name the starters in Nebraska's offensive interior for the 1973 Orange Bowl game. Hint: Two earned All-America honors, though not necessarily in 1972.

25. The Notre Dame linebackers coach in the 1973 Orange Bowl was an assistant on Bob Deveney's staff at the Gotham Bowl game in 1962. Name him.

Quiz 51: Osborne's Bowls, Briefly

1. Nebraska won the 1974 Cotton Bowl, Tom Osborne's first as head coach, defeating Texas 19–3. The Cornhuskers' first score, a 24-yard field goal, was set up by a 65-yard fumble return. Who returned the fumble? Who kicked the field goal, the first of two? Extra credit: What Longhorn running back fumbled the ball?

2. The Cornhuskers' touchdowns in the 1974 Cotton Bowl game also were set up by the defense. The first followed a 41-yard return of a blocked field goal attempt. The second was set up by a fumble recovery. Who returned the blocked field goal attempt? Who recovered the fumble?

3. Dave Humm struggled in his final game at Nebraska, the Sugar Bowl on December 31, 1974. Humm completed two of 12 passes for 16 yards with four interceptions before Osborne replaced him. Who replaced Humm and led the Cornhuskers to a 13–10 victory against Florida?

4. What Cornhusker won the most valuable player award in both the 1974 Cotton Bowl and the 1974 Sugar Bowl? What position did he play in each game? Where was he from?

5. Nebraska scored all 13 of its points in the fourth quarter of the 1974 Sugar Bowl. The last seven points were by a placekicker—an extra point and two field goals. Name the placekicker.

6. Quarterback Vince Ferragamo had to sit out the first game of the 1975 season because of something that occurred at the 1974 Sugar Bowl game. What occurred?

7. Ferragamo started the 1975 Fiesta Bowl, a 17–14 loss against Arizona State. He threw an interception on the first series of the game, however, and was replaced. Who replaced him?

8. Who kicked Arizona State's winning field goal in the 1975 Fiesta Bowl game?

9. Who recovered a fumble with 1:34 remaining in the fourth quarter to preserve Nebraska's 27–24 victory against Texas Tech in the 1976 Astro-Bluebonnet Bowl?

10. The Cornhuskers defeated North Carolina 21–17 in the 1977 Liberty Bowl to give Osborne a 4–1 bowl record. Whose picture was on the cover of the official game program?

11. Osborne coached his first victory against Oklahoma in 1978, a 17–14 upset of the top-ranked Sooners at Memorial Stadium. The Orange Bowl put a damper on that victory by setting up a rematch on New Year's night. Oklahoma won the rematch 31–24. The game wasn't that close, however. Nebraska scored a touchdown on the final play of the game. The play was a pass. Who threw it? Who caught it? Extra credit: How long was the pass?

12. Houston defeated Nebraska in the 1980 Cotton Bowl 17–14. The winning touchdown was scored with 12 seconds remaining, on a six-yard pass play. Who threw it? Who caught it?

13. Clemson limited Nebraska to 256 total yards in winning the 1982 Orange Bowl game 22–15. The Tigers' defense included a 6-foot-3, 295-pound freshman middle guard from Aiken, South Carolina, who wore jersey number 66 and had a unique nickname. Identify him and his nickname. The difference in the game was three field goals, kicked by a freshman from Anambra, Nigeria. Name him. Clemson's head coach played for Bear Bryant at Alabama. Name him.

14. Nebraska took a 7–3 lead midway through the first quarter of the 1982 Orange Bowl game on a 25-yard touchdown pass. Who threw the pass? Who caught it?

15. As long as we're name-dropping, LSU's starting right defensive tackle in the 1983 Orange Bowl game against Nebraska had a successful NFL career, mostly with the New York Giants. Identify him. Hint: He was no "Hollywood Square." He was from Franklin, Louisiana.

16. Nebraska might have won the national championship if two other bowl games had come out differently. As it was, the Cornhuskers finished number three in both polls, the same as they began New Year's Day. What were the two bowl outcomes that needed to be different?

17. The Cornhusker chosen as MVP of the 1985 Sugar Bowl game was awake most of the night before, suffering from the flu. It hit, full force, after he returned to the hotel with his teammates following the traditional night-before-the-game movie. Identify him. Hint: He started the first five games of the season but didn't start again until the Sugar Bowl, in part because of a shoulder injury. Extra credit: Who replaced him in the starting lineup from the sixth game on?

18. What player led Nebraska in rushing in both the 1985 Sugar Bowl victory against LSU and the 1986 Fiesta Bowl loss against Michigan? Did he rush for 100 or more yards in either game?

19. Two of Michigan's three touchdowns in the Wolverines' 1986 Fiesta Bowl game victory against Nebraska were scored by a player who went on to a career in the NFL. He's still playing. The touchdowns against Nebraska came on runs of one and 23 yards. Name him.

20. LSU's two touchdown drives against Nebraska in the 1987 Sugar Bowl game were the same length. The first came on the Tigers' first possession. The second came on their last possession. In between, the Cornhuskers scored 30 points to win handily. How long were LSU's two drives?

21. A 15-yard touchdown pass on fourth-and-goal with 3:07 remaining in the game gave Florida State a 31–28 victory against Nebraska in the 1988 Fiesta Bowl. Name the Seminole who threw the pass and the Seminole who was wide open in the end zone and caught it. Nebraska might have pulled out the victory if a 56-yard pass play hadn't been called back because of a penalty. Who threw that pass? Who caught it? For what were the Cornhuskers penalized? Extra credit: What well-known professional athlete was in the Seminole secondary?

22. Miami defeated Nebraska in the 1989 and 1992 Orange Bowl games. The Hurricanes shut down Nebraska's running game in both. Within 10, for how many yards did the Cornhuskers rush in each of those games? Extra credit: Who was Nebraska's leading rusher in each?

23. Florida State's quarterback set what was then a record for passing yards against Nebraska in the Seminoles' 41–17 victory in the 1990 Fiesta Bowl game. He completed 25 of 40 passes for 422 yards and five touchdowns. Name him. Extra credit: Who held the record he broke?

24. Florida State led the nation in total offense in 1993. How many touchdowns did the Seminoles score in their 18–16 victory against Nebraska in the 1994 Orange Bowl game? Who was the Cornhuskers' leading rusher in the game? Within five yards, how many did he have?

25. Florida State's Charlie Ward won the Heisman Trophy in 1993. But Nebraska's sophomore quarterback Tommie Frazier played him to a standoff in the 1994 Orange Bowl game. Which quarterback had the most yards of total offense in the game?

Answers

Quiz 47: It Must Have Been the Roses

1. Forrest Behm, who played alongside Alfson at tackle, also earned All-America recognition.

2. Albert wore jersey number 13, which proved to be bad luck for the Cornhuskers.

3. In 1899, A. Edwin Branch's team was 1–7–1. The only victory was against Drake at Des Moines, 12–6. Nebraska also tied the Kansas City

(Photo Courtesy of *Huskers Illustrated*)

Medics 6–6 and defeated Lincoln High School 6–0 in an exhibition at the beginning of the season. If you answered any part of this question correctly, you're a Cornhusker fanatic—even though Nebraska's football teams weren't called the Cornhuskers until 1900.

4. a. Ray Prochaska, b. Harry Hopp, c. Roy Petsch, d. Walter Luther, e. Royal Kahler

5. Walter "Butch" Luther was killed during World War II, a sad footnote to the Rose Bowl experience. On the night before the Cornhuskers boarded the train for Phoenix, Luther was engaged in a ceremony at the sorority house of his fiancée. The 1942 Rose Bowl game between Oregon State and Duke was played on the other side of the United States, in Durham, North Carolina. Duke is located in Durham.

6. Robert Taylor was from Filley. His real name was Spangler Arlington Brugh.

7. Shaughnessy played at Minnesota. In 1913, Stiehm's team beat the Gophers 7–0.

8. Vike Francis followed his brother, Sam, as a Cornhusker fullback.

9. Gotham Bowl, 1962, NU 36, Miami 34; Astro-Bluebonnet Bowl, 1976, NU 27, Texas Tech 24; Liberty Bowl, 1977, NU 21, North Carolina 17; and Citrus Bowl, 1991, Georgia Tech 45, NU 21.

10. January 1, 1974, Cotton Bowl: NU 19, Texas 2. December 31, 1974, Sugar Bowl: NU 13, Florida 10. January 1, 1980, Cotton Bowl: Houston 17, NU 14. December 27, 1980, Sun Bowl: NU 31, Mississippi State 17. Janu-

ary 2, 1996, Fiesta Bowl: NU 62, Florida 24. December 31, 1996, Orange Bowl: NU 41, Virginia Tech 21.

Quiz 48: Maybe You Do Remember

1. Sonny Jurgensen was a backup to Blue Devil starter Jerry Barger.

2. Charles Bryant, Jon McWilliams, and Sylvester Harris, who was from Kansas City, Missouri. Bryant was all over the field making tackles during the second half of the Orange Bowl game.

3. Ron Clark a 5-11, 175-pound senior from Ravenna, Nebraska, was the regular right halfback in 1954.

4. Don Comstock transferred to Alabama, with Glassford's help, following the 1954 season. Bill Comstock, his brother, lettered as an end at Nebraska in 1960, 1961, and 1962.

5. Bob Wagner and Bob Smith served as captains for the bowl game.

6. Richard Nixon, who came to Lincoln to proclaim Nebraska national champions for 1970

7. Lloyd Cardwell coached Omaha University, which is now the University of Nebraska–Omaha. Glenn Presnell coached Eastern Kentucky. The Tangerine Bowl became the Citrus Bowl. The Cornhuskers lost to Georgia Tech 45–21 in the 1991 Citrus Bowl.

8. Durham, North Carolina, where the 1942 Rose Bowl game was played because of World War II

9. Johnny Bordogna was the quarterback. George Cifra was the fullback. John Machisic, a senior guard in 1952, also was from Turtle Creek. He did not letter, according to Nebraska's records. Ralph Fife coached Loehr, Bordogna, Cifra, and Machisic in high school before coming to Nebraska.

10. Glassford lettered at Pittsburgh in 1934, 1935, and 1936. The Panthers defeated Nebraska in each of those seasons. Glassford's coach there was Dr. Bain "Jock" Sutherland.

Quiz 49: The Unforgettable Finish

1. Ken Calhoun, a junior for Titusville, Florida, tipped Gill's pass. He wore jersey number 2.

2. Bernie Kosar was from Youngstown, Ohio. He wore jersey number 20.

3. Okay, this was a trick question. Kyle Vanderwende, a sophomore from Palm Beach Gardens, Florida, was Kosar's backup for the Orange Bowl. But you're right, Vinnie Testaverde was also on the team. He was redshirted, however. Vanderwende played only sparingly. Kosar took most of the snaps. Miami had several talented freshmen, among them Jerome Brown, Daniel Stubbs, Melvin Bratton, Rick Tuten, Brian Blades, and Alonzo Highsmith.

Brown was the second-string defensive right tackle, behind sophomore Kevin Fagan, and Highsmith was Albert Bentley's backup at fullback.

4. Schnellenberger traveled by helicopter, which landed on the field at the stadium. He explained that the helicopter enabled him to avoid the holiday traffic jams in the metropolitan area. Right.

5. The Hurricanes snapped Nebraska's 22-game winning streak. The Cornhuskers hadn't lost since the third game of the 1982 season, when Penn State beat them at State College, Pennsylvania, 27–24.

6. Cornhusker guard Dean Steinkuhler ran 19 yards with an intentional fumble by quarterback Turner Gill for a touchdown. The NCAA made the "fumblerooskie" illegal following the 1992 season.

7. Jimmy Austin, who was from Miami

8. Monster Mike McCashland and cornerback Dave Burke traded jerseys. McCashland wore number 2 throughout the season. Burke wore number 33. In the Orange Bowl, those numbers were reversed. Nebraska was trying to confuse Kosar's reads, which were based on the positioning of the rover. "Obviously, it didn't make any difference," Nebraska assistant George Darlington said afterward.

9. Glenn Dennison. Albert Bentley and Alonzo Highsmith each ran for a touchdown.

10. Nebraska trailed Oklahoma State at halftime in Stillwater, Oklahoma, 10–7 but won 14–10.

11. The Pittsburgh Maulers made Rozier the first pick.

12. The Chicago Blitz drafted Fryar.

13. Coach Fred Akers's number two–ranked Texas Longhorns were 11–0 going into the Cotton Bowl game against Georgia. The Bulldogs won 10–9. Auburn, which defeated Michigan 9–7 in the Sugar Bowl to finish 11–1, was number three in the final rankings, followed by Georgia and Texas. Miami also was ranked behind 10–1 Illinois going into the bowls. But the Illini lost to UCLA in the Rose Bowl 45–9. This illustrates the likelihood that Nebraska could have been the national champion with a tie. The Cornhuskers would have been 12–0–1. Every other team would have had at least one loss. Miami would have been 10–1–1.

14. Miami lost its opener in 1983 to bitter rival Florida 28–3.

15. Nebraska fumbled six times against Miami but lost only the one by Smith.

16. Scott Livingston, a junior from Lakewood, Colorado, would have been called on to attempt the extra-point kick. Livingston replaced Dave Schneider as the number one placekicker midway through the season.

17. Smith caught six passes, two for touchdowns, in 1983. He did not catch a pass in the bowl game.

18. Nebraska had a slight edge in yardage, 459 to 430. The Cornhuskers

ran 86 plays to 63 for Miami, and they had an advantage in time of posses-sion of more than four minutes.

19. The Cornhuskers had played in nine Orange Bowl games. The 1984 game was their 10th.

20. Nebraska's first Orange Bowl victory was on January 1, 1964, against Auburn, 13–7.

Quiz 50: A Little Test on Bob and His Bowls

1. Baylor defeated Utah 24–9 in the first Gotham Bowl.

2. Bob Brown, a linebacker on defense and a guard on offense, inter-cepted the pass.

3. Dennis Claridge intercepted the first Mira pass.

4. Nebraska failed to run out the clock. Claridge punted, but Miami didn't return it and time elapsed.

5. Oklahoma lost to Alabama 17–0 in the Orange Bowl. Missouri de-feated Georgia Tech 14–10 in the Bluebonnet Bowl. Nebraska's only losses in 1962 were against Oklahoma and Missouri.

6. Osborne coached regular-season victories against the Hurricanes in 1975 and 1976. Both games were played in Lincoln, with the Cornhuskers winning 31–16 and 17–9. Former Nebraska assistant Carl Selmer was the Miami coach in each of those games. Osborne's record against Miami was 3–3. In addition to the two regular-season games, Osborne coached in four Orange Bowl games against Miami: a 31–30 loss, 1984 Orange Bowl, Howard Schnellenberger; a 23–3 loss, 1989 Orange Bowl, Jimmy Johnson; a 22–0 loss, 1992 Orange Bowl, Dennis Erickson; and a 24–17 victory, 1995 Orange Bowl, Erickson. Bill Glassford was the Cornhuskers' coach when the teams played in 1951 and 1953. The Cornhuskers lost the first game in the series at Miami 19–7. They won the second at Memorial Stadium 20–16.

7. Andy Gustafson was the head coach at Miami from 1948 to 1963. When he retired as coach following the 1963 season, the Hurricanes tried to hire Bob Devaney as his replacement.

8. a. East Brady, Pennsylvania, did not play against Nebraska; b. Youngstown, Ohio, played against Nebraska in 1984 Orange Bowl; c. El-mont, New York, did not play against Nebraska; d. St. Paul, Minnesota, played against Nebraska in 1989 Orange Bowl; e. West Palm Beach, Florida, did not play against Nebraska; f. Pinole, California, played against Nebraska in 1992 Orange Bowl

9. Devaney was 7–3 in bowl games. One of the seven victories came when he was the head coach at Wyoming. The Cowboys defeated Hardin-Simmons 14–6 in the 1958 Sun Bowl.

10. Devaney coached Nebraska to victories in his final four bowl games.

11. Quarterback Dennis Claridge ran 68 yards for a touchdown on the game's second play from scrimmage, before the late arrivers in a crowd of 72,647 had settled into their seats. Bob Brown and Lloyd Voss made key blocks on the play. Dave Theisen kicked a 31-yard field goal to break the Orange Bowl record of 22 yards, set by Tennessee's Bowden Wyatt in 1939. Then Theisen kicked a 36-yarder.

12. Jimmy Sidle

13. Frank Solich, who replaced Osborne as head coach in 1998, returned the punt. Bob Hohn made a key block to clear the way.

14. Jerry Duncan

15. Steve Sloan quarterbacked Alabama to the 39–28 victory against Nebraska. In the previous year's Orange Bowl, Sloan was replaced by Joe Namath, who directed the Crimson Tide comeback.

16. Nebraska quarterback Bob Churchich completed 12 of 17 passes for 232 yards and three touchdowns, two of them to end Tony Jeter. Alabama's Ray Perkins also caught two touchdown passes.

17. Ray Perkins caught the pass from Ken Stabler. Perkins had seven receptions for 178 yards and one touchdown in the game. Stabler was 12 of 18 passing for 148 yards.

18. Bob Churchich again was the Cornhuskers' starting quarterback for the 1967 Sugar Bowl. He was replaced late in the game by Wayne Weber, the uncle of Outland Trophy winner Zack Wiegert. Weber attempted four passes, one of which was complete. The other three were intercepted. Churchich also threw two interceptions against the swift, opportunistic Crimson Tide defense.

19. Paul Rogers

20. Rodgers scored four touchdowns, three by running and one on a pass reception, for 24 points.

21. Rodgers threw a touchdown pass to split end Frosty Anderson for 52 yards.

22. Tom Clements

23. Notre Dame wasn't expecting Rodgers to play I-back. The first play was a pitch to Rodgers, who gained 13 yards. He finished with 81 yards rushing on 15 carries and three receptions for 71 yards.

24. Daryl White and Marvin Crenshaw, the tackles, were All-Americans, White in 1972 and 1973, Crenshaw in 1974. Mike Beran and Dan Anderson were the guards. Doug Dumler was the center.

25. George Kelly

Quiz 51: Osborne's Bowls, Briefly

1. Steve Manstedt returned the Roosevelt Leaks fumble to set up Rich Sanger's field goal.

2. Safety Bob Thornton made the return. Middle guard John Bell recovered the fumble.

3. Terry Luck, a 6-foot-3, 212-pound junior from Fayetteville, North Carolina, replaced Humm and promptly directed a 99-yard touchdown drive, culminating in Monte Anthony's two-yard run.

4. Tony Davis was chosen as the MVP in Osborne's first two bowl games. Davis was an I-back as a sophomore in 1973. He was moved to fullback in 1974. He was from Tecumseh, Nebraska.

5. Mike Coyle

6. Ferragamo, a redshirt transfer from California, made the trip to New Orleans for the Sugar Bowl and suited up for the game, in violation of NCAA rules regarding redshirts.

7. Terry Luck replaced Ferragamo, as he had replaced Humm in the 1974 Sugar Bowl. Luck completed 12 of 22 passes for 90 yards against the Sun Devils.

8. Danny Kush, the son of Coach Frank Kush, kicked the 29-yarder with 4:50 remaining.

9. Reg Gast, a junior defensive end from Lincoln

10. Elvis Presley is pictured in a military uniform. The Liberty Bowl is played in Memphis, Tennessee.

11. Tom Sorley threw a two-yard touchdown pass to tight end Junior Miller.

12. Terry Elston threw the six-yard pass to Eric Herring.

13. William "the Refrigerator" Perry was Clemson's starting middle guard in the 1982 Orange Bowl game. Donald Igewbuike was the Tigers' placekicker. Danny Ford was Clemson's head coach.

14. I-back Mike Rozier threw the pass to wingback Anthony Steels.

15. Leonard Marshall. He was no relation to *Hollywood Squares* host Peter Marshall.

16. Number one Penn State, which handed Nebraska its only defeat, won against Georgia 27–23 in the Sugar Bowl, and number two Southern Methodist defeated Pittsburgh 7–3 in the Cotton Bowl.

17. Senior quarterback Craig Sundberg completed 10 of 15 passes for 143 yards and three touchdowns in the 28–10 Cornhusker victory. Travis Turner replaced him as a starter until the Sugar Bowl.

18. Doug DuBose carried 20 times for 102 yards against LSU, and he carried 17 times for 99 yards and a touchdown against Michigan. He caught a touchdown pass in each of the games.

19. Michigan quarterback Jim Harbaugh ran for two touchdowns.

20. The drives were 66 yards each.

21. Danny McManus threw the 15-yard touchdown pass to Ronald Lewis for the winning touchdown. Steve Taylor and Morgan Gregory teamed up on what would have been a 56-yard pass play to the Seminole two-yard line.

Bob Devaney and quarterback Dennis Claridge have happy smiles after Nebraska beat the University of Miami in the Gotham Bowl at Yankee Stadium 36–34. The game was played on December 15, 1962.
(Photo Courtesy of UPI/CORBIS-BETTMANN)

But the play was nullified by an illegal procedure penalty. The Cornhuskers didn't have enough players on the line of scrimmage. Deion Sanders was in the Florida State secondary.

22. The Cornhuskers were limited to 80 yards rushing in the 23–3 loss in the 1989 Orange Bowl. They managed 82 yards rushing in the 22–0 loss in the 1992 Orange Bowl. Ken Clark was Nebraska's leading rusher with 36 yards in the first of the two. Calvin Jones rushed for 69 in the second.

23. Peter Tom Willis broke the single-game passing yardage record against Nebraska previously held by the Seminoles' Danny McManus, who completed 28 of 51 for 375 yards in the 1988 Fiesta Bowl.

24. Florida State scored only one touchdown against Nebraska in the 1994 Orange Bowl game. William Floyd ran one yard for the touchdown early in the third quarter. Otherwise, the Seminoles had to depend on the field goals of Scott Bentley, whose fourth came from 22 yards with 21 sec-

onds remaining. Nebraska's leading rusher in the game was quarterback Tommie Frazier, who gained 77 yards on 14 carries.

25. Ward and Frazier each finished with 283 yards of offense. Ward passed for 286 yards and had a net of minus three yards rushing. Frazier passed for 206 yards and rushed for 77 yards.

9

FROM COWBOY TO CORNHUSKER:

The Bob Devaney Years

Even though the Cuban missile crisis was only a month away, six Russians were among the 26,953 at Memorial Stadium that Saturday afternoon in late September of 1962. The Russians were visiting the University of Nebraska during a cultural, educational, technical, and agricultural exchange.

The experience in question, the Nebraska football opener, was cultural.

"Russian football is much faster," one of the visitors told a Lincoln newspaper reporter. That's how it was between the United States and the Soviet Union then. Neither could match the other, even when comparing apples and oranges—or in this case American football and Soviet soccer.

"Most of these players just lie around on the ground," the Russian observer said.

Other than the Russian's assessment, there were few complaints about the speed with which the players in new scarlet jerseys moved across the field of natural grass. The majority of fans had come expecting to see a faster Nebraska team than those of recent seasons. And they weren't disappointed.

The Cornhuskers were big and swift, and they made short work of outmanned South Dakota, winning 53–0. With what enthusiasm she could muster, the Russian visitor cheered for South Dakota. It was more than just being contrary, she claimed. She was "always for the underdog," she said.

The year before, Nebraska might easily have been mistaken for the underdog, even in a game against South Dakota. The Cornhuskers had finished 3–6–1 in 1961. Their victories had come against North Dakota, Kansas State, and Iowa State, and they had tied Arizona State, or vice versa.

The losing season was Nebraska's sixth in a row and 17th since 1940, when Biff Jones's next-to-last Cornhusker team won eight of 10 and played Stanford in the 1941 Rose Bowl game.

Still, South Dakota was no threat. Dick Dunkel, whose rating system was popular at the time, made the Cornhuskers 44-point favorites. Bob Burns, South Dakota's first-year head coach, said, "If Nebraska shoots off a cannon after every touchdown, the crows may go home shell-shocked."

Bob Devaney gets a ride on the shoulders of fullback Jim Carstens (L) and tackle Larry Jacobson after defeating Alabama 38–6 in the 1972 Orange Bowl.

(Photo Courtesy of UPI/CORBIS BETTMANN)

Burns was right. And Dunkel's prediction proved to be conservative.

A 53–0 Nebraska victory against any opponent was cause for celebration. But this one had much greater significance because it was the Cornhusker coaching debut of Bob Devaney.

The skies were overcast, with the threat of rain, for the 2 P.M. kickoff. By the fourth quarter, however, as five o'clock approached and many fans headed for home, the sun was shining.

As they left the stadium, they talked of a new era in Nebraska football. Even so, they remained skeptical, which was understandable given two decades of frustration and failure.

The mounting tension between the United States and the Soviet Union over the Soviet missile buildup in Cuba dominated the national headlines in late September 1962. A month and a half before—on August 5, to be exact—actress Marilyn Monroe died of an apparent drug overdose. She was 36.

The Four Seasons' hit single "Sherry" was in its second of five weeks atop the charts. By the time "Sherry" finally gave way at the top to the "Monster

Mash," by Bobby "Boris" Pickett and the Crypt-Kicker Five, Devaney's team was 5–0. And the skeptics were becoming believers.

The world was on its way to becoming Marshall McLuhan's "global village," through advances in telecommunications. The first television transmission by satellite had occurred in July.

Television viewers in the United States were entertained by *The Beverly Hillbillies* and *Candid Camera.* The Academy Award for best motion picture went to *Lawrence of Arabia.*

The Cornhuskers' lopsided victory against South Dakota preceded, by three days, a heavyweight championship fight in Chicago between Floyd Patterson, the champion, and Sonny Liston, an ex-convict. South Dakota was able to hang in against Nebraska a little longer than Patterson hung in against Liston. The challenger knocked out the champ just two minutes and six seconds into the first round.

The Cornhuskers didn't deliver what was for all intents and purposes a knockout punch, in the form of a 20-yard touchdown pass, until nearly 12 minutes had elapsed in the first quarter.

The first two units for Devaney's first game as coach at Nebraska:

FIRST TEAM

Left end	**Larry Donovan**	6-0, 185, senior
Left tackle	**Tyrone Robertson**	5-11, 210, senior
Left guard	**Dwain Carlson**	6-2, 200, senior
Center	**Ron Michka**	6-0, 205, junior
Right guard	**Bob Brown**	6-5, 251, junior
Right tackle	**Lloyd Voss**	6-4, 225, junior
Right end	**Jim Huge**	6-1, 185, senior
Quarterback	**Dennis Claridge**	6-3, 210, junior
Left halfback	**Dave Theisen**	6-2½, 202, junior
Right halfback	**Dennis Stuewe**	6-0, 175, senior
Fullback	**Warren Powers**	6-1, 180, junior

SECOND TEAM

Left end	**Larry Tomlinson**	6-0, 205, junior
Left tackle	**Monte Kiffin**	6-2, 225, junior
Left guard	**John Kirby**	6-3, 205, junior
Center	**Jim Baffico**	6-1, 240, junior
Right guard	**Gary Toogood**	6-3, 220, senior
Right tackle	**Al Fischer**	6-1, 215, senior
Right end	**Dick Callahan**	5-11, 180, junior
Quarterback	**John Faiman**	6-2, 185, senior
or	**Doug Tucker**	5-11, 170, sophomore

Left halfback	**Willie Ross**	5-10, 195, junior
Right halfback	**Rudy Johnson**	5-11, 185, junior
or	**Kent McCloughan**	6-1½, 190, sophomore
Fullback	**Gene Young**	6-2, 197, junior

Quiz 52: The Devaney Era

Use the above list of players to answer the following questions.

1. Who scored the first touchdown of the Devaney era? Who threw the pass?

2. Nebraska's starting lineup included a transfer from Marquette, who intercepted a pass and returned it 27 yards for the fourth touchdown in the South Dakota game. Name him.

3. Another player who transferred to Nebraska after Marquette dropped football earned letters in 1963 and 1964. He was a lineman from Chicago and later became a judge. Name him. Also name the assistant coach on Devaney's first staff who came from Marquette. Hint: The coach was one of two carryovers from the previous staff. Extra credit: Who was the other carryover?

4. The top two units included nine players from Nebraska. Name them and their hometowns.

5. Of the 241 lettermen during Devaney's 11 seasons as head coach, 94 came from towns in Nebraska, including 24 from Omaha and nine from Lincoln. Columbus was third among Nebraska towns in producing De-vaney-era lettermen, with six. Name at least three of the six Devaney-era lettermen from Columbus. Give yourself extra credit if you can name all six, two of whom also earned letters under Tom Osborne.

6. One of the nine Nebraskans on the first two units for the South Dakota game was a cocaptain in 1962. Another was a cocaptain on Devaney's second team. Identify them.

7. The other cocaptain on Devaney's first team was recovering from a shoulder separation and didn't play in the opening game against South Dakota. As a result, his name is not listed on the top two units. He was a fullback on offense and a linebacker on defense. Who was he?

8. What was the alliterative nickname of the player in question number 7? He was from Libbey High School in Toledo, Ohio, and later coached a Cornhusker All-America defensive end at Scott High in Toledo. Who was the defensive end? Another Cornhusker senior and first-team All–Big Eight selection in 1962 was from Libbey High in Toledo. Who was he?

Time-out

While we're on the subject of nicknames, identify the following Devaney-era players by their nicknames. The first few should be the easiest.

1. Larry Jacobson, DT, 1969–71	1. Jake
2. Mike Beran, OG, 1970–72	2. Red Baron
3. Bob Newton, OT, 1969–70	3. Big Fig
4. Wally Winter, OT, 1968–70	4. Wall
5. Tom Penney, FL, 1966–68	5. Nickel
6. Bill Bomberger, FB-K, 1967	6. Bomber
7. Rich Glover, MG, 1970–72	7. Jersey
8. Ben Gregory, HB, 1965–67	8. Pope
9. Willie Harper, DE, 1970–72	9. T Sweet Willie
10. Willie Paschall, HB, 1962–64	10. Frenchy
11. Harry Wilson, RB, 1964–66	11. Lighthorse
12. Charlie Winters, FB, 1965–66	12. Choo-Choo
13. John Dutton, DT, 1971–73	13. Lurch
14. Willie Ross, HB, 1961–63	14. Twister
15. Walt Barnes, DT-MG, 1963–65	15. Crazy Horse
16. Jerry Murtaugh, LB, 1968–70	16. Rat
17. Dan Schneiss, FB, 1968–70	17. Baby Bull
18. John Dervin, G, 1962–64	18. Happy Tooth
19. Langston Coleman, DE, 1964–66	19. Trey
20. Joe Blahak, DB, 1970–72	20. Air Head
21. Ron Kirkland, HB 1964–66	21. Skinny
22. Doug Dumler, C, 1970–72	22. Goose
23. John Adkins, DE, 1970–71	23. Spider
24. Doug Jamail, C, 1970–71	24. Chalk-Chalk
25. Lynn Senkbeil, LB, 1964–66	25. Butch

9. Four of the players on Nebraska's top two units for the South Dakota game in 1962—as listed earlier—were from Minnesota. Name then and, for extra credit, their hometowns.

Falling into Place

Devaney accomplished a dramatic turnaround at Nebraska with players who had been recruited by his predecessor, Bill Jennings. He inherited considerable talent. Among the many reasons for his immediate success was his willingness to reward effort in practice with playing time in games.

"He had a system where the first team would play a little more than half a quarter," said Larry Kramer, a sophomore on the 1962 team. "The second-team guys got a chance, too."

Devaney expressed his philosophy in the Nebraska football media guide for 1962, written by John Bentley, the Cornhuskers' athletic news director. Bentley quoted Devaney: "We will try to build our football team . . . on a two-unit basis and to have a third unit which can spell the first two."

Devaney also avoided beating down his players in practice so they were fresh for games. He told the players he would limit practices to two hours, "and that's what he did," said Kramer, another of the carryover players from Minnesota (Austin) and a consensus All-America tackle in 1964.

"We shortened practices and did not have continual contact," Devaney once said.

He learned that lesson as a high school coach in Michigan. He scrimmaged his team against one from a bigger high school during the week of a game and did well. But when his team played the game, it played poorly. Afterward, the opposing coach told him, "You don't beat up guys during the week."

Devaney also made certain his players were successful during practice, so they would be confident during games. Fred Duda, a quarterback on Devaney's teams in the mid-1960s, also coached for Devaney as a graduate assistant. "If something didn't work, he'd just say to forget it," Duda has said. "He never tried to fix something in practice. He'd go back to the coaches' meeting, and if it couldn't be worked out there, he'd drop it. He knew how to keep players focused and positive."

10. Of the 147 out-of-state players to earn letters during the Devaney era, 13 were from Minnesota. But four states were better represented by lettermen under Devaney, including his home state of Michigan, which provided him with 17. That wasn't the most, however. Name the state, after Nebraska, from which the most Devaney-era lettermen came. Name the other two states that provided Devaney with more players than Minnesota. Hint: Duda came from one of the three states.

11. One of the players on Devaney's first team was from Reno, Nevada. Name him. Easy extra credit: Another player from Nevada lettered under Devaney. Name him and his hometown.

12. Devaney's teams had one letterman from each of the following states: Vermont (1970–71), North Dakota (1969–72), Arizona (1970–71), and Arkansas (1961–63). Name the lettermen from each of those states. What Devaney letterman came from the District of Columbia?

Husker Fact

Devaney was familiar with at least one Cornhusker when he arrived at Nebraska in 1962: senior end Larry Donovan. "Devaney almost talked me into going to Wyoming," said Donovan, who was recruited by the Cowboys as a high school senior in Scottsbluff, Nebraska—which is considerably closer to the Wyoming campus in Laramie than it is to Lincoln. Pressure from the home folks helped to persuade Donovan to pick Nebraska, however. As a result, he still ended up playing for Devaney.

What Goes Around

Nebraska's success in recent seasons is a result of the option offense, which replaced the more pass-oriented offense that helped earn Devaney national championships in 1970 and 1971. But the Cornhuskers also ran an option offense in Devaney's early years. Fred Duda, who earned letters in 1963, 1964, and 1965, was an option quarterback. He was more of a threat as a runner than as a passer.

In contrast, Bob Churchich, who lettered as a quarterback in 1964, 1965, and 1966, was more effective as a passer. "We just optioned off the fullback—not the triple option—fake to the fullback and read the end. The quarterback would keep or pitch," Churchich has said. "The only read was on the end."

Devaney joked that the fans at Memorial Stadium stood and applauded the first play of the South Dakota game in 1962 even though it was an incomplete pass because they were weary of the three-yards-and-a-cloud-of-dust offense to which they had become accustomed. By contemporary standards, however, his early teams were ground-bound, running from a full-house backfield behind an unbalanced line.

"Really, that offense was the beginning of the wishbone," said Churchich, who rewrote the passing section of the Cornhusker record book during his three seasons. For his career, including bowl games, he completed 220 of 408 passes (53.9 percent) for 2,935 yards and 19 touchdowns.

Bowl games are not included in official career statistics. Even so, Churchich still ranks among Nebraska's all-time top 10 passers, with 2,434 yards and 15 touchdowns.

Bob's Biggest Victory

Devaney's teams won 101 games and two national championships in 11 seasons. But he often said his most important victory at Nebraska was the second in 1962. The Cornhuskers' 25–13 victory against Michigan at Ann Arbor represented a turning point in Nebraska football history.

Defeating Coach Bump Elliott's Wolverines on their home field "got people believing," said John Melton, one of the assistant coaches who came with Devaney from Wyoming.

Prior to the season, Devaney and his assistants evaluated the schedule and concluded that before the seventh game, against Missouri, there was no opponent the Cornhuskers shouldn't beat.

Devaney placed special emphasis on winning the Michigan game because the Wolverines had tradition and because they played in the Big Ten, which enjoyed more national respect than the Big Eight. Devaney understood the dynamics of the situation. He was from Michigan and had coached for 14 years in Michigan high schools before becoming an assistant at Michigan State.

Devaney anticipated a drop-off at Michigan because of heavy graduation losses. Elliott had only 19 lettermen returning from a 6–3 team in 1961. Plus, the Cornhuskers would have the experience of one game, albeit against South Dakota, while the Nebraska game was Michigan's opener.

Even so, Dick Dunkel, who had made Nebraska a 44-point favorite against South Dakota, forecast a 10-point Michigan victory against the Cornhuskers, and Will Grimsley of the Associated Press predicted the Wolverines would win with relative ease, 22–7. Devaney couldn't have been more delighted.

The facilities at Nebraska weren't as good as those he'd left at Wyoming. But the players he inherited from his Cornhusker predecessor, Bill Jennings, were better—and more abundant.

"We couldn't believe the size and the speed of the kids here," said Jim Ross, another of the assistants who came with Devaney—and who had coached with him at the high school level.

Jennings's ability as a recruiter was unquestioned. "The ingredients were there, the athletes," said Warren Powers, who earned letters playing for Jennings as a sophomore and junior. The program "just needed a leader to drive it in the right way. Bob was great and masterful at handling people."

Because of the talent, as well as other reasons, Devaney was encouraged to take the job at Nebraska by his longtime friend Duffy Daugherty, for whom he had been an assistant at Michigan State before taking the job at Wyoming. "Duffy told me: 'If you go to Nebraska, you'll be at a school where you can win a national championship. That's not going to happen at Wyoming,'" Devaney once said.

Devaney had a plan, and winning at Michigan was essential to the plan. It was so important, in fact, that Devaney departed from his policy of not scrimmaging in practice the week before a game. South Dakota hadn't provided much of a challenge, and he wanted to be certain his players were ready.

On the Monday before the Michigan game, he had them scrimmage against his freshman team, which included future stars Frank Solich, Freeman White, Tony Jeter, Fred Duda, and Dick Czap.

Michigan Stadium wasn't as imposing as it might have been. The attendance was 57,254, well below the 101,000 capacity. Wolverine fans might have anticipated a letdown, or they may not have considered Nebraska an attraction. In either case, Nebraska benefited from their disinterest.

The first quarter was scoreless, even though Michigan had the ball deep in Cornhusker territory. Nebraska led 7–6 at halftime and increased the lead to 19–6 going into the fourth quarter. Michigan cut the deficit to 19–13. But Bill Thornton, the Cornhuskers' senior fullback, ended the suspense with a 16-yard touchdown run. He also scored Nebraska's second touchdown, on a one-yard plunge.

The Michigan victory was one of nine in Devaney's first season. And it came at the expense of a team that finished the season 2–7. Its importance, however, transcended those facts. "During different parts of Nebraska football history, there have been some big upsets," Devaney once said. "But we felt that to get the program going again, to sell people on what we were doing, we had to beat Michigan."

Quiz 53: Bob's First One

1. Bill Thornton missed Nebraska's opener in 1962 while recovering from a shoulder separation, and his availability for the Michigan game was in doubt until Devaney sent him in during the second quarter. He immediately made his presence felt by throwing a key block on Nebraska's first touchdown run. The player for whom Thornton made the block—and who led the Cornhuskers with 80 yards rushing that afternoon—had a son who played wide receiver for Virginia Tech in the 1996 Orange Bowl game. Who was this Nebraska halfback?

2. Four assistant coaches came with Devaney from Wyoming. Name them. Hint: Two are identified in the account of the Michigan game. So you have to name only two more.

3. Two of the four assistants who came with Devaney had been high school coaches in Wyoming. One of the four played collegiately at Notre Dame, under Coach Elmer Layden—who had been a member of the fabled Four Horsemen. One had been a star fullback at Wyoming, playing for Bowden Wyatt on the Cowboys' undefeated Gator Bowl team in 1950. Identify the Devaney assistants who coached at Wyoming high schools. Name the assistant who played for Layden at Notre Dame. Name the assistant who was a star fullback at Wyoming.

4. Devaney wasn't Nebraska's first choice as a replacement head coach. Tippy Dye, the Cornhuskers' new athletic director, came from Wichita State and tried to bring the coach there with him. Instead, the coach accepted the head coach's job at Texas A&M, and Dye had to look elsewhere. In addition to Devaney, Dye's list of candidates included two other coaches from the Skyline Conference. One was from Utah. The other was from Utah State. Name the coach who turned down Nebraska and went to A&M. Name the Utah and Utah State coaches.

5. Nebraska's interest in Devaney was a result of an endorsement by Michigan State coach Duffy Daugherty. Nebraska contacted Daugherty to see if he might have an interest in leaving East Lansing. Nebraska's chancellor had been a professor of agriculture at Michigan State and knew Daugherty. Who was Nebraska's chancellor when Devaney was hired? Hint: He served as U.S. secretary of agriculture under Richard Nixon.

6. The Michigan game was the first of 11 in which Devaney coached against a Big Ten school while he was at Nebraska. The Cornhuskers' non-conference schedules during his 11 seasons always included one Big Ten team. Yet he coached against only three Big Ten teams in those games. Name the three Big Ten teams. How many of the 11 games did Nebraska win?

206

7. Devaney's record at Nebraska for 11 seasons was 101–20–2, a winning percentage of .829. With what team or teams did the Cornhuskers tie? In what season or seasons?

8. In addition to reducing the length of practices and not wearing down the players with excessive contact work leading up to games, Devaney didn't use freshman players on scouting squads during practice. Instead he assigned two full-time assistant coaches to work with them, and they immediately began learning his offensive and defensive systems. Which two assistant coaches worked with the Cornhusker freshmen in 1962? Extra credit: Name the two graduate assistants on Devaney's first staff, who also worked with the freshman team.

9. Devaney never coached a football team, at the high school or college level, that finished with a losing record. He was a football coach for 14 years at four high schools in Michigan before joining the Michigan State staff as an assistant. He was a football assistant and the head baseball coach for one year in Saginaw. Name the other three Michigan towns/cities in which he coached at the high school level. Caution: Big Beaver was the name of a high school, not a town.

10. One of the baseball players Devaney coached in high school pitched for 15 seasons in the major leagues, mostly with the Milwaukee Braves. He pitched for them in the 1957 World Series. In high school, however, he was a weak-hitting first baseman, the position to which Devaney thought he was best suited. "That tells you the kind of baseball coach I was," Devaney said. Name him.

11. Devaney was ready to quit coaching and move on to something else when Duffy Daugherty contacted him about going to Michigan State to be an assistant coach in 1953. Daugherty wasn't the head coach at the time, however. Devaney coached the Spartan ends. One of the players he coached at Michigan State went on to become a coach in the Big Eight. Devaney's record against him was 3–3. Another Big Eight coach was an assistant at Michigan State with Devaney. Devaney's record against him was 5–4. Name the head coach at Michigan State when Devaney was hired. Name the player Devaney coached at Michigan State who went on to become a coach. Name the Big Eight coach who had been an assistant with Devaney at Michigan State.

12. Devaney's teams in 1964, 1965, and 1966 included two players from North Platte High School in Nebraska. One was a defensive back. The other was a fullback. Name them.

Hooray for Hollywood . . . Not

Devaney's teams had gone 32 games without defeat before Efren Herrera's 30-yard field goal with 22 seconds remaining produced a 20–17 upset by

UCLA in the 1972 opener at the Los Angeles Coliseum. The loss to UCLA also snapped a 23-game Cornhusker winning streak, which began after a 21–21 tie with Southern Cal at the Coliseum in the second game of the 1970 season.

Nebraska was a two-touchdown underdog to the number three–ranked Trojans that night. So Cornhusker fans were fairly pleased with a tie on the road. Even so, Nebraska had an opportunity to put the game out of reach in the fourth quarter by kicking a field goal that would have made the lead 24–14.

Because of a bad center snap, however, the 12-yard field goal attempt failed, leaving the door open to the Trojans, who tied the score with 6:44 remaining and then threw a 50-yard Hail Mary pass on the final play of the game in an attempt to pull out a come-from-behind victory.

The Cornhuskers moved from ninth to eighth in the Associated Press rankings the week following the tie. "Southern Cal . . . basically, they tied us," Johnny Rodgers said many years later.

Rodgers was a sophomore in 1970. The game was his second on the varsity. "We should have won the game, but we got more consideration because people saw that we should have won," he said.

As it turned out, the tie at the Coliseum was the only blemish on Nebraska's record in 1970. The Cornhuskers went on a 10-game winning streak to earn their first national championship.

Quiz 54: The Big Ones—Back to Back

1. Devaney matched strategy with another Hall of Fame coach in the 1970 USC game. Tom Osborne once asked the Trojan coach for a graduate assistant's job. Who was he?

2. Nebraska's senior placekicker in 1970 was from Rock Rapids, Iowa. He was 8 of 13 on field goal attempts for the season—including the Orange Bowl victory against LSU. He was 20 of 47 for his career, not counting bowl games. Who was he?

3. The Cornhuskers took a 21–14 lead late in the third quarter of the USC game, on a 67-yard touchdown run by a player who had been forced to sit out the 1969 season because of a knee injury. Name him. Extra credit: Name the running back who scored USC's final touchdown. He had the same last name as a more well-known Trojan tailback, who was a consensus All-American and runner-up to Archie Griffin in voting for the Heisman Trophy in 1974.

4. Juniors Jerry Tagge and Van Brownson alternated at quarterback for Devaney in 1970. The Cornhuskers' first touchdown against USC in 1970 came on a 17-yard pass, but it wasn't thrown by either Tagge or Brownson. It was one of two Nebraska touchdown passes that weren't thrown by quarterbacks in 1970. Both were caught by a senior split end described in the

Cornhusker media guide as "small but mighty." He stood 5-foot-9 and weighed 158 pounds. Name the "small but mighty" split end. Name the nonquarterback who threw the touchdown pass against USC. Name the other nonquarterback who threw a touchdown pass for Nebraska in 1970. Hint: One was a fullback; the other was an I-back.

5. Nebraska's passing attack was remarkably efficient in 1970. Not counting the Orange Bowl game victory against LSU, the Cornhuskers completed 61.4 percent of their passes, 154 of 251, for 2,080 yards and 20 touchdowns. Tagge was 104 of 165 passing. His .6303 percentage is a school single-season record for a minimum of 100 attempts. Brownson was even more accurate, completing 49 of 75 (.653). Besides the players to whom question number 4 refers, two other Cornhuskers attempted passes in 1970. One was a wingback whose name you'll know. The other was a reserve quarterback from Oaklawn, Illinois. Name the wingback. For extra credit, name the reserve quarterback, who never earned a letter at Nebraska. Hint: The reserve quarterback had the same name as a tackle from West Point, Nebraska, who lettered for Bill Jennings's final two teams and then for Devaney's second team in 1963. He was sidelined all of Devaney's first season after undergoing shoulder surgery.

I Am the President . . .

After Nebraska completed its 1970 national championship run by defeating Louisiana State 17–12 in the Orange Bowl game, President Richard Nixon came to Lincoln to proclaim the Cornhuskers national champions. A crowd of 8,000 packed the NU Coliseum to see and hear Nixon's proclamation.

Nixon read from a plaque that he then presented to Devaney and Nebraska's cocaptains: "The University of Nebraska, 1970 football team . . . Champions of the Big Eight Conference . . . Victors in the 1971 Orange Bowl . . . the Associated Press . . . No. 1 College Football Team in the Nation . . ."

6. Who were the Cornhusker cocaptains on the podium with Devaney when Nixon placed the presidential seal on Nebraska's first national championship?

7. A transfer from New Mexico Military Institute played on the Cornhuskers' back-to-back national championship teams. He played split end. Who was he?

8. Devaney's 1971 national championship team included three players from Green Bay, Wisconsin. You'll get two of them right away, and maybe the third without much thought. Name the three and the positions they played. Also identify which of the three were high school teammates. Extra credit: The three came to Nebraska together but didn't finish together. Explain.

9. What Devaney-era Cornhusker's wife competed in the 1968 Mexico

City Olympics? What position did he play? What is his wife's name? In what Olympic event did she compete? One of their sons played at Nebraska. Name him and the position he played.

10. The top three quarterbacks on Devaney's final team in 1972 were from Las Vegas, Ogallala, Nebraska, and Fayetteville, North Carolina. Name them. Extra credit: Two other quarterbacks, both sophomores, were listed on the preseason depth chart in 1972. One was from Des Moines, Iowa. The other was from Blue Springs, Nebraska. Neither played. If you can name one of the two without looking in the media guide, you are a certified Cornhusker fanatic.

An All-Time, All-Devaney Team

Jerry Tagge was the starting quarterback on the 1971 national championship team, after sharing the number one job with Van Brownson in 1970. But when it came to quarterbacks, Dennis Claridge was "maybe the best I ever had here," Devaney once said, looking back over his 11 seasons as coach at Nebraska.

Using that as the determining factor, here's an all-Devaney era Cornhusker team.

Remember, the NCAA didn't change its rules to allow two-platoon football until 1965, so the players on Devaney's first three teams at Nebraska went both ways. Also, the Cornhuskers' offensive and defensive schemes changed significantly during Devaney's 11 seasons.

This team is meant to be representative rather than definitive.

OFFENSE

Split end	**Freeman White**	1963–65, 6-5, 211
Line	**Bob Brown**	1961–63, 6-5, 259
Line	**LaVerne Allers**	1964–65, 6-0, 215
Line	**Larry Kramer**	1963–64, 6-2, 231
Line	**Bob Newton**	1969–70, 6-4, 248
Line	**Lyle Sittler**	1962–64, 6-0, 223
Tight end	**Jerry List**	1970–72, 6-0, 210
Quarterback	**Dennis Claridge**	1961–63, 6-3, 210
Running back	**Jeff Kinney**	1969–71, 6-2, 210
Running back	**Harry Wilson**	1964–66, 5-11, 196
Slotback	**Johnny Rodgers**	1970–72, 5-9, 173
Placekicker	**Paul Rogers**	1968–70, 6-0, 192

DEFENSE

Line	**Willie Harper**	1970–72, 6-2, 207
Line	**Larry Jacobson**	1969–71, 6-6, 247

Line	**Rich Glover**	1970–72, 6-1, 234
Line	**Wayne Meylan**	1965–67, 6-0, 239
Line	**Walt Barnes**	1963–65, 6-3, 252
Linebacker	**Jerry Murtaugh**	1968–70, 6-3, 212
Linebacker	**Bob Terrio**	1970–71, 6-2, 209
Back	**Larry Wachholtz**	1964–66, 5-8, 162
Back	**Bill Kosch**	1969–71, 6-0, 176
Back	**Joe Blahak**	1970–72, 5-9, 179
Back	**Dana Stephenson**	1967–69, 6-2, 183
Punter	**Rich Sanger**	1971–73, 6-0, 214

Sanger is included as the punter, but he also would be a good choice as the placekicker—as would Wachholtz. Stephenson also could be the punter, as could Claridge. This is a versatile team.

TIME-OUT

The NCAA defines consensus All-Americans as: "Those players who were first-team selections on one or more of the All-America teams that were selected for the national audience and received nationwide circulation." The following Devaney-era Cornhuskers were consensus All-Americans. Three of the 11 were double winners, and four were unanimous consensus selections. Identify the three double winners and the four unanimous selections. Extra credit: Identify the year(s) in which each was selected.

1. Bob Brown, guard
2. Larry Kramer, tackle
3. Freeman White, end
4. Walt Barnes, defensive tackle
5. LaVerne Allers, guard
6. Wayne Meylan, middle guard
7. Bob Newton, offensive tackle
8. Johnny Rodgers, wingback
9. Willie Harper, defensive end
10. Larry Jacobson, defensive tackle
11. Rich Glover, middle guard

In Memoriam

On April 10, 1997, 50-year-old Ben Gregory died after suffering a heart attack. Gregory, an assistant coach at Colorado at the time, lettered from 1965 through 1967, when he was a Cornhusker cocaptain. Gregory, a halfback, was "one of the best all-around football players we ever had at Nebraska," Devaney once said. He was "as good a football player as Johnny Rodgers."

Gregory's son Morgan was a Cornhusker football letterman from 1987 through 1989.

One That Got Away

Gale Sayers was among the best football players ever to come out of a Nebraska high school. The Omaha Central graduate packed his bags and went to Kansas in 1961. He was a consensus All-American in 1963 and 1964. Devaney was determined to keep the state's best football players at home and retained Clete Fischer from Bill Jennings's staff to ensure that. Fischer was popular among the state's high school coaches and had been endorsed by a group of them as Jennings's replacement.

Soon after arriving from Wyoming, Devaney and Fischer drove around the state, visiting high school coaches and establishing the lines of communication so important to recruiting.

Devaney also gave Fischer primary recruiting responsibility in the state.

Sayers ran a record 99 yards from scrimmage for a touchdown against Nebraska at Memorial Stadium as a junior in 1963. But the Cornhuskers had the last laugh, winning 23–9.

Quiz 55: Gale Sayers

1. Nebraska played Kansas twice at Lawrence during Sayers's three seasons as a Jayhawk. Did Kansas win either of those games at home? If so, which one?

2. Who punted the ball that was downed at the Kansas one-yard line preceding Sayers's touchdown run in 1963? Hint: He also opened the scoring by kicking a 32-yard field goal in the first quarter. Extra credit: In what quarter did Sayers make his record-setting run?

3. Did Sayers score any other touchdowns against Nebraska? If so, when?

4. The Kansas quarterback in the 1963 game became a major league baseball pitcher. He spent 15 seasons in the big leagues. Name him. Hint: He stood 6-foot-5.

5. Sayers's touchdown cut the score to 10–9, but the extra-point attempt failed. Nebraska added 13 points, the last coming on a 47-yard interception return. Name the Cornhusker who intercepted the pass and completed the scoring. Hint: He was from Beatrice, Nebraska.

6. Sayers's first appearance at Memorial Stadium was equally impressive. He was chosen the outstanding offensive player in the Nebraska Shrine Bowl high school all-star game in 1961, rushing for 95 yards on six carries and scoring four touchdowns to lead the South to a 32–0 victory. The North included a Cornhusker-to-be from Broken Bow, Nebraska. He also was a halfback. Name him. Extra credit: This is a tough one. Two other fu-

ture Cornhuskers played in the 1961 Shrine Bowl, a fullback from Falls City and a lineman from Lexington. Name them.

7. Several outstanding running backs who followed Sayers at Omaha Central came to Nebraska, including one recruited by Devaney in 1966. Name him. Extra credit: Name the three Omaha Central running backs who have earned letters at Nebraska since 1984.

Offense or Defense

After a decade of liberalizing substitution rules, the NCAA rules were changed in 1965 to allow wholesale changes between periods and after touchdowns, opening the way for the return of two-platoon play. Some players were being used primarily on offense or defense by 1964.

Devaney said the best two-way player he ever coached was Bob Brown, who was a guard on offense and a linebacker on defense. Tackle Larry Kramer was another outstanding two-way player.

"We probably made a mistake when we went offense-defense with him, however," Devaney wrote in his 1981 autobiography. "We put Larry on offense . . . but he was probably a better defensive player."

Ben Gregory played in the mid-1960s, when changes in NCAA substitution rules allowed teams to use offensive and defensive platoons. Because of his versatility, however, Gregory was still used on both at times. He began his junior season in 1966 as a defensive player but was moved to offense because of an injury to senior halfback Ron Kirkland. Gregory was primarily an offensive player as a senior.

An Irishman's Luck

Don Bryant, who served as Nebraska's sports information director for 31 years and now has the title sports information director emeritus, was given a red rabbit's foot after the Cornhuskers' 17–7 loss to Missouri at Columbia, Missouri, in 1969. A week later, before Nebraska played Kansas in Lincoln, Bryant encouraged Devaney to pat the rabbit's foot for luck.

The Cornhuskers, off to a 2–2 start, came from behind to defeat Kansas 21–17. Jeff Kinney scored the winning touchdown on a six-yard run with 1:22 remaining in the fourth quarter.

Devaney asked to stroke the red rabbit's foot the next week, before a 13–3 victory against Oklahoma State. Nebraska finished the season with seven consecutive victories and didn't lose again until the 1972 opener at UCLA—a 32-game unbeaten streak, which included two national championships.

Fast-forward to 1983 and the Cornhuskers' final regular-season game at Oklahoma. . . .

The Sooners had taken a 14–7 lead late in the first half, on a 73-yard pass play from Danny Bradley to Buster Rhymes, when Bryant realized he had left the red rabbit's foot in a briefcase in his rental car in the parking lot. No sooner had he retrieved the rabbit's foot than Nebraska scored for a halftime tie.

Oklahoma took a 21–14 lead midway through the third quarter, prompting Bryant to seek out Devaney in the visiting athletic director's suite in the press box. After all, Bryant reasoned, the luck had depended on Devaney's rubbing the rabbit's foot. As Devaney rubbed it, Cornhusker I-back Mike Rozier broke loose on a 62-yard run to the Oklahoma three-yard line. Turner Gill finished off the series from one yard out, and fullback Mark Schellen added the winning touchdown on a 17-yard run five minutes later.

Was it luck or coincidence?

On the Tuesday before his first game as Cornhusker head coach in 1973, Tom Osborne was persuaded to move Nebraska's lucky horseshoe to the tunnel leading from the new varsity locker room in the South Stadium. The horseshoe had hung in Schulte Fieldhouse during Devaney's tenure as coach.

No one seemed to know exactly when it was hung there. But the tradition was for players and coaches to tap the horseshoe for luck before they went onto the field. "I've never touched the horseshoe," Osborne told a Lincoln newspaper reporter. "Several of them [players] talked about wanting it moved to the new dressing room. . . . I've just never believed in that sort of thing or in any superstitions."

John Dutton and Daryl White, Osborne's first captains, convinced him the horseshoe needed to be moved, if for no other reason than Cornhusker opponents couldn't use it for luck.

"I've never believed in black cats, ladders, picking up pennies, or any of the usual superstitions," Osborne said. "Maybe after I've been a head coach a little longer, I'll acquire some."

Younger Than He Looked

The September 25, 1965, issue of *Newsweek* included a short feature on Devaney. According to the story, "the 60-year-old Nebraska head coach resembles Wallace Beery rather than Kirk Douglas." The next week, Devaney jokingly told a booster club he was considering a lawsuit against the magazine.

The basis for a lawsuit, however, wouldn't have been because of the comparison to Beery but rather because Devaney was 50 years old, not 60. The magazine editors issued an apology.

Dan Jenkins of *Sports Illustrated* compared Devaney to a "droll sheriff" in 1971, and John Underwood, Jenkins's associate at *Sports Illustrated*, described Devaney as "unpretentious" and "unassuming" with a "broad, pleasant potato face" and a "dumpy baker's build." The characterization fit, though maybe not entirely in the way Underwood intended. Devaney wasn't averse to rolling up his sleeves and immersing himself in baker's flour if that was what the situation demanded. As for his lack of pretension, Devaney lived in the same redbrick house on C Street from the time he arrived in Lincoln until his last couple of years.

He also never had an unlisted telephone number, a reflection of the times as well as his personality.

Moon over Miami

While he was at Nebraska, Devaney was contacted by several professional football teams about moving to the next level. Among those teams who showed an interest were the Los Angeles Rams, the Pittsburgh Steelers, the Denver Broncos, and, near the end of his coaching career, the New England Patriots.

Perhaps the closest Devaney came to leaving Nebraska, however, was in 1963, his second season, when Henry King Stanford, president of the University of Miami, tried to lure him to Miami.

Stanford had been impressed by Devaney when the Hurricanes played Nebraska in the ill-fated Gotham Bowl game at the end of the 1962 season, and Miami coach Andy Gustafson was set to retire from coaching and concentrate on duties as the Hurricanes' athletic director.

Devaney met with Stanford during a visit to Miami to make arrangements for the Cornhuskers' 1964 Orange Bowl game against Auburn. He returned for a second visit before announcing he would remain at Nebraska. His wife, Phyllis, had just purchased snow tires for their car, he jokingly explained.

It took more than new snow tires to keep Devaney at Nebraska, however. Miami boosters reportedly were raising $25,000 to lure Devaney. Nebraska was paying him an annual salary of $19,000, after rewarding him with a $2,000 raise and a five-year contract following the 9–2 season in 1962.

Also, a Cornhusker booster group was raising money to pay the premium on a $100,000 life insurance policy (about $60,000). Originally, the group had planned to purchase a policy worth $200,000.

Devaney's decision to stay earned him another raise. In addition to receiving the paid-up $100,000 life insurance policy from the boosters, he was made a tenured professor, with a new five-year contract at an annual salary of $21,000, by the Nebraska Board of Regents. He was well worth the investment.

It Doesn't Get Any Worse Than This

The low point in Devaney's coaching career came in November 1968, when the Cornhuskers were embarrassed by Oklahoma at Norman 47–0 to finish 6–4 for the second consecutive season.

Two weeks before the Oklahoma game, Nebraska was shut out at Memorial Stadium by Kansas State 12–0. Though the score wasn't as bad, the net effect was. Not only had the shutout come at home but also it had come against Kansas State, which hadn't won against Nebraska since 1959.

The Wildcats were having difficulty defeating anyone in the 1960s. They had posted records of 1–9 in 1967, 0–9–1 in 1966, and 0–10 in 1965. They hadn't won a conference game since 1964.

They had doubled their victory total, combined over the three previous seasons, when they came to Lincoln. But they were back to their old ways, in the form of a four-game losing streak.

Nebraska, in contrast, had been ranked in the Associated Press Top 20 early in the season before dropping out of the rankings after back-to-back losses against Kansas (23–14) and Missouri (16–14). On top of everything else, the Kansas State game was on Homecoming weekend, which meant the Cornhuskers were playing in front of the second-largest audience of the season.

The ignominy of losing to the Wildcats was compounded by the fact that they probably didn't play well enough to win, losing three fumbles and 125 yards in penalties. Yet the Cornhuskers could get no deeper into Kansas State territory than the 31-yard line, and they managed only 146 total yards.

Devaney's popularity was eroding to the point that boosters in Omaha circulated a petition calling for his ouster. The negative letters began to pile up in his office at the NU Coliseum.

However, "I actually didn't realize how irritated the fans were," Devaney wrote in his 1981 autobiography. His secretary began tossing the critical letters in the trash.

Athletes tend to be more resilient than their coaches and certainly the fans.

"There was no sense of urgency with us, as far as I can remember," said Adrian Fiala, who lettered at linebacker from 1967 to 1969. "We didn't sense any great concern. Coach Devaney never came to us and said: 'You got to win or my job's gone.' He never would have done that. He wasn't that way."

Quiz 56: More Bob

1. Nebraska was shut out only three times in Devaney's 11 seasons. The first shutout occurred in 1967. By whom were the Cornhuskers shut out? Extra credit: What was the score?

2. Kansas State's head coach in 1968 was in his second of eight seasons, during which his teams had a combined record of 33–52. He was a Florida State graduate, class of 1956. Name him.

3. On their first possession, the Wildcats scored a touchdown, set up by a 47-yard pass play that carried to the Nebraska six-yard line. Name the sophomore quarterback who threw the pass. Extra credit: Name the Wildcat who caught the pass. This is a tough one.

4. Nebraska had trouble with Kansas State in 1969, winning 10–7 after trailing at halftime 7–0. But the 1970 game was payback time at Memorial Stadium. The Cornhuskers won 51–13 and set a school record for intercep-

tions against the quarterback mentioned in question number 3. How many passes did they intercept? He completed 22 of 47 for 255 yards, by the way.

5. Devaney's conference record at Nebraska was 62–14–1. His Cornhusker teams never lost against two Big Eight opponents, and they were perfect against one of those two. Name the Big Eight team against which Devaney was 11–0. Name the team against which he was 10–0–1.

6. Devaney's record against Oklahoma was his worst in Big Eight play. What was his combined record against the Sooners? Against what conference team was his second-worst record?

7. How many conference championships did Devaney's teams win? All but one were outright. In what season did Devaney's Cornhuskers share the Big Eight title? With whom? What was Nebraska's worst conference finish under Devaney?

Air Force Assault

The crowd of 37,056 was late arriving because of a traffic jam, caused by football fans driving into Colorado Springs to see Nebraska play Air Force. The Cornhuskers were ranked number two in the nation by the Associated Press—they were *Sports Illustrated*'s preseason number one.

By the time many of the fans settled into their seats, Nebraska led 14–0. On the first play from scrimmage at the Cornhusker 20-yard line, fullback Frank Solich took a handoff from quarterback Bob Churchich, went off right guard, and kept on running, 80 yards for a touchdown.

Less than six minutes later, halfback Ron Kirkland scored Nebraska's second touchdown on a six-yard run. Before the quarter was finished, Solich scored a third touchdown on a 21-yard run. Kirkland threw a key block to clear the way for Solich. The Cornhuskers led 21–0, and it appeared the rout was on.

Air Force regrouped, however, and rallied, cutting the deficit to 21–17. Nebraska couldn't relax until Solich scored his third touchdown, on a 41-yard run, with 2:06 remaining in the game—the Falcons offered no resistance. The Cornhuskers lined up fourth-and-two, and even though the Air Force jumped offside, there was no whistle. The Falcon defenders let up, but Solich did not.

Solich, a senior from Cleveland, Ohio, finished with 204 rushing yards; he was the first Cornhusker—in modern history, at least—to rush for 200 or more yards in a game, breaking the previous record of 187, set by Bobby Reynolds in a 32–26 victory against Minnesota at Memorial Stadium in 1950.

Solich stood 5-foot-8 and was listed at 158 pounds in the Nebraska media guide for 1965. A story in the September 20, 1965, issue of *Sports Illustrated*—with no apologies to Tennessee Williams—said Solich "darts, dodges, and scurries among them [defenders] like a mouse on a hot tin roof."

Solich's picture was on the cover of that issue, which was on the newsstands the week before the Air Force game. So it was the dreaded *Sports Illustrated* jinx in reverse.

Devaney's 1965 team went through the regular season undefeated and untied. But the Cornhuskers' 10-game winning streak was snapped by Alabama 39–28 in the 1966 Orange Bowl game.

Answers

Quiz 52: The Devaney Era

1. Larry Tomlinson caught the pass, which was thrown by quarterback John Faiman.

2. Dave Theisen

3. Bernie McGinn was the lineman from Chicago. George Kelly was the assistant coach who came from Marquette. Clete Fischer was the other assistant retained by Devaney.

4. Donovan, Scottsbluff; Carlson, Fullerton; Michka, Omaha; Huge, Holdrege; Tomlinson, O'Neill; Kiffin, Lexington; Kirby, David City; Faiman, Omaha; and McCloughan, Broken Bow

5. Joe Blahak, 1970–72; Bill Bomberger, 1967; Bill Kosch, 1969–71; Marv Mueller, 1965–67; Terry Rogers, 1972–74; and Steve Wieser, 1972–74

6. Carlson, 1962; Kirby, 1963

7. Bill Thornton

8. Thunder. Willie Harper. Robertson was Thornton's teammate at Libbey High.

9. Voss, Magnolia; Claridge, Robbinsdale; Stuewe, Hamburg; and Fischer, Princeton

10. Duda was from Chicago. Based on a media guide survey, Devaney's out-of-state lettermen were from: Illinois 18; Michigan 17; Pennsylvania, California, 15 each; Minnesota, Iowa, Ohio, 13 each; Wisconsin 9; Kansas 6; Texas 5; South Dakota 4; Missouri 3; Indiana, New Jersey, Nevada, Wyoming, Colorado, 2; Vermont, North Dakota, West Virginia, Arizona, Arkansas, District of Columbia, 1 each.

11. Toogood was from Reno. Dave Humm was from Las Vegas.

12. Vermont: Jeff Hughes, Burlington. North Dakota: Bill Janssen, Grand Forks. Arizona: Carl Johnson, Phoenix. Arkansas: Willie Ross, Helena. Langston Coleman, 1964–65

Quiz 53: Bob's First One

1. Dennis Stuewe. His son Michael played against the Cornhuskers in the Orange Bowl.

2. John Melton, Jim Ross, Mike Corgan, and Carl Selmer

3. Melton and Selmer coached at Wyoming high schools, in Thermopolis and Worland, respectively. Melton played fullback on Wyatt's 1950

team. Selmer also played for Wyatt at Wyoming, by the way. Iron Mike Corgan played halfback and fullback at Notre Dame under Layden.

4. Hank Foldberg picked A&M—where he earned a football letter in 1942—over Nebraska. He coached the Aggies for three seasons, and his cumulative record was 6–23–1. Utah's Ray Nagel and Utah State's John Ralston also were interviewed for the Cornhuskers' coaching vacancy.

5. Clifford Hardin

6. In addition to Michigan, Nebraska played Minnesota and Wisconsin while Devaney was head coach. The Cornhuskers were 11–0 in those games, eight of which were against Minnesota.

7. Nebraska tied USC 21–21 in 1970 and Iowa State 23–23 in 1972.

8. John Melton and Clete Fischer were assigned to the freshmen. The graduate assistants who also worked with the freshmen were Dallas Dyer and, yes, Tom Osborne.

9. Devaney's first coaching job out of college was at Big Beaver High in Birmingham, Michigan. In addition to Saginaw, he also coached at high schools in Keego Harbor and Alpena.

10. Bob Buhl played first base for Devaney at Saginaw High School.

11. Biggie Munn was the head coach at Michigan State when Devaney joined the staff. Chuck Fairbanks was the Spartan end whom Devaney coached. Fairbanks and Devaney divided six games while Fairbanks was the head coach at Oklahoma. Dan Devine and Devaney were assistants together at Michigan State. Devine's Missouri teams were 4–5 against Devaney's Cornhuskers.

12. Larry Wachholtz and Pete Tatman were high school teammates in North Platte. Wachholtz was a defensive back and Tatman was a fullback in 1965 and 1966, when two-platoon football returned.

Quiz 54: The Big Ones—Back to Back

1. John McKay

2. Paul Rogers

3. Joe Orduna scored Nebraska's final touchdown. Clarence Davis scored Southern Cal's final touchdown, on a 10-yard run. Anthony Davis was the Heisman Trophy runner-up in 1974.

4. Guy Ingles was the "small but mighty" receiver. Senior fullback Dan Schneiss threw the pass to Ingles for Nebraska's first touchdown in the 1970 USC game. Senior I-back Joe Orduna threw a touchdown pass to Ingles in the Cornhuskers' 35–10 victory at Minnesota in 1970.

5. Johnny Rodgers threw one incomplete pass in 1970. Bob Jones, the reserve quarterback from Oaklawn, Illinois, was 1 for 5 passing in 1970. The Bob Jones from West Point spent one season with the NFL's Washington Redskins after being drafted in the 18th round in 1964.

6. Jerry Murtaugh and Dan Schneiss

7. Woody Cox

8. Quarterback Jerry Tagge, cornerback Jim Anderson, and monster or strong safety Dave Mason were from Green Bay. They all were teammates at West High School. They were freshmen at Nebraska in 1968, and they all lettered in 1969, when Mason was a split end. Mason redshirted in 1970 because of an injury. As a result, he completed his career a season later than Tagge and Anderson.

9. Larry Frost earned letters as a wingback from 1967 to 1969. Wife Carol competed in the discus at the Mexico City Olympics. Son Scott was the Cornhusker quarterback in 1996 and 1997.

10. Dave Humm, Las Vegas. Steve Runty, Ogallala. Terry Luck, Fayetteville. Dana Potter was from Des Moines. Bob Rutan was from Blue Springs. Potter and Rutan saw limited action as backups to Luck on the 1971 freshman team. Potter threw two touchdown passes. Rutan rushed for a touchdown. Rutan redshirted in 1972 and was listed as a defensive end in 1973. He didn't play in 1973 either.

TIME-OUT

1. 1963 unanimous,   2. 1964 unanimous,   3. 1965,   4. 1965,   5. 1966, 6. 1966 and 1967,   7. 1970,   8. 1971, 1972 unanimous,   9. 1971 and 1972, 10. 1971,   11. 1972 unanimous

Quiz 55: Gale Sayers

1. Nebraska won both: 40–16 in 1962 and 14–7 in 1964.

2. Dave Theisen punted the ball. Sayers's run was the fourth play of the fourth quarter.

3. Sayers didn't score in either the 1962 or the 1964 games.

4. Steve Renko

5. Bob Hohn

6. Kent McCloughan, Broken Bow; Bruce Smith, Falls City; and John Strohmeyer, Lexington

7. Joe Orduna earned letters in 1967, 1968, and 1970. He missed the 1969 season because of injury. Keith Jones, Calvin Jones, and Ahman Green all came to Nebraska from Omaha Central.

Quiz 56: More Bob

1. Kansas defeated Nebraska 10–0 at Lawrence in 1967.

2. Vince Gibson

3. Lynn Dickey threw the pass to Dave Jones.

WHERE THE WEST BEGINS

NEBRASKAland

OUTDOOR NEBRASKAland   January 1966   50 cents

1963 - GOTHAM BOWL
1964 - ORANGE BOWL
1965 - COTTON BOWL
1966 - ORANGE BOWL

Go Cornhuskers!

(Photo Courtesy of Author's Collection)

4. Nebraska intercepted seven Dickey passes.

5. Devaney's teams were 11–0 against Oklahoma State and 10–0–1 against Iowa State.

6. Devaney's teams were 5–6 against Oklahoma, and they were 7–4 against Missouri. His record against the remaining Big Eight teams was: Kansas 9–2, Colorado 10–1, and Kansas State 10–1.

7. Devaney coached Nebraska to eight conference championships: 1963, 1964, 1965, 1966, 1969, 1970, 1971, and 1972. The Cornhuskers shared the 1969 title with Missouri. Their worst finish in the Big Eight under Devaney was in 1967, when they tied for fifth place with a 3–4 record.

10

AN UNBEATABLE LEGACY:

The Tom Osborne Years

What impresses me about Tom and his staff is how hard they work when things don't go particularly well, when they don't meet their expectations. I think they've made a lot of adjustments through the years.

—Husker volleyball coach Terry Pettit on Tom Osborne

The practice was pretty much like any other during Tom Osborne's first season as head coach. For some reason, however, the 36-year-old Osborne was in a demonstrating mood.

He was going to run a post pattern to show his young charges how it was done in Nebraska. And if, in the process, he could show them that he could still go get the ball . . . well, that was fine, too. He had been a flanker for three seasons in the National Football League, after all. So he knew what he was doing.

Osborne was matched against senior safety Bob Thornton. The two raced down the field stride for stride as backup quarterback Steve Runty released the ball. The timing wasn't right, and the pass was just out of Osborne's reach. He made a desperate dive, stretching his arms to full length. Osborne and the ball both hit the ground. Thornton couldn't avoid contact and hit Osborne in the ribs.

Junior David Humm, a bemused onlooker and the number one quarterback, considered the demonstration's aftermath and smiled, as only he could. "Coach Devaney would have caught it," he said.

Humm was speaking in jest. But his comment underscored Osborne's burden in following his Hall of Fame predecessor, Bob Devaney, as head coach. "I felt when I took over for Bob it would be uphill. Just because of the contrast, I thought it would be difficult to last more than five years," Osborne has said. "My preference would have been to start out at a program that had been down."

Nebraska had not been down, of course. The Cornhuskers had just won national championships in 1970 and 1971. And Devaney's record at Nebraska was 101–20–2, a winning percentage of .829. The Cornhuskers also had won or shared eight conference championships in his 11 seasons.

Tom Osborne gets a hug from Jason Peter, after Peter and Grant Wistrom drench him with ice water with less than a minute remaining in the 1998 Orange Bowl victory against Tennessee.
(Photo Courtesy of *Huskers Illustrated*/Scott Smith)

The standard was high. But beyond that, Devaney's success had come on the heels of six consecutive losing seasons and the malaise that followed the 1940 team's trip to the Rose Bowl.

"Bob always had a built-in grace factor because he turned the program around," Osborne has said. "I wasn't going to have that opportunity because I was more of a caretaker."

Even so, Osborne accepted the challenge. "You only get so many chances to be a head coach," he said. "This is my home state, and it was a chance to give the program some continuity."

Despite his own equally remarkable success, Osborne always seemed to be beset by the job paranoia that is the constant companion of considerably less successful coaches. He was the winningest active football coach in Division I-A of the NCAA when he stepped aside after the 1998 Orange Bowl game. He led Nebraska to back-to-back national championships. And he reached 200 career coaching victories more quickly than any Division I-A coach in history.

In 25 seasons, Osborne's record was 255–49–3 (.836), better than Devaney's. He coached the Cornhuskers to three national championships in his final four seasons. Nebraska's record in his final five seasons was 60–3. Yet he was convinced that after a mediocre season or two, he would surely find a pink slip in his office mailbox.

"I've never felt very comfortable here," Osborne once said.

Quiz 57: Chasing the Record

1. What three NCAA Division I-A football coaches have reached 300 victories during their careers? How many does each coach have? How many seasons did he coach?

2. What two *active* NCAA Division I-A football coaches had more victories than Osborne when he retired?

Quiz 58: They Were Keepers

Tom Osborne's first staff in 1973 included 10 assistant coaches, seven of whom were carryovers from Bob Devaney's staff. Name all 10 assistants and identify which three were hired by Osborne. To help, here are the positions they coached.

1. Defensive coordinator, defensive line
2. Defensive ends
3. Linebackers, recruiting coordinator
4. Defensive backs
5. Offensive line, kickers
6. Offensive line
7. Tight ends, wingbacks
8. Quarterbacks, wide receivers
9. Offensive backs
10. Freshmen

Extra credit: Name Osborne's first two graduate assistant coaches.

In the Beginning . . . Coach Osborne's First Game

The motion picture *Paper Moon* was finishing its 10th "great week" in Lincoln, according to a newspaper advertisement. *American Graffiti*, which had even greater nostalgic appeal, was showing at the same theater complex. A handbill for the movie asked: "Where were you in '62?"

Tom Osborne would have answered by saying he had been in his first year as a graduate assistant on Bob Devaney's first coaching staff at Nebraska. Osborne may have seen both movies. According to a lengthy personality profile in

Lincoln's *Sunday Journal and Star* the week before his first game as head coach, Osborne's favorite leisure activities included "attending movies."

Devaney's hand-picked successor was "straight but certainly not a square," the profile said. Though he had a Ph.D. in educational psychology, he occasionally read "a Western novel as an escape."

Reading Western novels and going to the movies would have offered a brief escape from discussions of the Watergate scandal, which continued to dominate the headlines in September 1973.

John Ehrlichman and G. Gordon Liddy, prominent Watergate figures, were indicted in connection with the burglary of psychiatrist Daniel Ellsberg's office the week of Osborne's coaching debut.

Osborne was preparing his team for the season opener against UCLA on September 8. In March 1973, John Wooden had coached the Bill Walton–led Bruin basketball team to a record seventh consecutive NCAA championship. Now UCLA's football team was seeking national prominence.

A year earlier, the Bruins had ended Nebraska's 32-game unbeaten streak with a 20–17 upset at the Los Angeles Coliseum. The game was the first in Devaney's final season as head coach.

Devaney had been persuaded to stay on as head coach one more season, to try to lead the Cornhuskers to an unprecedented third consecutive national championship. Losing to UCLA, on a field goal in the closing seconds, was not a particularly good way to begin such a quest.

In 1973, the Bruins had to come to Lincoln, where Nebraska had played before 59 consecutive sellouts at Memorial Stadium, dating to early November of Devaney's first season.

A little over a month earlier, a rock concert at Watkins Glen, New York, attracted 600,000. UCLA didn't have to contend with such a mob. But Memorial Stadium was imposing, nonetheless.

The official attendance that Saturday was 74,966, consecutive sellout number 60. There is no way to know how many of the men in the crowd wore double-knit, bell-bottom slacks or leisure suits. But the color of choice for women as well as for men attending the game was most definitely red.

The day was the next-to-last in the Nebraska State Fair's 10-day run. It was promoted as "Super Saturday." Those who couldn't get tickets to the football game could watch on large-screen television sets in the Open Air Auditorium at the State Fairgrounds, then attend the *Stars of Lawrence Welk* show in the grandstand. The timing was right. Kickoff was 3:50 P.M. The Lawrence Welk show began at 7:45 P.M.

The football game was clearly the main attraction, however. In the State Fair livestock barns were two sheep with wool that had been dyed bright red with "Go Big Red" stenciled on their backs.

Those who couldn't get tickets for the game and weren't inclined to attend the State Fair could watch ABC's national telecast at home. That had a certain appeal, anyway, because of a threat of rain.

The day before, 3,000 sat in Memorial Stadium in a downpour at a pep rally staged for ABC's cameras. Osborne and cocaptains John Dutton and Daryl White spoke at the rally. The Cornhusker marching band performed, as did "watersoaked NU cheerleaders," according to a newspaper account. Red-and-white signs in the stadium "soon melted into light pink in the heavy rain."

The rain held off, for the most part, on Super Saturday, but UCLA encountered a figurative deluge of points scored by Nebraska, beginning with the Cornhuskers' first possession.

Senior quarterback Steve Runty directed them on an 11-play, 56-yard touchdown drive, which he capped with a one-yard sneak. Nebraska never let up, coasting to a 40–13 victory.

Sophomore I-back Tony Davis rushed for 147 yards and two touchdowns against the Bruins, who were regarded as national championship contenders . . . pending the game's outcome.

The starters for Osborne's first game were:

OFFENSE

Split end	**Frosty Anderson**	6–0, 176, senior
Left tackle	**Daryl White**	6–4, 247, senior
Left guard	**Tom Alward**	6–3, 230, junior
Center	**Rik Bonness**	6–4, 205, sophomore
Right guard	**Dan Anderson**	6–1, 232, senior
Right tackle	**Al Austin**	6–5, 219, senior
Tight end	**Brent Longwell**	6–3, 218, senior
Quarterback	**Steve Runty**	5–11, 196, senior
I-back	**Tony Davis**	5–11, 212, sophomore
Wingback	**Ritche Bahe**	5–10, 182, junior
Fullback	**Maury Damkroger**	6–2, 232, senior

DEFENSE

Left end	**Steve Manstedt**	6–2, 202, senior
Left tackle	**Ron Pruitt**	6–3, 234, sophomore
Noseguard	**John Bell**	6–0, 215, senior
Right tackle	**John Dutton**	6–7, 248, senior
Right end	**Bob Martin**	6–0, 182, sophomore
Linebacker	**Tom Ruud**	6–2, 216, junior
Linebacker	**Bob Nelson**	6–4, 233, junior
Left corner	**Zaven Yaralian**	5–11, 176, senior

Right corner	**Randy Borg**	5–11, 187, senior
Monster	**Wonder Monds**	6–4, 200, junior
Free safety	**Bob Thornton**	6–0, 173, senior

Quiz 59: A Little Quiz on Osborne's First Game as Head Coach

1. One of UCLA's star players went on to become a television–motion picture actor. He also had a famous father. Who was he? Who was his father? And for what was his father famous?

2. One of Nebraska's starters later became a full-time assistant coach on Osborne's staff. Who was he?

3. As indicated, the game was televised nationally by ABC. Who were Nebraska's offensive and defensive players of the game as chosen by ABC? In addition, two Cornhuskers shared the Associated Press award as National Player of the Week. Who were they?

4. What was Nebraska monster back Wonder Monds's real name?

5. Nebraska's starting lineup included 12 players from Nebraska. Who were the 12? And from what towns did they come? Ironically, none were from the state's largest city, Omaha.

6. Two of the Cornhusker starters would eventually be first-round NFL draft picks. Who were they? And by whom were they drafted?

7. Lefty David Humm was Nebraska's starting quarterback in 1972 as a sophomore. Why didn't he start the UCLA game? Extra credit: Humm's brother was on the 1972 team but didn't earn a letter. What was his name? What position did he play? And from where did the Humm brothers come?

8. Runty threw 11 of the Cornhuskers' 12 passes against UCLA. Who threw the other one?

9. While he was an assistant coach, Osborne's recruiting territory included California. Four Cornhusker starters for the UCLA game were from California. Who were they?

10. What was different about the way the Cornhuskers came onto the field before the UCLA game? Hint: They continued to do the same thing throughout Osborne's tenure as coach.

11. Nebraska defensive coordinator Monte Kiffin was extremely concerned about the type of offense UCLA ran because it had given the Cornhuskers problems in the past. What was the offense?

12. UCLA had 12 players who started the 20–17 upset of Nebraska in 1972 returning, including the placekicker who made the winning field goal. Who was the placekicker? How long was the game-winning field goal? And how much time remained on the clock at the Los Angeles Coliseum after he kicked it?

13. UCLA's colorful third-year coach was in sharp contrast to Osborne in personality. The week before the game, he told reporters he wouldn't lead

the Bruins onto the field with a somersault, explaining, "I don't do that on the road because I don't want to make anyone mad." Who was this coach?

14. The Bruin head coach also remarked that "Nebraska might have a better team than last year, but we'll kick the ball to their punt returner this year. Last year, we didn't." Why?

15. UCLA's aforementioned willingness to "kick the ball to their punt returner" proved to be a mistake. Nebraska's second touchdown came on a 77-yard punt return. Who returned it?

16. As a young assistant coach, Osborne set a goal of becoming a head coach by the time he was 35 years old. Did he meet that goal? How old was he the day of the UCLA game?

17. Despite the lopsided loss, UCLA was able to do something against Nebraska that no opponent had done in the previous 33 games. What was that?

18. Nebraska went into the UCLA game ranked number four nationally by the Associated Press. The Bruins were ranked number 10. After the decisive victory, the Cornhuskers moved up to number two in the AP poll and remained there until their first loss under Osborne. How many more games did they win before losing? To what team did they lose? Who was the opposing coach? And what was the score?

Quiz 60: Wizardry of Oz

For some of you, perhaps many, this might not be much of a challenge. This isn't an open-book test. Pop quizzes never are, you know. So you probably shouldn't use a media guide. See how you do.

1. Boyd Epley, Nebraska's assistant athletic director and director of athletic performance, was once a Cornhusker athlete. What was his sport? Be as specific as you can.

2. The video tribute to the late Brook Berringer, put together by Cornhusker video production specialist Jeff Schmahl, includes background music from what song, by what artist?

3. What former Cornhusker football player was the starting center on his junior high basketball team, ahead of Dave Hoppen, Nebraska's all-time leading scorer in basketball? What was his nickname?

4. Tom Osborne's teams were characterized by their consistency. During his 25 seasons as head coach, Nebraska lost only once to an opponent that finished its season with a losing record. In what season did that loss occur? What was the team? Who was the coach? And what was the score?

5. This one will take some thought. In how many of Tom Osborne's 25 seasons did the Cornhuskers lose their final regular-season game? Don't count the 1996 season's 37–27 loss to Texas in the Big 12 play-off.

6. Tom Osborne was shirttail relation to what former Cornhusker quarterback?

7. Assistant coach Ron Brown's description of his smallish receivers as the "itty bitty committee" became popular during the 1993 season. There were three main members of the committee, none of whom was taller than 5-foot-9, in 1993. Two others didn't play much but lettered. Who were the five?

Extra credit: Two of the five were listed at 5-foot-8. Which two were they?

8. Foreign athletes are commonplace in some intercollegiate sports. But they are rare in football. Even so, three foreign athletes earned football letters during Tom Osborne's 25 seasons as head coach. All three were walk-ons. Can you name them as well as the countries from which they came?

9. Despite his reputation for being conservative offensively, Tom Osborne's playbook has some imaginative entries—tomfoolery, if you will. One such entry, "the fumbleroosky," had to be removed from the Cornhusker playbook after the 1992 season because of a change in NCAA rules.

The center snapped the ball, which the quarterback touched, then the center put the ball on the ground for a guard to pick up and advance. Osborne had seen the play while watching film of a high school football game played in Texas. He added the fumbleroosky to Nebraska's playbook in 1979.

The fumbleroosky produced two touchdowns for the Cornhuskers over 14 seasons. Name the guards who scored the touchdowns, and the games in which they scored the touchdowns. Extra credit: Name the last Cornhusker to run the fumbleroosky and the year in which he did it.

10. In 1978, Tom Osborne considered a head coaching job offer from Colorado. He was serious enough about the opening that he and his wife, Nancy, flew to Boulder to discuss the position with Colorado athletic director Eddie Crowder. Osborne also interviewed for a head coaching job in 1969, while he was an assistant to Bob Devaney. The appeal of the job went beyond becoming a head coach. The Cornhuskers' 6–4 seasons in 1967 and 1968 were significant factors in his interest in finding employment elsewhere. "It was fairly ugly [in 1967 and 1968]," Osborne has said. Nonetheless, he acknowledges, "I knew very well what could happen, how it could change."

At what school was the head coaching job for which Osborne applied in 1969? Hint: It is a member of the Big 12 Conference. Extra credit: Name the coach who was hired for the job.

11. Osborne is often referred to, affectionately, as Dr. Tom because of his Ph.D. In what academic field did he earn his doctorate? And what was the title of his doctoral dissertation?

12. Osborne has undergone double-bypass heart surgery. When did he have the surgery? And who was the Lincoln doctor who performed the surgery?

More Tomfoolery

The fumbleroosky wasn't the first bit of "roosky" deception Tom Osborne's charges perpetrated against an opponent. Nebraska also used the "Bummeroosky" and the "bounceroosky," as well as the "swinging gate," under orders from Osborne. The Bummeroosky was the original "roosky" ruse, so named because Bum Phillips was credited by many with devising the play while he was an assistant to the legendary Paul "Bear" Bryant at Texas A&M. Osborne got the play from one of his assistants, Jerry Moore, who had used it while he was a high school coach in Texas.

Osborne used the Bummeroosky for the first time in a 30–7 victory at Missouri in 1975. His record as head coach against the Tigers was 0–2. The play, a fake punt, worked like this. The Cornhuskers had a fourth down at the Missouri 40-yard line late in the first half. They were leading 10–7. Punter Randy Lessman was sent into the game, as was running back John O'Leary, with whom Osborne sent instructions to call the Bummeroosky. Though the team had worked on the play during practice the previous week, the players thought it was only to break the monotony.

"Did I think we would ever run it? Not at all," O'Leary would recall years later.

Because of his reputation as a practical joker, O'Leary was concerned that his teammates wouldn't think he was serious when he said in the huddle that they were supposed to run the Bummeroosky.

Center Rik Bonness snapped the ball to Tony Davis, the up-back, instead of to Lessman. Davis then handed the ball forward, through O'Leary's legs. O'Leary was lined up as a blocking back.

After getting the ball to O'Leary, Davis turned and faked a handoff as if on a reverse to Monte Anthony, another running back who also had lined up as a blocker. Anthony ran to the right flank, along with the blockers and Lessman, who first leaped up as if the center snap had gone high.

O'Leary, with the ball hidden as best he could, delayed one count as a slanting Missouri defensive end crashed past him. The end saw the ball, but too late. O'Leary ran to the left, away from the flow of blockers and defenders, and kept running, 40 yards for the touchdown.

Osborne dipped into his bag of tricks and pulled out the bounceroosky during the Cornhuskers' 28–24 victory against Oklahoma at Memorial Stadium in 1982. Quarterback Turner Gill intentionally threw an incomplete pass in the direction of a split receiver. The pass was not thrown forward, however, making it a lateral, which meant it could be recovered by either team. Gill's toss

Zach Wiegert, 1994 Outland Trophy winner, holding up retired jersey at a spring game. Tom Osborne looks on.
(Photo Courtesy of *Huskers Illustrated*/John Waller)

skipped off the artificial turf and into the hands of the split receiver, who relaxed for an instant as if it were an incomplete pass, then threw down the field to a wide-open tight end. The play was good for 37 yards.

Quiz 61: The Bounceroosky

1. Who was the split receiver on the bounceroosky? And who was the tight end?

2. Nebraska led at halftime 21–10. But on the third play from scrimmage in the second half, an Oklahoma tailback ran 86 yards for a touchdown, his second of the game. Who was the tailback?

3. The Cornhuskers couldn't breathe easily until an interception in the end zone with 26 seconds remaining thwarted Oklahoma's final attempt at victory. Who made the interception?

As with the Bummeroosky, the Cornhuskers practiced the bounceroosky the week before the Oklahoma game. But it almost never worked during practice, prompting center Dave Rimington to say to Osborne, "I hope you don't use it until we're either 100 points ahead or behind."

The swinging gate was considerably less successful when Osborne pulled it out in a bowl game, with Nebraska lining up third-and-goal at the six-yard line late in the game. All of the Cornhuskers except one lined up about 15 yards to the left of the ball. The quarterback, who was on the line of scrimmage, was the only player near the ball. He flipped the ball sideways to the I-back, who was behind the wall of blockers. The I-back ran into the end zone for what would have been a touchdown. But the officials ruled the quarterback had picked up the ball instead of scooping it in one continuous motion, a violation.

The defense was offsides, however, so the down was replayed. Nebraska, which had trailed by a field goal, scored on a pass play to the tight end to take a four-point lead with just under four minutes remaining in the game. The Cornhuskers would lose the game, however, in the closing seconds.

Quiz 62: The Swinging Gate

1. Name the quarterback who lateraled the ball on the swinging gate play.
2. Name the I-back who caught the lateral and scored what would have been a touchdown.
3. Identify the bowl game in which the play was used, the opponent, and the final score. Extra credit: The bowl game was televised by CBS. Afterward, Osborne said he thought the opposition had anticipated Nebraska's trickery because a CBS analyst had watched the Cornhuskers practice and had discussed the play on the air. The analyst was a Heisman Trophy winner. Who was he?

In Memoriam

On April 18, 1996, 22-year-old Brook Berringer died in the crash of a light plane he was piloting. The crash occurred near Raymond, Nebraska, two days before the annual Red-White Game. Berringer, the handsome quarterback from Goodland, Kansas, had just completed his senior season at Nebraska and was preparing for the National Football League draft. Tobey Lake, the brother of Berringer's girlfriend, also died in the crash.

Quiz 63: Like Father, Like Son

Nebraska benefited from second-generation players during Tom Osborne's tenure as head coach, including three sons of Clete Fischer, a four-year Cornhusker football letterman from 1945 to 1948. Clete also served as an assistant coach at Nebraska from 1959 to 1985.

Clete played two seasons with the NFL's New York Giants before beginning his coaching career at the high school level—in his hometown of St. Edward, Nebraska. Sons Pat (1973), Tim (1976–78), and Dan (1980) all earned football letters under Osborne. Daughters Kerry and Kathleen also were involved in Husker athletics. Kerry lettered on the softball team, and Kathleen was a member of the Huskerettes, a spirit-dance team that performed during Nebraska basketball games.

And, hey, Doris, Clete's wife, deserves some credit here, too.

The Fischers qualify as the first family of Nebraska football. Clete's brothers—Ken (1948–49), Rex (1955), and Pat (1958–60)—were Cornhusker football lettermen, too.

The Porter family of Nebraska City deserves honorable mention. Scott Porter earned letters as a Cornhusker fullback in 1983 and 1984. His father, Mort, lettered as a fullback on A. J. Lewandowski's team in 1943. And his grandfather Grover lettered as a halfback on Coach Jumbo Stiehm's 7–0–1 team in 1914. Scott is believed to be the first third-generation Nebraska football letterman.

In addition, Scott's older brother, Budge, went to Nebraska on a football scholarship in 1974. But he suffered an injury during spring practice in 1976 that left him paralyzed from the chest down.

Here are some more of Osborne's second-generation Nebraska football players. See if you can name each player's father. For extra credit, identify the approximate year or years in which the father lettered.

And if you really want to show off, identify the position the father played.

1. Scott Frost, quarterback (1996–97)
2. Terry Rodgers, I-back (1986–89)
3. Chad Blahak, defensive back (1995–96)
4. Jesse Kosch, punter (1995–97)

Too easy? Keep going. They get a little tougher . . . and the optional stuff is harder.

5. Steve Damkroger, linebacker (1979–82)
6. Maury Damkroger, fullback (1971–73)
7. Freeman White, defensive back (1989)
8. David Edeal, center (1988–90)
9. Becky Hornbacher, goalkeeper (1996–present). Okay, so she's a Husker soccer player. But in some parts of the world, soccer is considered "football." She isn't a son, but no one said this would be easy. Besides, you may have been complaining about how easy this was.
10. Morgan Gregory, split end (1987–89)
11. Mike McCashland, defensive back (1982–84)
12. Gregg List, defensive back (1996–97)
13. Dave McCloughan, defensive back (1987–90) . . . Oops! How did a Colorado Buffalo letterman get on this list? Oh well, he's number 13, so it's Colorado's bad luck and his dad was a Cornhusker letterman. So try it. Sorry.

14. Andy Means, defensive back (1978–80)
15. Ryan Terwilliger, linebacker (1993–96)

Quiz 64: The Nebraska City Connection

Four of Scott Porter's Cornhusker teammates also were his teammates at Nebraska City High School. That's remarkable, given the fact Nebraska City's population was, and is, about 7,000 and its high school athletic teams compete in Class B, which is only the state's second-largest classification. Name the four teammates and the positions they played.

Quiz 65: Oh, Brother

When Nebraska played Northern Illinois at Memorial Stadium to open the 1989 season, it was Caliendo against Caliendo, Nebraska's Chris against Northern Illinois's Cary. They were twins who went different directions out of high school in Milwaukee but looked so much alike that Cary could pass himself off as Chris, which he did at least once the week before the Cornhuskers' 1989 Orange Bowl game. A reporter from a television station in Nebraska interviewed Cary in the lobby of the team hotel, thinking that Cary, who had made the trip to Miami to watch his brother play, was Chris.

The Caliendo brothers played at different schools. But just as it benefited from numerous second-generation players, Tom Osborne's program had its share of brother combinations.

The following players have had brothers on the Nebraska football team. Name the brother and identify either the year (or years) in which the brother lettered or, in lieu of that, which of the brothers was older. The list is not all-inclusive, certainly. Hint: In some cases, a brother did not letter.

1. Zach Wiegert, 1991–94
2. Scott Strasburger, 1982–84
3. Roger Craig, 1980–82
4. John McCormick, 1985–87
5. Robb Schnitzler, 1984–86
6. Kelvin Clark, 1976–78
7. Broderick Thomas, 1985–88
8. Mike Rozier, 1981–83
9. Jim Pillen, 1976–78
10. Danny Noonan, 1984–86
11. Aaron Penland, 1992–95
12. Bob Lingenfelter, 1974–76
13. Ritch Bahe, 1972–74
14. Andy Keeler, 1986–88

Which Johnson Was That Again?

Brad Johnson was the number one backup to Dave Rimington, Nebraska's Outland Trophy– and Lombardi Award–winning consensus All-American center in 1982. Brad Johnson was also a starting offensive tackle on the Cornhuskers' undefeated freshman team in 1982.

How could that be? Well, there were two Brad Johnsons on Nebraska's roster in 1982. One, a senior, was a walk-on from Harvard, Nebraska. He was Rimington's backup. The other, a freshman, was a scholarship recruit from Ralston, Nebraska. He played for Coach Frank Solich's 5–0 freshman team.

Quiz 66: What's in a Name?

1. Through the 1997 season, 16 players with a last name of Johnson had earned at least one football letter at Nebraska. Those 16 were tied for the most in Cornhusker history with what other last name? Include variant spellings in determining the answer, if necessary, for example: Thompson, Thomsen, or Thomson. There were eight of those through 1997, by the way. Hint: Twelve of the 16 played for Tom Osborne or Bob Devaney (10 for Osborne).

2. Eleven of the 16 Johnsons earned letters playing for Osborne or Devaney, or in one case, both. Can you name the Johnson who earned letters in 1972 and 1973 (and 1974)? Extra credit: Name as many of the Johnsons as you can. And name as many of the players with the other last name as you can. Anything over 50 percent is worth a grade of B. Anything over 12 on either name is worth an A-plus. If you can get them all, you've cheated and referred to the media guide.

3. Through the 1997 season, only two football lettermen had last names that began with the letter *U*. They were James Unrath (1966) and Ed Uptegrove (1934). There had been no football lettermen with a last name beginning with the letter *X*. And there had been only one football letterman with a last name beginning with the letter *Q*. Name the player and the Nebraska town from which he came. His high school has a unique nickname for its athletic teams, which is something of a clue. And if you really want to flex your Husker trivia muscles, identify the occupation of the *Q* player's dad.

4. I. M. Hipp was promoted by former Cornhusker sports information director Don Bryant as "college football's most famous walk-on" when he burst onto the scene in grand fashion by rushing for 1,301 yards as a redshirted sophomore in 1977. What do the initials I. M. stand for?

Quiz 67: What's in a Nickname?

Can you identify the Tom Osborne–era players whose nicknames follow?
1. Marvelous

2. Smiling Assassin
3. Slick
4. Tough Tony
5. Lumpy
6. Sandman
7. Twisted Steel
8. Too Strong
9. Bullethead
10. Wino

Quiz 68: (Don't) Walk on By

No other major college football program in the country depends on walk-on players as much as Nebraska. It is a haven for walk-ons, in fact. (A walk-on is a player who enrolls at Nebraska and goes out for the team even though he doesn't have a scholarship. Most successful walk-ons eventually earn scholarships. Nebraska doesn't give out its entire NCAA allotment of scholarships during recruiting for that reason.)

The walk-on program is "probably one way we've been able to survive against the Florida schools and the schools in the Sunbelt, schools in populated areas," Tom Osborne has said. "If we didn't have the walk-ons willing to come here, I think it wouldn't be long before we very quickly became a second-rate program. So they're very, very important to us."

Most Cornhusker walk-ons come from towns in Nebraska. But occasionally they come from other states, and even other countries. Walter Wallace came all the way from Aviano, Italy, in hopes of becoming a Cornhusker. He led the Nebraska freshman team in rushing in 1978, gaining 561 yards and scoring seven touchdowns on 85 carries. He never made it with the varsity, however.

These walk-ons all made it and earned letters. Can you identify from whence they came?

1. Terris Chorney (1990–92, center)
2. Mike Murray (1987–89, middle guard)
3. Kelly Saalfeld (1977–79, center)
4. Jared Tomich (1994–96, rush end)
5. Jimmy Williams (1979–81, defensive end)
6. Scott Strasburger (1982–84, defensive end)
7. Andy Means (1978–80, defensive back)
8. Mike Stigge (1989–92, punter)
9. I. M. Hipp (1977–79, I-back)
10. Matt Shaw (1992–94, tight end)
11. Mike McCashland (1982–84, defensive back)
12. Dale Klein (1984–86, placekicker)

If the list seems too easy, here are some extra-credit walk-ons for you to try. Be careful. Remember, you're identifying the walk-on's hometown, not the high school he attended.

13. Zeke Cisco (1991–93, defensive back)
14. Pete Buchanan (1988, linebacker)
15. Lance Gray (1991–93, defensive end/fullback)
16. Gerald Armstrong (1991–93, tight end)
17. Doug Welniak (1985–87, linebacker)
18. Cartier Walker (1987–88, defensive back)
19. Tom Werner (1990–92, wingback)
20. Jerry Dunlap (1989, quarterback)
21. Joel Cornwell (1991–92, quarterback)
22. Paul Potadle (1979, center)
23. Ric Lindquist (1979–81, defensive back)
24. Toby Williams (1980–82, defensive tackle)

More About Walk-ons

Walk-ons were an important factor in the success of Tom Osborne's teams. But Nebraska's walk-on tradition is usually traced to the early 1960s, when Langston Coleman and a friend hitchhiked from Washington, D.C., to Lincoln to earn a place on one of Bob Devaney's teams.

"We didn't know much about either one of them," Devaney once said.

Coleman was encouraged to go to Nebraska by his mom, who worked in the Washington, D.C., office of Ted Sorensen, an administrative aide to President John F. Kennedy and a Nebraska alum.

The 6-foot-2, 197-pound Coleman played defensive end, earning letters in 1964, 1965, and 1966, and developed a well-deserved reputation for intensity on the field. He was "one of the meanest football players we ever had at Nebraska," Devaney once said. "During practice, the other players used to hate being in drills with Langston because he'd beat the heck out of guys."

Coleman's friend decided not to play football at Nebraska, by the way.

Because of more generous NCAA scholarship limits, "we didn't have to worry about walk-ons. The walk-ons we had when I was head coach were more or less incidental," Devaney said.

Their arrivals may have been incidental, but their contributions were not. On the final play of the Oklahoma State game in 1965, the Cowboys' Walt Garrison broke free from the Nebraska 23-yard line and headed goalward, with the Cornhuskers clinging to a 21–17 lead. Garrison had a full head of steam, but he was brought down at the five-yard line as time ran out by Bill Johnson, a 5-foot-10, 187-pound defensive back. Johnson, the son of a Stanton, Nebraska, rancher, was a walk-on.

Nearly two decades after Coleman's unlikely journey to Nebraska, the

Cornhuskers got another outstanding walk-on defensive end from Washington, D.C., Jimmy Williams. He and his brother Toby, a defensive tackle, made the initial contact. They did not, however, hitchhike to Lincoln. Neither did I-back I. M. Hipp, who had to borrow money for a plane ticket in order to get to Lincoln so he could walk on.

Osborne-Era All-Walk-on Team

Here's an all-walk-on team from the Tom Osborne era. Even though transfers from other four-year schools are technically walk-ons, this team is limited to those players who came to Nebraska directly from high school. So some players who deserve consideration have been excluded.

The Cornhuskers changed base defensive alignments during Osborne's tenure as head coach, switching from a 5–2 to a 4–3. As a result, the distinction between defensive ends, rush ends, and outside linebackers is muddled. Jimmy Williams, for example, is included as a linebacker, even though his position was defensive end. Derrie Nelson is listed as a defensive lineman, even though, like Williams, he played defensive end, which was more like an outside linebacker now.

If you're having difficulty following this, check the chapter on defense. (The player's senior season is included in parentheses.)

OFFENSE	DEFENSE
SE—Todd Brown (1982)	DL—Jared Tomich (1996)
OL—David Edeal (1990)	DL—John Parrella (1992)
OL—Kelly Saalfeld (1979)	DL—Tim Rother (1987)
OL—Adam Treu (1996)	DL—Derrie Nelson (1980)
OL—Tim Roth (1985)	LB—Jimmy Williams (1981)
OL—Keven Lightner (1987)	LB—Mark Daum (1984)
TE—Matt Shaw (1994)	LB—Scott Strasburger (1984)
QB—Steve Runty (1973)	DB—Mark Blazek (1988)
IB—I. M. Hipp (1979)	DB—Ric Lindquist (1981)
FB—Joel Makovicka (1998)	DB—Charles Fryar (1988)
WB—Anthony Steels (1981)	DB—Andy Means (1980)
PK—Gregg Barrios (1990)	P—Mike Stigge (1992)

Any Coach Can Make a Mistake—but Sometimes It'll Cost 'Em

John Parrella, an all-conference defensive tackle in 1991 and 1992 and a Cornhusker cocaptain in 1992, signed a letter of intent with Colorado out of high school. But he never played a down for the Buffaloes. In fact, he never enrolled at Colorado. Bill McCartney, then the head coach of the Buffaloes, withdrew the scholarship Parrella had been offered, and Parrella came to Nebraska as a walk-on. Technically, would Parrella have been a transfer from Colorado? Probably not.

Quiz 69: If You Don't Like It There . . .

In a sense, players who transfer from other four-year colleges are like walk-ons because they have to make the initial contact. As a result, they don't have scholarships when they make the decision to become Cornhuskers. Scott Frost, the starting quarterback in 1996–97, transferred from Stanford, where he played both defensive back and quarterback for Coach Bill Walsh.

Identify the four-year schools from which these players transferred.
1. Jarvis Redwine (1979–80, I-back)
2. David Clark (1978–80, defensive tackle)
3. Vince Ferragamo (1975–76, quarterback)
4. Jimmy Burrow (1974–75, defensive back)
5. Bob Sledge (1986–88, offensive tackle)
6. Mark Schellen (1982–83, fullback)
7. Jim Scott (1990–92, center)
8. Allen Lyday (1981–82, defensive back)
9. Brian Blankenship (1983, 1985, offensive guard)
10. Dante Wiley (1986, linebacker)

Brains and Brawn

Nebraska leads the nation in football Academic All-Americans, which is appropriate given the fact that Tom Osborne taught for a time in the Department of Educational Psychology and Measurements while also serving as an assistant football coach under Bob Devaney.

The Cornhuskers' emphasis on academics also can be traced to Osborne, who handled the team's academic affairs before Dr. Ursula Walsh took that responsibility in the early 1970s.

Walsh left Nebraska in November of 1985 to work for the NCAA.

In January of 1978, the NCAA passed a rule allowing student-athletes to compete as graduate students. Prior to that, fifth-year players (those who had redshirted) were forced to delay graduation and enroll in undergraduate courses they didn't need to take in order to remain eligible.

Graduate-student football players are commonplace at Nebraska.

Quiz 70: It's Academic

1. Who was the first graduate student to play football for Nebraska? Hint: He was a captain and played defense.

2. What Cornhusker played as a graduate student in 1994, after making straight A's through his college career as well as in high school? What was his major?

3. Two Cornhuskers have earned first-team academic all-conference honors four consecutive seasons. Who were they and what positions did they play?

The Cornhusker All-Academic Team

Although there have always been outstanding students who represented Nebraska on the football field, the selection of Academic All-America teams is a fairly recent phenomenon. So it is appropriate that a Cornhusker All-Academic team for the modern era be included in the Tom Osborne chapter.

The Cornhuskers' success in the classroom "didn't start with any great and glorious plan to create scholars," Bob Devaney once said. "We just wanted to see the players graduate and stay eligible." Even so, he coached eight first-team Academic All-Americans during his 11 seasons at Nebraska.

Devaney credited former assistant Jim Ross, with whom he coached in high school in Michigan and then brought with him to Nebraska from Wyoming. "As it turned out, Jim took his job pretty seriously and got us started on the right track," said Devaney. "Then we got Tom Osborne."

As with any such team, deserving members must be omitted. Defensive tackle Larry Jacobson, for example, won the Outland Trophy and was a consensus All-American and an Academic All-American in 1971. But defensive tackles Terry Connealy and Rob Stuckey were two-time first-team Academic All-Americans and three-time academic all-conference honorees and could hardly be left off. (The year in which the player earned first-team Academic All-America honors is in parentheses.)

OFFENSE	DEFENSE
SE—Jim Huge (1962)	DL—Grant Wistrom (1996, 1997)
OL—Rob Zatechka (1993, 1994)	DL—Terry Connealy (1993, 1994)
OL—Randy Schleusener (1979, 1980)	DL—Rob Stuckey (1983, 1984)
OL—Dave Rimington (1981, 1982)	DL—George Andrews (1978)
OL—Mark Traynowicz (1984)	LB—Trev Alberts (1993)
OL—Aaron Graham (1995)	LB—Pat Tyrance (1990)
TE—Tony Jeter (1965)	LB—Scott Strasburger (1983, 1984)
QB—Dennis Claridge (1963)	
RB—Jeff Kinney (1971)	DB—Mark Blazek (1987, 1988)
RB—Pat Clare (1960)	DB—Ted Harvey (1976, 1977)
WB—Frosty Anderson (1973)	DB—Ric Lindquist (1981)
PK—Dale Klein (1986)	DB—Randy Reeves (1969)
	P—Mike Stigge (1991, 1992)

Rush end Grant Wistrom, the 1997 Lombardi Award winner, sacks the Colorado quarterback. Wistrom would be a lock on an all–Tom Osborne era team.

(Photo Courtesy of *Huskers Illustrated*/Doug DeVoe)

Fresh Faces and Jayvees

On October 8, 1993, at Memorial Stadium, Matt Turman, a redshirted freshman walk-on from Wahoo, Nebraska, completed nine of 11 passes for 182 yards and three touchdowns and rushed for 73 yards to lead Nebraska's freshman–junior varsity to a 49–20 victory against the Air Force Academy jayvees.

The audience was atypically small, not only because the game was played on a workday afternoon but also because some Cornhusker fans had yet to return from Stillwater, Oklahoma, where the previous night the Nebraska varsity defeated Oklahoma State 27–13 for Tom Osborne's 200th victory as head coach.

The Cornhusker jayvees had practiced together only once. Graduate assistants Gerry Gdowski and Bill Busch coached the team, which was made up mostly of players who hadn't made the trip to Stillwater. Redshirts couldn't play without sacrificing a season of eligibility.

Osborne scheduled the game as a favor to Air Force coach Fisher DeBerry, a friend. The Cornhuskers has discontinued their junior varsity program in February of 1991, in anticipation of an NCAA-mandated reduction in the number of football assistant coaches, which would go into effect in 1992.

Nebraska's makeshift jayvee team was to play the Air Force jayvees a second time at Colorado Springs in mid-November. The game was postponed and then canceled because of a snowstorm.

Thus, the Cornhuskers' remarkably successful freshman–junior varsity program, which had existed in one form or another for nearly 80 years, was committed to history, going not with a bang but a whimper. Even if Osborne had wanted to resurrect it, he couldn't have because the Big Eight Conference passed a rule, soon after, prohibiting member schools from fielding junior varsity football teams.

The purpose of the rule was cost containment.

Until its final seasons, Nebraska's junior varsity team was made up mostly of freshmen. Even after freshmen were allowed to play varsity football, the Cornhuskers kept most first-year players on the junior varsity. They would play one season, then redshirt before competing for varsity jobs.

The benefits of such a system were obvious. Players could gain experience and maturity, and they could develop a winning attitude that served them well on the varsity. That carryover eventually caused other conference coaches to refuse to schedule junior varsity games against Nebraska.

As a result, except for a continuing home-and-home series with the Air Force jayvees, the young Cornhuskers played junior college teams and junior varsity teams from small colleges in the late 1980s. That led to some serious mismatches. They defeated the St. Thomas, Minnesota, jayvees in consecutive seasons by a combined score of 148–3, and they won four games in a row against the Bethany, Kansas, junior varsity by scores of 65–0, 68–0, 76–0, and 45–0. The Air Force series was competitive, however, as were some games, both home and away, against nationally ranked junior college teams.

From 1956, when records were first kept for the freshman team, through 1990, the last regularly scheduled junior varsity season, Nebraska's freshman–junior varsity record was 120–17–1. Included in that total were 21 unbeaten and untied seasons—and only one losing season. In 1987, the Cornhusker jayvees finished 2–3, losing their final three games to the Air Force jayvees (21–19), Coffeyville (Kansas) Junior College (49–14), and Waldorf (Iowa) Junior College (42–36). The Waldorf game was in Lincoln.

"A lot of people benefited from the freshman program," Osborne said.

Quarterback Turner Gill and wingback Irving Fryar provided a preview of coming attractions as freshmen on the junior varsity team in 1980. Gill completed 34 of 52 passes for 679 yards and eight touchdowns, and Fryar caught 16 passes for 432 yards and five touchdowns.

That jayvee team finished 5–0, winning by an average score of 51–14.

Quiz 71: Jayvees

1. Success on the freshman–junior varsity team wasn't necessarily an indication of varsity success. Will Curtis, for example, set the jayvee record

for touchdowns in a season, by scoring eight as a freshman I-back in 1981. But he never went any further in the program. Sometimes players switched positions after a season on the junior varsity team. With that in mind, who was the leading rusher for the high-scoring freshman–junior varsity team in 1980? Hint: He played defense during his varsity career.

    2. Mike Rozier joined Gill and Fryar in the Scoring Explosion backfield. He didn't redshirt. Yet he didn't gain a yard for the Nebraska jayvees as a college freshman in 1980. Why not?

    3. Who was the Cornhuskers' freshman coach in 1980?

But Seriously, Folks . . . Osborne on His Career in the NFL

Tom Osborne often is described by those who don't know him as humorless, occasionally to the point of being Jonathan Edwards–like. Remember Edwards's "Sinners in the Hands of an Angry God" sermon you had to read in the early American literature class in college? No? That's just as well.

Anyway, Osborne has a sense of humor, which is never more apparent than those all-too-rare times when he talks about his short-lived professional football career.

Osborne spent three seasons in the National Football League. He was an 18th-round draft choice of the San Francisco 49ers in 1959, after a multisport career at Hastings College in Nebraska. He played quarterback at Hastings College, but 49ers coach Red Hickey immediately made him into a flanker because San Francisco already had two proven quarterbacks in Y. A. Tittle and John Brodie.

Osborne spent the 1959 season on the 49ers' inactive list. He traveled with the team, however, and his roommate on the road was a quarterback from Occidental College: Jack Kemp.

Osborne went to training camp with the 49ers in 1960 but was released before the season and picked up by the Washington Redskins. Kemp signed with the fledgling American Football League.

Osborne played two seasons for Redskin teams that compiled a 2–21–1 record under two head coaches: Mike Nixon in 1960 and Bill McPeak in 1961. Osborne was primarily a backup to Joe Walton in 1960, but Walton was traded and he became the starter in 1961, when he finished second on the team in pass receptions despite a hamstring pull that bothered him from training camp on.

Osborne has told these stories, in various forms, about his brief NFL career.

• The Redskins instituted a unique pay system based on merit. Players earned $100 for scoring a touchdown, $50 for catching a pass, and $15 for making a block or tackle. There were deductions for mistakes, including such things as fumbles and missed assignments. "To give you an idea of the kind of player I was, at the end of the first year, they called me in and added everything up and said I owed the team $34.50. They said I was the highest-paid player on the team."

- "The first recollection I had of being with the Redskins was in New York City. I joined the team there. I can remember standing out in front of the Waldorf-Astoria.

    "Being the high-class organization they were then, that's where the Redskins always stayed when they were in New York . . . out in front of the Waldorf-Astoria."

- "I got a copy of the *New York Times*. There was only a small item at the very back, in a corner. It said I had been acquired by the Redskins to be a fullback. This terrified me. I tore out the article and showed it to the head coach, who had never seen it before.

    "'Coach, this has to be a misprint or a practical joke or something.'

    "'No, Osborne, I want you to be our fullback.'

    "'Well, Coach, I'm 6-foot-4 and 185 pounds. Why in the world would you want a guy like that to be your fullback? Most pro fullbacks weigh at least 230 or 240.'

    "'Have you ever seen the Redskins play, Osborne? When you see the size of the holes our line opens up, well, you're the only kind of fullback who can get through.'"

Husker Fact

True grit is in the genes. Derrie Nelson, an All-America defensive end in 1980, came from tiny Fairmont, Nebraska, and walked on at Nebraska. His high school coach was Tim Turman, father of former Cornhusker quarterback Matt Turman, who also was a walk-on from Wahoo, Nebraska.

Doggone It

Broderick Thomas had a Chinese shar-pei puppy named Champ. One afternoon in fall 1987, Thomas and wingback Richard Bell drove to the South Stadium offices on an errand. They took Champ along and left him in Thomas's car, which they left running in the parking lot. The air-conditioning was on, so the windows were up. When they returned, Champ somehow had hit the power locks and activated the tape deck. Music blared, and Thomas and Bell couldn't get in. Champ playfully bounced from door to door while they tried to coax him to hit the locks again. Their efforts were in vain.

Finally, Thomas called campus security. Before an officer could arrive, however, Champ hit the locks, opening the doors. Thomas maintained Champ had locked the doors on purpose.

Quiz 72: What if? . . . The Osborne Era

There aren't right or wrong answers in this section (although there are questions that can be answered under each subject). The purpose is to consider how the course of Cornhusker football history might have been altered in major or minor ways if certain things had happened differently.

Tom Osborne wrote in his 1985 autobiography *More Than Winning* that one of the factors leading to his decision to retire from professional football after the 1961 season was the Washington Redskins' unwillingness to pay the players for exhibition games, in violation of league rules.

Instead of playing another season in the NFL, Osborne enrolled in graduate school at Nebraska and began his coaching career as an unpaid graduate assistant on Bob Devaney's first staff.

What if the Redskins Hadn't Withheld Players' Pay for Exhibition Games?

1. Although Osborne didn't get a paycheck as a graduate assistant, he was compensated for his work with the freshman receivers. What form did that compensation take?

Mike Rozier is Nebraska's all-time leading rusher. He gained 4,780 yards and ran for 49 touchdowns in his three seasons as a Cornhusker. He played his freshman year at Coffeyville Community College in Kansas because he didn't have enough credits to meet NCAA eligibility requirements. The problem stemmed, in part, from a teachers' strike in Camden, New Jersey, during his senior year in high school.

What if Rozier Had Been Eligible at Nebraska as a Freshman in 1980?

To refresh your memory, the Cornhuskers lost twice in 1980: 18–14 to Florida State and 21–17 to Oklahoma. They were ranked number seven in both major wire service polls after defeating Mississippi State in the Sun Bowl 31–17. With a victory against Oklahoma, they would have gone to the Orange Bowl.

2. Who led the Cornhuskers in rushing in 1980?

On a second-and-four at the Nebraska 17-yard line with time running out and the Cornhuskers leading Penn State 24–21 at State College, Pennsylvania, in 1982, the Nittany Lions picked up 15 yards and a first down at the two-yard line on a Todd Blackledge pass to his tight end. The tight end may have been out of bounds.

Afterward, he said, "The refs said I was in. I saw some of the Nebraska players, and they looked pretty confident that I was out. I was worried. But the ref came over and made the call."

On the next play, Blackledge threw his third touchdown pass of the game, to another tight end in the back of the end zone, to give Penn State a 27–24 victory. Only four seconds remained.

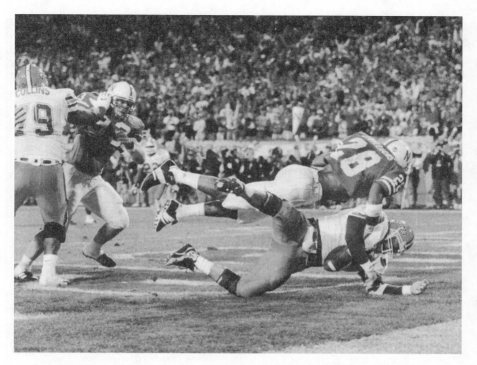

Jamel Williams sacks Florida quarterback Danny Wuerffel in the 1996 Fiesta Bowl game—which provided Tom Osborne with his second national championship.

(Photo Courtesy of *Huskers Illustrated*/Bob Berry)

What if the Reception at the Two-Yard Line Had Been Ruled Out of Bounds?

Penn State was voted the national champion for that season, after defeating Georgia in the Sugar Bowl game, 27–23. Georgia was undefeated, untied, and ranked number one going into the bowl game. Penn State was number two, even though the Nittany Lions had lost to Alabama decisively, 42–21, two weeks after edging Nebraska. The Cornhuskers finished the season 12–1 and ranked number three after a lackluster 21–20 victory against Louisiana State in the Orange Bowl game. Southern Methodist was ranked number two.

3. Can you name the Penn State tight end who made the controversial reception at the two-yard line? How about the tight end who caught the winning touchdown pass?

Here's a still-familiar topic. A conjecture section wouldn't be complete without it. Nebraska, with its Scoring Explosion offense, was undefeated and untied going into the 1984 Orange Bowl game against Miami. After junior I-back Jeff Smith, who was playing in place of injured Heisman Trophy winner Mike Rozier, scored his second touchdown of the fourth quarter to cut the deficit to

31–30 with 48 seconds remaining, Osborne made the decision to go for two points and the victory.

That dramatic decision, made without hesitation or remorse, helped to define Osborne's coaching career, almost as much as the national championships in 1994, 1995, and 1997.

What if Osborne Had Settled for an Extra-Point Kick and the Tie a Successful Kick Would Have Produced?

4. Who was the Cornhuskers' number one placekicker that night, and whom did he succeed in that capacity in the seventh game of the season against Missouri?

Early in the second quarter of Nebraska's game against Colorado in 1988, the Buffaloes' J. J. Flannigan broke free on a run up the middle, on a third-and-three from the Cornhusker 43-yard line. There was no score in the game, which was a defensive struggle throughout. Flannigan ran 24 yards before losing control of the ball, without a Nebraska defender close enough to stop or catch him. He managed to recover his fumble at the Nebraska 19-yard line. Colorado couldn't capitalize, however. The Buffaloes were penalized for holding, and then the Cornhuskers' Broderick Thomas tackled Jeff Campbell for a 19-yard loss on a reverse, forcing a fourth-down punt from—where else?—the Nebraska 43-yard line.

Nebraska finally scored in the third quarter to win 7–0.

What if Flannigan Had Not Lost Control of the Ball?

A week later, the Cornhuskers defeated Oklahoma in another defensive struggle, 7–3, to win the Big Eight championship and a berth in the Orange Bowl game. The loss was the only one in the conference for Coach Barry Switzer's Sooners. It was the last time Switzer coached against Osborne.

5. Nebraska's number one I-back in 1988 scored the touchdown against Colorado. He rushed for 1,497 yards that season as a junior. Who was he and from what high school did he come?

Osborne nearly left Nebraska to become the head coach at Colorado in 1978. "If it had been a plain business proposition, I'd have gone to Colorado," he said in announcing his decision to stay. "The financial opportunity and security were certainly greater at Colorado. But when I thought of the players . . . it would be difficult to tell them that I was going to go and coach against them."

What if Osborne Had Accepted the Colorado Job?

The coach Colorado hired to replace Bill Mallory spent only three seasons in Boulder. During those seasons, his teams had a combined record of 7–26. Included in the 26 losses were three against Osborne's Cornhuskers, by a combined score of 142–17. Bill McCartney was hired in 1982 and suffered through three losing seasons before finally getting the program turned around.

6. Who was the coach Colorado hired after the 1978 season?

Dave Rimington considered submitting his name for the NFL draft after his junior season at Nebraska in 1981. He was serious about it. "This didn't just come up overnight," he said following the Cornhuskers' 22–15 loss against Clemson in the 1982 Orange Bowl game. "A lot of my teammates in the offensive line think I should declare hardship." Rimington could have done so because the NCAA had granted him a fifth season of eligibility after he was sidelined by knee surgery as a freshman in 1978. The Outland Trophy–winning center was plagued by injuries throughout his career, which was a significant factor in his consideration of leaving early for the NFL.

What if Dave Rimington Had Left Nebraska After His Junior Season?

With Rimington back for his senior season in 1982, the Cornhuskers went 12–1 and finished number three in both major wire service polls. With Rimington anchoring the offensive line, Nebraska led the nation in total offense, rushing, and scoring. He won a second Outland Trophy and the Lombardi Award. He was a consensus All-American, and he was picked in the first round in the 1983 NFL draft.

7. What team drafted Dave Rimington?

Tommie Frazier's final recruiting visit was to Nebraska. He already had made visits to Notre Dame, Syracuse, Colorado, and Clemson and had grown weary, so much so that he considered canceling the trip to Nebraska and picking from among the other four schools. Most recruiting analysts speculated that his decision would come down to Notre Dame and Clemson, anyway. Frazier's mom made him take the trip to Nebraska, however. "I told Tommie that I didn't know exactly where Nebraska was, but I was going to drag him out there if I had to. Your word is your bond," Priscilla Frazier told the *Omaha World-Herald*.

Tommie visited Nebraska just before letters of intent could be signed in early February 1992. The weather was unseasonably warm in Lincoln. "I told him it was unusually cold for this time of year," Osborne said, jokingly, at a news conference to announce the Cornhusker recruits.

What if Frazier's Mom Hadn't Made Him Keep His Word and Visit Nebraska?

During his visit to Colorado, Frazier was told that he needed to make a decision while he was in Boulder because the Buffaloes were recruiting another top high school quarterback in Texas.

8. Who was the quarterback in Texas?

This isn't a final exam in the traditional sense. It's not a comprehensive exam, based on what you may or may not have learned throughout this chapter. Rather, it is a collection of questions that come at the end of the chapter, hence the designation "final" exam. Just so there's no confusion . . .

SECTION I: WHO AM I?

1. I was a Cornhusker cocaptain and Associated Press All-America offensive guard in 1987. While I was in Fort Lauderdale, Florida, with the other AP All-Americans for a videotaping of a Bob Hope television Christmas special, I tried to intervene in an argument involving Oklahoma offensive lineman Mark Hutson and Miami defensive end Daniel Stubbs. The Sooners and Hurricanes were going to play in the Orange Bowl game. Stubbs inadvertently punched me instead of Hutson. It was no big deal. Who am I?

2. I was among the most publicized members of Tom Osborne's 1983 recruiting class. I was a running back from a small high school in Havre de Grace, Maryland, a suburb of Baltimore. I played well enough as a freshman at Nebraska, averaging 6.3 yards per carry and scoring four touchdowns in four junior varsity games. But for various reasons, I never played for the Cornhusker varsity. Who am I?

Extra credit 1: Despite my per-carry average, I wasn't the Cornhusker junior varsity's leading rusher in 1983. A freshman walk-on from Arlington, Texas, was. What was his name?

Extra credit 2: Nebraska recruited another highly publicized running back from a small high school in Ridgeway, Ohio, in 1977. Like me, he never achieved success as a Cornhusker, playing sparingly as a freshman on the jayvee team before leaving. Who was he?

3. Tom Osborne is well-read. No great insight there. I am a character in a Herman Melville novel. Osborne compared himself to me after a practice in 1987 to emphasize that he wasn't driven to win a national championship. Who am I? What is the novel in which I am a main character?

4. I was the first quarterback from Lincoln, Nebraska, to start a game for Tom Osborne. In fact, the last time a quarterback from Lincoln had started a game for the Cornhuskers was in 1955. I was the fifth quarterback listed on the depth chart going into preseason camp my senior year, 1979. I was a walk-on. I started the Penn State game, which was nationally televised, and I led Nebraska to a 42–17 victory, completing 14 of 22 passes for 215 yards and two touchdowns. Who am I? From what Lincoln high school did I come? Who was my high school coach? And who was Nebraska's quar-

terback from Lincoln in 1955? Extra credit: Who were the four listed ahead of me on the preseason depth chart in 1979?

5. I began the 1994 football season as a freshman student manager. But the Cornhuskers were thin at quarterback. Ben Rutz had transferred. Jon Elder had left the team, and school. Monte Christo was injured, and Matt Turman was less than full speed, leaving only Tommie Frazier and Brook Berringer healthy. So quarterbacks coach Turner Gill asked if I would be interested in playing quarterback on the scout team. I had played quarterback for my high school team in Lake Havasu, Arizona. My dad was my high school coach. I got in the Pacific game, carrying once for four yards and throwing an incomplete pass. Who am I?

Extra credit: When I went into the Pacific game, the fans cheered, "Rudy! Rudy!" Why? Also, what was my jersey number? Hint: It was the same number that cornerback Tyrone Williams wore.

6. I was a member of Nebraska's 1985 recruiting class, which included, among others, Steve Taylor, Broderick Thomas, and LeRoy Etienne. At least one recruiting analyst rated our class the best in the nation. I spent just a few days in fall camp, practicing with the freshmen, before leaving.

I enrolled at a junior college in the Kansas City area and didn't play football that season. I missed it, however, and played at Coffeyville Community College in Kansas in 1986. I began as a running back in Coffeyville's wishbone offense but was moved to fullback about midseason. In 1987, I returned to Nebraska. I lettered three seasons for the Cornhuskers, also as a fullback. Who am I? Hint: I teamed with Gerry Gdowski on a 51-yard touchdown pass to stun Colorado a minute and a half into the game at Boulder, Colorado, in 1989. Even so, we lost to the Buffaloes, 27–21.

7. I was recruited by Nebraska primarily as a linebacker but ended up playing fullback. I sang with a Lincoln band called Brain Hammer. I didn't want people to think that my singing in a band was a big deal, that I was some kind of rock-and-roll singer. But Rick Telander wrote about Brain Hammer and my being a singer in a story for *Sports Illustrated* the week after we defeated UCLA 42–33. If you don't believe me, check out the story in the September 21, 1987, issue of the magazine. My name's in there.

For fun, I liked to watch the World Wrestling Federation. You could have seen me at ringside during a match or two at Pershing Auditorium. I also was a good student, by the way. Who am I?

8. I was a 6-foot-6, 260-pound offensive tackle from Leawood, Kansas. I was bothered by a ruptured disc and didn't earn a letter until my senior season in 1979. About a month after the Hawaii game in 1978, I decided to fly to Toronto to be injected with an enzyme extracted from unripe papaya. The enzyme helped to dissolve the disc, which, in turn, allowed me to play without pain. I had to go to Canada because the procedure wasn't allowed in the United States at the time. Who am I?

SECTION II: SHORT ANSWERS, MOSTLY OSBORNE

1. As mentioned earlier, Tom Osborne was a roommate of Jack Kemp for road trips in 1959, when the two were players on the San Francisco 49ers' taxi squad. Osborne wrote in his 1985 autobiography *More Than Winning* that Kemp's "studiousness was a great influence on me." He has joked that some of the 49ers considered Kemp an "intellectual" because he read what magazine?

2. At the end of training camp, after the 49ers told Osborne he had made the team but would spend his rookie season on the taxi squad, he briefly tried something else before deciding he wanted to concentrate on football, even if it meant being on the 49ers' taxi squad. What did he try?

3. Osborne played for the Washington Redskins in 1960 and 1961. He considered enrolling at the George Washington School of Law in Washington, D.C., during his first off-season with the Redskins. He changed his mind, however, and took graduate classes in psychology at another university, where he lived in the athletic dorm and kept tabs on the players. He asked the football coach if the program had an opening for a graduate assistant. It did not. What was the school? Who was the coach?

4. In October 1980, a Lincoln newspaper used a headline on a story about a speech Osborne made at a meeting of an Omaha booster club that made it appear he might be thinking about going to another school to coach. The school, which has a nationally prominent football program, was looking for a new head coach. The local story was picked up by the national wire services, causing Osborne considerable concern. The headline said: NU'S OSBORNE WOULD CONSIDER _____. Fill in the blank.

5. Before the Cornhuskers boarded the buses for Sun Devil Stadium and their national championship game against Florida in the 1996 Fiesta Bowl, Osborne read a passage from what book during a team meeting at the hotel? Extra credit: What was the essence of the passage?

6. Nebraska played a four-game home-and-home series with Penn State beginning in 1979. The series matched the coaching genius of Osborne and that of Penn State's Joe Paterno for the first time. Paterno was the winningest active major college coach by percentage when the teams played in 1979.

Nebraska won the first game decisively, 42–17. When Osborne met Paterno on the field to shake hands, he told his friend and coaching rival, "Sorry about the score." Cornhusker cocaptain Tim Smith presented Osborne with the game ball on behalf of the players afterward.

How many of the remaining three games in the series did Nebraska win? When was the next time the Cornhuskers played Paterno's Penn State team, and what was the outcome of that game?

7. When Nebraska played Penn State for the first time under Osborne in 1979, security was increased on the sidelines at Memorial Stadium during the game. Why?

8. Osborne and Florida State's Bobby Bowden, another coaching legend, matched strategy for the first time in a four-game series that began in 1980. All four games were played in Lincoln. Bowden established the national reputation his program now enjoys by scheduling top teams on the road. The Seminoles defeated third-ranked Nebraska 18–14 in 1980. How many of the remaining three games in the original series did Florida State win? When did the teams play next?

9. Florida State came back from a 14–0 deficit midway through the second quarter to upset the Cornhuskers in 1980. The Seminoles drove 72 yards on 14 plays to set up a 32-yard field goal late in the first half, setting the stage for what would happen in the second half. They scored three more field goals in addition to a touchdown and an extra point after the intermission.

Nebraska almost pulled out a victory. The Cornhuskers got to the Florida State three-yard line in the closing seconds of the game, but a Seminole linebacker tackled quarterback Jeff Quinn, forcing a fumble, which Florida State recovered. The linebacker finished with 18 tackles, including 12 unassisted. What was his name? And what was the name of the Seminole placekicker who made the four field goals?

Extra credit: Afterward, Florida State's quarterback complimented Nebraska's fans: "That was my first experience of going on the road and being treated well by first-class fans." What was his name?

10. If you've done fairly well in answering most of the questions in this book, there's one more section coming up to test you. As a preview, try this one. What was Osborne's jersey number with the Washington Redskins in 1961? Okay. So the final questions aren't THAT tough. Even Osborne might not remember. . . .

Then again, maybe you know his Redskins jersey number, which would be pretty scary.

Answers

Quiz 57: Chasing the Record

1. Bear Bryant, 323 in 38 seasons; Pop Warner, 319 in 44 seasons; and Amos Alonzo Stagg, 314 in 57 seasons

2. Joe Paterno, Penn State, 298 after the 1997 season, and Bobby Bowden, Florida State, 281 after the 1997 season

Quiz 58: They Were Keepers

1. Monte Kiffin, 2. George Darlington, 3. Rick Duval, 4. Warren Powers, 5. Cletus Fisher, 6. Bill Myles, 7. John Melton, 8. Jerry Moore, 9. Mike Corgan, 10. Jim Ross. Moore, Darlington, and Duval were hired by Osborne. The others were on Devaney's staff. Osborne's first two graduate assistant coaches were former players Guy Ingles and Jim Anderson.

Quiz 59: A Little Quiz on Osborne's First Game as Head Coach

1. Bruin quarterback Mark Harmon became an actor. His father, Tom, was a football All-American at Michigan in the late 1930s and played professionally for the Los Angeles Rams. He also earned the Silver Star and Purple Heart in the United States Air Force during World War II.

2. Bob Thornton coached the Cornhusker defensive backs from 1981 to 1985.

3. Steve Runty, offense, and John Dutton, defense, ABC; Runty and Tony Davis, AP

4. Wonderful Monds Jr.

5. Frosty Anderson, Scottsbluff; Rik Bonness, Bellevue; Dan Anderson, Fremont; Al Austin, Lincoln; Brent Longwell, Homer; Steve Runty, Ogallala; Tony Davis, Tecumseh; Ritch Bahe, Fremont; Maury Damkroger, Lincoln; Steve Manstedt, Wahoo; Bob Martin, David City; and Randy Borg, Alliance

6. John Dutton was a first-round pick of the Baltimore Colts in 1974. Tom Ruud was a first-round pick of the Buffalo Bills in 1975. Bob Nelson, who played linebacker alongside Ruud, was the Buffalo Bills' second-round draft pick in 1975. Both Ruud and Nelson were from Minnesota.

7. Humm was recovering from strained knee ligaments and wasn't full speed. Osborne indicated he might be available if he was needed. But he was not. Runty was a more than capable replacement, completing nine of 11 passes to set a school and Big Eight Conference record for completion percentage, .818. Tom Humm was a wide receiver. The Humm brothers were from Las Vegas, Nevada.

8. I-back Tony Davis threw a pass, which was incomplete.

9. Ron Pruitt, Compton; John Bell, Anaheim; Zaven Yaralian, Inglewood; and Bob Thornton, Lomita

10. Prior to 1973, the varsity locker room was located in the Schulte Fieldhouse at the north end of Memorial Stadium. The South Stadium locker room was completed and used for the first time in 1973. So the Cornhuskers ran onto the field from the south end instead of the north end. They also warmed up in the south end zone instead of the north end zone, of course.

11. The Bruins ran a wishbone offense. Quarterback Mark Harmon was a better runner than passer, and UCLA had outstanding running backs, including Kermit Johnson, James McAlister, and Eddie Ayers.

12. Efron Herrera kicked a 30-yard field goal with 22 seconds remaining for the victory.

13. Pepper Rodgers, who also coached against Nebraska while at Kansas

14. The Cornhuskers' Johnny Rodgers, the Heisman Trophy winner, was a game-breaking punt returner. He completed his eligibility in 1972.

15. Randy Borg

16. Yes. Osborne officially became the head coach immediately after the Orange Bowl game victory against Notre Dame on January 1, 1973. He celebrated his 36th birthday on February 23, 1973. So he was 36 the day of the UCLA game.

17. The Bruins scored a touchdown in the first quarter against the Blackshirts. The last time an opponent had scored a first-quarter touchdown against the Blackshirts was the Minnesota game in 1970, when the Gophers' Ernie Cook ran 45 yards to score. Kansas and Oklahoma State each scored first-quarter touchdowns against the Cornhuskers in 1970, but both were on kickoff returns. In 29 of those 33 games, the opposition didn't score at all in the first quarter. Prior to the 1973 game, UCLA was the last team to score in the first quarter against Nebraska, on a 27-yard field goal by Efron Herrera in the 1972 upset.

18. The Cornhuskers won three more games before losing at Missouri 13–12. The Tigers, who were ranked number 12 by the AP at the time, were coached by Al Onofrio.

Quiz 60: Wizardry of Oz

1. Epley was a pole vaulter on the track-and-field team. His involvement in strength and conditioning was a result of a serious back injury. He was Nebraska's first 15-foot pole vaulter indoors.

2. "Because You Loved Me," by Celine Dion

3. Lee Jones, defensive tackle, 1985–87, nickname "Killer"

4. The season was 1992. The team was Iowa State. The coach was Jimmy Walden. The score was 19–10.

5. Nebraska lost its final regular-season game under Osborne 11 times. All but one of those 11 were against Oklahoma. The years: 1973, 1974, 1975, 1977, 1978, 1979, 1980, 1984, 1985, 1986, and 1990. The only non-Oklahoma loss was in 1978, when Missouri defeated the Cornhuskers 35–31.

6. Matt Turman, 1994–96

7. Corey Dixon, Abdul Muhammad, Reggie Baul, Brendan Holbein, and Riley Washington. Dixon and Baul were listed at 5-foot-8. The others were listed at 5-foot-9.

8. Peter Buchanan, lettered 1988, outside linebacker, Canada; Terris Chorney, lettered 1990–92, center, Canada; and Brett Popplewell, lettered 1992–93, split end, Australia

By the way, if you included George Achola among the three, give yourself a little extra credit even though he didn't walk on. Technically, he fits otherwise. He lived in Kenya until he was six years old. His family moved to the United States, and he stayed when his parents later returned to Kenya. He was a Cornhusker scholarship recruit following an outstanding high school career at Omaha Creighton Prep. "My nationality is Kenyan, but I'm an American for all practical purposes," he once said. He is an American for the purposes of this answer as well. Achola, who concentrated on soccer until he was an eighth-grader, lettered as an I-back for the Cornhuskers in 1990 and 1991. He rushed for 490 yards and scored six touchdowns during his career.

Bobby Newcombe, a freshman sensation at wingback in 1997, was born in Sierra Leone, Africa.

9. Randy Schleusener scored on a 15-yard run against Oklahoma in 1979. The Cornhuskers lost 17–14. Dean Steinkuhler scored on a 19-yard run against Miami in the 1984 Orange Bowl. Nebraska lost 31–30. Will Shields gained 16 yards on the fumbleroosky in 1992, the final season the play was legal.

10. After Nebraska's 45–7 victory against Georgia in the Sun Bowl at El Paso, Texas, in 1969, Osborne went to Lubbock to interview for the head coaching job at Texas Tech. The job was not offered to him. The Red Raiders hired Jim Carlen to replace J. T. King. Devaney subsequently picked Osborne as his successor at Nebraska. Originally, Devaney planned to retire after the 1971 season. But he was persuaded to stay in 1972 so that he could attempt to coach a third consecutive national championship team.

11. Osborne's doctorate is in educational psychology and measurements. He understands test stress better than most of us because he wrote a doctoral dissertation on "The Effects of Instructions on Situational Anxiety Level and Examination Performance." Presumably he took those factors into account when he administered his weekly tests to the Cornhusker quarterbacks.

12. Dr. Deepak Gangahar, who also handled Tommie Frazier's blood clot problems in 1994, was the lead cardiovascular surgeon for the operation, which lasted some three hours on February 5, 1985. Gangahar was assisted by Dr. Stephen Carvath.

Quiz 61: The Bounceroosky

1. Wingback Irving Fryar scooped up the ball and passed to tight end Mitch Krenk.
2. Marcus Dupree
3. Defensive end Scott Strasburger

Quiz 62: The Swinging Gate

1. Jeff Quinn
2. Jarvis Redwine
3. Nebraska used the swinging gate against Houston in the 20–17 1980 Cotton Bowl loss. The analyst was Paul Hornung, who won the Heisman Trophy at Notre Dame.

Quiz 63: Like Father, Like Son

1. Larry Frost, wingback, 1967–69
2. Johnny Rodgers, wingback/slotback, 1970–72
3. Joe Blahak, defensive back, 1970–72
4. Bill Kosch, defensive back, 1969–71
5. Ralph Damkroger, end, 1947–49
6. Ralph Damkroger, see above. Yes, Steve and Maury are brothers. Just checking.
7. Freeman White, end, 1963–65. The father is Freeman White II. The son is Freeman White III.
8. Russell Edeal, tackle, 1958
9. Bill Hornbacher, middle guard, 1968–69
10. Ben Gregory, halfback, 1965–67
11. Dick McCashland, fullback, 1956–58
12. Jerry List, tight end, 1970–72
13. Kent McCloughan, halfback, 1962–64
14. Arden Means, guard, 1943, 1947–49
15. Marlin Terwilliger, defensive back. You're right, Marlin didn't earn a letter at Nebraska, but he was on the team for a time in the late 1960s. He was an outstanding multisport athlete at Grant High School in Nebraska, graduating in 1966. He also was Ryan's football coach at Grant.

Quiz 64: The Nebraska City Connection

Mitch Krenk, tight end; Bret Clark, safety; Greg Orton, guard; and Chad Daffer, linebacker. Krenk was a Cornhusker senior in 1982, when Porter, Clark, and Orton were sophomores and Daffer was a freshman.

Quiz 65: Oh, Brother

1. Erik Wiegert, 1989–91
2. Matt Strasburger, 1985
3. Curtis Craig, 1975–77
4. Kevin McCormick, did not letter, was older
5. Craig Schnitzler, 1987
6. David Clark, 1978–80
7. Will Thomas, 1989–90
8. Guy Rozier, 1983–85, and Bill Rozier, did not letter, was older
9. Clete Pillen, 1974–76
10. David Noonan, 1990–93
11. Matt Penland, 1990–92
12. Bruce Lingenfelter, did not letter, was younger
13. Chip Bahe, 1987–89
14. Mike Keeler, 1981–83

Quiz 66: What's in a Name?

1. There were 16 players with the last name Brown who had earned at least one football letter at Nebraska through the 1997 season, including four on the 1997 team: Kris Brown, Lance Brown, Ralph Brown, and Mike Brown. There was only one Johnson letterman in 1997, Eric. Ardell Johnson, who walked on, lettered for Devaney's final team in 1972, then lettered for Osborne's first two teams in 1973 and 1974. He was a cornerback from Chillicothe, Missouri.

2. The Johnson lettermen, through the 1997 season, non-Osborne-Devaney era in CAPS:

Ardell Johnson (1972–74)
Brad Johnson (1980–82)
Brad Johnson (1985–86)
Carl Johnson (1970–71)
Clester Johnson (1993–95)
Craig Johnson (1978–80)
Doug Johnson (1970)
F. W. JOHNSON (1907–1909)
HARRY JOHNSON (1954–55)
JOHN JOHNSON (1944)
Monte Johnson (1970–72)
ROGER JOHNSON (1945)
Rudy Johnson (1961–63)
W. M. JOHNSON (1900–1905)
William (Bill) Johnson (1963–65)
Eric Johnson (1996–present)

The Brown lettermen, through the 1997 season, non-Osborne-Devaney era in CAPS:

Brian Brown (1989–91)
Clint Brown (1993–94)
DAN BROWN (1952–54)
Derek Brown (1990–92)
Kris Brown (1995–present)
Lance Brown (1995–present)
James Brown (1964–65)
JERRY BROWN (1955–57)
JOHN BROWN (1925–27)
Kenny Brown (1975–79)
LEWIS BROWN (1930–31)
Robert (Bob) Brown (1961–63)
Todd Brown (1979–82)
Willis Brown (1993)
Mike Brown (1996–present)
Ralph Brown III (1996–present)

Other common last names of lettermen over the course of Cornhusker football history, through the 1997 season: Fischer/Fisher (12), White (11), Williams (11), and Anderson (10).

3. Jeff Quinn (1978–80) came from Ord, Nebraska, to play quarterback for Tom Osborne. The nickname of his high school team was the Chanticleers. And his father was a highway patrolman.

4. I. M. Hipp's full name was Isaiah Moses Walter Hipp. His nickname was "Zeke." There were two theories about the genesis of "Zeke." According to one, it was short for "Ezekiel," one of a couple of biblical names used by Cornhusker running backs coach Mike Corgan. He also called Hipp "Israel." The other theory, offered by Hipp, was that "Zeke" was a reference to the title of the Isaac Hayes album *Zeke the Freak*. Said Hipp, "The players think I do some weird things, so they call me 'Zeke.'"

Weird? Zeke was so committed to lifting that the training staff had to make sure he didn't sneak into the weight room on the mornings of home games to get in some repetitions.

Quiz 67: What's in a Nickname?

1. Jarvis Redwine, I-back, 1979–80. The nickname rhymed with his first name, and he was an outstanding back.

2. George Andrews, defensive end, 1976–78. Andrews was easygoing off the field but a terror on it. He always had a smile, in either case.

3. Anthony Steels, wingback, 1979–81. Steels once explained that he was given the nickname while he was in high school. "I used to be

bald-headed," he said. "But I prefer being called 'Slick' to being called 'Tony.'"

4. Tony Davis, running back, 1973–75. The nickname alliterates with Tony, who was from Tecumseh, Nebraska, and had the reputation for being one of the toughest Cornhuskers of his or any time.

5. Lance Lundberg, offensive tackle, 1991–93. This one is self-explanatory, probably. It alliterates with both his first and last names.

6. Broderick Thomas, outside linebacker, 1985–88. Thomas said he brought the nickname with him from Madison High School in Houston, where a teammate first called him that because he "put ball carriers to sleep" when he tackled them.

7. Neil Smith, defensive tackle, 1985–87. Smith was given this nickname by teammates because he took welding classes at Southeast Community College (the campus is located in Lincoln, Nebraska).

8. Rod Horn, defensive tackle, 1977–79. Horn was among the most committed weight lifters on the team. He also befriended the girl who distributed desserts in the serving line at the Cornhusker training table. He could eat.

9. Lance Gray, defensive end, fullback, 1991–93. Gray, among Nebraska's many walk-ons, earned his nickname for reckless play on special teams. He was the wedge breaker. He set the standard for kickoff team players.

10. Kerry Weinmaster, middle guard, 1976–79. The nickname was a play on his last name, not a reflection of drinking habits.

Quiz 68: (Don't) Walk on By

1. Ituna, Saskatchewan, Canada; 2. Chicago, Illinois; 3. Columbus, Nebraska; 4. St. John, Indiana; 5. Washington, D.C.; 6. and 7. Holdrege, Nebraska; 8. Washington, Kansas; 9. Chapin, South Carolina; 10. and 11. Lincoln, Nebraska; 12. Seward, Nebraska. Extra credit: 13. Monroe, Michigan; 14. Quebec, Canada; 15. Owego, New York; 16. Ponca, Nebraska; 17. Elyria, Nebraska (you were close if you said Welniak was from Ord, Nebraska; he went to Ord High School); 18. Atlantic City, New Jersey; 19. Tilden, Nebraska; 20. Ventura, California; 21. Carrollton, Missouri; 22. Tekamah, Nebraska; 23. Plattsmouth, Nebraska; 24. Washington, D.C.

If you got more than half right on the second section, you show definite signs of being a Husker fanatic.

And you also might want to consider getting a life.

Quiz 69: If You Don't Like It There . . .

1. Oregon State, 2. Texas–El Paso, 3. California, 4. Mississippi, 5. South Dakota, 6. University of Nebraska–Omaha, 7. Kearney State Col-

lege (now University of Nebraska–Kearney), 8. Texas Southern, 9. University of Nebraska–Omaha, 10. Pittsburgh

Quiz 70: It's Academic

1. Defensive end George Andrews in 1978, the first season grad students were eligible
2. Offensive tackle Rob Zatechka had a perfect 4.0 grade-point average. His major was biological sciences.
3. Rob Zatechka, 1991–94, offensive tackle, and Mike Stigge, 1989–92, punter

Quiz 71: Jayvees

1. Dave Burke, who lettered in 1982, 1983, and 1984 as a cornerback, began his Cornhusker career as an I-back. He led the jayvees in rushing in 1980, with 332 yards, and scored four touchdowns.
2. Rozier spent his freshman year at Coffeyville Community College in Kansas.
3. Frank Solich, who succeeded Mike Corgan as varsity running backs coach in 1983

Quiz 72: What If? . . . The Osborne Era

1. Osborne was allowed to eat at the training table.
2. Jarvis Redwine ran for a team-high 1,119 yards.
3. Mike McCloskey's fourth reception of the game was good for the first-and-goal at the two-yard line. Kirk Bowman's second touchdown reception won the game for the Nittany Lions.
4. Senior Scott Livingston, who had kicked a 34-yard field goal to tie the Orange Bowl game at 17 early in the third quarter, was the number one placekicker at season's end. Dave Schneider began the season as the number one placekicker. Livingston was 35 of 37 on extra-point kicks and 2 of 3 on field goals. Schneider was successful on Nebraska's only other field goal attempt of the season, in the opener against Penn State in the Kickoff Classic. The Cornhuskers were too busy scoring touchdowns to kick field goals.
5. Ken Clark, who was from Omaha Bryan High School
6. Chuck Fairbanks
7. Cincinnati Bengals
8. Koy Detmer

Quiz 73: The Osborne Years—A Final Exam

Section I: Who Am I?

1. John McCormick. Miami won the Orange Bowl, by the way, 20–14.
2. Novell Jackson. Extra credit 1: Pat Woodruff. Extra credit 2: Greg Whetsel
3. Captain Ahab. The novel was *Moby-Dick*. Osborne's allusion was: "People feel that somehow I'm like Captain Ahab chasing Moby Dick, that I'm obsessed. It's not that way with me. . . ." If you're not familiar with *Moby-Dick* and don't want to purchase the Cliffs Notes or can't find a copy of the Classic Comics version, Osborne fared considerably better than Captain Ahab.
4. Tim Hager came from Lincoln Southeast High School, where Frank Solich was his coach. Don Erway was the Cornhuskers' quarterback in 1955. He was a graduate of Lincoln High School.

   Extra credit: In order, they were: Jeff Quinn, junior; Mark Mauer, sophomore; Bruce Mathison, sophomore; and Steve Michaelson, sophomore. Quinn was injured, providing Hager an opportunity on which he capitalized. He also started the next six games after the Penn State victory.
5. Adam Kucera, whose father, Bill, had been a Cornhusker graduate assistant. Extra credit: *Rudy* was the title of a movie about a football walk-on at Notre Dame. Kucera wore number 8.
6. Bryan Carpenter
7. Micah Heibel, who lettered in 1986 and 1987
8. Mark Goodspeed

Section II: Short Answers, Mostly Osborne

1. *Time.* On a more serious note, Osborne has said of Kemp: "He read some very conservative stuff. Ayn Rand was one of his favorite authors, and she was very conservative."
2. Osborne began studies at a Presbyterian seminary in San Anselmo, California. He had been awarded a Rockefeller Grant, which was intended to pay a year's expenses at a seminary for those who were considering the ministry but who still weren't certain about making it their life's work. Osborne also applied for a Rhodes Scholarship while finishing at Hastings College but wasn't chosen.
3. Southern California. John McKay
4. Notre Dame. Osborne later said of his speech to the booster club, "I talked for about 20 minutes and spent about two minutes of that time answering a fan's questions about the Notre Dame situation. I don't think a

262

Tom Osborne and players are greeted by enthusiastic fans at the Bob Devaney Sports Center immediately following their return from the 24–17,
1995 Orange Bowl game victory against Miami—which provided Osborne
with his first national championship.

(Photo Courtesy of *Huskers Illustrated*/Bob Berry)

single person left that meeting feeling that I was looking for a job at Notre
Dame." The Fighting Irish were looking to replace Dan Devine, who was
headed for the Green Bay Packers after the 1980 season. Notre Dame hired
an Ohio high school coach, Gerry Faust, on November 24, 1980.

5. Osborne read from the Bible, 2 Timothy 1:7. Depending on the version of the Bible, it says: "For God hath not given us the spirit of fear; but
of power, and of love, and of a sound mind."

6. Nebraska also won the second game in the series, 21–7 at State College in 1980. But the Nittany Lions roared back to win 30–24 at Lincoln in
1981 and 27–24 in a controversial game at State College in 1982. The teams
played again in 1983, in the first Kickoff Classic. Nebraska won 44–6.

7. A Cornhusker, whom Osborne did not identify, had received a
telephone threat. "It's tough enough playing on national television without worrying about someone making a threat on your life," Osborne said.
"We figured it was an idle threat. But you've got to take those things seriously."

8. The Seminoles won one of the remaining three. Nebraska won
34–14 in 1981, Florida State won 17–13 in 1985, and Nebraska won 34–17
in 1986. The teams next played in the 1988 Fiesta Bowl, with the Seminoles

winning 31–28. They have won three more bowl games against Nebraska since.

9. Paul Piurowski was the linebacker. Bill Capece was the placekicker. Rick Stockstill was the Florida State quarterback.

10. Osborne, an end or flanker, wore jersey number 84 in 1961.

11

BEGINNING A NEW ERA:

Frank Solich, Head Coach

Matt Hoskinson and Josh Heskew, offensive linemen on Nebraska's 1997 national championship team, were discussing Frank Solich, the Cornhuskers' new head coach, in the South Stadium varsity lounge.

"I wouldn't mess with the guy," Hoskinson said. Heskew agreed.

The 6-foot-1 Hoskinson weighed 280 pounds, as did the 6-foot-3 Heskew. Both were in their twenties. The 5-foot-8 Solich, 53 at the time, weighed what he did as a player, just under 160 pounds.

It was a solid just-under-160 pounds. He still works out regularly in the weight room. "I do not do a lot of cardiovascular work that maybe some people do, but I still do work out," Solich had said a few minutes earlier, after being announced as Tom Osborne's successor as head coach.

"It's a modified program, but the workouts I do, I try to make sure there's not a lot of rest in between. So hopefully I get a little bit of cardiovascular work. . . . I feel my energy level is good. I feel my endurance is good. I've got no health problems that I know of."

Solich appears to be much younger than he is. That coupled with his intensity would explain why much bigger and younger student-athletes would be hesitant to "mess with" him.

He has their respect, and affection. After Osborne announced that he would be stepping aside after 25 seasons as Nebraska's coach, junior fullback Joel Makovicka addressed reporters at a news conference. "I guess if you ask the question 'How do you replace arguably the greatest coach of all time in college football?' the answer is to get the next-greatest in college football, Coach Solich," he said. "I've had the privilege to be under Coach Solich the last three years. He's my position coach. Coach Solich instills the same thing as Coach Osborne, the work ethic and the values. To the recruits and all the young guys, the people who are thinking about coming to Nebraska, Coach Solich is going to do a great job. I guarantee you that with Coach Solich leading us, we'll keep Nebraska football going."

Solich came to Nebraska in 1979, after 13 seasons as a high school coach. He became the Cornhusker running backs coach in 1983, and he was given the

Frank Solich and Tom Osborne at the December 10, 1997, press conference to announce Osborne's retirement and Solich's ascension.
(Photo Courtesy of *Huskers Illustrated*/Michael Warren)

title assistant head coach in 1991. He was long regarded as Osborne's heir apparent—assuming Osborne ever decided to step aside.

That Solich would follow him as head coach was a significant fact in Osborne's decision to retire. Osborne was given that assurance by athletic director Bill Byrne and university chancellor James Moeser. "They agreed that Frank would be the logical choice, so there was never any arm-twisting or negotiations or anything like that," Osborne said in announcing his decision. "I really appreciate the chancellor and Bill doing what they did and recognizing the importance of continuity in this place.

"Nebraska's a little bit unique. You don't have mountains and you don't have beaches, you don't have warm weather, and you don't have a lot of people. So I think the guy who's been here, who knows the ins and outs of recruiting, who knows how practice has to be structured, is crucial.

"I could see a guy with all kinds of credentials coming in and not having a good understanding of what would work here. I know that Frank knows what to do. That's why I feel very good about it."

Continuity was essential to continued success, according to Osborne, who was hand-picked by his predecessor, Bob Devaney, who had that authority because he also was the athletic director.

"Here I was 35, and there were some guys who had been with Bob for 20 years," Osborne said, recalling his selection as Devaney's successor. "I didn't know, probably, which end was up."

The record indicates otherwise. Osborne was immediately successful as a head coach, though it took him several years to emerge from Devaney's shadow. Now Solich faces a similar task.

"I don't know that you replace Tom Osborne as much as you follow him," said Solich. "I don't know if intimidation and fear are the right words, but there's a lot of anxiety right now about taking over. I know this: I will not equal what he's done in 25 years; I can promise you that.

"I will not be coaching for 25 years."

You look at him, though, and you wonder why not. He has aged well.

Quiz 74: Frank Facts

1. Frank Solich coached at the high school level for 13 years before being hired by Tom Osborne to coach the Cornhusker freshmen. At what high schools did Solich coach?

2. Solich was a three-year letterman at fullback for Bob Devaney from 1963 to 1965. He was a Cornhusker cocaptain as a senior. Who was the other cocaptain in 1965?

3. Solich was offered a job as offensive coordinator and assistant head coach by a former Cornhusker teammate. Tom Osborne made him assistant head coach after he turned down the job offer. Who was the former Cornhusker teammate? At what school was he the coach?

4. Solich was sidelined by a broken ankle during his sophomore season at Nebraska in 1963. Who was the Cornhuskers' starting fullback in 1963?

5. Solich became the Cornhuskers' running backs coach in 1983. Whom did he follow?

6. Solich was born in Pennsylvania and grew up in Ohio. But "I feel like I'm a Nebraskan," he said. "I came here in 1962, came with two other players at my high school. We drove out here in a station wagon. I don't believe they even had the interstate system then—even in thought; I'm not sure. But it seemed like an awful long trip. I've spent my life out here since that time. Without question, in my mind I'm a Nebraskan." His wife, Pam, is. What was her hometown?

7. How many times during Solich's 15 seasons as running backs coach did the Cornhuskers lead the nation in rushing offense? Identify as many of the seasons as you can.

8. Solich set what is still the Orange Bowl single-game record for kickoff return yards as a senior. He returned four kickoffs. Within five yards, how many kickoff return yards did he have? Also, the fact that he returned four kickoffs is an indication Nebraska didn't do particularly well defensively in the game. Against whom did the Cornhuskers play? What was the score?

9. Who was Solich's position coach at Nebraska?

10. Solich took an educational psychology class when he was a student-athlete at Nebraska. Who was his well-known instructor in the educational psychology class?

Answers

Quiz 74: Frank Facts

1. Holy Name in Omaha for two years and Southeast in Lincoln for 11 years

2. Mike Kennedy

3. Barry Alvarez tried to hire Solich for his staff at Wisconsin.

4. Rudy Johnson

5. Mike Corgan, who retired

6. Pam Solich is from Beatrice.

7. Nine times: 1983, 1985, 1988, 1989, 1991, 1992, 1994, 1995, and 1997

8. Solich returned four kickoffs for 130 yards in a 39–28 loss against Alabama.

9. Mike Corgan, whom Solich succeeded as running backs coach

10. Tom Osborne taught the class. "I don't remember him being exceptionally tough," Solich has joked. "I was sitting in the back of the room, trying to hide most of the time."

JUST WHEN YOU THOUGHT YOU WERE A TRUE HUSKER FANIAC:

25 Really Tough Questions

In case you haven't had enough or you thought this stuff was too easy, the following ought to bend your mind a little. If you get half of the answers to these obscure challenges, you need to consider whether or not you're spending too much time thinking about Cornhusker football or whether you should become a sportswriter so you can get paid for it.

Get Red and get ready. It's showtime.

1. The Philadelphia Eagles and Brooklyn Dodgers played the first pro football game ever televised, on October 22, 1939. Brooklyn's coach was later the head coach at Nebraska. Name him.

2. Frank Solich is the 26th head football coach at Nebraska. He is only the fourth Cornhusker head coach also to have lettered on the Nebraska football team. The other three had a combined record of 12–32 over five seasons, a winning percentage of .273. Name them.

3. Perhaps the most ignominious loss in Nebraska football history occurred on September 17, 1955, when Hawaii, a 50-point underdog, upset the Cornhuskers 6–0 at Memorial Stadium. Name the player who scored the Hawaii touchdown. Extra credit: What was his position?

4. Some fans were calling for Bob Devaney's ouster as head coach after the Cornhuskers endured 6–4 seasons in 1967 and 1968. "I actually didn't realize how irritated the fans were," Devaney once said. That's because Devaney's wife, Phyllis, asked his secretary to screen the office mail and discard the critical letters. Name Devaney's secretary at the time.

5. The first high school athlete in the state of Nebraska to clear 14 feet in the pole vault went on to play defensive back for the Cornhuskers. Name him.

6. Tippy Dye was the athletic director who hired Bob Devaney to be the head football coach at Nebraska in 1962. What was Tippy Dye's full given name?

7. Who gave Tom Novak the nickname "Trainwreck"?

8. Among Devaney's closest friends was a wealthy businessman from Vicksburg, Mississippi, who regularly flew on his own plane to Nebraska

games. Once he flew from Turkey to attend a game. Name this business-man, who avoided publicity and never granted interviews.

9. The Cornhusker team that played Stanford in the 1941 Rose Bowl game included only one non-Nebraskan on its roster. Name him and his hometown.

10. Lyell Bremser was the radio voice of the Cornhuskers from 1940 through 1983, after doing color commentary in 1938 and 1939. During that time, Bremser broadcast every Nebraska game except the 1941 Rose Bowl. He did color commentary on a national broadcast of the 1955 Orange Bowl game. For whom was he the color commentator on Nebraska broadcasts in 1938 and 1939? Extra credit: With whom did he work on the 1955 Orange Bowl broadcast? Hint: The Orange Bowl broadcaster was best known for Brooklyn Dodgers' baseball.

11. Tom Osborne met his wife, Nancy, at Nebraska in 1962, when he was a Cornhusker graduate assistant. They were introduced by a mutual friend, who was a Cornhusker football letterman from 1958 to 1960. He also was one of Nebraska's first academic All-Americans in 1960. Like Osborne, he was from Hastings. Name him and his occupation. He's still in Lincoln.

12. Osborne could have had a scholarship for football or for basketball at Nebraska following his graduation from Hastings High School in Nebraska, but he opted to attend Hastings College. Who was the Cornhusker football coach when he graduated? For whom would he have played had he decided to accept a football scholarship from Nebraska? Extra credit: Osborne has said although he wasn't interested in becoming a Cornhusker, he would have readily accepted a football scholarship from another Big Seven school—had it offered him one. Name that school.

13. In a *Sports Illustrated* story on Nebraska's 42–33 victory against UCLA in 1987, writer Rick Telander pointed out that one of the Corn-huskers played in a local rock band, prompting the senior fullback to re-mark, "I don't want people to think that's a big part of my life, that I'm some sort of rock-and-roll singer." Name the player. Extra credit: Name the band.

14. Name Nebraska's opponent in the first night game ever played at Memorial Stadium. In what season was the game played? What was the fi-nal score?

15. One of the best-known photographs in Nebraska football history is of quarterback Jerry Tagge reaching the ball across the goal line for the win-ning touchdown with 8:50 remaining in the 1971 Orange Bowl game against LSU. The victory gave Nebraska its first national championship. The touch-down capped a 68-yard drive. Name the center behind whom Tagge tried to sneak. Extra credit: What famous *Sports Illustrated* photographer took the picture?

16. Two high school teammates were cocaptains for one of Devaney's teams at Nebraska. Name them. In what season were they captains? From

what high school did they graduate? Really tough extra credit: Name their high school coach.

17. In 1971, Nebraska and Oklahoma dominated the Associated Press All–Big Eight Conference first team, nabbing 17 of 22 positions on offense and defense. The five who weren't Cornhuskers or Sooners included a tight end from Kansas, an offensive lineman from Kansas State, a defensive lineman from Colorado, and linebackers from Kansas and Iowa State. Name at least one of the five.

18. What former Nebraska assistant caught a 54-yard touchdown pass against the Cornhuskers in the 1968 opener? Hint: Nebraska had to rally from a 10–0 deficit to defeat Wyoming 13–10.

19. Rush end Mike Rucker threw a memorable block on a 54-yard punt return for a touchdown in number two–ranked Nebraska's 49–25 victory against number eight–ranked Kansas State at Memorial Stadium in 1995. Name the Cornhusker who returned the punt for a touchdown. And name the Wildcat whose helmet was knocked off by the force of Rucker's block.

20. Guy B. Chamberlin was Nebraska's first consensus football All-American. For what did the initial "B" stand? What was Chamberlin's nickname?

21. Who followed Bob Devaney as head coach at Wyoming in 1962, after he came to Nebraska?

22. Bob Devaney coached the College All-Stars in their once-annual summer charity game against the Super Bowl champions at Chicago's Soldier Field in 1972. To whom did the College All-Stars lose in that game? What was the score? Extra credit: Five Cornhuskers played for the All-Stars. Four were selected and one was added because of an injury. Name the five.

23. Ahman Green, the second-leading rusher in Cornhusker history, is the nephew of a former Nebraska cocaptain. Who is his uncle? Tough extra credit: Green was given a nickname by Clinton Childs when they were students at Omaha's North High School. They were later teammates at Nebraska. What was the nickname that Childs gave Green?

24. Nebraska's first nationally televised football game was played at Memorial Stadium. It was the opener for what season? Whom did the Cornhuskers play? What was the score? Really tough extra credit: NBC televised the game. Who were the two well-known announcers? Hint: One is probably more familiar as a voice of the New York Yankees.

25. The final play in the Tom Osborne era at Nebraska was also the last play of the 1988 Orange Bowl game victory against Tennessee. The Cornhuskers had the ball, second-and-nine at the Tennessee 44-yard line. Appropriately, the play was a run. Who carried the ball? Tough extra credit: What was the net gain, or loss, on that final play?

1. George "Potsy" Clark coached the Dodgers in 1939. He coached the Cornhuskers during the 1945 season and again during the 1948 season. His record at Nebraska was a combined 6–13.

2. Glenn Presnell lettered from 1925 to 1927 under Coach Ernie Bearg. Presnell coached Nebraska to a 3–7 record in 1942. A. J. Lewandowski lettered in 1928 and 1929 under Bearg and D. X. Bible. He coached the Cornhuskers to records of 2–6 in 1943 and 1944. Bernie Masterson lettered from 1931 to 1933 under Bible. Nebraska was 3–6 and 2–7 under Masterson's direction in 1946 and 1947.

3. Hartwell Freitas, a fullback, scored the touchdown.

4. Dee Bykerk was Devaney's secretary.

5. Randy Reeves, who cleared 14–2½ as a senior at Omaha Benson High School in 1965, lettered for Devaney's teams in 1967, 1968, and 1969. He was an academic All-American in 1969.

6. William Henry Harrison Dye

7. Novak's high school coach, Corny Collin, gave him the nickname "Trainwreck."

8. F. L. Cappart, "Cappie"

9. Robert McNutt, a reserve lineman, was from Colby, Kansas.

10. Bremser was color commentator alongside announcer Bob Russell on Cornhusker broadcasts in 1938 and 1939. He worked with Red Barber on the 1955 Orange Bowl game broadcast.

11. Dr. Don Fricke, a dentist, introduced Osborne to Nancy Tederman, who was from Holdrege.

12. Bill Glassford told Osborne a football scholarship was his for the taking. Glassford was replaced in 1956 by Pete Elliott, who was replaced in 1957 by Bill Jennings. So Osborne would have been a freshman under Glassford, a sophomore under Elliott, and a junior and senior under Jennings. Osborne said he would have accepted a football scholarship from Oklahoma, which was in the midst of its NCAA-record 47-game winning streak under Coach Bud Wilkinson when Osborne graduated from Hastings High.

13. Fullback Micah Heibel sang in the band Brain Hammer.

14. The Cornhuskers defeated Florida State 34–17 in the first night game at Memorial Stadium. The game was Nebraska's opener in 1986. It was nationally televised on September 6.

15. Doug Dumler, a sophomore from Melrose Park, Illinois, snapped the ball to Tagge. Walter Ioss of *Sports Illustrated* snapped the photograph of Tagge's game-winning stretch across the goal line.

16. Jerry Tagge and Jim Anderson were Cornhusker cocaptains for the

1971 national championship team. They were teammates at West High School in Green Bay, Wisconsin, where their coach was Jerry Dufek. And yes, Dave Mason, another Cornhusker, also was their teammate at West High.

17. John Schroll, tight end, Kansas; Mo Latimore, offensive line, Kansas State; Herb Orvis, defensive line, Colorado; Kenny Page, linebacker, Kansas; and Keith Schroeder, linebacker, Iowa State

18. Gene Huey caught the touchdown pass.

19. Mike Fullman returned the punt. Kansas State's Joe Gordon lost his helmet.

20. Guy Berlin Chamberlin was nicknamed the Champ.

21. Lloyd Eaton, a Devaney assistant, succeeded him as head coach. The Cowboys were 5–5 in 1962.

22. Devaney's College All-Stars lost to the Dallas Cowboys 20–7. Jerry Tagge, Van Brownson, Jeff Kinney, and Larry Jacobson were chosen to play in the game. Dick Rupert was added.

23. Green's uncle was Mike Green, a fullback and Cornhusker cocaptain in 1969. The nickname Childs gave Green was "Emilio." Green explained that Childs couldn't remember Ahman. It came out "Armand" and "Amen." So he settled on something he could remember, "Emilio." It stuck with Green at Nebraska, although few people outside the team were aware of the nickname.

24. The Nebraska-Oregon game at Memorial Stadium was televised on September 19, 1953. Oregon won 20–12. The NBC announcers were Mel Allen and Lindsey Nelson.

25. True freshman I-back Correll Buckhalter carried for a five-yard gain on the final play of Osborne's final game as Nebraska's head coach.